Economics-Driven Software Architecture

Edited by

Ivan Mistrik

Rami Bahsoon

Rick Kazman

Yuanyuan Zhang

AMSTERDAM • BOSTON • HEIDELBERG • LONDON
NEW YORK • OXFORD • PARIS • SAN DIEGO
SAN FRANCISCO • SINGAPORE • SYDNEY • TOKYO

Morgan Kaufmann is an imprint of Elsevier

Acquiring Editor: Todd Green
Editorial Project Manager: Lindsay Lawrence
Project Manager: Punithavathy Govindaradjane
Designer: Maria Inês Cruz

Morgan Kaufmann is an imprint of Elsevier
225 Wyman Street, Waltham, MA 02451, USA

Library of Congress Cataloging-in-Publication Data

Economics-driven software architecture / edited by Ivan Mistrik, Rami Bahsoon, Rick Kazman, Yuanyuan Zhang.
    pages cm
  ISBN 978-0-12-410464-8
 1. Computer software–Development. I. Mistrik, Ivan.
  QA76.76.D47E295 2014
  005.3—dc23

                                              2014006136

British Library Cataloguing-in-Publication Data
A catalogue record for this book is available from the British Library.

ISBN: 978-0-12-410464-8

For information on all MK publications
visit our website at www.mkp.com

This book has been manufactured using Print On Demand technology. Each copy is produced to order and is limited to black ink. The online version of this book will show color figures where appropriate.

Economics-Driven Software Architecture

Contents

PART II   ECONOMICS-DRIVEN ARCHITECTING: DESIGN MECHANISMS AND EVALUATION

CHAPTER 5   Economics-Driven Software Architecting for Cloud 83

Funmilade Faniyi and Rami Bahsoon

PART III   MANAGING ARCHITECTURAL ECONOMICS

CHAPTER 8   Toward Collaborative Software Engineering Leveraging the Crowd 159

Benjamin Satzger, Rostyslav Zabolotnyi, Schahram Dustdar, Stefan Wild,
Martin Gaedke, Steffen Göbel, and Tobias Nestler

CHAPTER 9   Architectural Debt Management in Value-Oriented Architecting .. 183

Zengyang Li, Peng Liang, and Paris Avgeriou

PART IV   LINKING ARCHITECTURE INCEPTION AND EVOLUTION TO ECONOMICS: EXPERIENCES AND APPROACHES

Acknowledgments

The editors sincerely thank the many authors who contributed to this collection. The international team of anonymous reviewers gave detailed feedback on early versions of chapters and helped us to improve both the presentation and accessibility of the work. Finally, we would like to thank the Elsevier management and editorial teams, in particular Todd Green and Lindsay Lawrence, for the opportunity to produce this unique collection of articles covering the wide range of areas related to economics-driven and value-oriented software architecture.

About the Editors

Ivan Mistrik is an independent researcher in software-intensive systems engineering. He is a computer scientist interested in system and software engineering (SE/SWE) and in system and software architecture (SA/SWA), in particular: life-cycle system/software engineering, requirements engineering, relating software requirements and architectures, knowledge management in software development, rationale-based software development, aligning enterprise/system/software architectures, value-based software engineering, agile software architectures, and collaborative system/software engineering. He has more than 40 years of experience in the field of computer systems engineering as an information systems developer, R&D leader, SE/SA research analyst, educator in computer sciences, and ICT management consultant. In the past 40 years, he has been working primarily in R&D institutions in the United States and Germany and has done consulting on a variety of large international projects sponsored by ESA, the EU, NASA, NATO, and the UN. He has also taught university-level computer science courses in software engineering, software architecture, distributed information systems, and human—computer interaction. He is the author or co-author of more than 90 articles and papers in international journals, conferences, books, and workshops, most recently having contributed a chapter in *Requirements Engineering for Sociotechnical Systems*, a paper in *IC on Global Software Development*, and a paper in *Expert Systems Knowledge Engineering*. He has also written over 120 technical reports and presented over 70 scientific/technical talks. He has served on many program committees and panels of reputable international conferences and organized a number of scientific workshops, most recently two workshops on Knowledge Engineering in Global Software and Development at the International Conference on Global Software Engineering 2009 and 2010 and the IEEE International Workshop on the Future of Software Engineering for/in the Cloud (FoSEC) held in conjunction with IEEE Cloud 2011.

Mistrik was the guest-editor of *IEE Proceedings Software: A Special Issue on Relating Software Requirements and Architectures* published by IEE in 2005 and the lead editor of *Rationale Management in Software Engineering* (Springer, 2006). He was also the co-author of *Rationale-Based Software Engineering* (Springer, May 2008). In addition, he was the lead editor of *Collaborative Software Engineering* (Springer, 2010); *Relating Software Requirements and Architectures* (Springer, 2011); the lead editor of *Aligning Enterprise, System, and Software Architectures* (IEEE, 2012); the lead editor of the *Expert Systems Special Issue on Knowledge Engineering in Global Software Development* (IEEE, 2013); and the co-editor of the *JSS Special Issue on the Future of Software Engineering for/in the Cloud* (IEEE, 2013).

Rami Bahsoon is a senior lecturer in software engineering and founder of the Software Engineering for/in the Cloud interest groups at the School of Computer Science, University of Birmingham, UK. His group currently comprises nine PhD students working in areas related to cloud software engineering and architectures. The group's research aims at developing architecture and frameworks to support and reason about the development and evolution of dependable, ultra-large, complex, and data-intensive software systems, in which the investigations span cloud computing architectures and their economics. Bahsoon had founded and co-organized the International

Software Engineering Workshop series on Software Architectures and Mobility held in conjunction with ICSE and the IEEE International Software Engineering for/in the Cloud workshop in conjunction with IEEE Services. He was the lead editor of two special issues of Elsevier's *Journal of Systems and Software*—one on the Future of Software Engineering for/in the Cloud and another on Architecture and Mobility. Bahsoon has co-edited a book on economics-driven software architecture, to be published by Elsevier in 2014 and co-edited another book, *Aligning Enterprise, System, and Software Architectures*, published by IGI Global in 2012. He is currently acting as the workshop chair for IEEE Services 2014, the Doctoral Symposium chair of IEEE/ACM Utility and Cloud Computing Conference (UCC 2014), and the track chair for Utility Computing of HPCC 2014. He holds a PhD in Software Engineering from University College London (UCL) for his research on evaluating software architecture stability using real options. He has also read for MBA-level certificates with London Business School.

Rick Kazman is a professor at the University of Hawaii and a Visiting Scientist (and former senior member of the Technical Staff) at the Software Engineering Institute of Carnegie Mellon University. His primary research interests are software architecture, design and analysis tools, software visualization, and software engineering economics. He also has interests in human–computer interaction and information retrieval. Kazman has created several highly influential methods and tools for architecture analysis, including the *SAAM* (Software Architecture Analysis Method), the *ATAM* (Architecture Tradeoff Analysis Method), the *CBAM* (Cost-Benefit Analysis Method), and the *Dali* architecture reverse engineering tool. He is the author of over 100 papers and co-author of several books, including *Software Architecture in Practice* and *Evaluating Software Architectures: Methods and Case Studies*.

Kazman received a BA (English/Music) and M.Math (Computer Science) from the University of Waterloo, an MA (English) from York University, and a PhD (Computational Linguistics) from Carnegie Mellon University. How he ever became a software engineering researcher is anybody's guess. When not architecting or writing about architecture, Kazman may be found cycling, playing the piano, gardening, practicing Tae Kwon Do, or (more often) flying back and forth between Hawaii and Pittsburgh.

Yuanyuan Zhang is currently a postdoctoral researcher in the CREST center, SSE Group, UCL. She received her PhD in software engineering from Kings College London in 2010. She has been working on multi-objective requirements selection and optimization for release planning problem. The research work proposes a search-based requirements selection and optimization framework. The aim is to widen and explore the scope of requirements engineering decision-making support as a problem for search-based software engineering (SBSE), a topic on which she has published 12 refereed publications, including the *RE, RE Journal*, and the GECCO 2007 best paper.

List of Contributors

Paris Avgeriou
University of Groningen, Groningen, The Netherlands

Rami Bahsoon
University of Birmingham, Birmingham, UK

Yuanfang Cai
Drexel University, Philadelphia, PA, USA

Hong-Mei Chen
University of Hawaii, Honolulu, HI, USA

Schahram Dustdar
Vienna University of Technology, Vienna, Austria

Funmilade Faniyi
University of Birmingham, Birmingham, UK

Claudiu Farcas
University of California, San Diego, CA, USA

Emilia Farcas
University of California, San Diego, CA, USA

Marios Fokaefs
University of Alberta, Edmonton, AB, Canada

Steffen Göbel
SAP AG, Dresden, Germany

Martin Gaedke
Technische Universität Chemnitz, Chemnitz, Germany

Rick Kazman
University of Hawaii, Honolulu, HI, USA

Ingolf Krüger
University of California, San Diego, CA, USA

Anand Kumar
Tata Consultancy Services, Pune, MH, India

Zengyang Li
University of Groningen, Groningen, The Netherlands

Peng Liang
Wuhan University, Wuhan, China

Doji Samson Lokku
Tata Consultancy Services, Pune, MH, India

Paul R. Messinger
University of Alberta, Edmonton, AB, Canada

Ivan Mistrik
Independent Consultant, Heidelberg, Germany

Swaminathan Natarajan
Tata Consultancy Services, Pune, MH, India

Tobias Nestler
SAP AG, Dresden, Germany

Kesav Vithal Nori
Tata Consultancy Services, Pune, MH, India

Benjamin Satzger
Vienna University of Technology, Vienna, Austria

Carlos V.A. Silva
Federal University of Bahia, Bahia, Brazil

Michael Stal
University of Groningen, Groningen, The Netherlands

Eleni Stroulia
University of Alberta, Edmonton, AB, Canada

Alistair Sutcliffe
University of Lancaster, Lancaster, UK

T. Maruthi Padmaja
K. L University, Vaddeswaram, AP, India

Sarah Thew
University of Manchester, Manchester, UK

Anil Kumar Thurimella
Harman Automotive Division and TU, Munich, Germany

Steve Tockey
Construx Software, Bellevue, WA, USA

Stefan Wild
Technische Universität Chemnitz, Chemnitz, Germany

Lu Xiao
Drexel University, Philadelphia, PA, USA

Rostyslav Zabolotnyi
Vienna University of Technology, Vienna, Austria

Yuanyuan Zhang
University College London, London, UK

Foreword by John Grundy
Economics-Driven Software
Architecting

Software architecting has become a critical part of most software systems' development projects. However, as popularized in the seminal papers by Shaw and Garlan (1996) and Kruchten (1995), most software architecture research and practice have historically been focused on the technical aspects of the task, not on value-driven or value-creation aspects (Boehm and Sullivan, 2000; Bahsoon and Emmerich, 2008). Given the huge impact software architecture choices have on system performance, scalability, and maintainability, not to mention the actual adoption and deployment of systems, it has become accepted that software architecting can no longer ignore economics-driven imperatives (Bass et al., 2003; Kruchten et al., 2006).

So saying, there is a need to both incorporate an economics-driven perspective into the software architecting of systems and to balance this with continuing to solve increasingly challenging technical problems. There are several major areas for incorporating a software economics perspective in the architecting process:

- *Requirements Constraints* (particularly Quality of Service on software architecture) on architecture—requirements are increasingly challenged to meet with increased demand on scaling, reliability, robustness, and security. Most, if not all, of these constrain the architectural solution space, sometimes in conflicting ways. Meeting some implies more costly, less flexible and less extensible architectural solutions. Expected or unanticipated changing QoS can have dramatic impact on architecture, including rendering a particular architecture choice no longer tenable.
- *Technical Constraints* on architecture—technical choices may be constrained by a range of issues and are not limited to cost of solution platform (software, hardware, network, third-party applications); availability; open versus proprietary; and likely future technological change (e.g., the emergence of the cloud computing paradigm). Once commitment has been made to one set of technical solutions, change is almost invariably expensive.
- *Deployment environment* constraints—architectural solutions make heavy use of other applications and components in their deployment environment, as well as platform hardware and networks. With the advent of cloud computing, a variety of platform-as-a-service and infrastructure-as-a-service, with elastic availability, have complicated this aspect further. Different platforms offer different technical and QoS constraints, but they also come with differing cost models.
- *Process constraints* greatly impact software architecting—the advent of agile methods with the concept of the "emergent" architecture has some strong cost incentives: Implement only as much as you have to and no more. Unfortunately, as applications and user requirements evolve, sometimes dramatic re-architecting and reengineering become necessary, with attendant cost implications.

- *Team constraints* are an increasingly interesting area. Sometimes many of the above decisions are actually made due to team or organizational preferences, biases, and prior experiences. Sometimes dominant individuals or politically or economically powerful lobbies hold sway over key architectural solution decisions, disregarding some of the factors above and including cost and longer term software economic implications. Sometimes architecture choices are driven by the concept of "value" to the team, for example, a reason for exploring interesting new technologies and solving interesting technical problems, instead of value to business, stakeholders, or even maximization of the actual value of the software itself.
- Finally, *business constraints* must be taken into account. These constraints include limitations on purchase or usage of hardware and software, desire to leverage value in the future if not the present, balancing cost versus opportunity, and potentially increasing the attractiveness of the product due to architectural decisions that appeal to likely or potential stakeholders. Simply choosing the "cheapest" options often turns out to be a false economy. Similarly, massively overengineering applications and the consequences of cost and loss of time-to-market edge can have severe economic and value implications.

The concept of economics needs to be incorporated into the software architecting process itself. Traditionally, most, if not all, of the practice of software architecture has been technical in focus. However, many constraints impacting on architectural decision making have major implications for platform and software costs, team costs, enhancement of software value, enhancement of company value and capability, and positioning of product and organization for (un)anticipated future demand. Following are some suggestions on how each area described above might be advanced.

Requirements impact on architecture economics

Architectures must realize the functional and nonfunctional requirements that have been set for them. As several recent works have stated (Avgeriou et al., 2011), many now think software architecting and requirements engineering must proceed hand in hand rather than the former rigidly follow the later. In fact, architectural choices often constrain the requirements as often as not (Tang et al., 2011; Woods and Rozanski, 2011). Quality of Service (QoS) constraints have a major impact on the economics of software architecture, both in terms of the expense of its solution and the value inherent to the solution.

Typically, the higher the QoS expectations e.g. greater the throughput, reliability, security, and scalability needed by stakeholders for their application, greater the complexity, implementation and cost required. However, a simple, cheap, quick-to-build web application that is intended to manage highly mission-critical or sensitive data is going to have much less—if any—value, than one demonstrably safe, secure, robust and clearly meeting the QoS requirements set for it. Similarly, an over-engineered solution that will never be required to scale, be as secure, manage highly private data, or face a range of difficult deployment environment conditions, will waste design, development, testing and deployment resources to little or no added value.

Balancing the current QoS needs against architectural decisions that meet these, but do not greatly exceed them, is challenging. In particular, as many QoS constraints and suitable architectural solutions conflict, trade-off analysis can be very challenging. Factoring in cost in terms of development time, testing, required platform support and business value needs to be a part of decision making, not just technical solutions (Bahsoon and Emmerich, 2011).

A major difficulty is changing requirements. Adding or modifying functionality is difficult, but incorporating potentially massive QoS constraint changes usually presents a much greater challenge. With the complexity and connectedness of today's applications, this is probably going to get even more difficult. Architectural solutions allowing for more flexible QoS changes are likely to be ever more necessary (Allen et al., 1998).

Technology impact on architecture economics

Different technical solutions for software architectures come with different inherent costs: Some are free (e.g., open-source versus bought solutions). Some are easily modified and configurable, whereas others are very constrained, saving expense if built-in functionality is required but incurring cost if extension is needed. Some require expensive hardware or third-party software investment, whereas others allow for an elastic, demand-driven pay-as-you-go infrastructure. Some are widely used and thus embody well-known and supported approaches; others are bespoke solutions, possibly optimized but potentially with poorly known or undiscovered weaknesses.

Technology choice will therefore impact architectural economics dramatically in terms of both cost (both to build and to maintain), and value (e.g., is the solution able to be deployed with a wide range of off-the-shelf components, or does it require purchase of expensive, third-party components, putting off potential buyers?). Some technology choices are more costly up front, for example, cost to purchase, more difficult to use, more time consuming for the team, requiring more costly deployment environmental support. However, they enable an architecture to be more "robust" under requirements change; for example, they provide dynamic load balancing and runtime component switching, enable elastic resource management, and so on. As with requirements change, anticipating future technology demands is difficult in many situations but may enable more cost-effective (in the long run) architecture choices to be made and may maximize software value.

Environmental impact on architecture economics

Software does not run in isolation; it is deployed on hardware, networks, and with other third-party applications and services. These may well impact architecture choices and themselves impact the cost effectiveness of solutions and the value of the system as a whole. A major traditional cost has been overengineering solutions, not just the software architecture itself but its deployment environment— for example, massive overallocation of compute nodes, data storage, network capacity. Sometimes this overallocation is actually capacity that is needed very rarely, for example, once a day/month/year peak processing.

The advent of the cloud computing model has gone some way toward addressing this overallocation by enabling elastic provisioning and multitenant solutions, incorporated into the engineering of software systems (Grundy et al., 2012). However, variable cost models, immaturity of the platforms, and development methods, as well as other issues such as legislative constraints on data location, can impact the usefulness of this solution in terms of software economics. Understanding of different platform implications on running costs, ability to scale up/down resource demand, robustness on failure, loss of control over security and load balancing, and other concerns make impact on software architecting still very unclear.

Process impact on architecture economics

Traditionally, architecting has largely been performed before large-scale implementation and testing, and re-architecting has only been attempted when major problems occur (scale and performance being the most common). However, the advent of agile development processes and the concept of "agile architecting" have gained prominence. Originally, architectural spikes and an "emergent" architecture resulted. However, emergent architecture is a bit like emergent behavior or constraints for a software system: unpredictable, hard to control, hard to plan and manage, and hard to cost.

Any development process for a software system needs to factor in architecture design, analysis, and—often—evolution. As many technologies and deployment environments themselves greatly constrain architectural solutions, so they will constrain architecting in the development process. Software cost estimation and management have become well-recognized areas of software engineering [Refs].

Team impact on architecture economics

Team dynamics, organizational context and constraints, and socio-technical aspects of software development may all play an overly large role in architecture choices and hence cost and value implications. Developers may prefer architectural solutions and technologies familiar to them. Conversely, they may prefer "new" or "interesting" options whose value to them is in their technical attractiveness but economically may have suboptimal value to the software project, application, stakeholders, and organization. Architectural choices may be constrained by organizational and/or stakeholder preferences that have little basis in sound technical—or economic—rationale. Attempting a project with a new technology that the team, organization, and stakeholder have little or no experience with is a classic high-risk strategy.

By far the major cost for most software projects is personnel—developer time and related overheads. Hence, software architecture decisions that have positive or negative impact on developer time have great potential to impact a project economically. Factoring in impact on the team into architectural decision making would seem an important area for research and practice.

Business impact on architecture economics

Finally, software is normally developed for a purpose: to assist people (and increasingly, machines) in carrying out their activities more effectively, efficiently and in a satisfying way. Business constraints relating to software economics are of course myriad: constraints on investment in developing the software itself; constraints on platform capabilities to host the software; short-term development versuslong-term maintenance costs; time-to-market challenges; changing business models; and changing legislative context. Value offered by software is also multifaceted: improving efficient use of resources; reducing costs; enabling quick response to market demand; opening up previously unavailable business opportunities; and even enabling future software and business development by improved team skill set, system integration, and solidity of underlying software architecture. Software architecting incorporating business context and need is thus likely to better meet these needs and live within necessary constraints. Equally, software economics that carefully considers architecture as a fundamental software value enabler is necessary.

John Grundy
Swinburne University of Technology

About the Author

John Grundy is Professor of Software Engineering and Deputy Dean, Faculty of ICT, at the Swinburne University of Technology, Melbourne, Australia. He has published over 250 refereed papers on software engineering tools and methods, automated software engineering, software architecture, visual languages and environments, collaborative work systems and tools, aspect-oriented software development, user interfaces, software process technology, and distributed systems. He has made numerous contributions to the field of software architecture, including numerous innovative architecture modeling tools, performance engineering tools, software architecture visualization, and various novel software architecture frameworks and realizations for collaborative work, service-oriented systems, and cloud-based systems. He is Associate Editor of the *IEEE Transactions on Software Engineering, Automated Software Engineering journal and IEEE Software.* He has been Program Chair of the IEEE/ACM Automated Software Engineering conference and the IEEE Visual Languages and Human-Centric Computing Conference, and has been a PC member several times for the International Conference on Software Engineering.

References

Allen, R., Douence, R., Garlan, D., 1998. Specifying and analyzing dynamic software architectures. Fundam. Approaches Softw. Eng. 21−37.

Avgeriou, P., Grundy, J., Hall, J.G., Lago, P., Mistrík, I., 2011. Relating Software Requirements and Architectures. Springer, Berlin.

Bahsoon, R., Emmerich, W., 2008. An economics-driven approach for valuing scalability in distributed architectures. Seventh Working IEEE/IFIP Conference on Software Architecture. IEEE, WICSA 2008, pp. 9−18.

Bahsoon, R., Emmerich, W., 2011. Economics-driven architecting for nonfunctional requirements in the presence of middleware. In: Avgeriou, et al., (Eds.), Relating Software Requirements and Architectures. Springer, Berlin, Chapter 20.

Bass, L., Clements, P., Kazman, R., 2003. Software Architecture in Practice. Addison-Wesley, New York.

Boehm, B.W., Sullivan, K.J., 2000. Software economics: a roadmap. In: Avgeriou, et al., (Eds.), Proceedings of the Conference on the Future of Software Engineering. ACM, pp. 319–343.

Grundy, J., Kaefer, G., Keong, J., Liu, A., 2012. Software engineering for the cloud. Softw. IEEE 29 (2), 26–29.

Kruchten, P.B., 1995. The 4 + 1 view model of architecture. Softw. IEEE 12 (6), 42–50.

Kruchten, P., Obbink, H., Stafford, J., 2006. The past, present, and future for software architecture. Softw. IEEE 23 (2), 22–30.

Shaw, M., Garlan, D., 1996. Software architecture: perspectives on an emerging discipline. Prentice Hall.

Tang, A., Liang, P., Clerc, V., van Vliet, H., 2011. Traceability in the co-evolution of architectural requirements and design. In: Avgeriou, et al., (Eds.), Relating Software Requirements and Architectures. Springer, Berlin, Chapter 4.

Woods, E., Rozanski, N., 2011. How software architecture can frame, constrain and inspire system requirements. In: Avgeriou, et al., (Eds.), Relating Software Requirements and Architectures. Springer, Berlin, Chapter 19.

Foreword by Len Bass

Economic analysis of software architecture has great promise, and the chapters in this book propose a number of different approaches. One missing element, however, is the management of uncertainty. Economic analysis is either predictive or explanatory. In either case, there is uncertainty due to the assumptions of the models being used, the difficulty of gathering sufficient data, or the judgments of the architect. Uncertainty can be managed, however, and bounded. In this Foreword, I will discuss some of the causes of uncertainty, the various types of uncertainty, and techniques for bounding different types of uncertainty.

Economists make a distinction between microeconomics—focusing on the behavior of individual households and firms—and macro economics—which focuses on the economy as a whole. Translating these concepts to the software architecture of a system, I see a distinction between the granularity of applying economic analysis to the whole system or to individual design decisions. When considering the whole system, typical questions are: How much should we invest in performance, how much to security, how much to paying down technical debt, how much to including various features, and how much to risk mitigation? The responses to these questions are then translated into meaningful business attributes for the organization developing the system—improved sales, quicker time to market, reduced development cost—and used to make decisions. When one is considering individual design decisions, the questions are, for each of the options: What is the utility of each choice, what is the impact on schedule, what is the cost, and what is the risk introduced? The software architect then uses the responses to these questions to guide the response to a particular design choice.

I will use two examples—one from a macro perspective and one from a micro perspective—to add concreteness. "How much of the technical debt should the current iteration pay down?" is the macroeconomic example. "Should an intermediary be inserted, or is the performance penalty too high?" is the microeconomic example.

For both of these examples, uncertainty comes from

- Accommodating different stakeholders. The number of different types of stakeholders is very large. One list includes 19 different types ranging from developer to end-user to maintenance to network administrator. Each of these types of users has a different set of interests. Paying down technical debt is a means of reducing the future cost of modifications. The resources used in paying down technical debt are unavailable to apply to other qualities of interest, such as time to market, features included in the current iteration, or overall quality of the system. Introducing an intermediary will reduce the cost of future modifications at the cost of slower performance. Both of these choices involve the stakeholders of maintenance personnel, end-users, and potentially other classes. Balancing the wishes of the various classes of stakeholders is something that the decision makers for a project must do routinely, but analytic techniques for doing so (e.g., the analytic hierarchy process) introduce uncertainty. Ad-hoc techniques for balancing the wishes of different stakeholders also introduce uncertainty.
- The impracticality of surveying all of the different stakeholders for technical or managerial decisions. Consequently, these decisions are made utilizing stakeholder representatives or utilizing a decision maker's intuition. Stakeholders do, however, provide input when

requirements for a system are defined. Whether those requirements are in the form of user stories or some other form is immaterial. The stakeholders at that point can specify, for each feature, their limits in terms of the various qualities—for example, what are acceptable performance limits for response time or throughput, what modifications might be expected in the future, how sensitive is this feature to security concerns, and so forth. This information can be used not to weight different stakeholders but, at least, to indicate their desires in particular situations.

- The ability to predict the results of a decision. Predicting the results of a decision is inherently uncertain. Paying down technical debt makes assumptions about the types of modifications that are going to occur in the future and the cost of making the specified changes. Introducing an intermediary also makes assumptions about the types of modifications and their costs. In both of these cases, a model of modifiability can be used to predict the cost of potential modifications, but uncertainty is introduced both by the use of a model and by the assumptions on the type of modifications that will occur.
- Translation to the meaningful business attributes of a decision. Organization decision makers are concerned with time to market, cost, benefit, and risk of the construction of a system. Deciding the benefit of paying down or not paying down technical debt involves its impact on future costs and the impact of the alternatives on sales and time to market. It is similar for introducing an intermediary. The situation gets more complicated on the micro level. Consider determining the impact on performance from inserting an intermediary. How large an impact does it take for a stakeholder to care? It may be that the impact on performance is within a stakeholder's tolerance and increasing the response time marginally will not affect a business attribute. On the other hand, it may be that increasing the response time marginally is unacceptable to stakeholders.
- Evaluating the risk introduced by a decision. Decisions involve risks. Risks are discussed in terms of cause, impact, and probability. Each risk has a cause, and if it occurs it will have a particular impact. Each risk also has a probability of occurrence. Impact and probability provide a two-dimensional scale for categorizing risks. Low-impact, low-probability risks are not usually considered further. High-impact, high-probability risks should be mitigated immediately. Risks in the other two categories require some analysis to determine the extent of the mitigation desired. Identifying the risks associated with a particular project and then mitigating them is a key managerial activity. Again, however, it involves prediction and hence uncertainty.

Helton, (1997) classifies uncertainty into two types: *stochastic* uncertainty and *subjective* uncertainty. Stochastic uncertainty arises from the inherent randomness in the behavior of the system. Subjective uncertainty comes from the lack of knowledge about an appropriate value to use in the analysis.

In the examples above, both types of uncertainty arise. Deciding how much technical debt to pay down, for example, involves humans performing some activities. Predicting the cost of these activities is going to have some element of randomness. Performance prediction always has an element of randomness whether it comes from network interference, variations in workload, or sporadic failures of hardware components.

Subjective uncertainty in these examples comes, for example, from the models used and the assumptions made within the models.

Techniques exist to manage some causes of both types of uncertainty. One technique for managing stochastic uncertainty is to use results derived from different sources. Meta analysis (Wikipedia) utilizes results from different studies to attempt to derive patterns. If researchers made available the data that they use to justify their analysis, others could compare and contrast the different types of analysis and develop bounds for stochastic uncertainty.

One source of subjective uncertainty is the occurrence of rare events that are outside of the assumptions of the analysis. Analyzing technical debt, for example, requires making assumptions about the types of modifications that can be made. Disruptive technology introduction, however, will be outside of these assumptions. Managing this type of uncertainty is different than managing stochastic uncertainty, but disruptions rarely come without warning. Understanding the types of analysis that enable the management of subjective uncertainty in the area of economic analysis of software architecture is an open problem.

In summary, economic analysis of software architecture shows promise of providing important tools to the architect. Making these tools more effective will require identification and management of various types of uncertainty. I look forward to researchers addressing these problems.

Len Bass
NICTA, Sydney

About the Author

Len Bass is a Senior Principal Researcher at National ICT Australia Ltd. (NICTA). He joined NICTA in 2011 after 25 years at the Software Engineering Institute (SEI) at Carnegie Mellon University. He is the co-author of two award-winning books in software architecture, *Software Architecture in Practice, 3rd edition* and *Documenting Software Architectures: Views and Beyond, 2nd edition*, as well as several other books and numerous papers in computer science and software engineering on a wide range of topics. Len has almost 50 years of experience in software development and research in multiple domains, such as scientific analysis systems, embedded systems, and information systems.

References

Helton, J.C., 1997. Uncertainty and sensitivity analysis in the presence of stochastic and subjective uncertainty. J. Stat. Comput. Simul. 57, 3—76.
Wikipedia. Meta Analysis <http://en.wikipedia.org/wiki/Meta-analysis>.

Preface

In this publishing project we are editing a book titled Economics-Driven Software Architecture (EDSA). The main goal of this book is to outline some of the current thinking on the processes and practices for economics- and value-oriented software architecting. These orientations have many commonalities, and they often overlap in practice. There are many gray areas in which the expertise of more than one of these orientations is required in the planning and design of a system. Practicing software engineers, software architects, all researchers advancing our understanding and all students wishing to gain a deeper appreciation of underpinning theories, issues and practices within this domain will benefit from this book.

Introduction

Architects regularly make architectural design decisions but are usually unable to evaluate the economic impact of those decisions. Management, on the other hand, is often interested in product-level decisions (such as features and quality) but not in the technical details of how those decisions are reached. These differing interests lead to inconsistencies between how managers view value and how architects can enable or disable those value propositions through their design decisions. This lack of communication can result in poor decisions. Clearly, it is in the best interests of all stakeholders to make informed and technically feasible value-driven design decisions. Thus, architects need tools and techniques for applying economic-driven principles to software architecture to make better decisions and to better justify those decisions.

Current practice in architecting software systems does not often make economic and strategic considerations explicit. Architectural design decisions tend to be driven by ways that are not connected to, and usually not optimal for, value creation. Factors such as flexibility, time to market, cost, and risk reduction often have a great impact on value creation (Sullivan et al., 2001). Such ignorance is in stark contrast to the motivation and objectives of architecture-centric approaches to development and systematic evolution (e.g., model-driven architectures, domain-specific software architectures and product lines, component-based and middleware-induced architectures), where managing complexity, cost reduction, risk mitigation, evolvability, strategic planning, and long-term value creation are among the major drivers for adopting such approaches. This urges the need for economics-driven and value-based models and metrics, which provide the architect with insights into the long-term and strategic viability, cost effectiveness, and sustainability of the architecture design decisions. We argue that these metrics and models should be in the heart of the architecting process: inception, elaboration, composition, evaluation and analysis, implementation and deployment, maintenance and evolution of architectures. Such provision is important; it assists the objective assessment of the lifetime costs and benefits of evolving systems, and helps identify legacy situations, where an architecture or a component is indispensable but can no longer be evolved to meet changing needs at economic cost. Such consideration will form the scientific foundation for reasoning about the economics of nonfunctional requirements in the context of architectures and architecting.

Issues in economics-based and value-oriented software design

Software design, in some cases carried out across entire industry sectors, including open-source projects, university projects, and individual contributions, acts as a complex adaptive system, strongly driven to converge economically on, and to maintain, good architecture. Today we have few tested theories or practices either of design software-intensive systems for economic value or of how to establish economic forces that promote good architecture, such as through new contracting and acquisition structures. We therefore need research on **harnessing economics** to **promote good architecture** leading to a deeper understanding of how to organize architectures and design to maximize value and of how to create economic conditions that predictably provide incentives to create and sustain valuable architectures.

One of the questions that has arisen is how do we **align architectures** and **industry structures** to harness economic forces in the service of discovering and meeting key requirements of software-intensive systems? Another question is how do we model interaction with a social context in a way that offers guidance for how to design and support software-intensive systems? One of the most important questions focuses on how to relate the design of software-intensive systems to **business goals** and **value objectives** in general.

Architectures create value in at least two ways. First, they can support the delivery of certain properties for which people are willing to pay. Second, they create options to make follow-on investments to adapt or evolve a design to deliver even more valuable properties. Figuring out how to put a value on these options—on the flexibility to vary or adapt a design—is a real challenge, especially when benefits are uncertain. How much should one invest in architecture? The emerging field of *real options* has the potential to provide an intellectual and mathematical handle on such questions. That said, traditional real options techniques (e.g., using Black–Scholes or binomial options pricing techniques) cannot be used directly because they make deep assumptions about the nature and measurability of the underlying uncertainties. These assumptions are generally not valid in the setting of design of unprecedented systems.

The chapters in this volume address these issues, and more. In so doing, they deepen our understanding of economics-driven software architecture and highlight the potential for new tools and new ways for architecting software-intensive systems.

Book overview

The focus of this book is on architecting of software-intensive systems from two closely interrelated points of view: economics and value creation considerations. We have divided this book into four parts, with a general editorial chapter providing an overview of the domain of economics-driven software architecture and a conceptual framework for economics- and value-oriented software architecting.

Part 1—Fundamentals

In Part 1 we survey different software architecting models to deal explicitly with value-creation considerations, explore and identify areas of commonalities and differences, and discuss the role of various approaches in preparing an objective assessment of the lifetime costs and benefits of evolving systems.

The three chapters in this part deal with economic models for product line architecture; aspects of software valuation; and the design implications of users' values for system and software architecture.

Architecture is the central part of product line engineering. Product line architecture should be modeled by considering the economics-related and value-based concerns so that organizations can maximize return on investments on product line technologies. Chapter 2, by T. Maruthi Padmaja and Anil Kumar Thurimella, identifies relevant approaches in software economics and value-based engineering and reviews the suitability of these approaches in the context of product line architecture. Their review provides an overview of the existing support for software economics and value-based approaches for researchers and practitioners. The approaches are assessed based on their support for adoption, domain engineering, application engineering, and decision making. Based on this review, the following open issues are determined:

1. There is a sound support for economic calculations for making strategic decisions on software product line adoptions. However, there is no support for architecting issues (e.g., cost-benefit analysis, architecture evaluation) in these economic models.
2. Domain engineering has been the focus of most of the approaches, and there is little focus on architectural issues in application engineering.

The decision-making approaches for domain engineering should consider inputs from architectural design and architectural reengineering.

Basing software technical decisions on economics has not been generally recognized as important in the software industry. However, because most software is being developed and maintained in a business context, the business consequences of technical choices must be considered. A commercial software development project, a low-cost payroll processing application targeted at small businesses, is used to introduce the basic elements of economic analysis for software projects. Development of the software in an automated test equipment (ATE) system is then used to illustrate the same elements for internally developed software. The approach is then generalized using a decision to invest in refactoring an existing customer relationship management (CRM) code base as an example. Finally, the decision to capitalize software development costs is analyzed to illustrate that it is not as good an idea as some people think it is. Using the techniques described in Chapter 3 by Steve Tockey, software professionals will be able to evaluate the business consequences of their technical alternatives and, thus, be able to make appropriate business decisions about their software projects.

In Chapter 4, Alistair Sutcliffe argues the case for investigating users' values as important influences on the design of software architecture. First, definitions of values in the psychological and sociological literature are reviewed, followed by a derived taxonomy of values relevant to software engineering domains, such as trust, cooperativeness, privacy, and creativity. Stakeholder values are related to nonfunctional requirements or system quality attributes. The architectural implications for user values are described by linking values to design for autonomy, monitoring/awareness and other architectural components. Implications are explained in terms of software and system (i.e., socio-technical) architecture by relating software components to operations in a system design with human factors and organizational concerns. Methods for eliciting user values in the requirements analysis process are explained, and the implications for the future of value-based software architectures are discussed. Application of the value-based requirements engineering and architecture design method is illustrated in a case study of a medical research support system.

Part 2—Economics-driven architecting: design mechanisms and evaluation

The three chapters in this section provide insights into the following topics: economics-driven software architecting for cloud; economics-driven modularity evaluation; and the economics of architecture refactoring.

The market-based control paradigm is a promising approach for architecting large-scale, elastic cloud software systems. In Chapter 5 Funmilade Faniyi and Rami Bahsoon survey principles and practices in economics and cloud computing to motivate the usefulness of market primitives as viable tools for architecting cloud software. The resource allocation problem in cloud service provision is highlighted as one of the key challenges in cloud-based systems. This chapter takes the view that the software architecture is the right level of abstraction to engineer resource allocation mechanisms to address this problem. Using a novel posted offer market, an innovative cloud software architecture that utilizes the market mechanism for self-adapting components interaction at runtime is presented. Simulation studies are performed under representative scenarios to demonstrate the architecture's resilience, adaptive, and scalability properties. Lastly, the chapter poses some open challenges that are crucial for future research in the economics-driven software architecting domain.

As software matures, should we refactor or just keep adding features? Such questions present a recurring dilemma to software practitioners. While the costs of modularization activities, such as refactoring, are significant and immediate, their benefits are largely invisible, intangible, and long term. As a result, it is hard to justify an investment in modularization activities. But the technical debt caused by modularity decay causes huge losses over time in terms of reduced ability to provide new functionality and fix bugs, operational failures, and even canceled projects. The problem is that there is little help for architects, managers, and developers to make the long-term benefits of modularization activities explicit and quantifiable. The goal of Chapter 6 by Yuanfang Cai, Rick Kazman, Carlos Andrade, Lu Xiao, and Hong-Mei Chen is to provide a scientific foundation for explicitly manifesting the economic implications of software modularization activities so that the costs and benefits of such activities can be understood, analyzed, and predicted in a way that is amenable to both engineers and managers. This chapter presents the underpinnings for such a model—an integrated economics-driven modularization evaluation framework that combines code-level analysis, design-level analysis, expert stakeholder elicitation, and history-based cost-benefit analysis. They further show how this framework can be realized as a decision-support system (DSS) and present some of our progress in fleshing out the framework and DSS.

Some organizations regard software architects as advanced software engineers with a high-technology bias but without any expertise in business and strategy. Even software architects themselves often believe they are exclusively responsible for technology and design decisions, but not for economic aspects. This attitude leads to solutions that are technically sound but unable to deliver the expected return on investment. If software architects do not understand economics and the business, they cannot come up with economic solutions that support the business case and business strategy. This is why large and mission-critical projects often do not achieve their business goals, thus incurring high additional costs such as nonconformance penalties. Or as Cem Kaner once put it, "A program which perfectly meets a lousy specification is a lousy program." It is not only an insufficient specification that causes trouble, but also a "lousy" understanding of the specification and economic context by architects. Such projects frequently fail or at least experience significant problems. Although this holds for other engineering disciplines as well, the "softness" of software seems to increase the risks.

In Chapter 7, Michael Stal provides guidance and advice for coping with the economic challenge software architects face. It is not based on empirical or conceptual academic studies, but on experiences of a large international company. The experiences were systematically analyzed and collected from existing and historical projects to identify common causes of failure and to extract guidelines for software architects to avoid such failure.

Part 3—Managing architectural economics

In Part 3 we present a set of views on how to manage architectural economics. The three chapters in this part address the following topics: software engineering leveraging the crowd; architectural debt management in value-oriented architecting; and the value matrix framework for software architectures.

Chapter 8 by Benjamin Satzger, Rostyslav Zabolotnyi, Schahram Dustdar, Martin Gaedke, Stefan Wild, Steffen Göbel, and Tobias Nestler discusses how crowdsourcing can be leveraged for developing and maintaining software products. Crowdsourcing promises a highly flexible on-demand workforce and is compelling to many companies. For a widespread adoption of crowdsourcing for software development, it is crucial to adapt current software project management approaches and development tools to the new requirements on collaboration, decentralization, and scale. A high degree of automation for distributing tasks to developers or teams with the right skill set and expertise is another important aspect. The chapter describes how currently available approaches and tools can be combined with existing research results to get closer to the vision of crowd-enabled software development.

Chapter 9 by Zengyang Li, Peng Liang, and Paris Avgeriou proposes a conceptual model of architectural technical debt (ATD) and an ATD management process that applies this conceptual model to facilitate the decision making in value-oriented architecting. This approach (i.e., the ATD management process and the ATD conceptual model) helps to achieve a controllable and predictable balance between the value and cost of architecture design in the long term. The authors demonstrate how the ATD management process can be employed in architectural synthesis and evaluation in a case study. The outcome of this work provides architecture practitioners a ready-made solution for managing ATD in their architecting context.

In Chapter 10 Anand Kumar, Kesav Vithal Nori, Swaminathan Natarajan, and Doji Samson Lokku present their value matrix framework for software architectures. The basis of the value matrix framework is the "value viewpoint" for creating and describing software architectures. This framework includes identifying the need for architects to understand value creation processes, describing the value and quality concerns to be addressed at each level of development, defining appropriate form/structures for realizing value, and establishing traceability between value, quality, and architecture. In the value matrix framework, the discussion centers on the role of architects with respect to value and qualities, techniques for modeling the context and value influences, and use of the models to establish the relationship between value and qualities.

The core ideas behind the value matrix, as illustrated in Table 1, are the four different perspectives that are substantiated by the use of corresponding metaphors for each perspective. Its scope includes improving stakeholder value, solution lifetime, and consistency with solution environments and the critical concerns that need to be tackled. These concerns are: (1) dialoging with stakeholders in terms of desired benefits, (2) translating benefits to solution qualities, (3) defining the solution profile in terms of qualities, (4) defining the architecture in terms of architecture descriptions, and (5) realizing the architecture description and validating it for value and quality delivery. An X-matrix representation is used to capture the traceability from stakeholder value to features and quality attributes to architectural decisions.

Table 1 Summary of the Value Matrix Framework

Perspective	Metaphors	Guidelines
Value Proposition	Comprehend	Identify stakeholders
		Understand stakeholders value creation context
		Understand situation context
	Conceptualize	Define problem space
		Define solution space
		Define solution value creation context
Qualities Specification	Converge	Redefine stakeholders value requirements
		Define system configuration
		Define system quality characteristics and its correlation to value
	Co-Create	Create system breakdown structure
		Create quality breakdown structure
		Create usage processes
Architecture Description	Co-Convert	Identify architecture styles
		Define architecture rationales
		Define architectural models
	Communicate	Create architectural views and viewpoints
		Translate to architecture description
		Qualities conformance
Architecture Instance	Commit	Architecture realization
		Architecture analysis and improvement
	Co-Evolve	Qualities analysis and improvement
		Value analysis and improvement

Part 4—Linking architecture inception and evolution to economics: experiences and approaches

Part 4 contains three chapters that look at a variety of industrial cases and practices. The chapters in this section present practical approaches and cases. Chapter 11 presents a model of interactions and decision-making processes during the evolution of a system using a game-theoretic approach. Chapter 12 introduces a value-based methodology that allowed the authors to successfully architect, implement, and operate multiple CyberInfrastructures in multiyear projects. Chapter 13 proposes a framework for architectural design of self-aware adaptive systems to bridge the gap between requirements and user views and software engineering software architecture.

The architecture of service-oriented systems is defined by the services involved and the network of their usage interdependencies. Changes in an individual service may lead to the evolution of the overall architecture, as (a) different or new interactions may become possible and (b) existing partners may leave the network if their dependency needs are no longer fulfilled. Therefore, studying the evolution of a service and the impact it may have on services and business partners that depend on it is essential to studying software-architecture evolution in the age of service-oriented architecture. In such an environment with different and possibly independent parties, there may exist conflicting goals; for example, one party may aim for evolution while another may desire stability. In Chapter 11, Marios Fokaefs, Eleni Stroulia and Paul R. Messinger model the interactions and decision-making process during the evolution of a system using a game-theoretic approach and explore how variations in the dependencies and the information flow between the service provider and the clients impact the provider's decision-making process regarding the evolution of the service.

Chapter 12 by Emilia Farcas, Claudio Farcas, and Ingolf Krüger is an example of the techno-economic challenges facing modern CyberInfrastructure (CI) research in emerging fields such as E-Health that provide tremendous opportunities for innovation with high societal impact. In this chapter, the authors introduce a value-based methodology that allowed them to successfully architect, implement, and operate multiple CIs in multiyear projects from this domain. They detail aspects of value-based service elicitation, requirements negotiation and prioritization, cost trade-off analysis, domain modeling, logical and deployment architectures, and iterative architecture evaluation. They include appropriate discussions of the existing approaches, where they work or don't, the rationale for their approach, and how it helped them overcome the specific obstacles they encountered in practice. The chapter also describes the authors' CI projects, a typical architecture from this field, and how they addressed specific requirements, from data acquisition and management through system deployment and operation.

In Chapter 13, Alistair Sutcliffe proposes a framework for architectural design of self-aware adaptive systems (SAAS) to bridge the gap between requirements and user views and software engineering software architecture. The conceptual architecture consists of components for monitoring events, interpreting events and information, then adapting the system or providing information for human in the loop adaptation. Taxonomies of models for each component are described, with generic requirements and design issues for each model family. The framework is applied to design of the system architecture for a health-care application for monitoring and analysis signs of mild cognitive impairment from users' e-mail and computer use. Feedback aims to persuade the user to self-administer themselves for medical advice. The architecture is tested in a reuse exercise, applying it to another health-care application. The economic trade-offs and exploitation paths of development via generic architectures are reviewed.

Software architecture is widely recognized as the keystone of the development of complex software-intensive systems. Until recently, however, software architects have been operating in a largely technical domain, where their primary concern was with system functionality and quality attributes. This is, of course, only half the story. A successful architect is constantly faced with the trade-offs surrounding economics. No software architectural decision is taken in a vacuum. The prudent architect knows this and always considers cost and benefit, both in the near term and the long term, in making technical decisions.

This book is a first attempt to collect a body of knowledge that can guide a software architect in making such decisions. We hope that you find it useful and enlightening.

Ivan Mistrik
Heidelberg, Germany

Rami Bahsoon
Birmingham, UK

Rick Kazman
Honolulu, HI, USA

Yuanyuan Zhang
London, UK

Reference

Sullivan, K., Griswold, W., Cai, Y., Hallen., B., 2001. The Structure and value of modularity in software design, Vienna, Austria. pp. 99–108. Proceedings of the 9th ACM SIGSOFT Symposium on the Foundations of Software Engineering. ACM, New York

Economics-Driven Software Architecture: Introduction

1

Rick Kazman[1], Rami Bahsoon[2], Ivan Mistrik[3], and Yuanyuan Zhang[4]

[1]*University of Hawaii, Honolulu, HI, USA*
[2]*University of Birmingham, Birmingham, UK*
[3]*Independent Consultant, Heidelberg, Germany*
[4]*University College London, London, UK*

1.1 Introduction

Architects regularly make architectural design decisions but are usually unable to evaluate the economic impact of those decisions. Management, in contrast, is often interested in product-level decisions (such as features and quality) but not in the technical details of how those decisions are made. These differing interests lead to inconsistencies between how managers view value and how architects can enable or disable those value propositions through their design decisions. This lack of communication can result in poor decisions.

Clearly, it is in the best interests of all project stakeholders to make informed and technically feasible value-driven design decisions. Thus architects need practical, validated tools and techniques for applying economics-driven principles to software architecture. They need these tools and techniques to make better decisions and to better justify those decisions to their stakeholders.

Current practices in architecting software systems do not often make economic and strategic considerations explicit. Architectural design decisions tend to be driven by ways that are not connected to, and usually not optimal for, value creation. Factors such as flexibility, time to market, cost, and risk reduction often have high impact on value creation (Sullivan et al., 2001). But the sad reality is that such considerations are seldom included in architectural planning. The state of the practice is that systems are typically designed by thinking about functionality first and considering architecture, if at all, only when problems arise.

Such ignorance is in stark contrast to the motivation and objectives of architecture-centric approaches to development and systematic evolution (e.g., model-driven architectures, domain-specific software architectures and product lines, component-based and middleware-induced architectures, etc.), where managing complexity, cost reduction, risk mitigation, evolvability, strategic planning, and long-term value creation are among the major drivers for adopting such approaches. This suggests an urgent need for economics-driven and value-based architectural models and metrics, which can provide the architect with insights into the long-term and strategic viability, cost-effectiveness, and sustainability of the architecture design decisions made (or not made).

We believe that these metrics and models should be at the heart of the "architecting" process: inception, elaboration, composition, evaluation and analysis, implementation and deployment, maintenance, and evolution of architectures. Such a perspective is important; it assists the objective assessment of the lifetime costs and benefits of architectural decisions made for evolving systems. It also helps to identify legacy situations, where an architecture or a component is indispensable but can no longer be evolved to meet changing needs at a reasonable, sustainable cost. Such considerations will form the scientific foundation for reasoning about the economics of quality attribute requirements and project requirements in the context of architectures and architecting.

This book seeks to gather together a coherent set of research and experience on the following topics.

- Architecture-based economic models, particularly cost modeling and benefit modeling
- Architecture and its relationship to project inception and evolution
- Economic aspects of architecture-based project management
- Architecture and its effects on risk management, particularly as it relates to technical debt
- Architecture and agility
- Tools and techniques for analyzing the economic implications of architectural decisions

1.2 Architecture and project management

Architecture is most commonly used in medium to large-scale projects—projects that have multiple teams and too much complexity for any individual to fully comprehend. Such projects typically involve substantial investments and have multiyear durations. For such projects, the various teams (which may be distributed) need to coordinate their efforts. In these projects, upper management often demands both short time to market and adequate oversight. Thus the use of architecture as a tool for project management is becoming increasingly necessary and commonplace.

The project manager is responsible for the business side of the project. This responsibility involves providing appropriate and sufficient resources to the project; negotiating, creating, and overseeing the budget and schedule; negotiating requirements and constraints with stakeholders; and ensuring overall project quality. The software architect, working closely with the project manager, is responsible for the technical side of the project. This involves: designing to achieve specific quality attributes, determining and enacting appropriate technical oversight, reviewing requirements for feasibility, and day-to-day leadership of the development team.

Once an architecture has been designed, it can be used to define the project structure and organization. The structure of a project and the structure of the team that realizes the project need to be reasonably congruent. This is known as Conway's Law (Conway, 1968) or the Mirroring Hypothesis (Colfer and Baldwin, 2010). Once implementation of a project commences, the project manager and architect have a series of decisions to make involving trade-offs, incremental development, and risk management. The project manager and architect need to negotiate any trade-offs, particularly those arising from new requirements, as these will affect one or more of cost, schedule, and quality. The project plan also defines the schedule, which has enormous implications for the architecture since it has to accommodate internal "releases" of subsets of the project's functionality, leading up to a (hopefully) successful complete implementation. And through it all the project manager must track progress. This tends to occur through some combination of personal contact with developers (which does not scale up well), through formal status meetings, through the collection of metrics, and through risk management.

1.3 **Architecture-based economic modeling**

An economic model in any domain is a simplification—an abstraction. For economic modeling to be tractable, the modeler must ignore many details of the domain being modeled and choose the most salient details to model, all the while maintaining as high a degree of fidelity as possible. Every model is an approximation, and the better the approximation the more useful the model is, all other things being equal. But all other things are never equal. They must be based on readily available, traceable, and verifiable data; they must be computationally tractable; and they must make sense to the model's stakeholders.

An architecture is an ideal place to bring cost modeling (as well as benefit modeling, risk management, and project management, as we will see). The architecture forms a large part of a software-intensive project's work breakdown structure and so it guides the architect and developers in doing both top-down and bottom-up cost estimates.

For example, Dan Paulish and colleagues at Siemens Corporation have developed a number of rules of thumb for doing top-down estimation of project costs (Paulish, 2002). Some rules of thumb that they have used in medium-sized ($\sim$150 K SLOC) projects are:

- Number of components to be estimated $\sim$150
- Paper design time per component $\sim$4 hours
- Times between engineering releases $\sim$8 weeks
- Overall project development allocation
  40% design—5% architectural, 35% detailed
  20% coding
  40% testing

Once an initial architecture design has been produced, then leads for the pieces of the architecture are assigned and the teams can be built. At this point, bottom-up estimates from the team leads can be produced. This bottom-up estimate is usually much more accurate than the top-down estimate, but there may also be significant differences due to differing assumptions. These differences between the top-down and bottom-up estimates need to be discussed and negotiated. An experienced project manager knows to avoid committing costs to upper management until the bottom-up estimates (and project schedule) have been developed and negotiated through this bottom-up/top-down process.

Numerous cost models have been developed over the past three decades. Perhaps the best known of these models are the COCOMO (COnstructive COst MOdel) family of models (Boehm and Turner, 2003) and Function Points (Albrecht, 1979). The original COCOMO model was a regression model that predicted a project's cost based on a number of "factors"—project, process, hardware, and personnel attributes—that affected a project's complexity and hence cost. Function points attempted to estimate a project's size and complexity, and hence cost, by looking at the complexity of business requirements and processing requirements. While neither of these models is explicitly about architecture, their concerns and levels of abstraction were consistent with those of software architectural analyses.

1.4 **Architecture-based benefit modeling**

In the final analysis, the goal of economics-driven architecting is to create the maximum amount of value. Value should be our guide in making any architecture-related decisions. We need value-based activities and strategies that are practical and easily implemented that have a principled basis and that have a simple and clear rationale.

What is value? This is, in itself, a complex issue when dealing with software. Value is how much a product or service is worth to a stakeholder, and this worth is often relative to other things. It is typically measured in money, but it does not always have to be. Value can also be an evaluation of what something could or should be worth, or an explanation of its actual market value (price); this is the purpose of using stock prices to value a company on the open stock market. Furthermore, we have to consider such facts as productivity, evolvability, and reputation, all of which are indirect ways in which a product or service might create value. These are frequently trickier to measure than "price" or "profit," but they are extremely useful measures nonetheless! Finally, value in software is not just a function of costs such as personnel or material inputs; it reifies what the software is worth to a wide variety of stakeholders: the consumer, the producer, maintainer, and so on. For example, how valuable is it for the software architect to have an evolvable design?

When creating or evolving a software or system architecture, the architect needs to focus on value. Design is, in its essence, a search through a (virtually infinite) space of possible alternatives, choosing the one that maximizes expected value, given the project's available resources, the schedule or deadline, and the set of project constraints (interfaces that must be complied with, resources that must be employed, Commercial Off-The-Shelf (COTS) packages that must be used, strategic agreements with partners, abilities of the development team, backward compatibility, etc.).

Shooting for the absolute "maximum" amount of value is not achievable in practice. Instead, in any value-based problem, we aim for something slightly less optimal but vastly more achievable: Pareto-optimality (also known as 80–20 rules). What is an 80–20 rule? In 1906 Vilfredo Pareto noted that 80% of income in Italy went to 20% of the population. He noted many such unequal distributions. For example, he reported that 20% of the pea plants in his garden produced 80% of the peas. He saw this as an optimization problem: How can one find the 20% in advance and concentrate one's resources and efforts on this population?

Given a set of alternative allocations and a set of individuals, a movement from one allocation to another that can make at least one individual better off, without making any other individual worse off, is called a Pareto improvement. An allocation of resources is Pareto optimal when no further Pareto improvements can be made. How do we achieve this in practice? In software engineering such 80–20 rules have also been noted. For example, 80% of the defects are found in 20% of the code, or 80% of the value is found in 20% of the features. Of course, there is nothing magical about the numbers 80 and 20; it could be 90–10 or 60–40. The point is that we would like to be able to optimize our efforts and focus on the 20% of tasks that lead to 80% of the value. We would like to be able to predict where to spend our time. And this boils down to cost/benefit estimation and decision making.

One technique that is being adopted from the field of financial economics is use of the theory of real options to provide an estimate of value. An architectural decision, such as the application of a pattern, is analogous to a financial derivative. In financial markets a derivative is an instrument whose value depends on, or derives from, the values of basic underlying assets. For example, a stock option is a derivative whose value is dependent on the price of the stock. The stock is the underlying asset for the option.

Real options theory can be employed to analyze the value of architectural patterns in terms of the quality attributes, and hence value, that can be achieved with them (Ozkaya et al., 2007).

Options are valuable when there is uncertainty. The theory is typically applied in situations when uncertainty is large enough that it is necessary to wait for more information. Waiting can be valuable when it allows investments to be postponed until uncertainty is resolved. The components of real options analysis include the decision to make, characterization of the uncertainty, and the decision rule. The decision rule can be viewed as a simple mathematical expression that will serve as a guide on when to exercise the decision. The decision rule also helps identify the critical parameters that need to be observed in making the decision.

Clearly, the real options formulation is applicable to architectural design decisions: Investments are frequently contingent on prevailing and future market conditions (e.g., the addition of a new tier in an n-tier architecture makes it easier to make changes to business rules). In addition, there is typically a large degree of uncertainty in the future that makes it advisable to wait for more information before making a decision.

1.5 Architecture and risk management

Architectural design and analysis are intimately tied to risk management, which in turn supports project management. When making architectural decisions, the architect needs to consider the level of certainty of the requirements and how any consequent architectural decisions might change in the future. Each of these is, in essence, an estimate of risk.

Real options are one way of managing risk, by attempting to quantify the consequences of architectural decisions. Other forms of architectural risk management are creating performance models, building simulations of critical system behavior, and building architectural "experiments" to test out important new concepts or pieces of system infrastructure. These kinds of risk management typically focus on the runtime aspects of a system's behavior.

But the non-runtime aspects can have an equally important impact on a system's eventual success. Consider modifiability, for example. If the system is not "appropriately" modifiable, then it will likely fail. If, on the one hand, the system is hard to modify then it will not satisfy its user's demands in the future and will fall behind competitive offerings. If, on the other hand, the system is designed to be extremely modifiable, it may take a very long time to reach the market, and it may be very expensive to create and highly complex to test.

The metaphor of "technical debt" (Brown et al., 2010) was created to describe the situation when developers make short-term suboptimal decisions that need to be "paid back" later in a project. The most common form of technical debt is related to modularity or, more precisely, the lack of modularity. By not modularizing functionality, developers can quickly develop code but typically at the expense of later modifiability. This debt accumulates over the life of a project, and it is only paid down by refactoring activities, which can be seen as a kind of investment in the existing software corpus. Numerous techniques have been suggested to attempt to locate and diagnose technical debt, including "code smells" (Fowler, 1999), modularity violation detection (Wong et al., 2011), clone detection (Kim Notkin, 2009), and various coupling and cohesion metrics (Chidamber and Kemerer, 1994). Each of these techniques is aimed at determining architectural "hot spots"—locations in the system where technical debt has accumulated.

Of course, other types of technical debt are possible as well, such as the extravagant use of resources in a first implementation, which then needs to be tuned and refined as a system matures and attempts to scale. Whatever the source and form of the technical debt, it is essentially an economic decision: Is it a choice of "how much architecture" and "how much risk mitigation" up-front versus getting a release to market more quickly, albeit with less-than-optimal quality attributes?

1.6 Architecture and agility

Agile processes were initially employed on small- to medium-sized projects with short time frames and enjoyed considerable early success. In the early years, Agile processes were not often used for larger projects, and Agile projects eschewed up-front planning, including architectural design.

Agile processes, when they first appeared, were a response to a need for projects to:

- be more responsive to their stakeholders.
- be quicker to develop functionality that users care about.
- show more and earlier progress in a project's life cycle.
- be less burdened by documenting aspects of a project that would inevitably change.

These needs, however, are not in conflict with architecture. The question for a software project is not "Should I do Agile or architecture?" The Agile manifesto claimed to prefer individuals and interactions over processes and tools, working software over comprehensive documentation, customer collaboration over contract negotiation, and responding to change over following a plan. Is any of this inimical to the use of architecture?

In fact, the question for a software project is not "should I do Agile or architecture?", but rather, "how much architecture should I do up-front versus how much should I defer until the project's requirements have solidified somewhat?", or "when and how should I refactor?", "how much of the architecture should I formally document, and when?" and "should I review my architecture and, if so, when?".

Boehm and Turner (2003), for example, have looked at the trade-offs between "agility" (the ability to quickly respond to changes) and discipline (up-front work on architecture and risk resolution). The more up-front work that you do, the more cost that you add, up-front, to a project. For small projects—say, 10,000 lines of code—this discipline simply never pays off. However, for medium (100,000 lines of code) and large (1,000,000 lines of code) projects, up-front work does pay off. In fact, the larger the project, the more that up-front work pays dividends. Every project has a sweet spot between agility and discipline. Bohem and Turner's analysis helps to find this spot.

1.7 Runtime economics-driven architecting

The work on EDSA has also been concerned with dynamic and self-adaptive architecting for value creation. We describe research effort under this category as *runtime EDSA*. Runtime EDSA stems from the belief that the ability of a design decision to create value tends to be limited; it can be sensitive to dynamic changes in context, inputs from the environment, and users' requirements. Research under this category has primarily been concerned with self-organization and self-optimization of the architecture, with the objective of delivering an added value through optimal modes of architectural compositions, which are best "fit" to the runtime changes in requirements and the environment. In EDSA at runtime, value creation through optimization is formulated as a "dynamic search" problem. The search continuously evaluates and optimizes the structure, where value can be linked to behavior and context requirements, technical debt analysis and reduction, energy efficiency, risk mitigation for compliance, and improved Quality of Service (QoS). Design time decisions form a "portfolio" of possible strategies, which can be automatically searched and exercised at runtime if a strategy promises an added value. In this context, value creation is treated as a moving target, which can be self-optimized through feedback loops, measurement and control leading to self-organization, and self-management of the structure.

The application of runtime EDSA has been appealing to service-centric and cloud-based architectures in particular. Let us have a closer look at cloud-based architectures and how they can benefit from runtime EDSA by referring to (Nallur and Bahsoon, 2013; Faniyi Bahsoon, 2012). Given the unpredictable, highly dynamic, elastic and on-demand nature of the cloud, priory knowledge and design time strategies for value creation are mere difficult to formulate. It would be unrealistic to assume that optimal strategies for value creation can be predicted at design time as value is heavily dependent on dynamics in the infrastructure inducing these architectures.

Cloud-based architectures can be composed of web services, which can be leased off the cloud. The value of the application and its underlying architecture is a function of the value of the individual web services composing the application. These architectures can "trade" instances of abstract web services off the cloud, which can serve as a basis for dynamic synthesis and composition of the architecture. That is, for a given abstract service A, there exist multiple concrete services $A_i \ldots$ A_n in the c market offering comparable functionalities but differing in their price and QoS provisions. We view the cloud as a marketplace. Cloud-based architectures encompass a set of strategies and tactics that can be viewed as goods to be traded in this market. We argue that market-based control can contribute to the foundation of the runtime EDSA. Economics and markets have intrinsic properties that make them of interest in this setting, namely, decentralization, scalability, adaptiveness, and robustness. Market mechanisms lend themselves neatly to the notion of valuation of cost and benefits via utilities. "Buyers" are cloud-based architectures, and sellers are vendors and providers of the services, which realize quality attributes, functional requirements, and price and environmental constraints (Faniyi Bahsoon, 2012).

In a dynamic and continuously evolving context, the challenge is to understand how value can be captured, modeled, and analyzed and to discover the various trade-offs involved and their evolution trends as the system is executing. A common way of representing value for an architecture tactic (e.g., provision of resource to improve QoS) is to formulate the value using utility functions. This effort could take different forms (e.g., additive utility), where each formulation impacts the market's ability to reach desirable emergent state(s). There are many existing market mechanisms in the micro-economics literature. Each theoretically studied mechanism can be shown to reach some known solution concept (e.g., Nash equilibria). A self-adaptive mechanism, which uses these utility models, can assist analysts, architects, and enterprises in providing built-in support for an autonomic architecture management supporting continuous evolution for value added. The inputs to these modes can be continuous data and feeds available via published benchmarks (e.g., cloudharmony.com; spec. org), which can continuously steer the selection and composition of such architectures.

1.8 Final thoughts

A book such as this can only be a snapshot of a complex and growing field. We have attempted to survey the major historical and current research areas within economics-driven software architecture, but such a picture will always be incomplete and subject to revision. Such is life.

References

Albrecht, A.J., 1979. Measuring application development productivity. Proceedings of the Joint SHARE, GUIDE, and IBM Application Development Symposium, IBM Corporation, pp. 83−92.

Boehm, B., Turner, R., 2003. Balancing Agility and Discipline: A Guide for the Perplexed. Addison-Wesley, Reading, MA.

Brown, N., Cai, Y., Guo, Y., Kazman, R., Kim, M., Kruchten, P. et al., November 2010. Managing technical debt in software-reliant systems. 2010 FSE/SDP Workshop on the Future of Software Engineering Research at ACM SIGSOFT FSE-18, Santa Fe, NM.

Chidamber, S., Kemerer, C., 1994. A metrics suite for object oriented design. IEEE Trans. Software Eng. 20 (6), 476−493.

Colfer, L., Baldwin, C., 2010. The mirroring hypothesis: theory, evidence and exceptions. Harvard Business School Finance Working Paper No. 10−058.

Conway, M.E., 1968. How do committees invent? Datamation 14 (4), 28−31.

Faniyi, F., Bahsoon, R., 2012. Self-Managing SLA compliance in cloud architectures: a market-based approach. Proceedings of the International ACM Sigsoft Symposium on Architecting Critical Systems, Bertinoro, Italy. ACM Press, New York, USA.

Fowler, M., 1999. Refactoring: Improving the Design of Existing Code. Addison-Wesley, Reading, MA.

Kim, M., Notkin, D., 2009 Discovering and representing systematic code changes. 31st International Conference on Software Engineering, 309−319.

Nallur, V., Bahsoon., R., 2013. A decentralized self-adaptation mechanism for service-based applications in the cloud. IEEE Trans. Software Eng. 39 (5).

Ozkaya, I., Kazman, R., Klein, M., 2007. Quality-attribute-based economic valuation of architectural patterns. Technical Report. CMU/SEI-2007-TR-003. Carnegie Mellon Software Engineering Institute. <http://www.sei.cmu.edu/pub/documents/07.reports/07tr003>.

Paulish, D., 2002. Architecture-Centric Software Project Management: A Practical Guide. Addison-Wesley, Reading, MA.

Sullivan, K., Griswold, W., Cai, Y., Hallen, B., 2001. The structure and value of modularity in software design. Proceedings of the 9th ACM SIGSOFT Symposium on the Foundations of Software Engineering. ACM, Vienna, Austria, pp. 99−108.

Wong, S., Cai, Y., Kim, M., Dalton, M., May 2011. Detecting software modularity violations. Proceedings of the 33th International Conference on Software Engineering (ICSE 2011).

Fundamentals of Economics-Driven Software Architecture

Economic Models and Value-Based Approaches for Product Line Architectures

2

Anil Kumar Thurimella[1] and T. Maruthi Padmaja[2]
[1]Harman Automotive Division and TU, Munich, Germany
[2]K. L University, Vaddeswaram, AP, India

2.1 Introduction

Software product line engineering (SPLE) (Weiss and Lai, 1999) supports the development of a family of systems by customizing artifacts from a set of core assets. A *software product line* (SPL) is a set of software-intensive systems that share a common, managed set of features satisfying the specific needs of a particular market segment or mission and that are developed from a common set of core assets in a prescribed way (Clements and Northrop, 2006). An asset is an artifact that can be used in the development of several systems of a SPL.

SPLE provides several advantages such as improved reuse, quicker time to market, improved cost savings, and decreased defect rates. Based on these advantages, SPLs are beneficial for economical software development. Many companies have already recorded success stories by adopting and practicing SPL approaches; some of these success stories are available at the Product Line Hall of Fame (Product Line Hall of Fame).

Software economics (Boehm et al., 2000) support models for analyzing various use cases such as return on investments (ROI) and cost-benefit analysis. For example, based on the COnstructive COst MOdel (COCOMO) (Boehm et al., 2000), managers may analyze if the costs of creating assets are recovered while developing products. Another related area is *value-based software engineering* (VBSE) (Biffl et al., 2005) which associates business value with artifacts.

Companies do not develop SPLs from scratch; rather, they usually transition from a single-system development to SPLE. This transition is often incremental and evolutionary and requires significant initial investments (Schmid and Verlage, 2002). In addition, transitioning also requires significant investments because of the switch in the paradigm (single-system development to SPLE). Therefore, before adopting product line approaches, companies have to decide if SPLE provides a good ROI for them. Later, a transition plan should be developed for adopting SPLE approaches.

Transitioning involves technical challenges in terms of architecting across various application domains, companies, and product families. Let us consider a simple case in which a company has been developing a family (or a set of related products) with N products by pragmatically reusing (e.g., through copy and paste followed by modifications) specifications and repositories. In this situation, justifying an economic case would be based on relatively simple ROI calculations. In particular, a product line manager could argue that costs for asset creation and reuse are significantly less than costs for maintaining N different repositories. Due to different historical reasons as well as future perspectives, making decisions on transitioning to SPLE is also complex in some situations. Let us consider the case of companies getting new products and markets by new acquisitions. Suppose that a company X has been developing a software system SYS1 in C++. The company X acquires another company Y that developed SYS2, which has been developed in Java or FOTRAN and shares significant functionality with SYS1. In this situation, product line managers also have to ensure value-based considerations for creating architectural models.

In order to understand the landscape of SPL architecture, economics, and VBSE, we first review the support for these aspects in the literature. In particular, we address the following research questions:

- RQ1: What are the relevant economic models and approaches that support value-based considerations?
- RQ2: What is the relevance of these approaches for product line architecture?

Providing an overview of a wide variety of economic models and value-based approaches is helpful for industry people in selecting relevant approaches for their usage. Understanding their relevance to product line architecture can improve understanding of the landscape by assessing the support for economic architecting in the literature. A comparative analysis of the economic models is already available in the literature (e.g. Ali et al. (2009)). Similarly, Lim (Lim, 1996) has produced another comparative survey of economic models. Software architecture and VBSE have not been the focus of these reviews.

Because this chapter focuses on architecture, we could have restricted our discussion to RQ2. The rationale for considering both RQ1 and RQ2 is as follows. Architecting involves design decisions based on the outputs of economic models. Therefore, there is a need to identify relevant approaches for both the economic models and value-based communities. Existing reviews (Ali et al., 2009; Lim, 1996) assess only the economic models. Therefore, RQ1 focuses on identifying relevant approaches, and RQ2 focuses on reviewing their relevance to software architecture. Without identifying the relevant approaches, we could not have reviewed them in the context of software architecture.

This chapter is organized as follows. Section 2.2 provides background information on product lines and software economics. Section 2.3 presents the research framework used for the review process within this chapter. In addition, we provide overviews of the papers reviewed here. The approaches reported in the reviewed papers are described in sections 2.4 and 2.5, respectively. In particular, section 2.4 describes the economic models, and section 2.5 reviews the value-based approaches. All these approaches are discussed in section 2.6. In the discussion, we use examples to highlight open issues. Related work is presented in section 2.7. Section 2.8 concludes the chapter with a list of open issues.

2.2 Background

In this section, we provide background information relevant to understanding the concepts of this chapter. In particular, we present background information on topics such as SPLE, software economics, and software architecture.

2.2.1 **Fundamentals of SPLE**

A *platform* is a collection of reusable artifacts called assets. SPLE includes two high-level processes: domain engineering and application engineering. *Domain engineering* is responsible for developing reusable platforms in which the commonality and variability of the product lines are defined and realized. *Application engineering* is responsible for developing product line applications from the platform by reusing assets as much as possible.

The term *variability* means the ability to change; it is defined and identified during domain engineering. Variability is introduced as an abstraction during the product management for allowing customization and reuse of assets. Variability is identified during domain engineering and is exploited (i.e., instantiated) during application engineering for allowing software reuse. Variability management covers the identification and representation of variability, its instantiation for specific products, as well as variability evolution, which deals with the change of variability.

In the SPLE context, a variation point abstracts variability. The variation point is defined as the variability subject within the domain artifacts enriched by contextual information (Pohl et al., 2005). Modeling variability in SPLE is essential for building a flexible architecture (Griss, 2000).

2.2.2 **Economic models**

In this chapter we review several economic models and access them for their applicability to software architecture (see RQ1). Therefore, we present some generic models in this area.

COCOMO MODEL (Boehm et al., 2000): The constructive cost model was used by thousands of software project managers. There are two popular versions of the COCOMO model. The initial version is the Basic COCOMO model or COCOMO81. Later, an advanced version, COCOMO II models, was created to estimate modern software development projects.

1. Basic COCOMO: This model estimates the software development effort as a function of program size (SLOC). The equations for basic COCOMO model are:

$$Effort\ Applied(E) = a_b(KLOC)^b b[man - months] \qquad (2.1)$$

$$Development\ Time(D) = c_b(E)^d b[months] \qquad (2.2)$$

$$People required(P) = E/D[count] \qquad (2.3)$$

Here *KLOC* is lines of code in terms of thousands. The coefficients a_b, b_b, c_b, and d_b are predefined constants (Van der Linden, 2002) and vary depending on project class. Although basic COCOMO presents a quick estimate of software costs, it lacks cost driver estimates such as hardware constraints, personnel quality, and experience.

2. COCOMO II: The effort applied in person-months E in COCOMO II is estimated as

$$E = a_i(KLOC)^{b_i}.EAF \qquad (2.4)$$

Here, *EAF* is the Effort Adjustment Factor, which is an effort multiplier rating on a six-point scale that ranges from "very low" to "extra high"(Van der Linden, 2002). The coefficients a_i and b_i are constants and vary according to project class.

2.2.3 Software architecture

Architecture is the central part of SPLE. In a general sense, software architecture is a structured solution that can optimize common quality attributes such as performance, security, and manageability in order to meet all the requirements. It involves a series of decisions based on a wide range of factors, and these decisions have an impact on quality attributes (Ali Babar et al., 2009). Good architecture reduces the business risks associated with building a technical solution. The successful maintenance of any complex software-intensive system depends on selecting appropriate series of business-critical architecture design decisions.

Architectural description languages (ADL) are often used to represent software architecture. A classification of architecture design languages is reported in Medvidovic and Taylor, 2000. Unified modeling language (UML) supports abstractions for software design. Patterns (Martin, 2000) provide reusable solutions for software design. All these architectural modeling techniques have been used in the context of product line architectures (Lutz and Gannod, 2003; Gomaa, 2004).

Software product lines are usually not developed from scratch. Typically, architecture is recovered from legacy systems. Later, the recovered architecture is evolved into product line architecture. The architecture recovery techniques are also used as analysis techniques to find gaps in architecture. For example, Lutz and Gannod (2003) recover product line architecture based on a set of tools and specify the architecture in an ADL notation. By formally checking ADL specifications, gaps in the architecture are identified. Product line architecture evaluation is used to access qualities such as modularity, extensibility, and portability (Breivold et al., 2012).

Architecting (architecture analysis and design as described above) involves decision making. Architectural knowledge management (Ali Babar et al., 2009) is an emerging area of study. Here, the challenge is to capture the design decisions and to manage the tacit knowledge behind these decisions. Zimmermann et al. (2012; 2009) presents a meta-model, a formal representation and a tool for modeling architectural design decisions. In addition, design decisions are also used as assets (Zimmermann, 2011). However, these contributions do not focus on product lines.

Among possible design decisions, identifying optimal software architecture for a software-intensive system is an important issue in SPLE. Here, software economics plays a critical role in making business-oriented architecture design decisions. The main concern of economics for product line architectures is to improve return on investment (ROI) by making better architectural decisions. In addition, architects should consider the value (e.g., benefits for the cost of implementing a decision) for making design decisions. Therefore, both of these perspectives are reviewed in this chapter.

2.3 Research framework

In this section we present our research framework with an overview of the approaches examined in this chapter in the form of two tables: Table 2.1 summarizes the mathematical models for performing economics related calculations, and Table 2.2 presents a preview of the relevant SPL approaches, with a focus on architecture, or includes value-based considerations at least partially. The approaches discussed in both of the tables are complementary to each other.

We identified the approaches by searching for relevant papers in the literature as follows. In order to identify relevant approaches on economic models and value-based approaches in the context of product lines, we searched for relevant papers in Google as well as in digital libraries

Table 2.1 An Overview of SPL Economic Models Reviewed in this Contribution

Nr	Author(s)	Publication	Economics-related Substance	Related Section
1	Poulin 1997	*Journal of Applied Software Technology,* 1997.	A model for estimating the financial benefits (e.g., ROI) of software development for product lines.	Section 2.4.1
2.	Boehm et al., 2004	ISESE, 2004.	This article discusses a new product line life-cycle economics model, Constructive Product Line Investment Model (COPLIMO). for addressing the issue of underestimation of return on investments.	Section 2.4.2
3.	Böckle et al., 2004	IEEE Software 2004	Based on a simple mathematical model, this approach supports economic considerations for seven different scenarios.	Section 2.4.3
4.	Clements et al., 2005	Carnegie Mellon University, 2005.	The Structured Intuitive Model for Product Line Economics (SIMPLE), which supports a cost model for various product line development scenarios.	Section 2.4.4
5.	In et al., 2006	Communications of the ACM, 2006.	A quality-based product line life-cycle cost estimation model, called qCOMPLIMO, and investigates the effect of software quality cost on the ROI of SPL.	Section 2.4.5
6.	Withey, 1996	Carnegie Mellon University, 1996	An investment analysis approach for SPL assets.	Section 2.4.6
7.	Cohen, 2003	Carnegie Mellon University, 2003	A prediction model based on applications, benefits, and costs.	Section 2.4.7
8.	Pohl et al., 2005	Software Product Line Engineering Foundations, Principles, and Techniques, Springer 2005	Different transition strategies such as incremental, tactical, pilot project, and big bang are presented in order to switch from single-system development to SPLE.	Section 2.4.8

(IEEE, ACM). For the literature search, we used keywords such as software product lines AND economic models OR cost models for Table 2.1 and software product lines AND value-based OR decision making for Table 2.2. After getting the initial publications, we filtered them on the basis of the following criteria:

- Relevance and context of the keywords used in the papers. For example, the term *product line* is used across different communities (e.g., operations management) and can be used in different senses. We excluded the papers where the keywords are used in a different context and have a different meaning.
- The paper should report a novel approach. We excluded papers that reported a literature review.

Table 2.2 An Overview of value-based Approaches Reviewed in this Contribution

Nr	Author(s)	Publication	Economics Related Substance	Related Section in this Chapter
1.	Clements and Northrop, 2006	Framework for Software Product Line Practice-Version 4.2	This online article discusses measurement activity for a SPL via data collection for different metrics in order to track their risks.	Section 2.5.1
2.	Lago and van Vliet, 2005	ICSE 2005	This approach enables architectural design decisions in the context of SPLs by enriching feature models with assumptions.	Section 2.5.2
3.	Rabiser, et al., 2008	VaMOS 2008	An approach that combines variability management, value-based software engineering, and collaborative software engineering.	Section 2.5.3
4.	Thurimella and Bruegge, 2012	IST, 2012	Decision support for variability management as well as managing the rationale behind decisions.	Section 2.5.4
5.	Muller, 2011	SPLC '11	Introduced a Value-Based Portfolio Optimization in order to make critical business decisions to improve return on investment.	Section 2.5.5

- We only included approaches that were at least partly evaluated. We excluded papers where authors were not able to demonstrate their claims.
- Papers that have relevance to software architecture; that is, the report should either address architecture-related issues or can be tailored to product line architectures.

After filtering based on the above described criteria was completed, the relevant papers obtained were classified into economic models and value-based groups, depending on the content of the papers. We summarized all the papers by displaying evidence using homogeneous tables. Each table consists of paper number (Nr), authors, publication details, economics/value-based substance reported in the paper, and the corresponding section in the paper where the content of the reviewed paper was elaborated.

From the economic models community, we sampled Poulin's paper on ROI calculation (Poulin, 1997), the Constructive Product Line Investment Model (COPLIMO) from Boehm et al. (2004), economic calculations for seven different scenarios from Böckle et al. (2004), the SIMPLE cost model from Clements et al. (2005), qCOMPLIMO for identifying the effect of software quality cost on the ROI, investment analysis from Withey, (1996), the applications, costs, and benefits model (Cohen, 2003), and transition strategies from Pohl et al. (2005).

From the value-based community we sampled the following approaches: product line framework from Clements and Northropm (2006), feature model enriched with assumptions (Lago and van Vliet, 2005), value-based elicitation (Pohl et al., 2001), issue-based variability management (Thurimella and Bruegge, 2012), and value-based portfolio optimization (Muller, 2011). Relevant publications are summarized in Table 2.2. These approaches are complementary to the approaches in Table 2.1.

The assessment criteria are followed to evaluate existing economic models against the following industrial needs:

- Support for adoption: transitioning from single-system architecture to SPL architecture.
- Architectural decision making: performing architectural decisions and dealing with tacit knowledge behind them.
- Support for domain engineering architects: various architectural strategies, architectural maintenance, conflicts between qualities and costs, and so on, n the domain engineering context.
- Support for application architects: architectural considerations while instantiating products from SPL architecture.

At a different level, we also reviewed for use cases supported on the basis of economic calculations (e.g., ROI calculations, focus on transition strategies), applicability to product line architectures, and association between value-based considerations and economic calculations.

2.4 Economic models for software product lines

The following sections describe the economic models mentioned in Table 2.1. At the end of this section, we provide a discussion and summarization of the reviewed approaches.

2.4.1 Poulin's measuring software reuse

Poulin's model (1997) is based on two parameters for estimating the efforts of reuse.

1. The relative cost of reuse (RCR): This is the ratio of effort needed to reuse the software without modifying the original costs that are normally associated with the development of the same software for a single use.
2. The relative cost of writing for reuse (RCWR): This is the cost associated with creating RCR assets; that is, the value relates the costs of creating reusable software to the cost of writing one-time-use software.

This model uses RCR and RCWR parameters to calculate two more parameters that are responsible for predicting the cost saving of entire project.

The reuse cost avoidance (RCA) is the cost saving of reusing assets over writing the equivalent software for a single use. The RCA further computed with development cost avoidance (DCA) and the service cost avoidance (SCA). DCA is calculated as

$$DCA = RSI * (1 - RCR) * (\text{cost of single\_use code}/\text{Lines of code[LOC]}) \qquad (2.5)$$

Here, reused source instructions (RSI) value comes from

$$\%reuse = \frac{reused\_source\_instructions}{total\_source\_instructions} * 100\% \qquad (2.6)$$

SCA represents the maintenance cost by eliminating repair cost and is calculated as

$$SCA = RSI * (\text{Error\_Rate}) * (\text{Error\_Cost}) \tag{2.7}$$

The additional development cost (ADC): It is based on RCWR

$$ADC = (RCWR - 1) * RSI * (\text{new codecost}) \tag{2.8}$$

Finally, Poulin's approach calculates return on investment value as

$$ROI = \sum_{i-1}^{n} RCA_i - ADC \tag{2.9}$$

Here i represent the successive usage of the reusable software.

In the following, we illustrate Poulin's economic calculations so that readers can obtain a more concrete understanding of economic models. Due to space restrictions, we only illustrate Paulin's approach. However, similar examples can be built for the other economic models reviewed in this chapter.

For developing a new application, let us assume that a company needs 18,000 (18 K) instructions out of which 10,000 (10 K) instructions could be reused from existing software modules. Therefore, % of reuse based on Equation (2.6) is 10K/18K*100 = 55%.

Assume that roughly 25% of the code is to be modified. On this basis, RCR is 0.4.

Let us suppose that the cost of developing for single use is 2000,000 USD and the lines of code 21 K.

$$DCA = 55 * (1 - 0.4) * 2000,000/21,000 = 31428.5 \text{ USD. (See Equation 2.5.)}$$

Let us suppose that the cost of fixing an error is 300 USD and the error rate is 0.2. Based on Equation (2.7), SCA = 55*0.2*1000 = 3300 USD.

$$RCA = DCA + SCA = 31428.5 + 3300 = 34728.5 \text{ USD.}$$

Assuming RCWR is 1.5 implies 50% of additional cost to write the rest of the software with 8 K instructions. Based on this assumption, DCA is calculated as follows.

$$ADC = 0.5 * 0.55 * 50,000 = 13750 \text{ USD}$$

$$ROI = 34728.5 - 13750 = 20978.5 \text{ USD.}$$

Poulin only considers cost saving based on estimated development of individual products and reuse costs. Furthermore, Poulin's method does not consider the effects of time on the reuse costs and necessary changes on those reuse costs.

2.4.2 COPLIMO

The underlying model behind the COPLIMO (Boehm et al., 2004) economic model is COCOMO, which estimates development effort in terms of code size and cost drivers. In COCOMO the code size is represented in terms of KLOC, whereas in COPLIMO a series of equations are used to generate code size for the given asset of a product line.

The COCOMO model generates development effort using Equation (2.4), whereas COPLIMO also uses the same equation for generating relative cost of reuse (RCR) and relative cost of writing for reuse (RCWR). But the model is needed to calculate two factors:

1. a cost model for product line development
2. an annualized postdevelopment life-cycle extension

A cost model for product line development. This model calculates the values similar to RCR and RCWR in Poulin's model. In order to calculate RCWR, COPIMO uses the cost drivers of the COCOMO model—namely, development for reuse (RUSE) and two constraints from COCOMO: (1) required reliability (RELY) and (2) degree of documentation (DOCU). From these constraints and cost drivers, the RCWR is modeled as

$$RCWR = (1 + RUSE) * \text{cost of reliability} * \text{cost of documentaion} \qquad (2.10)$$

The RCR in COPLIMO is calculated as an equivalent size of code using a factor known as assessment and assimilation (AA). The RCR calculation again considers two cases: (1) black-box reuse and (2) white-box reuse.

Black-box reuse: For black-box reuse, the factor is in the 0.02−0.08 range. The amount of code reused and multiplied by this factor generates an equivalent code size.

White-box reuse: White-box reuse includes several factors, including:

- the amount of design modified (DM) and code modified (CM)
- the integration effort (IM)
- the system understanding factor (SU) and programmer unfamiliarity (UNFM)

  Adaptation adjustment factor (AAF), a quantification for modifications in the white-box reuse is based on the design and code modification plus integration effort:

$$AAF = (4 * DM) + (3 * CM) + (3 * IM) \qquad (2.11)$$

- Adaptation adjustment multiplier (AAM), where $AAF < = 50$ is calculated as

$$AAM = \frac{AA + AAF(1 + (0.02 * SU * UNFM)}{100}$$

where $AAF > 50$,

$$AAM = \frac{AA + AAF + (SU * UNFM)}{100} \qquad (2.12)$$

The AAM multiplied by the amount of code reused gives the equivalent code size in the white-box-based RCR calculation in COPLIMO.

Once the code size (PSIZE) is calculated, the estimated effort is calculated using Equation (2.4) as

$$E = a_i(PSIZE)^{b_i}.EAF \qquad (2.13)$$

An Annualized Life-Cycle Model in COPLIMO: The life-cycle cost in COPLIMO is calculated by adding the initial development cost (in person-months) to the maintenance costs based on the number of years in maintenance. The maintenance costs use the annual change traffic (ACT) or the fraction of a product's software that changes per year, system understanding (SU), and unfamiliarity factors (UNFM). The formula for size is:

$$AMSIZE = PSIZE * ACT\left(1 + \frac{SU}{100} + UNFM\right) \tag{2.14}$$

COCOMO converts the AMSIZE into a maintenance formula as

$$PM(N, L) = PM(N) + L * N[A * (AMSIZE)^B * \prod(EM)] \tag{2.15}$$

Here, N is the number of products under maintenance, L is the number of years, and EM is the effort multiplier. COPLIMO applies Equation (2.15) for each of the three categories of new, reused, and adopted assets. The results are summed to give a total maintenance value.

Thus considering variations in the cost of reuse and considering maintenance make the COPLIMO reuse model better than the Poulin model. But the performance of the COPLIMO depends on the range of parametric values that must be accurately calibrated. This limits the attractiveness of the mode for a nontechnical audience.

2.4.3 Calculation model from Böckle et al.

Böckle et al. (2004) proposed the following model.

$$C_{org} + C_{cab} + \sum_{i=1}^{n_l}(C_{unique}(p_i) + C_{reuse}(p_i)) \tag{2.16}$$

C_{org} – The cost to an organization of adopting the product line approach for its products.
C_{cab} – The cost to develop a core asset base suited to support the product line being built.
C_{unique} – The cost to develop unique software that isn't based on a product line platform.
C_{reuse} – The cost to reuse core assets in a core asset base.

The Böckle model has been used in the following scenarios, some of which are also covered by SIMPLE (Clements et al., 2005) (see section 2.4.4 below).

Scenario 1. An organization has a set of products in the market that were developed more or less independently. It wishes to explore the possibility of transitioning to SPLE
Scenario 2. An organization plans to bring its products into market. A possibility of bringing them to a SPL should be explored.
Scenario 3. An organization plans to bring a set of products to the market as a software product line. It wants to explore building a core asset base to support at least a subset of products.
Scenario 4. An organization wants to explore the possibility of merging two or more software product lines that appear to overlap.
Scenario 5. An organization plans to bring a new product to market. It wants to know the cost implications of developing this product under the auspices of an existing product line versus building it in a stand-alone fashion.
Scenario 6. An organization wants to start a new software product line on the basis of an existing one. Here, managers want to make a decision from a cost perspective.
Scenario 7. A manager wants to know the financial implications of killing one of the products in a product line.

2.4.4 **SIMPLE**

The SIMPLE (Clements et al., 2005) cost model incorporates the time stamp events in the Böckle et al. (2004) cost estimation model. This cost model comprises a set of cost and benefit functions that can be used to construct equations in order to achieve the following goals:

1. Is adopting the SPLE approach the best option for development? In that case, what is the ROI for this approach?
2. Is merging the already existing product lines feasible? In that case, what is the cost on benefit?
3. Is adding new products to already existing product lines feasible? In that case, what is the cost on benefit?

2.4.4.1 The four basic cost functions of SIMPLE

$C_{org}()$: This function returns the cost of adopting SPLE for an organization. This cost includes reorganization, process improvement, training, and whatever other organizational remedies are necessary.

$C_{cab}()$: This function returns the cost for developing a core asset base for software product line. This cost includes performing a commonality/variability analysis; defining the product line's scope (Clements et al., 2005); designing and then evaluating a generic (as opposed to one-off) software architecture; and developing the software so designed. It also includes building the production plan, establishing the development environment, and producing a testing architecture and other artifacts that are reusable across the family.

$C_{unique}()$: This function returns the cost for developing unique parts of a product that are not based on assets in the core asset base. It includes the cost of locating a core asset, checking it out of the repository, tailoring it for use in the intended application, and performing the extra tests associated with reusing core assets.

$C_{reuse}()$: This function returns the cost for reusing the core assets in a core asset base.

Along with these four functions which represent the basic approach, three other cost functions are added to the model.

$C_{prod}()$: This function returns the cost of developing the products in stand-alone fashion.

$C_{evo}()$: This function returns the cost of producing the new version of the original product in the non-SPLE regime.

$C_{cabu}()$: This function returns the cost of updating the core asset base as a result of releasing a new version of a product.

The SIMPLE cost estimation model is very much supportive toward reactive product line development (Boehm et al., 2000) schemes in which time periods of a particular events could be incorporated. Here the SIMPLE model is explained with different scenarios that occur in real-world situations (in an organization).

The basic cost model that is described in SIMPLE is

$$\text{Cost of Building a Product Line} = C_{org}(t) + C_{cab}(t) + \sum_{i=1}^{n}(C_{unique}(product_i, t) + C_{reuse}(product_i, t))$$

$$(2.16)$$

$$\text{Cost of Building a Product as a stand-alone product} = \sum_{i=1}^{n} C_{prod}(product_i, t) \qquad (2.17)$$

$$\text{Return on Investment (ROI)} = \frac{Cost\ savings}{Cost\ of\ Investments} \qquad (2.18)$$

ROI achieved after one round of evolution of a product line

$$= \sum_{i=1}^{n} C_{evo}(product_i) - \frac{C_{org}() + C_{cab}() + \sum_{i=1}^{n}(C_{unique}(product_i) + C_{reuse}(product_i))}{C_{org}() + C_{cab}()} \qquad (2.19)$$

ROI achieved after second round of evolution of a producr line =

$$\sum_{i=1}^{n}(C_{evo}(product_i)) - \frac{\sum_{i=1}^{n}(C_{cabu}(product)_i + C_{unique}(product)_i + C_{reuse}(product)_i}{C_{org}() + C_{cab}()} \qquad (2.20)$$

The ROI after p rounds of updates where $(p > 1)$ is Equation (2.19) plus $(p - 1)$ rounds of Equation (2.20)).

Scenario 1: The cost of producing a set of products as a software product line.

Scenario 2: Choosing between building a set of products as a software product line and building them as a set of stand-alone products that do not share core assets.

Scenario 3: The cost of releasing a new version of a product in a software product line that is already in existence.

Scenario 4: An organization has a set of existing stand-alone products undergoing periodic evolutionary updates. Its managers might wish to know which is cheaper:

* Option A: converting them to a product line and continuing their evolution in that form.
* Option B: continuing to evolve them separately and foregoing the cost of setting up the product line.

Scenario 5: An organization wishes to know the ROI after the first round of evolution and after subsequent rounds.

Scenario 6: An organization has zero products and wishes to know the cost saving of S_1 products developed in nbr_periods over constructing and evolving them in a stand-alone fashion.

Scenario 7: An organization has n product lines, each comprising a set of products, and also has $s1$ stand-alone products. The organization wishes to transition to the state in which it has m product lines, each comprising a (perhaps different) set of products, and also $s2$ stand-alone products. The organization wishes to determine the optimum division of products among the optimum number of product lines to minimize the cost of initial construction and maintenance for the expected number of periods.

Scenario 8: An organization has n product lines, each comprising a set of products, and also has $s1$ stand-alone products. The organization intends to add k products. It wishes to determine the optimum allocation of the k products over the existing product lines based on foreseeable maintenance costs over the next "nbr_periods" time periods.

2.4.5 qCOPLIMO

The qCOPLIMO (In et al., 2006) cost estimation model is made up of COPLIMO (Boehm et al., 2000) and COQUALMO (Chulani et al., 1999) models and consists of the following two cost models: relative cost of writing for reuse (RCWR) for initial product line development and relative cost for reuse (RCR) for the following product development cases. Most of the SPLE models do not consider software quality cost, which is spent on removing undetected defects once after the product is released. The underlying model behind qCOPLIMO in calculating RCR and RCWR is COPLIMO, and in that model, COQUALMO (Poulin, 1997) is incorporated to identify the number of residual defects.

RCWR: The relative cost of writing the software most cost effectively that can be reused across SPLE is calculated as

$$
\begin{aligned}
C_{RCWR} = {} & \text{Labor Rate} * COPLIMO_{RCWR} + \text{Software Quality Cost}_{RCWR} \\
= {} & \text{Labor Rate} * [COCOMO \text{ baseline(initial software size)} * \text{Effort Adjustment for } RCWR] + \\
& [\text{Cost per Defect} * (1 - \text{Testing Effectiveness}) * COQUALMO(\text{initial software } size, EM_{PL})]
\end{aligned}
$$
(2.21)

Here EM_{PL} is the effort multiplier from the COCOMO II model cost drivers for SPLE.

RCR: The cost of reusing the software in a new application with product line family is calculated as

$$
\begin{aligned}
C_{RCR} = {} & \text{Labor Rate} * COPLIMO_{RCR} + \text{Software Quality Cost}_{RCR} \\
= {} & \text{Labor Rate} * [COCOMO \text{ baseline (software size for reuse)}] + \\
& [\text{Cost per Defect} * (1 - \text{Testing Effectiveness}) * COQUALMO(\text{software size for reuse}, EM_{PL})]
\end{aligned}
$$
(2.22)

The estimated cost for developing N products is

$$
C_{PL}(N) = C_{RCWR} + (N - 1) * C_{RCR}
$$
(2.23)

The majority of quantitative software product line models only address development and life-cycle costs. In contrast, *qCOPLIMO* estimates the effect of software quality cost on potential savings and return on investment.

2.4.6 Withey's cost estimation model

Withey's (Withey, 1996) cost estimation method proposes an investment analysis approach in order to solve the resource allocation issues for defining and evaluating appropriate investment value. In this approach, the scope for calculating the economics for SPLE is as follows.

- When fewer inputs are needed to produce a greater variety of products.
- When fewer inputs are needed to produce greater quantities of a single product.

The investment analysis is carried out by calculating each activity cost for each allocation resource. The activity cost calculation includes the following formula calculation:

$$\text{Opportunity cost of current process } S_M = \sum_{i}^{M} \sum_{j}^{V} Y_{ij}$$

$$\text{current } W_{ij} \text{ current} - \sum_{i}^{M} \sum_{j}^{V} Y_{ij} \text{ assets } W_{ij} \text{ assets}$$

$$(2.24)$$

Here

M = set of assets
V = number of planned products
Y = quantity of product
W = hourly rate

The investment analysis is carried out in two steps:

- Asset portfolio construction
- Estimate portfolio investment

Asset portfolio construction is carried out by characterizing product variety, choosing screen patterns, selecting assets, and evaluating the constructed portfolio for resource allocation.

The portfolio investment estimation is carried out by calculating dynamic net present value.

The traditional net present value is calculated as

$$NPV = \sum_{t=0}^{n} \frac{C_t^{inflow} - C_t^{outflow}}{(1 + r)t}$$

$$(2.25)$$

Here

C^{inflow} = Cash inflows for period t
$C^{outflow}$ = Cash outflows for period t
R = opportunity cost of capital
T = time period
N = number of periods in the planning horizon

If NPV is positive, then the stakeholders should invest; else not.

2.4.7 Applications, benefits, and costs (ABC)

Most of the economic models that are reviewed so far (e.g. Clements et al., 2005; Poulin, 1997; Clements and Northrop, 2002; Lim, 1996) are based on the assumption that an organization should develop assets and reduce the cost of developing software applications for a domain or for a product line or else develop the products in stand-alone fashion. The applications, benefits, and costs (ABC) (Cohen, 2003) uses the time period over which the organization will apply the assets, which is measured with a refresh rate. In particular, the refresh rate is the particular time period over which the core asset base completely changes to accommodate new technology or consumer demands.

In this model, ABC is described as follows.

- Applications (A): Applications are the different software systems that an organization plans to develop using product line assets over the time period of the business case.
- Benefits (B): The cost saving or any other kind of returns obtained by using product line assets. The benefits are again of two types: tangible and intangible. The tangible benefits are measured directly; these benefits are like quality, profitability, and performance of the derived products. The intangible benefits cannot be measured in terms of product metrics; these benefits include customer satisfaction and professional satisfaction.
- Costs (C): The actual costs of reuse that an organization pays to develop and use the assets.

The main idea behind this model is incrementally increasing the degree of reuse (DOR) of core assets which can incrementally bring down the cost of reuse (COR).

- If the refresh rate is short, applications are changing rapidly and the asset base must be rebuilt frequently to accommodate that change as new products are developed.
- If the refresh rate is long, assets have longer shelf lives and undergo less change with each new product, COR can be brought down through investment in tools.
- If the assets are never refreshed, DOR decreases rapidly over time and COR increases due to necessary changes in existing assets.

Initially, it was through this model that part of the core asset base was developed, including the architecture and some of the components. Later, one or more products would be developed. In the next increment, A portion of the rest of the core asset base and additional products can be developed. Over time, more of the core asset base can be developed in parallel by evolving new products.

2.4.8 Transaction strategies

Pohl et al. (2005) discuss four transition strategies for adopting the cost models to initiate product lines in an organization: (1) Incremental introduction; (2) tactical approach; (3) pilot project strategy; and (4) big bang strategy.

Incremental Introduction: This strategy starts small and extends incrementally. The extension can be done in two ways.

- Expanding organizational scope: starts with a small group with sound domain knowledge and strong technical experience. If this group succeeds in instantiating product lines, then other groups are added incrementally.
- Expanding investments: starts with small selected investments. If this increment attains high ROI, then the funds are further added accordingly.

With this strategy, the ROI by the adopting model (Pohl et al., 2001) is calculated as

$$ROI = \frac{(C_{conv} - C)}{C} \tag{2.26}$$

Here

C_{conv} is building k product in a stand-alone fashion, that is, k*Equation (2.17).

C = total cost from all increments, that is, $C = C_1 + C_2$ (for two increments).
C_1 = cost for creating the whole asset base and building the s old products

$$C_1 = C_{org} + C_{cab} + \sum_{i=1}^{s}(C_{unique}(p_i) + C_{reuse}(p_i)) \tag{2.27}$$

C_2 = cost of building the k other products based on the asset developed so far

$$C_2 = C_{org} + C_{cab} + \sum_{i=1}^{s}(C_{unique}(p_i) + C_{reuse}(p_i)) \tag{2.28}$$

Tactical Approach: In this strategy, only specific subprocesses and methods of the existing stand-alone process are changed to adopt product lines.

Pilot Project Strategy: The development of a new project with this strategy can be accomplished in one of these alternative ways.

- A new product can be started as a first member of the SPL process.
- A new product can be an extension of a series of existing products.
- A new product can be developed as a toy product.
  - This can be beneficiary when developing a new product is too costly.
- A new product can be developed as a prototype.

In this strategy the ROI and C_{conv} calculations are similar to those in the incremental strategy, The cost for developing prototype (C_1), rebuilding k_1 products, and developing k_2 (C_2) products using the core asset base is:

$$C_1 = C_{org} + C_{cab} + C_{unique}(p_i) + C_{reuse}(p_i) \tag{2.29}$$

$$C_2 = C_{org} + C_{cab} + \sum_{i=1}^{k_1+k_2}(C_{unique}(p_i) + C_{reuse}(p_i)) \tag{2.30}$$

Big Bang Strategy: In this strategy, the transition to SPLE is performed at one time. The first domain engineering process is accomplished in order to build a platform. Later, new products are derived from the existing platform during application of the engineering process.

In this strategy, the ROI and C_{conv} calculations are similar to those in the incremental strategy. The cost of developing k applications at a stretch is calculated as

$$C_2 = C_{org} + C_{cab} + \sum_{i=1}^{k}(C_{unique}(p_i) + C_{reuse}(p_i)) \tag{2.31}$$

2.4.9 Discussion and summary

Calculating cost savings from reuse of artifacts is helpful in deciding on product line adoption. Poulin's model (1997) is a fundamental approach useful for measuring reuse. However, this model only considers cost saving based on estimated development costs and reuse costs. The effects of time on the reuse costs and necessary changes on those reuse costs are not considered in Poulin, (1997). COMPLIMO (Boehm et al., 2004) models variations in the cost of reuse. By considering maintenance parameters, the COPLIMO reuse model is better than the Poulin model. However, COPLIMO's performance depends on the range of parametric values that must be accurately calibrated. Therefore, the applicability is limited. Poulin's models and COMPLIMO only focus on development and life-cycle costs. In contrast, qCOPLIMO estimates the effect of software quality cost on potential savings and return on investment. ABC (Cohen, 2003) differs from all the above discussed models by using the time period over which the organization will apply the assets, which is measured with the refresh rate. The refresh rate is the particular time period over which the core asset base completely changes to accommodate new technology or consumer demand.

Investment analysis is orthogonal to the above discussed reuse calculations. Withey (1996) proposes an investment analysis approach in order to solve the resource allocation issues for defining and evaluating appropriate investment value.

ROI calculations aid decision making on product line adoption. In Böckle et al. (2004) cost calculation, models are presented for product line adoption in seven different scenarios. SIMPLE (Clements et al., 2005) is a cost-benefit model for merging two product lines and adding new products to an existing product line. Both Böckle et al. (2004) and Clements et al. (2005) support ROI calculations based on the organization's situation.

An organization has to use a product line strategy for transitioning to SPLs after deciding on the product line adoption. Pohl et al. (2005) discuss four transition strategies for adopting the cost models for initiating product lines in an organization: incremental introduction, tactical approach, pilot project strategy and big bang strategy.

2.5 Relevant value-based approaches for SPL

In the following, the value-based approaches mentioned in Table 2.2 are reviewed in detail. At the end of this section, we provide a discussion and summary of the reviewed approaches.

2.5.1 Framework for product line practice

The framework for product line practice is based on patterns that have been traditionally used to solve recurrent problems in software engineering. For example, design patterns have been used for designing and implementing various software modules. The framework uses patterns to solve the product line engineering problems at three different levels:

- The context is the organizational situation.
- The problem is what part of a software product line effort needs to be accomplished.
- The solution is the grouping of practice areas and the relations among them that together address the problem for that context.

Overall, the framework uses 12 different patterns (Clements and Northrop, 2002). For example, the Essentials Coverage pattern gives a mapping of each practice area to each of the three essential product line activities: core asset development, product development, and management. The

Product Builder pattern consists of practice areas that should be used whenever any product in the product line is being developed. The economic models discussed in the previous section could be applied for relevant patterns. For example, SIMPLE economic model can be applied for calculating ROI for developing new products in the Product Builder pattern.

2.5.2 Feature models enriched with assumptions

Design decisions often determine the development, deployment, and evolution of a system and provide the earliest place for assessing architecture. Lago and van Vliet (Lago and van Vliet, 2005) model assumptions to reason about variability and invariability as well as architectural design decisions. The authors argue that enriching variability with assumptions provides a more complete picture of the SPL. For example, the assumption "modularity is business driven" creates variability by impacting the design of the functionality for common services and service specific functionality.

The approach (Lago and van Vliet, 2005) models relationships between features and assumptions. For example, an assumption can impact a feature. Similarly, a feature can realize an assumption. Modeling assumptions provides several advantages.

- Assumptions provide a strong link between requirements and design. Therefore, modeling assumptions improves forward and backward traceability.
- Hinders implementation of changes that go against assumptions made at architecting time.
- Assumptions are useful for improving management of architectural knowledge. For example, externalizing the documentation assumptions is helpful in their reuse for multiple projects.

2.5.3 Value-based elicitation of variability

Bridging business and technology is receiving increasing attention in the software engineering community. For example, value-based software engineering (VBSE) (Biffl et al., 2005) aims to associate a value (e.g., business value) for artifacts. In this context, value-based variability modeling would mean considering the business value and the associated risks during decision making on variability.

Extracting tacit variability knowledge about product line architecture is a collaborative process (Dhungana et al., 2006). In particular, software engineers/architects involved in developing the reusable assets as well as people from business and marketing (e.g., people involved in selling these assets) are in the process.

The value-based process (Rabiser et al., 2008) for eliciting product line variability aims at integrating three research areas:

- SPLE, with a focus on variability modeling and management
- VBSE, particularly the question how much is enough in variability modeling?
- Collaborative software engineering (Finkelstein et al., 2010) with patterns of collaboration that enable different people working together to produce mutually satisfactory results

The value-based elicitation process (Rabiser et al., 2008) was implemented using structured workshops. Based on the workshops, various lessons were learned. Here are the relevant findings for software architecture:

- Different levels of variability decisions are identified, which include decisions on customer and sales, systemwide, subsystemwide, component level, and low-level parameterization
- Complementary results with variability recovery tools such as parsers analyzing existing architecture models and configuration files

2.5.4 Issue-based variability management

Issue-based variability management methodology (IVMM) (Thurimella and Bruegge, 2012) supports decision making on variability management based on concepts such as questions, options, and criteria (QOC). In addition, the methodology enables capture of the rationale behind variability decisions. In the IVMM meta-model, a criterion is modeled based on a business goal (e.g., price) or a nonfunctional requirement (e.g., maintainability). Therefore IVMM relates value-based considerations to variability at the modeling level. IVMM supports decision making on variability in three different use cases:

- UC1: Variability identification: For deciding on the creation of variation points, stakeholders evaluate possible variations against a set of criteria. In particular, stakeholders collaborate and decide on mandatory, optional, and alternative variations.
- UC2: Variability instantiation: Instantiating variability models involves selecting a subset of variants for a new product of a product line. For instantiating variation points, stakeholders evaluate the possible options of a variability model against product-specific quality concerns. For example, stakeholders would be able to reason about the value of a feature for a particular market segment.
- UC3: Variability evolution: Stakeholders evaluate alternative change requests for changing assets and reason about the variability changes.

IVMM allows capture of rationale during the decision-making process. The captured rationale information is reused to solve similar issues that occur during variability management. For example, a variation point is instantiated for multiple products of a product line. The tacit knowledge that is captured while instantiating a variation point for a product could be reused for instantiating the same variation point for other products. Similarly, the tacit knowledge captured is also reused for the evolution of variability models.

2.5.5 Value-based portfolio optimization

Value-based portfolio optimization (Muller, 2011) addresses the problem of identifying and prioritizing the most important features to be realized. In particular, the approach portfolio optimization (Muller, 2011) addresses the problem by applying an optimization technique called simulated annealing. The basic idea is to understand how the entities such as features, assets, customers, and market segments affect profits. Based on this idea, the approach models a mathematic utility function for profits with the dependent variables, such as customers, market segments, features, and their costs. Based on the mathematical optimization, the approach suggests

- the features that should be implemented and
- the starting price for the products.

2.5.6 Discussion and summary

The Framework for Product Line Practice (Clements and Northrop, 2002) addresses product line architecture issues based on patterns. Here, architects have the possibility to apply a set of patterns that give value and economic benefits to the organization.

Identifying the value for creating variation points and making the value explicit are other important topics. Value-based elicitation adds value to artifacts (Biffl et al., 2005) during variability elicitation. Value-based portfolio optimization (Muller, 2011) helps to decide on features to be implemented and their initial price. This technique uses mathematical optimization.

Architectural knowledge management is a related area. Issue-based variability management (Thurimella and Bruegge, 2012) supports decision making and rational management during the identification, instantiation, and evolution of variability. The approach can incorporate value-based criteria. Enriching feature models with assumptions (Lago and van Vliet, 2005) provides value by improving traceability, preventing unanticipated changes, and aiding architectural knowledge management.

2.6 Discussion on architectural issues

No explicit focus on architecture with a possibility for tailoring. Of all the reviewed approaches, only the Framework for Product Line Practice (Clements and Northrop, 2006) and feature models enriched with assumptions (Lago and van Vliet, 2005) address software architecture-related issues. In particular, (Clements and Northrop, 2006) uses patterns for addressing organizational, SPL and grouping related issues and (Lago and van Vliet, 2005) models assumptions for enhancing the design of a software product line. Therefore, the focus on SPL architecture from the value-based and economics communities is apparently little.

The other approaches do not focus primarily on software architecture. However, they can be tailored to architecture or used in the context of software architecture. For example, Thurimella and Bruegge (2012) uses QOC to support decision making on variability and requirements. The same methodology can be used to decide on design issues as well. In the following, we illustrate the usage of IVM for product line architectures. This example is also used to highlight other topics of the discussion section.

Let us consider an example in which a company is transitioning to SPL-based development from single-system development. In designing the product line architecture, an architect wants to decide on the extensibility of the architecture based on plug-ins. As part of the company's business model, several third-party companies intend to develop plug-ins for the platform. A plug-in is a software module that contains implementations for a set of functions. By installing the plug-in, the platform functionality will be extended. In the running example, the architect considers two options for supporting plug-in based extensibility:

- Traditional plug-in architecture. Developers would be able to develop a plug-in for the platform that offers the core functionality. The platform architecture itself is not plug-in based.
- Pure plug-in architecture. Similar to Eclipse, all the platform modules would be designed as plug-ins.

The architect evaluates the two options together with the other platform architects (follow Table 2.3). The criteria considered for the evaluation are configurability, value, and ROI. The

Table 2.3 Justification Matrix for Extensibility of a product Line Architecture	Configurability	Value	ROI
Issue: How should we support extensibility for the product line architecture?			
Option1: Traditional plug-in architecture	−	+	++
Option2: Pure plug-in architecture	++	−	− −
Decision: The product line architecture will be based on traditional plug-in architecture (Option1) because of better assessments for value and ROI.			

assessments are given based on + (supports), + + (supports strongly), 0 (no affect), − (hinders) and − (hinders strongly). In the pure plug-in approach, all software modules are based on plug-ins. This is advantageous for configuring software while instantiating the platform software for creating products. However, the traditional plug-in approach has better assessments than the pure plug-in approach:

- The pure plug-in approach does not create a value for the company in our example because the existing third-party companies would have to make an additional effort to understand the new pure plug-in based architecture.
- The pure plug-in architecture would need significant refactoring investments. The ROI assessments show option 1 is better than option 2.

Based on the assessments, the architect decides on the traditional plug-in based architecture. Value-based portfolio optimization (Muller, 2011) uses simulated annealing to optimize assets for price. A design element is also an asset. The optimization technique (Muller, 2011) can be used for optimizing features by considering the costs of classes and components.

The economic models reviewed in section 2.4 consider development and reuse costs, with a focus on source code. Although architecture has not been the direct focus for these economic models, they can be tailored to software architecture. For calculating ROI based on Paulin's approach, costs of creating architecture can be included to the development costs, and costs for reusing architecture can be added to the reuse costs.

The reviewed economic models support SPL adoption (Böckle et al., 2004; Clements et al., 2005) and selection of transition strategies (Pohl et al., 2005). Both adoption and transition strategies influence the evolution of product line architecture. In this sense, the economic models are also related to software architecture.

No explicit architectural considerations in the economic calculations. In section 2.4 we have reviewed a set of economic models from the literature. The basic idea behind the reviewed economic models is to provide mathematical models from which product line managers calculate factors such as ROI.

- These approaches present different considerations. Some models include basic considerations, while some make advanced considerations. For example, Poulin provides (Poulin, 1997) a basic model, while COMPLIMO uses advanced considerations such as cost of reliability and cost of documentation for calculating the cost of writing for reuse. qCOMPLIMO considers quality aspects for calculating reuse costs.

- The scenario coverage of the approaches has been different as well. For example, Poulin supports calculations only for SPLE adoption, while some support the life-cycle considerations (qCOMPLIMO). Furthermore, economic models such as Boeckle et al. and SIMPLE support multiple scenarios.
- Pohl et al. (2005) (see section 2.4.8) focuses on transition strategies, while approaches discussed between 4.1 and 4.7 focus on calculations for ROI and NPV and so on. However, ABC has a major focus on incremental adoption strategy, while the approaches do not focus on a particular adoption strategy.

To summarize: The economic models help product line managers make strategic decisions on the adoption of SPLE. However, the economic models do not support explicit architectural considerations, which form a significant portion of costs for asset creation (e.g., cost of reuse and cost of writing for reuse). Not all the reviewed economic models have considerations for architecture-related use cases/aspects such as modularity, cost-benefit analysis for SPL architecture, refactoring single-system architecture for supporting SPLs, SPL architecture evaluation, alternative architectural strategies, and architectural decision making. Systematic guidance should be provided so that an architect can perform quantitative analysis of architectural issues. In the running example, the ROI calculations for both traditional and pure plug-in approaches would be needed.

Little focus on application engineering. The domain engineering activities such as managing assets, variability, scoping, and adoption are well addressed in the literature. The framework (Clements and Northrop, 2006) supports patterns for managing assets. Value-based elicitation focuses on variability identification and product line adoption. Feature modeling enriched with assumptions (Lago and van Vliet, 2005) enhances variability by modeling assumptions. Value-based portfolio optimization improves product line scoping based on mathematical optimization. Only IVM (Thurimella and Bruegge, 2012) supports both domain and application engineering activities. In particular, variability identification and variability evolution are supported in domain engineering, and product instantiation is supported in application engineering. Therefore, the reviewed approaches cover domain engineering activities, while application engineering has not been addressed sufficiently.

Little support for explicit value-based considerations. Only two approaches directly support explicit value-based considerations: the elicitation process (Rabiser et al., 2008), which relates business value for identifying variation points and (Lago and van Vliet, 2005) which optimizes a mathematical function of features and costs for profitability. In making design decisions, architects can include value-based assumptions in the approach reported in Lago and van Vliet (2005) and value-related criteria in IVM (Thurimella and Bruegge, 2012). Moreover, Lago and van Vliet (2005) and Thurimella and Bruegge (2012) support value-based considerations implicitly; that is, there is no systematic guidance to make value-based design decisions. Based on this we conclude that (i) SPL architecture approaches should support explicit value-based considerations; (ii) there should be guidance for architects to perform value-based analysis, and (iii) case studies and industrial experiences in this area should be reported in the form of conferences and journal papers.

Missing link between value-based approaches and economic models. Another issue is the missing link between the economic models and the architecting. The models reviewed in section 2.4 do not make an association with the value-based approach reviewed in section 2.5 and vice versa. In particular, the issue of interest is "how the costs that were estimated for creating and reusing assets have been associated with architecting." Similarly, the value-based approaches also fail to make a link to economic models. This issue is critical because while they are designing assets, architects should be able to evaluate multiple options with respect to price, ROI, and economic benefits. A value-based approach should recommend a set of economic models and should demonstrate the usage of economic models together with the value-based approach. In the IVM illustration, an architect needs to evaluate ROI for the traditional plug-in and pure plug-in extensibility. It should be demonstrated how Paulin's should be used for ROI calculations in the context of IVM. Similarly, the Framework (Clements and Northrop, 2006) could support economic calculations by embedding SIMPLE for adoption and scoping.

2.7 Related work

According to Boehm and Sullivan (2000), the fundamental goal of a good design is to create maximal value added for any given investment. Furthermore, Boehm and Sullivan, (2000) proposed a roadmap that contains two relevant items for this chapter: (1) primary focus on benefits and value instead of costs and (2) resolution of uncertainty. In this chapter, in addition to the cost calculation approaches, we reviewed papers on value-based and uncertainty resolution. Based on this material, we argue that the roadmap supports the research issue elicited from our discussion of the "missing link between value-based approaches and economic models."

In an operations management journal paper (Hopp and Xu, 2005), the authors conclude that reducing product development costs based on modularity aids product variety. Therefore, modularity has a positive effect on variability and cost reduction. From the software engineering community, Sullivan et al. (2001) emphasized the importance of the structure and value of modularity. Modularity is an important concern for product line architecture. Unfortunately, the SPL papers reviewed in this chapter do not focus on these relationships.

In addition to the modularity, recent contributions emphasize bridging the communication gaps for reducing failures (Cataldo and Herbsleb, 2013) and understanding human factors for improving design reuse and maintenance (Thurimella and Brügge, 2013; Zanetti, 2012). In this chapter, we reviewed papers on tacit knowledge (Thurimella and Bruegge, 2012; Lago and van Vliet, 2005).

VULCAN is a tool available for product line architectures. This tool supports instantiating products from assets in the context of global projects by employing patterns (Lee and Yang Kang). Problem frames are used to provide mapping between feature models and reusable components (Dao and Kang, 2010). Neither of these contributions on product line architectures focuses on economics or value-based considerations.

2.8 Conclusion

This chapter reviews state-of-the-art software economics and value-based software engineering for product line architectures. We have provided an overview of the existing support on software economics and value-based considerations in the context of SPLs. In addition, we have accessed these approaches with a focus on support for adoption, domain engineering, application engineering, and decision making. Based on the review, we conclude the following open issues:

- There is sound support for economic calculations for making strategic decisions on SPL adoptions. However, there is no support for architecture issues (e.g., cost-benefit analysis, architecture evaluation) in these economic models.
- Domain engineering has been the focus of most of the approaches, whereas there is little focus on architectural issues in application engineering.
- There is no link between economic models and value-based approaches.

References

Ali, M.S., Babar, M.A., Schmid, K., 2009. A Comparative Survey of Economic Models for Software Product Lines EUROMICRO-SEAA, pp. 275–278.

Ali Babar, M., Dingsøyr, T., Lago, P., Vliet, H., van, H. (Eds.), 2009. Software Architecture Knowledge Management: Theory and Practice. Springer, Heidelberg.

Biffl, S., Aurum, A., Boehm, B., Erdogmus, H., Grünbacher, P., 2005. Value-Based Software Engineering. Springer, New York.

Böckle, G., Clements, P., McGregor, D., Muthig, D., Schmid, K., 2004. Calculating the ROI for software product lines. IEEE Softw. 21 (3), 23–31.

Boehm, B., Abts, C., Brown, A.W., Chulani, S., Clark, B.K., Ellis Horowitz, R., et al., Software Cost Estimation with COCOMO II. Prentice-Hall, Englewood Cliffs, NJ.

Boehm, B., Brown, A.W., Madachy, R., Yang, Y., 2004. A software product line life cycle cost estimation model. In: International Symposium on Empirical Software Engineering (ISESE '04), pp. 156–164.

Boehm, B.W., Sullivan, K., 2000. Software Economics: A Roadmap, Conference on the Future of Software Engineering, at the International Conference on Software Engineering, Limerick, Ireland, pp. 319–343.

Breivold, H.P., Crnkovic, I., Larsson, M., 2012. Software architecture evolution through evolvability analysis. J. Syst. Softw. 85 (11), 2574–2592.

Cataldo, M., Herbsleb, J.D., 2013. Coordination breakdowns and their impact on development productivity and software failures. IEEE Trans. Softw. Eng. 39 (3), 343–360.

Chulani, S., Boehm, B., Steece, B., 1999. Bayesian analysis of empirical software engineering cost models. IEEE Trans. Softw. Eng. 25 (4), 573–583.

Clements, P., Northrop, L., 2002. Software Product Lines: Practices and Patterns. Addison-Wesley, Reading, MA.

Clements, P., Northrop, L., 2006., URL: <http://www.sei.cmu.edu/prodvolnuctlines/framework.html> A Framework for Software Product Line Practice-Version 4.2 [online]. Carnegie Mellon, Software Engineering Institute, Pittsburgh, PA.

Clements, P.C., McGregor, J.D., Cohen, S.G., 2005. The Structured Intuitive Model for Product Line Economics (SIMPLE). Software Engineering Institute, Carnegie Mellon University.

Cohen, S., 2003. Predicting When Product Line Investment Pays. Software Engineering Institute, Carnegie Mellon University.

Dao, T., Kang, K., 2010. Mapping features to reusable components: a problem frames-based approach. SPLC 377–392.

Dhungana, D., Rabiser, R., Grünbacher, P., Prähofer, H., Federspiel, C., Lehner, K., 2006. Architectural knowledge in product line engineering: an industrial case study. Proceedings of the 32nd Euromicro

Conference on Software Engineering and Advanced Applications (SEAA). IEEE Computer Society, Cavtat/Dubrovnik, Croatia.

Finkelstein, A., Grundy, J., van der Hoek, A., Mistrík, I., Whitehead, J. (Eds.), 2010. Collaborative Software Engineering. Springer Verlag, Heidelberg.

Gomaa, H., 2004. Designing software product lines with UML: from use cases to pattern-based software architectures. Addison-Wesley Obj. Technol. Ser.

Griss, M.L., 2000. Implementing product line features with component reuse. 6th International Conference, ICSR-6, Vienna, Austria. June 27–29, pp 137–152. <http://www.springer.com/computer/swe/book/978-3-642-02373-6>.

Hopp, W., Xu, X., 2005. Product line selection and pricing with modularity in design. J. Oper. Manag. 7 (3), 172–187.

In, H.P., Baik, J., Kim, S., Yang, Y., Boehm, B., 2006. A quality based cost estimation model for the product line life cycle. Commun. ACM 49, 85–88.

Lago, P., van Vliet, H., 2005. Explicit assumptions enrich architectural models. 27th International Conference on Software Engineering (ICSE). IEEE, pp. 206–214.

Lee, H., Jin-seok, Y., Kang, K.C., 2012. VULCAN: architecture-model-based workbench for product line engineering. In: Proceedings of the 16th International Software Product Line Conference - Volume 2 (SPLC '12), vol. 2. ACM, New York, NY, USA, pp. 260–264.

Lim, W.C., 1996. Reuse economics: a comparison of seventeen models and directions for future research. ICSR '96: Proceedings of the 4th International Conference on Software Reuse. IEEE Computer Society, pp. 41–50.

Lutz, R., Gannod, G., 2003. Analysis of a software product line architecture: an experience report. J. Syst. Softw. 66 (3), 253–267.

Martin, Robert C., 2000. Design principles and design patterns. <http://www.google.de/url?sa=t&rct=j&q=&esrc=s&source=web&cd=1&ved=0CCsQFjAA&url=http%3A%2F%2Fscm0329.googleode.com%2Fsvn-history%2Fr78%2Ftrunk%2Fbook%2FPrinciples_and_Patterns.pdf&ei=2_sVU4XsGsnS4QSViIDIAw&usg=AFQjCNGqS4zIupvokMk-CE6W0DTUoIHNsg&sig2=4FHVdb89m4SMSzJvmdyZYQ&bvm=bv.62286460,d.bGE&cad=rja>.

Medvidovic, N., Taylor, R.N., 2000. A classification and comparison framework for software architecture description languages. IEEE TSE 26 (1), 70–93.

Muller, J., 2011. Value-based portfolio optimization for software product lines, pp. 15–24. Proceedings of the 15th International Software Product Line Conference (SPLC '11). IEEE Computer Society, Washington, DC.

Pohl, K., Bockle, G., Clements, P., Obbink, H., Rombach, D. (Eds.), 2001. Proceedings Dagstuhl Seminar Product Family Development. University of Essen, Germany.

Pohl, K., Böckle, G., van der Linder, F., 2005. *Software Product Line Engineering Foundations, Principles, and Techniques*. Springer, New York.

Poulin, J.S., 1997. The economics of product line development. Int. J. Appl. Softw. Technol. 3, 20–34.

Product Line Hall of Fame, SEI, URL: <http://splc.net/fame.html>.

Rabiser, R., Dhungana, D., Grünbacher, P., Burgstaller, B., 2008. Value-based elicitation of product line variability: an experience report. VaMoS 73–79.

Schmid, K., Verlage, M., 2002. The economic impact of product line adoption and evolution. IEEE Softw. 19 (6), 50–57.

Sullivan, K., Griswold, W.G., Cai, Y., Hallen, B., 2001. The Structure and Value of Modularity in Software Design, European Software Engineering Conference, held Jointly with ACM SIGSOFT International Symposium on Foundations of Software Engineering (ESEC/FSE), Vienna, Austria, pp. 99–108.

Thurimella, A.K., Bruegge, B., 2012. Issue-based variability management. IST 54 (9), 933–950.

Thurimella, A.K., Brügge, B., 2013. A mixed-method approach for the empirical evaluation of the issue-based variability modeling. J. Syst. Softw. Available online 16 March 2013.

Van der Linden, F., 2002. Software product families in europe: the ESAPS and CAFÉ projects. IEEE Softw. 19 (4), 41−49.

Weiss, D., Lai, C.T.R., 1999. Software Product Line Engineering—A Family-Based Software Development Process. Addison-Wesley, Reading, MA.

Withey, J., 1996. Investment Analysis of Software Assets for Product Lines Software Engineering Institute. Carnegie Mellon University, CMU/SEI-96-TR-010-010.

Zanetti, M.S., 2012. The co-evolution of socio-technical structures in sustainable software development: lessons from the open source software communities, 1587−1590.

Zimmermann, O., 2011. Architectural decisions as reusable design assets. IEEE Softw. 28 (1), 64−69.

Zimmermann, O., Koehler, J., Leymann, F., Polley, R., Schuster, N., 2009. Managing architectural decision models with dependency relations, integrity constraints, and production rules. J. Syst. Softw. 82 (8), 1249−1267.

Zimmermann, O., Miksovic, C., Küster, J.M., 2012. Reference architecture, meta-model, and modeling principles for architectural knowledge management in information technology services. J. Syst. Softw. 85 (9), 2014−2033.

Aspects of Software Valuation

Steve Tockey

Construx Software, Bellevue, WA, USA

3.1 Introduction

Many books, papers, blogs, and the like have been written on topics such as software architecture selection and technical debt. The vast majority treats these topics purely from a technical perspective. What's missing is a treatment of these topics from a business perspective. Just because one architectural alternative makes more technical sense than another, is it also necessarily guaranteed to be in the best interest of the corporation's stockholders? Is it always in the best interest of a corporation to reduce technical debt? Since most software is being developed and maintained in a business context, the business consequences of these kinds of technical choices also need to be considered.

When making business decisions, investment needs to be compared to return on that investment. Estimating investment in software situations isn't trivial, but it's not that difficult. Estimating the return on that investment is much less obvious. This chapter will describe a process for determining the business value of software, whether it is a commercial product or in-house. Nontrivial examples of each are provided. By following the process described in this chapter, organizations will be able to understand the business values of their software alternatives and, thus, be able to make appropriate business decisions about software.

In addition, a recent trend in corporations has been to "capitalize" software costs. This chapter shows that software capitalization may not be in the best interest of the business.

3.2 Basics of economic analysis

A prerequisite for discussing software valuation is an understanding of the basic elements of economic analysis and business decision making. Several such elements will be presented here for readers who are not already familiar with them:

- Alternatives
- Cash flow streams
- Cash flow diagrams
- Interest
- Present worth, PW(i)
- Comparing alternatives

Of course, the complete subject of economic analysis and business decision making is much more involved (see, for example, DeGarmo et al., 1993; Eschenbach, 2003; Grant et al., 1990; Thuesen and Fabrycky, 1993, or Tockey, 2005). Readers already familiar with these basics can skip this section.

Making a business decision starts with the concept of an *alternative*.[1] An alternative is an option being considered, like carrying out a particular software development project. Another alternative could be to enhance an existing program, and yet another might be to redevelop that same software from scratch. Alternatives represent mutually exclusive units of choice—either you choose to carry out that alternative or you choose not to. The purpose of business decision making is to decide which technically viable alternatives should be carried out and which ones should not.

To make a business decision about an alternative, that alternative will need to be evaluated from a business perspective. *Cash flow instances* and *cash flow streams* are used to describe the business perspective of an alternative. A cash flow instance is a specific amount of money flowing into or out of the organization, as a consequence of some alternative, at a specific time. Examples of cash flow instances in a software organization might include:

- In an alternative to develop and launch product X, the payment for new development computers, if needed, would be an example of an outgoing cash flow instance. Money would need to be spent to carry out that alternative.
- The sales income from product X in the second year after market launch could be an example of an incoming cash flow instance. Money would be coming in because of carrying out the alternative.

A cash flow stream is a set of cash flow instances, over time, caused by carrying out some alternative. The cash flow stream is the complete financial perspective of that alternative.

A *cash flow diagram* is a graphical view of a cash flow stream. Figure 3.1 shows an example cash flow diagram for an alternative that will be presented below.

A cash flow diagram shows the cash flow stream in two dimensions. Time is shown from left to right, and amounts of money are shown vertically. The time axis is divided into units that represent years, months, weeks, and so on, as appropriate. Each cash flow instance is drawn at a horizontal position relative to its timing. The amount of the cash flow instance is shown as an arrow. Upward arrows represent income and downward arrows represent expense. The length of the arrow is usually drawn proportional to the amount of the cash flow instance. The actual amounts are normally written on the diagram next to the arrows.

Typically, many separate, individual cash flow instances will happen during any single time period, particularly when periods represent months or years. The individual cash flow instances within a period will be added, and a single "net cash flow instance" for that period will be drawn on the diagram. By convention, cash flows are shown at the end of the corresponding period. The initial investment is shown "at the end of period zero".

One of the most important concepts in business decision making is that money has time value. A given amount of money at one time almost always has a different value than the same amount of

---

[1]More properly, one should start with "proposals" as the unit of choice and then gather sets of proposals into mutually exclusive alternatives. For the purposes of this chapter, it is better to just start with the idea of alternatives as the unit of choice. Proposals and creating mutually exclusive alternatives are described in detail in (DeGarmo et al., 1993) through (Tockey, 2005).

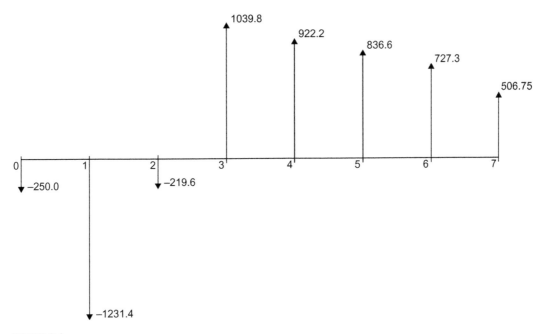

FIGURE 3.1

An example cash flow diagram ($thousands).

money at another time. The concept of *interest*, the cost of being able to use someone else's money, has existed since the dawn of recorded human history. Anyone making a business decision will need to understand interest and how it affects business decisions. A set of formulae (see, for example, DeGarmo et al., 1993, through Tockey, 2005) allows converting money at one time to an equivalent-valued amount of money at another time given an interest rate. One such formula is the "Single-payment Present-worth" formula.

$$P = F\left[\frac{1}{(1+i)^n}\right]$$

This formula translates a future value, F, at a time n interest periods in the future into a present value, P, using interest rate, i. For example:

$$P = \$5k\left[\frac{1}{(1+0.07)^8}\right] = \$2910.05$$

At an annual interest rate of 7%, $5000 eight years in the future has the same value as $2910.05 today. This kind of problem is very common in business decision making, and a shorthand notation exists:

$$P = \$5k \overset{P/F,7\%,8}{(0.58201)} = \$2910.05$$

Table 3.1 Calculating PW(i) for the Cash Flow Stream in Figure 3.1 ($thousands)

Year	Net Cash Flow	Single-Payment Present-Worth Factor	Present Worth
0	−$250	P/F,7%,0 (1.000)	−$250
1	−1231	P/F,7%,1 (0.9346)	−1150
2	−220	P/F,7%,2 (0.8734)	−192
3	1040	P/F,7%,3 (0.8163)	849
4	922	P/F,7%,4 (0.7629)	703
5	836	P/F,7%,5 (0.7130)	596
6	727	P/F,7%,6 (0.6663)	484
7	507	P/F,7%,7 (0.6228)	316
			PW(7%) = $1,356

The shorthand notation shows that the constant 0.58201 is used to convert a future value to a present value when the interest rate is 7% and the time difference is eight interest periods. Tables of such constants are available widely (for example, in DeGarmo et al., 1993, through Tockey, 2005).

The Single-Payment Present-Worth formula can be applied to an entire cash flow stream. If each cash flow instance is converted back to its value the beginning of that stream (i.e., the end of period zero), and then each of them is added together, the result will be the *present worth, or PW (i)*, of that cash flow stream. Present worth is sometimes called *Net Present Value, or NPV*. The formula for calculating the PW(i) of a cash flow stream is

$$PW(i) = \sum_{t=0}^{n} F_t(1+i)^{-t}$$

where n is the number of interest periods in the cash flow stream, F_t is the net cash flow instance in period t, and i is the interest rate per period. Table 3.1 shows how PW(i) is calculated for the cash flow stream in Figure 3.1. This table shows that at 7% interest, the cash flow stream is financially equivalent to receiving a one-time net income of $1.356 million today.

Expressed in PW(i) terms, any two cash flow streams can be meaningfully compared. Imagine that a mythical company, Alpine Software, receives two alternative offers from one of its customers. That customer offers to buy one of Alpine's products at the full price of $8000 today and also offers to instead pay $1000 annually at the end of each of the next 10 years. As shown in Table 3.2, this looks like a simple choice between $8000 today and $10,000 later. It might seem like the $1000-each-year alternative is better by $2000.

Table 3.2 The Cash Flow Streams for Alpine Software's Purchase Alternatives		
End of Year	**$8000 Today**	**$1000 Over 10 Years**
0	$8000	$0
1	0	1000
2	0	1000
3	0	1000
4	0	1000
5	0	1000
6	0	1000
7	0	1000
8	0	1000
9	0	1000
10	0	1000
Apparent total income	$8000	$10,000

This analysis, however, incorrectly assumes an interest rate of 0%. If Alpine Software chooses $8000 today, it can realize a return from investing that money. What would that money be worth after those same 10 years? If a more realistic interest rate is used, say 7%, the picture is very different and the better alternative becomes obvious. The $8000 today has a present worth of $8000, while $1000 annually for the next 10 years has a present worth of $7023.58. Interest—the time value of money—causes the $8000 today alternative to be the better choice.

3.3 Valuation of software

Much has been written on the topic of technical debt and refactoring. From a business perspective, refactoring to reduce technical debt is a good idea only if it leads to increased profitability. Clearly, some kind of economic analysis should be made of the alternatives: Is it better for the business to refactor to reduce technical debt, or is it better to ignore the technical debt and just continue adding more functionality (while possibly increasing technical debt along the way)?

The cost of refactoring should be relatively easy to estimate: Of the available software development budget, how much will be allocated to technical debt reduction—thus taking away from the near-term capacity to deliver business functionality. As an example, with an annual development budget of $10 million, if we allocate $1.5 million (15%) for refactoring, then only $8.5 million is available to add the functionality the business wants added. The question becomes, "what is the value of the deferred functionality compared to the value of the technical debt reduction?"

Understanding the business value of software can be difficult, so some authors have simply assumed the value of the software is what it costs to create it. If a company spends $5 million to develop some application, then it assumes the value of the application to the business must be $5 million. While this approach is simple to understand, it can easily lead to very mistaken conclusions. Any proper businessperson should reasonably expect that the value of that software should be much greater than $5 million; otherwise, why was the money spent on developing it?

The value of software is not what it cost to acquire it; the value is what effect the software has on the revenue and expenses of the organization. Two different situations will be examined next, commercial products and in-house (internally developed) software.

3.3.1 Valuating a commercial software product

Recall mythical Alpine Software, above. Assume that Alpine is considering redeveloping a new low-cost payroll processing application targeted at small businesses. Alpine predicts that the payroll product will need to be completely rewritten after seven years, and business decisions will be based on an interest rate of 7%. To the selling organization, Alpine Software in this case, the value of the software product is the profit it generates. Remember the basic equation:

$$\text{Profit} = \text{Income} - \text{Expense}$$

Income from selling a software product can be generated in several forms:

- Sales to new customers
- Upgraded sales to users of previous versions
- Maintenance and support contracts
- Product training and consulting
- . . .

Table 3.3 shows estimates for development and maintenance staffing for the project, together with estimated units for each of the anticipated income elements. Estimates can—and should, if at all possible—be based on actual historical results from past, similar products.

Table 3.4 shows per-unit cost and income for each element of the project.

Alpine also estimates that an initial investment of $250,000 will be needed to purchase and install the software development environment for the project team. Creating the project's cash flow stream is now simply a matter of arithmetic. Table 3.5 shows the estimated cash flow elements for the payroll project, together with the net cash flow instance for each interest period. This net cash flow stream is the same one diagrammed in Figure 3.1.

Table 3.3 Component Estimates for Alpine Software's Proposed Payroll Project (units)

Year	Staffing	New Sales	Upgrades	Maintenance Contracts	Training Classes
1	9	1250	80	80	3
2	9	2750	450	320	8
3	3	2500	725	540	8
4	3	2250	875	660	8
5	3	2000	1200	880	8
6	3	1750	1375	1040	8
7	3	1500	750	1150	5

Alpine Software's total investment in this project is $7.675 million. The total income generated by the payroll project is $10.007 million. Considering Alpine's interest rate of 7%, the project has a present worth of $1.356 million. Using $7.675 million as the "value" of the project would clearly be very misleading.

3.3.2 Valuating in-house (Internally Developed) software

To the seller, the value of a commercial product is the profit it generates. What about software that is developed for internal use? Valuation of this kind of software can be less obvious because the effect of the software on the using organization's finances is usually much more subtle. The organization is not selling the software; it is using that software in the production of its own products and services. How does one put a value on the software in this case?

The situation is more abstract, but there is still a straightforward approach. Again, remember the basic equation:

$$\text{Profit} = \text{Income} - \text{Expense}$$

Profit obviously increases when income goes up and expense stays the same. Just the same, profit also goes up when income stays the same and expense goes down. This is "cost avoidance."

Table 3.4 Estimated Unit Cost and Revenue for Alpine Software

Element	Unit Cost/revenue
Staffing	−$225,000
New sale	600
Upgrade	100
Maintenance contract	145
Training class	8000

Table 3.5 Cash Flow Estimates for Alpine Software's Proposed Payroll Project ($thousands)

Year	Initial Investment	Staffing Cost	New Sales Income	Upgrade Income	Maintenance Income	Training Income	Net Cash Flow
0	−$250	$0	$0	$0	$0	$0	−$250
1		−2025	750	8	12	24	−1231
2		−2025	1650	45	46	64	−220
3		−675	1500	73	78	64	1040
4		−675	1350	88	96	64	922
5		−675	1200	120	128	64	837
6		−675	1050	138	151	64	727
7		−675	900	75	167	40	507

Instead of considering revenue generated, consider the reduction in the cost of providing products and services to the market.

One obvious cost reduction is in automating work that would otherwise have to be done by people.[2] As an example, consider a manufacturer of commercial airplanes. Commercial airplanes are very complex and need to be tested extensively to ensure that they have been assembled correctly and will be safe to fly. If the airplane manufacturer wants to open a new production line (perhaps for a brand-new airplane type), then testing of those airplanes in the factory will be necessary. Assume that, based on experience, the company can estimate a staff of 61 shopfloor mechanics would be required if the testing were to be done manually. At an average fully burdened cost of $180k per staff-year, the organization would need to spend $10.98 million annually in labor costs to test manually.

By developing and using a software application (which, in this case, is embedded in a hardware instrumentation platform), the manufacturer can test the airplanes with only 36 mechanics. The value of the software (and hardware) is that it reduces staffing by 25 mechanics, which reduces labor costs by $4.5 million annually. Now, the same testing job is done for a labor cost of only $6.48 million per year. Assume that over the planned 20-year production life of the factory, the investment in developing and maintaining the test equipment software and hardware totals $49 million. The total cost avoided in shopfloor mechanic labor is $85.5 million. At an interest rate of 7%, the present worth of the test equipment would be $11.3 million. Again, the value of the software is very different from what was spent creating it.

Another, albeit less obvious, cost reduction is reducing waste by doing work more accurately. Consider the IT department of a large, multinational corporation that is responsible for placing wireless access points in office buildings that are being constructed or remodeled. The corporation might build a software application that helps place the access points to achieve maximum coverage with the fewest access points. Wireless access point placement is a very complex job, and many factors, including the building structure itself, metal air ducts, power lines, and plumbing, all affect optimum access point placement. Assume that a network engineer is responsible for determining access point placement in a 100,000-square-foot (9300-square-meter) facility. Done by hand in the limited time available, at best the network engineer might end up requiring 45 access points to provide adequate coverage. By using placement analysis software, the network engineer could provide adequate coverage with only 30 access points. At a cost of $900 per commercial-grade wireless access point, the company is saving $13,500 on this one installation alone.

In practice, cost avoidance can be due to a combination of reduced headcount and increased accuracy. Consider numerically controlled milling machines (NC Machines) that execute part-machining programs to mill metal blocks into a desired shape. The NC Machine software (and related hardware) not only reduces the machinist headcount—one machinist can run several milling machines at a time instead of just one—but also the accuracy of the milled parts can be increased, thus reducing waste from improperly machined parts.

---

[2]Not necessarily laying the people off if they are already employed—instead, one hopes that they would be reassigned to work that generates more income elsewhere at the same expense.

3.3.3 **Generalizing the valuation approach**

The approach described above can, of course, be generalized. What is the business value of

- Adding new functionality?
- Refactoring?
- Fixing certain defects?
- Selecting one architectural / design alternative over another?
- Allocating functionality to software or hardware in embedded devices?
- . . .

The business value of doing anything lies in the difference between the cash flow stream of doing it and the cash flow stream of not doing it. Take refactoring as an example. Are we better off refactoring, or are we better off using the resources that would have been spent on refactoring to deliver more business functionality? A number of factors will come into play:

- How much functionality could be delivered in either case (refactoring vs. not)?
- What is the business value of delivering the functionality or not?
- What effect does refactoring (or not) have on the rate at which functionality is delivered?
- Is some of the desired functionality not implementable without refactoring first?
- . . .

As another example, assume mythical Alpine Software has an existing Customer Relationship Management (CRM) application that is also targeted at small businesses. The code base is three years old and has accumulated significant technical debt. Table 3.6 shows estimates—assuming no refactoring is done—for maintenance staffing, together with estimated units for each of the relevant income elements for the remaining four years of the code base's expected life.[3] Alpine anticipates that there will be no effect on training income for the CRM product, so this can be safely ignored.

The per-unit cost and income are the same as the payroll project (as shown in Table 3.4). Table 3.7 shows computation of the cash flow stream if no refactoring is done. The cash flow diagram is shown in Figure 3.2.

Table 3.6 Component Estimates for Alpine Software's CRM product without Refactoring

Year	Staffing	New Sales	Upgrades	Maintenance Contracts
1	6	3100	825	775
2	6	3200	975	875
3	6	3250	1050	950
4	6	2500	675	650

---

[3]The study period for this analysis was arbitrarily limited to only 4 to save space in this chapter. Successful refactoring could cause the software to have a longer practical lifetime. But a longer study period would mean more estimates and so on and would introduce some other complexities that are tangential to the point being made. This section serves to describe HOW the analysis is done. The relevant case-specific factors will need to be included in any given situation.

Table 3.7 Cash Flow Estimates for Alpine Software's CRM product without Refactoring ($thousands)

Year	Staffing Cost	New Sales Income	Upgrade Income	Maintenance Income	Net Cash Flow
1	−$1350	$1860	$83	$112	$705
2	−1350	1920	98	127	794
3	−1350	1950	105	138	843
4	−1350	1500	68	94	312

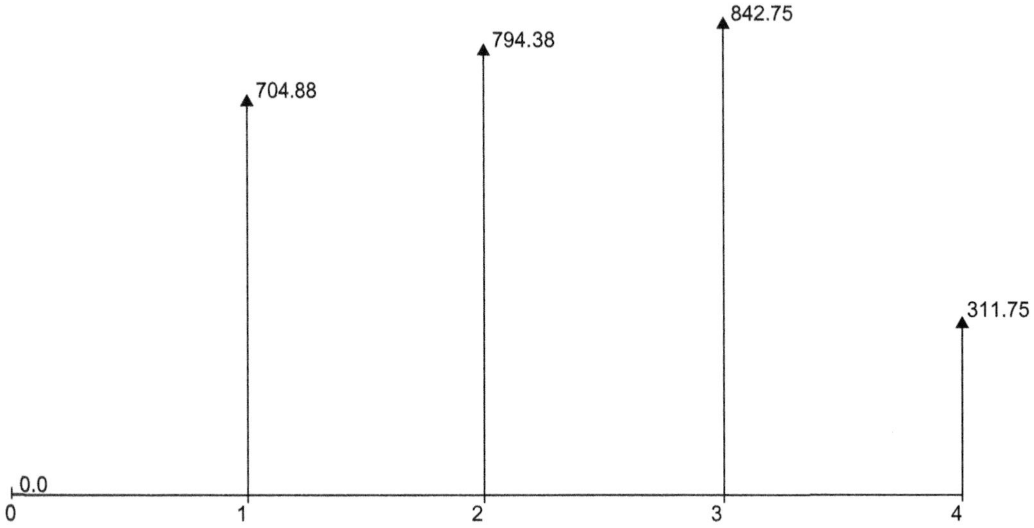

FIGURE 3.2

Cash flow diagram for the no refactoring alternative ($thousands).

The present worth, PW(7%), of the cash flow stream for the CRM project without refactoring is $2.28 million.

The software lead on the CRM project has proposed allocating 15% of next year's development resources to refactoring. In the short term, this means less customer-valuable functionality can be delivered, reducing sales. On the other hand, the long-term ability to deliver functionality is expected to increase, leading to higher sales later. Table 3.8 shows estimates, assuming refactoring is done, for the remaining four years of the CRM code base's useful life.

Table 3.9 shows computation of the cash flow stream if refactoring is done. The cash flow diagram is shown in Figure 3.3.

The present worth, PW(7%), of the cash flow stream for the CRM project with refactoring is $2.16 million. Alpine will be better off not refactoring the code base because the short-term

Table 3.8 Component Estimates for Alpine Software's CRM product with Refactoring

Year	Staffing	New Sales	Upgrades	Maintenance Contracts
1	6	2825	750	700
2	6	3000	875	750
3	6	3400	1175	1000
4	6	2650	775	775

Table 3.9 Cash Flow Estimates for Alpine Software's CRM Product with Refactoring ($thousands)

Year	Staffing Cost	New Sales Income	Upgrade Income	Maintenance Income	Net Cash Flow
1	−$1350	$1695	$75	$102	$522
2	−1350	1800	88	109	646
3	−1350	2040	118	145	953
4	−1350	1590	78	112	430

decrease in sales is not adequately compensated by increased sales later. The story could easily be different in any particular real-world situation:

- More or less refactoring may be needed.
- The effect on the delivery rate may be greater or lesser.
- More or less functionality may depend on prior refactoring.
- The effect on income or expense may be greater or lesser.
- . . .

In the end, the specifics of any given situation will need to be considered. Refactoring is not always a bad idea from a business perspective, but then neither is it always a good idea. Sometimes it makes sense, and sometimes it does not.

Evaluating architecture / design alternatives can be approached in a similar manner. The significant characteristics of each alternative would feed into estimates of required investment and return on that investment. For example, CPU load, memory, and disk use characteristics could feed into an estimate of hardware platform acquisition and operating and maintenance costs. Runtime characteristics such as throughput and reliability could drive an estimate of revenue generated or cost avoided. The technical complexity of the alternative could feed into an estimate of time-to-market. Scalability could drive an estimate of how quickly and easily the organization can react to significant changes in demand. Modularity, cohesion, and the like could drive an estimate of the rate at which business-relevant functionality could be delivered over the lifetime of the code base, and so on. Each of these estimates can then be combined into a cash flow stream representing the business perspective of that alternative. Once a cash flow stream for each alternative has been developed, it is simply a matter of finding the alternative with the most favorable present worth.

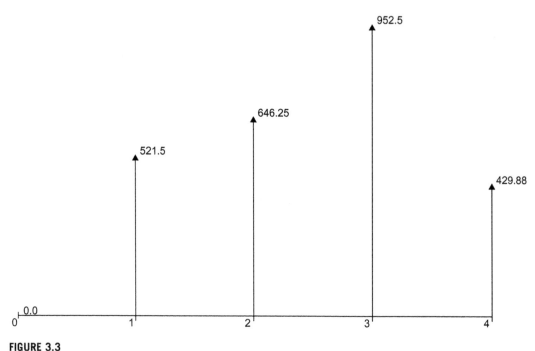

FIGURE 3.3

Cash flow diagram for the refactoring alternative ($thousands).

3.4 Capitalize software investments or not?

A recent trend in corporations has been to "capitalize" software development costs (see, for example, Aboody and Lev, 1998; Ben-Menachem and Gavious, 2007; de Groot, 2011; Gentle, 2011; Mulford and Roberts, 2006, and Muntor, 1997). First, what does it mean? Second, what effect does it have on the organization's profitability? This discussion will be in the context of corporations in the United States. The tax laws in other countries will almost certainly be different to some extent, but the same general principles will likely still apply.

3.4.1 What is capitalization?

The term *income tax* is actually quite misleading. Corporations are taxed on profit (net income), not gross income. Expenses must be subtracted ("written off") from gross income before taxable profit is known. If a corporation buys a box of paper for a photocopier, we can safely assume that the paper will be used within the tax year it was purchased, so it is safe to write off the cost of that paper in that tax year. But what about expensive things the corporation buys that last much longer than one year, like a computer that will be used for several years? Generally speaking, any item acquired by the corporation that

- is used in a business or trade,

- is used for producing income, and
- has a known life span of more than one year

is considered a "depreciable asset" for income tax purposes.

If the corporation were allowed to write off the entire cost when a depreciable asset was acquired, the income taxes for that year would be unrealistically low while the income taxes for the remainder of the asset's life would be unrealistically high. Just the same, if the corporation could only write off the actual expense (acquisition cost minus salvage value) after the asset had been sold or scrapped, then the early years' income taxes would be unrealistically high while the income taxes in the year of disposal would be unrealistically low. *Capitalization*, and its companion *depreciation*, are part of the process of spreading that asset's cost over several tax years. They are the tax authorities' attempt to make each year's income taxes as realistic as possible.

The term *depreciation* has two very different meanings in business decisions. First, it refers to how an asset will lose value over time due to wear and tear and obsolescence. This can be more precisely called *actual depreciation*. Second, it refers to how the organization accounts for that loss in value for income tax purposes. This can be more precisely called *depreciation accounting*. Depreciation accounting is an important factor in decision analyses that need to address the effects of income taxes.

The expenses written off in any tax year should accurately reflect the actual expenses incurred during that year. Those expenses should include at least an approximation of the actual depreciation of the assets the company owns. Through depreciation accounting, the tax authorities are trying to make the accounting and tax recognition of an asset's loss in value be as close as reasonably possible to when that loss actually happens.

Depreciation accounting effectively treats the acquisition cost of an asset as a prepaid expense. Instead of charging the entire cost as an expense when that asset is bought, depreciation accounting spreads the cost over the expected life of the asset. A $2 million NC machine would not be written off as a $2 million expense in the year that machine was bought. Instead, the $2 million would be spread systematically over the life of the machine. Depreciation accounting tries to approximate actual depreciation based on assumptions about how the asset loses value over time.

3.4.2 **Basic depreciation accounting**

As stated, actual depreciation (the real loss in value) of an asset is rarely the same as depreciation accounting (how value loss is accounted for by the corporation for income tax purposes). Actual depreciation is essentially impossible to determine. In practice, it can only be estimated by using one of a set of predefined methods. Three of those methods are explained here. If there is a difference, when the asset is sold or scrapped, between the asset's actual value and the value estimated by depreciation accounting, that difference needs to be addressed in the corporation's taxes.

A *Value-Time Function* is a formula that estimates how an asset loses value over time. The simplest value-time function is *straight line*. This function assumes that the value of the asset decreases at a constant rate (i.e., as a fixed percentage of its original value) over its lifetime. An asset that originally cost $50,000 and has a 10-year expected life is assumed to lose value at a rate of $5000 each year. The straight-line value-time function is shown in Figure 3.4.

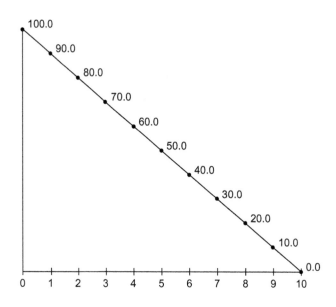

FIGURE 3.4

Straight-line value-time function.

Table 3.10 An Example of Straight-line Depreciation

End of Year	Depreciation Amount in Year	Remaining Value at End of Year
0	–	$11,000
1	$1500	9500
2	1500	8000
3	1500	6500
4	1500	5000
5	1500	3500
6	1500	2000

As an example, consider a computer system with an acquisition cost of $11,000, a useful life of six years, and an expected salvage value of $2000. The depreciation schedule and the remaining value at the end of each year are shown in Table 3.10.

The depreciation amount is a constant $1500 over the six-year useful life. The asset ends its expected life with a $2000 value on the corporation's books, which is the expected salvage value.

The second value-time function to consider is *declining balance*. In this case the depreciation amount is a constant percentage, α, of the remaining value of the asset at the beginning of the tax year. As the remaining value decreases, so does the depreciation amount. Under the current United States tax code, the maximum α is double the straight-line rate. An asset with a useful life of n years is limited to

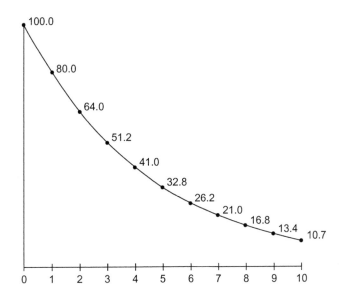

FIGURE 3.5

200% Declining-balance value-time function.

Table 3.11 An Example of 200% Declining-balance Depreciation

End of Year	Depreciation Amount in Year	Remaining Value at End of Year
0	–	$11,000
1	0.33 * $11,000 = $3667	7333
2	0.33 * 7333 = 2444	4889
3	0.33 * 4889 = 1630	3259
4	0.33 * 3259 = 1086	2173
5	0.33 * 2173 = 724	1449
6	0.33 * 1449 = 483	966

$$\alpha \leq \frac{2}{n}$$

A six-year asset would have a maximum α of 0.333, and a 20-year asset would have a maximum α of 0.10. Using this maximum depreciation rate is called the *double-declining-balance method* or the *200% declining-balance method*. Unlike straight-line depreciation, declining-balance depreciation ignores the salvage value of the asset. The 200% declining-balance value-time function is shown in Figure 3.5.

Table 3.11 shows the same $11,000 computer system depreciated using the 200% declining-balance method.

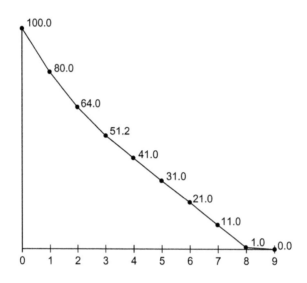

FIGURE 3.6

200% Declining-balance switching to straight-line value-time function.

$$\alpha = \frac{2}{6} = 0.33$$

The remaining value will never reach $0, and falls below the estimated salvage value of $2000 in year 5.

The last value-time function to consider is *declining-balance switching to straight-line depreciation*. In this method, the greater of the declining-balance and the straight-line amounts will be used. Declining-balance will be used early in the asset's life, and straight-line will be used for the rest. The switch from declining-balance to straight-line occurs when the declining-balance depreciation amount is less than the straight-line amount. This is shown in Figure 3.6.

The first four years in Figure 3.6 are identical to the 200% declining-balance value-time function in Figure 3.5, but years 5 through 8 follow the straight-line function in Figure 3.4. The switch happens in the fifth year, when the declining-balance amount ($8.2) becomes less than the straight-line amount ($10.0). Like the declining-balance function, this function ignores the asset's salvage value. Table 3.12 shows the same $11,000 computer system depreciated using the double-declining balance switching to straight-line method.

The switch from declining-balance to straight-line depreciation is in year 4, when the declining-balance depreciation amount ($1086) is less than the straight-line amount ($1500).

3.4.3 Effect of depreciation accounting on profit

Under depreciation accounting—and, therefore, capitalization—there is a significant effect on the profitability of the corporation. Alpine Software's payroll redevelopment project will be analyzed under three different scenarios—two where software costs are capitalized and depreciated using

Table 3.12 An Example of 200% Declining-Balance Switching to Straight-line Depreciation

End of Year	Depreciation Amount in Year	Remaining Value at End of Year
0	–	$11,000
1	0.33 * $11,000 = $3667	7333
2	0.33 * 7333 = 2444	4889
3	0.33 * 4889 = 1630	3259
4	0.33 * 3259 = 1086 so switch to 1500	1759
5	1500	259
6	259	0

different depreciation methods and a third where costs are not capitalized. Be aware that this example is somewhat unrealistic:

- The initial investment of $250k certainly includes real depreciable assets (specifically, the computer hardware for the development environment), but this depreciation is ignored in this example because it introduces unnecessary complexity.
- Only the first year's software development costs will be capitalized. In reality, if any software development costs are capitalized, then all software development costs would need to be capitalized. Capitalizing all software development costs introduces unreasonable complexity in having to deal with depreciation beyond the seven years of the project.

These scenarios illustrate the effect of any capitalization and depreciation accounting; more capitalization / depreciation simply magnifies the effect.

Assume that Alpine Software has an effective combined income tax rate (including federal, state, and local) of 38% and is profitable overall.

The first scenario will capitalize the first year software development cost and depreciate it using the straight-line method over the remaining six years of the project. This is shown in Table 3.13. The straight-line annual depreciation amount is $2,025,000 / 6 = $337,500. The after-tax cash flow diagram is shown in Figure 3.7.

The second scenario will capitalize the first-year software development cost and depreciate it using the 200% declining-balance, switching to the straight-line method over the remaining six years of the project. The computation is shown in Table 3.14, and the after-tax cash flow diagram is shown in Figure 3.8.

Table 3.15 shows computation of the after-tax cash flow stream when the first-year software development cost is not capitalized, so there is no depreciation. The after-tax cash flow diagram is shown in Figure 3.9.

Table 3.16 summarizes the consequences of the three different scenarios in terms of the present worth, PW(i), of the three after-tax cash flow streams.

From an after-tax perspective, no depreciation is clearly the best alternative because it leads to the highest present worth. Under both depreciation methods, the after-tax present worth of the project is negative—it would even be a bad idea to do the project in the first place. The difference is because more income taxes are being avoided earlier, and the time value of money makes the

Table 3.13 Computing Alpine Software's after-tax Cash Flow Stream using Six-year Straight-line Depreciation ($thousands)

(A) End of Yr	(B) Before-Tax Cash Flow Stream	(C) Depreciable Investment	(D) Depreciation Expense	(E) Taxable Income B + D	(F) Income Tax Cash Flow Stream-Rate*E	(G) After-Tax Cash Flow Stream B + C + F
0	−$250	$0	$0	−$250	$95	−$155
1	−1231	−2025	0	−1231	468	−2788
2	−220		−376	−558	212	−8
3	1040		−376	703	−267	773
4	922		−376	585	−222	700
5	837		−376	500	−190	647
6	727		−376	390	−148	579
7	507		−376	169	−64	442

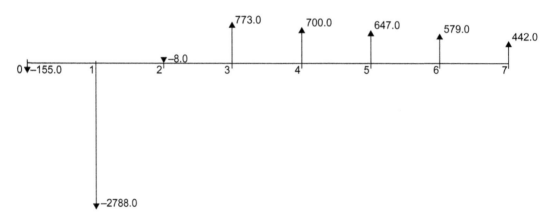

FIGURE 3.7

Cash flow diagram for the after-tax cash flow stream using six-year straight-line depreciation ($thousands).

resulting near-term profit worth more. 200% declining-balance switching to straight-line is better than straight-line depreciation for the same reason: More is written off sooner, so the time value of money is working in the corporation's favor. All other things equal, writing off sooner is better than later. Depreciation by any method (as a direct, unavoidable consequence of capitalization) necessarily delays the write-off, meaning that interest causes the business value to decrease. This is why—even though software has not traditionally been capitalized and depreciated—it is actually in the corporation's favor to keep it that way.

It is clearly advantageous to not depreciate at all, if you do not have to. Corporations would be much better off treating money spent on depreciable assets as expenses and writing off the entire

Table 3.14 Computing Alpine Software's after-tax Cash Flow Stream using 200% Declining-balance Switching to Straight-line Depreciation ($thousands)

(A) End of Yr	(B) Before-Tax Cash Flow Stream	(C) Depreciable Investment	(D) Depreciation Expense	(E) Taxable Income B + D	(F) Income Tax Cash Flow Stream-Rate*E	(G) After-tax Cash Flow Stream B + C + F
0	−$250	$0	$0	−$250	$95	−$155
1	−1231	−2250	0	−1231	468	−2788
2	−220		−675	−895	340	120
3	1040		−450	590	−224	816
4	922		−338	585	−222	700
5	837		−338	500	−190	647
6	727		−225	502	−191	536
7	507		0	507	−193	314

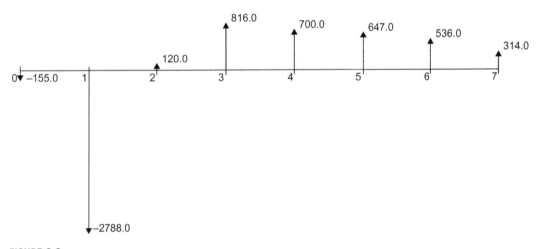

FIGURE 3.8

Cash flow diagram for the after-tax cash flow stream using 200% declining-balance switching to straight-line depreciation ($thousands).

acquisition cost in the year the asset is acquired. Corporations are not being <u>allowed</u> to depreciate assets; they are <u>required</u> by law to depreciate them.

3.5 **Additional comments**

The preceding analyses are all based on estimates: estimates of sales figures, estimates of head-count, estimates of project duration, estimates of cost, estimates of interest rate, and so on. It should

Table 3.15 Computing Alpine Software's after-tax Cash Flow Stream using no Depreciation ($thousands)

(A) End of Yr	(B) Before-Tax Cash Flow Stream	(C) Depreciable Investment	(D) Depreciation Expense	(E) Taxable Income B + D	(F) Income Tax Cash Flow Stream -Rate*E	(G) After-tax Cash Flow Stream B + C + F
0	−$250	$0	$0	−$125	$95	−$155
1	−1231			−1231	467	−763
2	−220			−220	84	−136
3	1040			1040	−395	645
4	922			922	−350	572
5	837			837	−318	519
6	727			727	−276	451
7	507			507	−193	314

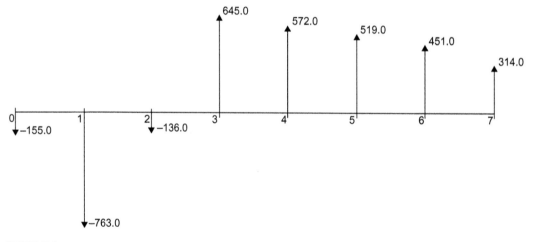

FIGURE 3.9

Cash flow diagram for the after-tax cash flow stream using no depreciation ($thousands).

be clear that if the actual values differed from these estimates, then the desirability of that alternative could easily be different. There isn't space in this chapter to discuss how to address the potential inaccuracy of estimates; however, techniques such as *analyzing ranges of estimates, sensitivity analysis,* and *delaying final decisions* are recognized approaches (see, for example, DeGarmo et al., 1993; Eschenbach, 2003; Grant et al., 1990; Thuesen and Fabrycky, 1993, or Tockey, 2005).

The preceding analyses also assumed that beyond technical feasibility, there was a single business decision criterion: money. Money is almost always the most significant business decision

Table 3.16 Comparing the after-tax present Worth of the three Scenarios ($thousands)

Depreciation Method	PW(7%) of after-tax Cash Flow Stream
Straight-line	−$480
200% declining-balance switching to straight-line	−442
No depreciation	842

criterion, but it is not always the only criterion. Again, space in this chapter is limited, but systematic multicriteria decision techniques such as *dominance, lexicography, additive weighting*, and *Analytical Hierarchy Process (AHP)* exist when there are multiple decision criteria (see, for example, Eschenbach, 2003, or Tockey, 2005).

The examples in this chapter show how to make financially sound technical decisions in for-profit organizations. Financially sound decisions also need to be made in not-for-profit organizations such as governments. Again, space in this chapter is limited, however techniques such as *benefit-cost analysis* and *cost-effectiveness analysis* are recognized approaches in these situations (see, for example, DeGarmo et al., 1993; Eschenbach, 2003; Grant et al., 1990; Thuesen and Fabrycky, 1993, or Tockey, 2005).

Finally, it should be stated that all of the techniques discussed in this chapter are standard, recognized elements of *Engineering Economy*. These techniques have been in use for well over 100 years in organizations where real engineering is done: Ford, Deutche Telekom, Alstom, Boeing, Toyota, Royal Dutch Shell, and the like. This is what real engineering is all about. Insofar as engineering can be defined as (The American Heritage Dictionary, 1983):

the application of scientific and mathematical principles to practical purposes, such as the design, construction, and operation of efficient and economical structures, equipment, and systems

the two key elements of engineering are:

- Using relevant science and math to generate a set of theoretically viable solutions to a real-world problem
- Selecting from the set of theoretically viable solutions, the one solution that is the most cost-effective

Economic decision making is central to engineering. Engineering Economy is the set of recognized techniques for addressing the second key element on real projects in the real world. It should follow, then, that for software engineering to be recognized as a legitimate, peer engineering discipline, then software technical decisions—including decisions about software architecture—must be made using these same business-relevant techniques.

3.6 Conclusion

When making business decisions, investment needs to be compared to return on that investment. Given a set of alternatives, the alternative with the best return-on-investment generally is preferred.

The value of a piece of software is not what it cost to create; the value is in the cash flow difference between doing something and doing something else. Placing a business value on software is not trivial, but it can be done. The process for doing so was outlined here; one has to just work through that process.

In addition, it was shown through example how capitalization—and thus, depreciation—of software development costs can actually be a bad idea from a business perspective.

References

DeGarmo, E., Sullivan, W., Bontadelli, J., 1993. Engineering Economy. ninth ed. Prentice Hall, Upper Saddle River, NJ.

Eschenbach, T., 2003. Engineering Economy: Applying Theory to Practice. second ed. Oxford University Press, New York.

Grant, E., Ireson, G., Leavenworth, R., 1990. Principles of Engineering Economy. eighth ed. Wiley, New York.

Thuesen, G., Fabrycky, W., 1993. Engineering Economy. eighth ed. Prentice Hall, Englewood Cliffs, NJ.

Tockey, S., 2005. Return on Software. Addison-Wesley, Boston, MA.

Aboody, D., Lev, B., 1998. The value-relevance of intangibles: the case of software capitalization. J. Account. Res. 36 (Suppl.), 161−191.

Ben-Menachem, M., Gavious, I., 2007. Accounting software assets: a valuation model for software. J. Inf. Systs. 21 (2), 117−132.

de Groot, J., 2011. Incorporating software quality in the capitalization of software as an asset. Master's Thesis, Leiden Institute of Advanced Computer Science (LIACS).

Gentle, M., 2011. Capitalizing software development costs—waterfall, agile and cloud. IT Project Financials. <http://itprojectfinancials.com/insights/2011/06/05/capitalizing-software-development-costs-from-sdcl-to-agile/>.

Mulford, C., Roberts, J., 2006. Capitalization of software development costs−a survey of accounting practices in the software industry. Georgia Tech. College Manage. <http://scheller.gatech.edu/downloads/2006/ga_tech_software_dev_2006.pdf>.

Muntor, P., 1997. Accounting for internal use software. CPA J. <http://www.nysscpa.org/cpajournal/1997/0297/features/f16.htm>.

The American Heritage Dictionary, 1983. Houghton Mifflin, Boston, MA.

An Architecture Framework for Self-Aware Adaptive Systems

Alistair Sutcliffe

University of Lancaster, Lancaster, UK

4.1 Introduction

Computer systems are evolving to include more intelligent, adaptive and location-aware processes. While there has been increasing recognition of the intertwining of requirements and architectural concerns in the software engineering community (Nuseibeh, 2006), the implications for mobile and context-aware applications have not been investigated per se. "Awareness requirements" (Souza et al., 2011) have been proposed to specify monitoring functionality in adaptive systems, so that systems can adapt their functionality depending on the feedback gained from awareness monitors. Others have proposed that systems could adapt to different nonfunctional requirements of service quality, depending on context awareness of the system environment (Ghezzi and Tamburrelli, 2009). Established approaches to modeling uncertainty, and changing relationships between requirements and the system environment (Fickas and Feather, 1995; Robinson, 2006), have been extended by Whittle et al. (2010), who argued for linguistic approaches to handle uncertainty in requirements, while also pointing out that self-adaptive systems needed complex decision-making abilities to resolve conflicting requirements and explanation facilities for humans in the loop adaptation. Given the growth of mobile and ubiquitous computing, the design of system architecture for context-aware, adaptive systems has become a concern in many domains (Dix et al., 2000).

Given this commonly occurring theme, it is surprising that no architectural framework has been proposed for this class of system. Architectural framework and other standardized architectures have been adopted in product lines and enterprise resource plans (ERP) systems (Pohl et al., 2005; Keller and Teufel, 1998), enabling rapid development by reuse. Since context awareness is a cross-cutting concern that could apply to a wide variety of application domains (Sawyer et al., 2010), a context-aware, adaptive systems architecture could produce considerable benefits. The economic implications are for empowering reuse, as standardized architectures can reduce development times and cost.

This chapter proposes a reference architecture for context-aware applications and explores its application in health care domains which involve monitoring people and providing adaptive feedback for decision making: a human-in-the-loop self-aware, adaptive system. Another aim is to investigate the nature of abstraction in system architecture modeling in response to a design goal to maximize the reuse of the context-aware architecture in similar health-related applications, and if possible more wide-ranging reuse in other domains. This reuse goal implies investigation into the level of abstraction and architectural modularity to support a wide range of reuse.

Three research goals motivated the work reported in this chapter: first, to develop a new generic architecture of self-aware adaptive systems (SAAS) from a user-centered perspective; and second, to investigate pathways to reuse and the economic implications of developing a generic architecture for reuse in an adaptive health care management application. The third goal, to bridge the gap between requirements and design in system architecture, motivates the user-centered perspective and specification of conceptual (i.e., application problem focused) rather than software design (solution-focused) architecture. In subsequent sections of this chapter, first the background and related research are reviewed, followed by explanation of the context-aware systems' architecture framework. The architecture is applied in a health care management case study for detecting early signs of mild cognitive impairment. The final section of the chapter discusses the approaches to abstraction in generic conceptual models and implications thereof for design of system architectures.

4.2 Background and related research

Application frameworks (Fayad and Johnson, 2000) and product lines, or families of reusable software components (Arango et al., 1993), are architectural genres that extend the scope of applications beyond single domains. However, methods and processes for developing reusable components (e.g., Pohl et al., 2005; Clements and Northrop, 2001) supply little guidance about cost-benefit analysis when specifying reusable architecture components. Furthermore, domain analysis and engineering analysis methods such as Feature Oriented Development Analysis (FODA) (Simos and Anthony, 1998; Vici et al., 1998) approach system specification simply as an exhaustive exercise in identifying and cataloguing functions within a particular domain, without considering architectural issues.

Rapanotti et al. (2004) have explored these implications by positing "architecture frames" based on Jackson's (2001) problem frames, whereby the system functions address different aspects of the security problem space, with assumptions annotated on to the specification. The system architecture is described in terms of processes for checking identity to prevent unauthorized access, audit trails to enable diagnosis of attacks, and so on, which are specified to satisfy the safety nonfunctional requirements within the bounds of assumptions made about the behavior of users and external threats.

Software architecture at the design implementation level is well known from Garland and Shaw's foundations (1993). Architectural styles have been proposed as heuristics and patterns for synchronization, concurrent pipelines, abstract data repository, publish/subscribe, and the like, to address design quality and implementation concerns (Bass et al., 2003). These styles were applied to sensing problems in the sea-buoy monitoring case study to address design of synchronization in multistream data capture. Architecture tactics are related heuristics for trade-off decisions advising on queuing, scheduling, and related concerns (Bachman et al., 2003). A generic stimulus response architecture-modeled system interfaces with domain artifacts and informs trade-offs on nonfunctional requirements such as performance time, reliability, input demand management and arbitration, allocating resources, and modifiability. Structural architecture patterns for design of collaborating classes (Gamma et al., 1995) included the observer pattern for design of monitor/sensor object collaborations. More extensive collections are described in the pattern-oriented system architecture series (Buschman et al., 2007). However, many architectural frameworks and patterns deal with implementation issues and performance quality trade-offs, so they do not support design of architecture at the application requirements level, a necessary precursor to design-level system architecture.

Within limited domains, for example, engineering applications, product lines have demonstrated the success of architecture templates with variations for adaptation and reuse (Clemens and Northrop, 2001; Pohl et al., 2005). Component-based conceptual architectures have evolved in the ERP genre (Keller and Teufel, 1998, Scheer and Habermann, 2000), where modularity was determined by business process models. However, reuse has to be supported by considerable adaptation effect, and solutions have often proven inflexible for adaptation to different cultures and user requirements (Krumbholz and Maiden, 2001; Ramos and Berry, 2005). The close relationship between requirements specifications and system architecture noted by Nuseibeh (2006) and Sutcliffe (2009) was synthesized in Jackson's problem frames (Jackson, 2001), which encapsulate the dependencies between domain artifacts and the software system. Four problem frames were proposed as goal-oriented abstractions dealing with control of devices in the domain, interaction with users, data updating, and general data transformations. However, these abstractions are difficult to map to applications.

Fowler's analysis patterns (Fowler, 1997) describe conceptual models closer to the application level, while more extensive libraries of conceptual models for application-level architectures have emerged in web service patterns (Endrei et al., 2004) and Oracle service-oriented architecture (SOA) patterns. IBM service patterns at the application level describe abstractions of service relationships, for example, user to user, user to business, user to data (information kiosk).Most patterns, however, are oriented to design implementation concerns such as client-server partitions. Oracle SOA patterns, within an application development framework, facilitate creation of reporting and database querying interfaces, with some limited support for transaction processing. Requirements patterns (Withall, 2007) provide 37 patterns organized into eight families, covering process issues such as documentation, user interface design, information and data modeling, user-oriented functions, access control, and nonfunctional requirements such as performance and flexibility; however, application-oriented problems and transactions are not covered. Transaction-oriented conceptual models are described in the domain theory (Sutcliffe, 2002), which proposed 13 families of conceptual models ranging from transactions such as reservation and sales order processing to sensing monitoring functions, agent control, progress tracking, and the like.

In their review of self-aware and adaptive systems, Salehie and Tahvildari (2009) note that several software design-level patterns exist for adaptation ranging from GOF (gang of four) patterns (Gamma et al., 1995) such as Wrapper and Proxy to Reflection (Buschman et al., 2007). At a higher architectural level, different strategies have been adopted such as component-based software engineering (CBSE), aspect weaving, plug-in architectures, and multi-agent systems. They reviewed 16 adaptive architecture projects using the MAPEK framework (Monitor, Analyze, Plan, Execute, Knowledge) (Kephart and Chess, 2003), concluding that only a few projects provided good support for all framework components. Self-aware adaptive architectures are closely related to autonomic systems where the "self" properties (optimizing, healing, protecting, adapting) characterize adaptive systems with increasing degrees of autonomy and adaptability (Kephart and Chess, 2003; IBM, 2004). Salehie and Tahvildari (2009) describe significant research challenges in design for adaptation, architecture of adaptation engines, and the interaction between software components and human agents.

Huebscher and McCann's (2008) review of autonomic computing reported similar issues as Salehie and Tahvildari (2009), although they focused on autonomic software toolkits such as

IBM's ABLE (IBM, 2004) and KX (Parekh et al., 2003) which present separate architectural components that may be applied to a variety of applications and legacy systems. They noted considerable research challenges in the level of autonomy, ranging from the core application system to more autonomous adaptation driven by higher-order system goals. Using a slightly different reference model (Collect-Analyze-Decide-Act), Cheng et al. (2009) argue for adaptive control-loop architectures and a more goal-oriented view to deal with multiple goals for adaptation; they also note the need for reference architectures and higher-order natural adaptation where humans are in the cycle of evolution. A more detailed requirements view (Sawyer et al., 2010) proposes a framework for "requirements reflection" where systems monitor their own behavior and goals, leading to requirements for adaptation and change, while pointing to the need for new modeling languages to deal with uncertainty and change in adaptive systems.

To summarize: Several conceptual-level sets of patterns and models have been proposed covering design and middleware concerns with some business-oriented patterns, but no application-oriented architectures have emerged. While reference models (e.g., MAPEK) and review frameworks have been reported for SAAS and applied to several projects in adaptive systems (Huebscher and McCann, 2008; Salehie and Tahvildari, 2009; Cheng et al., 2009), most projects have focused on general toolkits or middleware/system software. Few general reference architectures exist for SAAS applications, and user-centred perspectives on awareness and adaptation seem to have been ignored.

4.3 SAAS architecture framework

The framework is intended as a conceptual architecture to bridge the gap between requirements specification and architectural design. Since the term *system architecture* covers a wide range of concerns mainly focused on implementation and operation, the term *conceptual system architecture* is used as a more user-focused, requirements-based view of a prospective system design (Sutcliffe, 2009). This viewpoint originates from problem frames and Jackson's theory of requirements engineering (Zave and Jackson, 1997), which draw attention to the dependencies between the requirements, the software specification, and the domain. Problem frames describe four deep abstractions based in this conception: Required Behavior, any software that responds to events in the world and takes appropriate action (essentially a stimulus-response machine); Commanded Behavior, a stimulus-response (SR) machine where a human user is the origin of the stimulus; Workpieces, an SR machine for editing/database updating; and Transformation, a machine that changes the stimulus into a new output. A wider range of abstract conceptual models proposed in the domain theory (Sutcliffe, 2002) describes goal-oriented models and transformations for transaction processing, tracking, monitoring, simulation, and so on, in 13 fundamental families, based on a priori conceptual abstractions.

Both of these approaches have informed specification of the SAAS architecture framework. Other approaches for developing the architecture framework include elicitation of deep analogies of computational problems from expert software engineers (Sutcliffe and Maiden, 1998), scenario analysis of prospective components to vary inputs, and contextual models to investigate how robust components were in the presence of contextual variation.

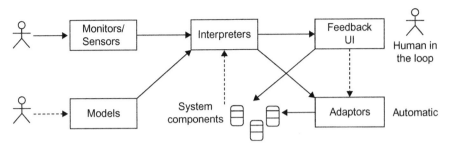

FIGURE 4.1

Basic conceptual architecture for self-aware adaptive systems.

The SAAS framework consists of three fundamental components: *monitors/sensors*, which detect events in the world; *interpreters*, which make sense of events and data about the environment; and *adaptors*, which provide feedback to human agents or take adaptive action (see Figure 4.1).

The rationale for the modularity of the architecture is separation of concerns and hence separability for reuse. Monitors and sensors are responsible for detecting events and changes in the external world. This component includes hardware sensors and software that convert device measures into processable data streams (e.g. analogue to digital converters). Monitors output data streams of processable events, which are passed to interpreters for sense making or for inferring higher-order information and patterns from basic event streams. In simple SR systems, interpreters may not be necessary as detection of the event may trigger an adaptor device directly (e.g., a safety monitor for a critical pressure value triggers shutdown in a process control plant). Interpreters make sense of data either with models of the external phenomena or with pattern analysis algorithms, for example, in data and text mining. The output from interpreters is sent to the adaption mechanisms, which will vary according to the type of SAAS system. In robots and systems equipped with physical actuators, adaptation is effected by system behavior controlling a device. Acting in the world may require further models of the system itself to plan action.

In human-in-the-loop system feedback, information is supplied to support decision making, learning, persuasion, or entertainment. Software systems adapt themselves automatically by parameter changes, selecting different methods and algorithms, or by configuring software components. Inevitably, boundary issues arise between these basic components; for instance, how much event preprocessing does a monitor perform, or should transforming events into higher-order information be the responsibility of interpreters? In spite of boundary issues, the framework establishes a general guide to modularity that can inform design for reuse. The components have many specializations that are reviewed in more depth in the following sections.

4.3.1 Monitor/Sensor conceptual models

Three modeling perspectives are presented: The first focuses on the nature of events and how they are captured; the second concerns the nature of the monitored object; while the third augments the first perspective with variations in strategies for data capture.

4.3.1.1 Event capture

The first perspective considers the nature of change that is being detected. In simple monitors only a semaphore is detected (e.g., signal present/absent), or a discrete event (e.g., dot-dash Morse code), or change in the value of a variable (e.g., temperature degrees). More complex monitors require a model of the external device and the input events to capture useful data, such as a keyboard monitor capturing ASCII alphanumeric text using a model of keystroke events. An almost infinite number of events and state combinations can be detected from environmental variables, so creating a detailed taxonomy would not be productive. However, some abstractions based on human error theory (Reason, 1990; Hollnagel, 1998) can inform design of monitors for human behavior. When event types are known and expected, event sequences can be specified a priori, and event pattern recognizers can detect omissions (events not present in an expected sequence), commissions (duplicated events), and inappropriate events in a sequence. When timing is added, events can be too early or too late; further specializations are possible for durations and concurrency if two or more event sequences are being compared. Monitors at the event level have many applications in trapping human operational errors, slips and lapses, when we forget to perform an action, or do the right action in the wrong context, and so on (Norman, 1999; Reason, 1990).

4.3.1.2 Awareness-performance monitors

The time period during which events are monitored and aggregated prior to analysis leads to the distinction between awareness monitors and performance monitors, as follows:

> *Awareness monitors*: capture events or event streams over a short time duration, where sense making and adaptation are at runtime.
> *Performance monitors*: capture events or event streams over a longer time period, where sense making and adaptation are at design time for configuration and decision-support requirements.

Awareness monitors that trap events and process them for an immediate system response are present in all adaptive control systems that respond to environment events. In contrast, performance monitors create datasets or histories of events and event sequences for longer-term analysis. These monitors feed existing data and text-mining software (Maimon and Rokach, 2005; Ananiadou and McNaught, 2006) or more complex interpreters that are dealt with in following sections. The duration of monitoring has no sharp boundary, since small datasets may be accumulated for discovering event patterns in limited timescales. Scaling up dataset collections for classifiers and more complex interpreters will depend on the application requirements; the architectural consideration is to plan for event databases, and controls for data sampling and duration.

The second perspective classifies monitors according to the external phenomena being observed.

4.3.2 Object-sensing models

This classification distinguishes between monitors of external entities, which may be human or artificial agents, natural entities, or properties of the general environment. The family tree of object-sensing monitors is illustrated in Figure 4.2. The first branch divides monitors that detect motion of objects within an environment from those that monitor properties of the object (or the whole environment) itself. Following the motion branch, further distinctions are between the nature of the

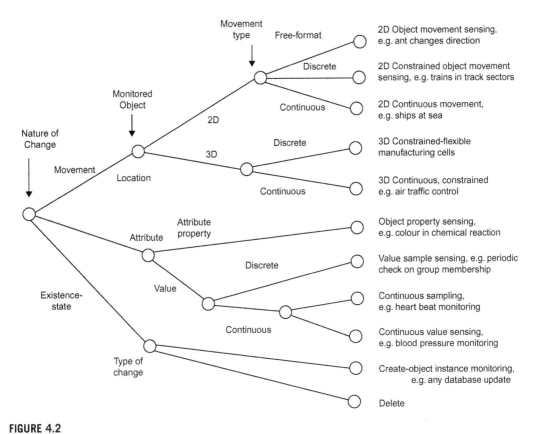

FIGURE 4.2

Monitor object-sensing models family tree.

space—two-dimensional (2D) planes or three dimensions—and then how motion is detected with reference to the environment, either discrete when transitions over boundaries are detected or continuous motion tracking. Further specializations, not represented in the taxonomy, are possible according to the nature of the spatial environment; this may be a topographic map as in geographic information systems, a Cartesian space without internal detail, or a topographical abstraction such as segments in air lanes or railway tracks. The final division in this branch describes monitors where there is no reference to the external environment (free format), so the monitored object is tracked in a Cartesian space from a reference point.

The nonmotion branch distinguishes between monitoring the existence of object instances and monitoring attributes. Following the attribute branch, monitors detect change either in values, with discrete or continuous variables, or as enumerated sets. Attribute monitoring can be specialized according to the monitored entity (e.g., human or artificial agent, natural entity) or applied to properties of the environment such as temperature, pressure, radiation, and so forth. Spatial specialization can segment the environmental properties into subspaces. The final type of change branch models Create, Replace, Update, Delete (CRUD) operations for creating or deleting object instances.

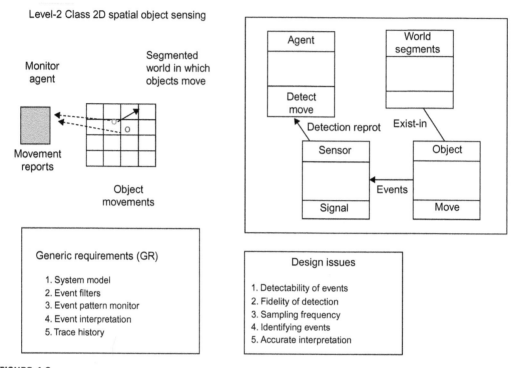

FIGURE 4.3

Object-sensing conceptual model—2D movement detection variant.

Each leaf node of the tree is linked to detailed conceptual models describing the nature of the monitoring problem, as illustrated in Figure 4.3, which shows the object-sensing model for the 2D spatial movement subfamily.

The conceptual model shows the generic objects for the subfamily, in this case the object of interest; the world in which it moves, which is segmented in this case; the sensor; and the report object it produces. An informal sketch helps to explain the conceptual model to end-users, and the model contains design advice specific to the problem class as well as generic requirements and design issues shared with other monitor classes, such as fidelity of event detection, sampling frequency, and how to identify events.

Space precludes elaboration of further submodels, but more detail is given in Sutcliffe (2002). The following section describes the third perspective on monitors, which poses the distinctions about how events are captured.

4.3.3 Hard and soft monitors

Hard monitors are familiar sensory technology, either detecting properties of the environment (e.g., temperature, pressure, radiation), properties of an agent (e.g., human blood pressure, heart rate, respiratory rate), movement of an agent (e.g., direction, speed, coordinate position), or behavior of

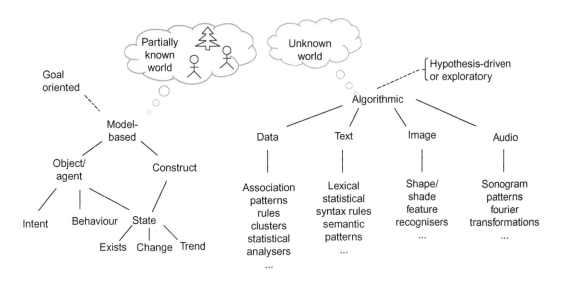

FIGURE 4.4

Interpreter component family tree.

an agent/artifact (e.g., keystrokes on a computer). However, data can be captured indirectly via people; we refer to these methods as "soft monitors." Soft monitors capture data either from people directly in question-answering and form-filling dialogues or via paper-based methods such as questionnaires. The advantage of soft monitors is that the human carrying out the data capture can act as a preprocessor to interpret data before data entry. For instance, the verbal response in an interview on product marketing could be interpreted on a 1 to 7 scale from linguistic expressions ranging from awful, okay, reasonable to excellent. While hard monitors are desirable to reduce the burden on human data entry (e.g., online questionnaires), the choice between hard and soft monitors revolves around the precision of the information to be captured and the sophistication of preprocessing necessary before software interpreters can act. When language-based information or complex behavior needs to be captured, soft monitors are advisable. Hard monitors could be built, but they also need sophisticated interpreters, such as text-mining and natural language processing for linguistic input, video motion capture and model-based scene recognition for complex behavior, and intelligent image analysis for complex scenes.

4.3.4 Interpreters

The second main architecture component takes input from monitors and carries out sense-making analysis to create higher-order information from input event data. As with many taxonomies, the distinction between components is not absolute. Elements of interpreters could be embedded within monitors, although separating interpreters is advisable when analysis tasks become more complex. The family tree of generic interpreter components is illustrated in Figure 4.4.

Two subfamilies are model-based sensing making, which relies on a model of the phenomena being analyzed, and exploratory analyses that do not need a model of the domain. In the model-based family, the system architecture will need components for model acquisition and updating. One subfamily branch includes object/agent interpreters that attempt to infer behavior, state, or intent of agents. For behavioral analysis, a model is necessary to link monitored events to actions and higher-order behavioral patterns, for example, mouse movements and clicks recorded as event streams with screen coordinates are interpreted with a user interface model to identify user actions from clicking on icons and from there to actions in the user's application task. Analysis of states might be modeled in the same way to detect which operational mode the user is in, for example, compose message, send, or read message in an e-mail application. Interpreting intent is more complex and depends on a model linking goals to behavior patterns and agent actions. An example might be to infer an agent's intent to attend to a message using eye-tracking data with coordinates and time to perform a sequence analysis to determine that the message had been read.

The other subfamily branch in the model-based side analysis constructs or semantic-ontological knowledge rather than information pertaining to agents. These interpreters tend to take text input rather than event data, although some constructs, for example, "importance," can be inferred from event frequencies or durations in eye-tracking data. However, most model-based construct interpreters will have a partial ontology of the phenomena being analyzed and attempt to refine or extend the model by syntactic/semantic analysis of text, possibly combined with behavioral data. Spatial and temporal contexts can be added to either family branch, which entails components for spatial interpretation, usually with topographic models and maps, whereas temporal analysis depends on the objectives for analyzing trends and temporal patterns.

Model-based interpreters become more complex with performance and soft monitors where there is a larger data volume for inference. Instead of simple algorithms, pattern classifiers, and rule-based interpreters, performance interpreters may analyze behavioral metrics to determine whether a threshold or goal has been attained. Inference of intent, identity, and higher-order knowledge might be driven by model-based data/text mining, for example, identifying personality types from text analysis of statements for sociability, extroversion, openness, and so on.

In the nonmodel-based, exploratory subfamily, no model of the phenomena exists, so sense making might be completely exploratory or partially directed by hypotheses. The subfamilies of algorithmic analyzers are specialized by modality. Data-value-based interpreters may use statistical routines to calculate trends, difference, clustering, or complex relationships between agent or other entities. Alternatively, this subfamily employs data-mining algorithms (Maimon and Rokach, 2005) to cluster data and identify patterns. The text modality subfamily includes simple word spotters to more sophisticated text-mining routines that can identify ontological structures and high-order meanings. The image modality contains various image-processing techniques from shape detection to shading, motion detection whereas the audio modality covers sonographical analysis and conversion to either text input from speech or semantic construct data for natural sounds, animal calls, and so forth. As this branch becomes more sophisticated, it converges with the model-based branch. This is especially true for image processing where most analysis requires a model of the scene for high-order sense making, while text miners are frequently seeded with a domain ontology. Performance monitor-interpreters with large volumes of data may employ learning algorithms to detect patterns, clusters, or higher-order information. Learning routines usually require seeding with a partial domain model or human assistance for model creation in explanation-based learning, for example, experts mark up input text for semiautomated text-mining inference tools.

4.3.5 Adaptors, actuators, and feedback components

The third part of the SAAS architectural framework is the adaption components. Three top-level families differ according to the phenomena that are changed by the system:

Self adaptation: The system changes itself in response to the environment. This family models software architectures where adaptation may vary from small-scale changes to the user interface look and feel, to adaptation by method parameterization, algorithm selection, and finally component-level adaptation.

Actuator response: The system takes action in the world by an actuator device. This may be simple control of devices such as turning heating on in a thermostatic control system to complex actions by robots where the system becomes an autonomous, adaptive component in the environment.

Human-in-the-loop: Adaptation in sociotechnical systems where the adaptive response is delegated to people. The system provides information, suggestions, advice, or a range of controls, leaving the ultimate choice to the user. In variations of this family the relationships between the system and the user change, that is, when the system's goal is to persuade or control the user.

Adaptive agent components are based on agent control models in the domain theory which describes command action relationships between two or more agents as a set of abstractions pertaining to command and control systems as well as to SAAS architectures. The top-level adaptive agents families are illustrated in Figure 4.5. This is slightly orthogonal to the first classification, with the human-in-the-loop being combined with the information-based adaptation, while the command-based branch subsumes both the system self-adaptation and actuator families. The agent

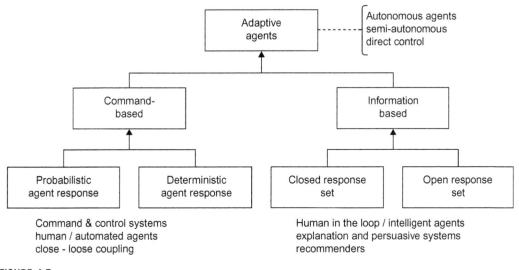

FIGURE 4.5

Adaptive agent components.

control family distinguishes between command coupling and data (information) coupling and then the dependency of the adapting agent's response.

In the command-based subfamily, human-in-the-loop systems will generally be characterized by a probabilistic agent response, since 100% compliance is usual even in systems with highly trained personnel (e.g., military, safety-critical systems). Deterministic agent response implies an agent whose response set is known and reliable, that is, actuator devices, or software under the system's control. The information-based family will generally involve human-in-the-loop adaptation. In multi-agent systems where another agent responds according to the content of a data message, the adaptation may be considered as data/information coupled. The subfamilies in this branch discriminate between the adapting agent where the response set is known and those where it is not. The design connotation of this distinction is that feedback information can be tailored toward the possible response in the closed case, but it has to be more open-ended, and hence frequently more comprehensive in the other.

As in the sense-monitoring family, more detailed conceptual models are given for each agent control/adaptation subfamily, as illustrated in Figure 4.6, which gives the information open-response agent model.

This model includes components for selecting, filtering, and explaining information since the response set is open. Hence, the receiving agent will probably need more information. The design issues involve user interface design expertise in choosing the media and representation messages, structuring arguments, and personalizing the delivery. Specialization of the subfamily adds components and further requirements for persuading users to take a specific action or decision, although this specialization is more common in the closed-response subfamily where the target response is known.

This concludes the description of the SAAS architectural framework. The detail of framework models is limited by space in this chapter as well as forming part of the future research agenda.

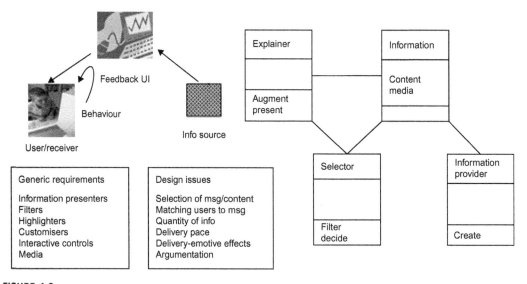

FIGURE 4.6

Adaptive agent information feedback model, open response set.

However, the set of abstractions and perspectives on conceptual systems architecture can be applied in design, as explained in the next section where the architecture framework is applied to a SAAS development case study in health care monitoring.

4.4 **Case study: health care management**

The SAMS project (Software Architecture for Mental Health Self-management) is developing software tools to help people monitor their own mental health and detect early signs of mild cognitive impairment (MCI), a harbinger of Alzheimer's disease. The top-level goals are to monitor users' computer use and e-mail traffic, and to analyze the records with data- and text-miner software to predict possible signs of MCI. The system is a loosely coupled human-in-the-loop self-adaptive system that provides feedback to users to encourage them to self-administer online follow-up tests and then, if necessary, refer themselves to their doctor for further tests and diagnosis. Nonfunctional requirements are to produce a low-cost solution with respect for users' privacy concerns and security, with accurate analysis of MCI signs and low rates of false-positive indications. The software also needs to be portable between different PCs and possibly other devices (tablets, mobile phones).

As well as developing a specific application, a secondary aim of the project is to develop a reusable architecture for related health care applications, such as monitoring for signs of mental illness in e-mail content and computer use. The SAAS architecture framework was applied to the project to develop the system architecture and reuse strategy.

The top-level system architecture is illustrated in Figure 4.7.

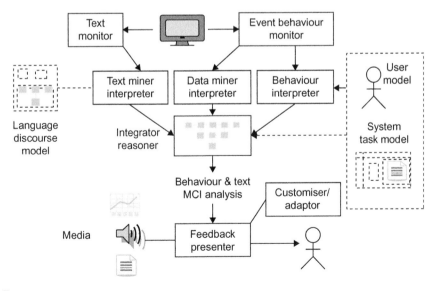

FIGURE 4.7

SAMs system architecture.

Rectangles framed with solid lines denote architecture components, while rectangles framed with dashed lines are models used by system functions. The following sections discuss the design rationale and architectural choices we made in the course of applying the SAAS architecture framework to specify components for functional and nonfunctional requirements. System input starts with monitors in the user's PC or tablet device.

4.4.1 Monitors

Two monitors capture events from mouse and keyboard interaction (event monitor) with conversion of keystrokes into text (text monitor). Other monitors such as image and audio capture could be implemented, assuming the user's computer has a camera and microphone. However, image and audio analysis would require complex interpreters; furthermore, these data streams would not add essential information for detecting MCI. The text monitor implements filters for privacy, so that either only user-authored text is captured or the user's text and e-mail replies are visible, depending on agreement of the participants. This illustrates the impact of nonfunctional requirements and stakeholders' views on architectural decisions.

The monitors were selected from the agent monitor subfamily to capture values, states, and properties of agents. Modeling choices were to monitor human agents directly or indirectly via computers. Direct monitoring of EEG (electroencephalogram) brain activity is the most direct means of analyzing cognitive activity, but the capture devices are an unacceptable intrusion into people's lives. Monitoring behavior by video and motion-tracking devices is less intrusive and has been adopted in assistive technology for Alzheimer's patients; however, this data was unlikely to yield sufficient sensitivity for detecting early signs of MCI. Accordingly, we chose indirect monitoring of computer use and e-mail content since these data provided a low-cost and relatively unobtrusive solution.

4.4.2 Interpreters

The SAMS objective is to detect early indications of cognitive pathology by interpreting event data and e-mail content. Rules and heuristics for detecting MCI were elicited from researchers who specialize in Alzheimer disease, the literature, and existing on- and offline tests. Diagnostic strategies and details do not concern the architectural decisions in this chapter. However, to place the choice of interpreters in the perspective of the requirements analysis and medical expertise, three principal analytic strategies emerged: detecting problems in memory, behavior, and emotional responses. These mapped on to the three interpreter classes, event awareness which analyzed behavior over short timescales, with data- and text-miner modules acting as performance interpreters by analyzing data over longer timescales.

4.4.2.1 Behavior activity interpreter

The behavior interpreter works in close conjunction with the user-task model to make sense of lower-level data, interpret events into actions via the system model, and compare interpreted data against benchmarks in the user model. This component processes keyboard event streams to produce low-level activity-event data for subsequent data mining (e.g., keystrokes, mouse clicks, response latencies, and movement durations); and subsequent mapping of keyboard and mouse events on to user's actions. Some of this data is captured from the object management system of the application (e.g., web browser, e-mail application) via Application Program Interfaces (APIs), so mouse moves and clicks are returned as user actions in a sequence. The action sequence data are then interpreted against the application task model that contains valid operational sequences (i.e., in e-mail, composing new messages, reading, filing, deleting messages, replying or forwarding). Word processing editing actions within a message are also interpreted at the level of typing and editing words. Action sequences are compared to detect deviations from normal usage patterns, repetitions, and omissions, with frequency and duration data to analyze changes in e-mail use. Three levels of analysis provide indications relevant to detecting memory and behavioral aspects of MCI:

Activity-motor indications: long response times, erratic event sequences, changes in activity timing
Behavior-task problems: deviations from normal task patterns, incomplete tasks, unnecessary repetitions
Errors: missing actions, repetitions, transposed events, changes in timing.

These outputs are passed to the Bayesian reasoner-integrator component.

4.4.2.2 Data miner interpreter

The data miner component is hypothesis-driven by expected indications of MCI derived from clinical expertise, but it may also be used in exploratory mode as a research tool. In hypothesis mode, this component accesses the user model for target expectations of performance relevant to MCI. The data miner uses historical datasets collected over many usage sessions. Both low-level event frequencies and durations are processed as well as higher-level task action sequences, applying Markovian analysis to investigate the probabilities of regular and infrequent sequences. Association, cluster, and rule-based analyzers are used to detect possible MCI signs from changes in activity levels, response times, and usage behavior patterns. These performance-level interpreters compare each individual against population benchmarks for normal behavior and against an individual baseline to detect changes over time. Statistical analyzers (e.g., regressions) are used for investigating temporal changes. Outputs are similar to those of the behavior interpreter, although data mining adds more sophisticated analyses comparing performance over time and benchmarking individuals against normal performance levels and longitudinal trend analysis

4.4.2.3 Text miner interpreter

The text miner inputs preprocessed e-mail content from the text monitor. Like the data miner, it needs high volumes of historical data and may operate with individual content in analysis mode or population-level content in research or configuration mode. It accesses external linguistic resources for semantic-lexical patterns (i.e., WordNet) as well as more specialized models for discourse patterns to detect emotional problems in sentiment analysis. Text input is processed for low-level information on word counts, message complexity metrics, and vocabulary diversity, then for topic focus continuity to detect pragmatic dysfunctions when the sender and receiver have misunderstandings, or topics get lost in an exchange. Finally, sentiment analysis aims to track affective indications in conversations for "flaming" or emotionally laden words and phrases that are evidence of distress, frustration, anxiety or other emotions. Output from the text miner, as with other interpreter models, provides evidence for memory and behavior indications of MCI. Furthermore, it adds evidence for the affective component. These outputs are passed to the Bayesian reasoner-integrator.

4.4.3 Interpreter reasoner-integrator

This component was not part of the reference architecture but was motivated by the multistream sense making that could have been presented to the user as a complex evidence set. Such complex evidence was unlikely to be comprehensible to nonexpert users, so a reasoner-integrator component was added. Inclusion of this component was also motivated by the need to improve diagnostic fidelity. Bayesian nets were chosen for this component since diagnostic reasoning is probabilistic, depends on prior assumptions grounded in medical expertise, and uses a causal model linking multiple sources of evidence. Briefly, Bayesian nets (BNs) are a mature technology that allows causal models to be implemented for probabilistic reasoning, taking prior knowledge into account which is added to the net during the configuration process. The BN reasons over inputs from the data, text miner, and behavior analyzer to produce a set of probabilities that the chance of the user having MCI are high ($p = .7$), medium ($p = .2$) or low ($p = .1$). Continuous variables have to be converted into discrete intervals, although the number of intervals is the analyst's choice. The probability distribution output is used to configure the feedback user interface and adaptation components.

4.4.4 Feedback and adaptation

The SAMS feedback component was based on the agent information closed-response family, with nondeterministic agents. Agent control by delegation was a possibility since notifying the user's doctor directly might have the advantage of improving the MCI detection rate; however, this could infringe the user's privacy and run the risk of doctors spending too much time on false alarms. The strategy of persuading the user to take self-administered online tests was preferred, with the eventual aim of encouraging self-referral to medical experts in memory clinics or local general practitioners. The user's response was partially anticipated by role playing and scenario analysis of emotion.

Adaptation was dominated by configuration at design time, with choices in the user's interface styles, media, and presentation of feedback. Presentation options were use of avatar characters to give spoken feedback; simple text messages; explanations of the system's conclusions; and comprehensive feedback with interactive visualizations using graphs and diagrams to explain how the measures were derived. Storyboard and prototyping exploration of design options indicated that the interface should be configured under user control, as some users preferred simple messages while others wanted more information. Furthermore, preferences for character-based interaction were mixed. Other decisions concerned the degree of persuasion to use in composing messages where rhetorical styles and choice of media (Reeves and Nass, 1996; Fogg, 2003) could influence users to take follow-up tests or self-refer. A persuasive style was used, although customization facilities were designed so that the user could select more or less persuasion. Nonfunctional requirements for personalization and usability with design guidelines from human-computer interaction determined architecture choice in this component.

4.4.5 **Design for reuse**

The SAMS architecture was packaged and documented with configuration points where each component could be adapted by initialization files. A paper-based reuse and redesign exercise was carried out to test the generalizability and flexibility of the architecture. Reuse and adaptation to a mental health tracking application, to detect early signs of depression by computer use, was investigated. Although this was a relatively modest test with a closely analogous application, it led to improvements in design and packaging the generic architecture.

The monitors could be adapted relatively easily to detect different event patterns in text and event data streams by loading new parameters into the system model. Since analysis methods had been constructed as declarative rule sets, new recognizer rules could be added with minimal change to existing code when parameterization of recognition rules was insufficient. Interpreters required more extensive adaptation for reuse, because tracking mental health problems such as depression needed specialized interpreters to detect different emotions and behavior patterns. Decreases in e-mail traffic over time, shorter messages, decreasing social interaction and emotional signs of withdrawal and loneliness were required to detect depression. Existing interpreters for behavior and event patterns could be adapted with modest changes, although new sentiment analyzers had to be developed to detect signs of emotion associated with depression in e-mail text. The feedback user interface component was adapted with ease since most changes were in the content of messages, explanations, and graphics. The design rationale of personalized feedback applied in the new application.

Overall, the architectural decision had proved to be robust when tested in a reuse scenario. The architectural structure was effective and flexible, although interpreter components were identified as the components where more substantial redesign was necessary. Design of a generic architecture with reuse in mind should make production of future application variants more efficient and economic.

4.5 **Economic implications**

The SAMS architecture was designed with multiple exploitation routes in mind. This section describes the economic motivations underlying exploitation planning. The first and most conventional route is delivery of a specific application for health care monitoring and self-management of MCI, with limited customization for individual users. From the socioeconomic perspective of architecture (Sutcliffe, 2008), this route has relatively low development costs, and while a large number of users could potentially benefit, exploitation is limited to the single application perspective.

The second route, tested in the design for reuse scenario, aims to deliver a configurable monitoring-decision support architecture for more general health care management in a range of mental health applications. The configurable architecture has slightly increased development costs, but a large range of application targets. Hence this is a more attractive proposition for software developers specializing in the medical Information & Communications Technology (ICT) area. However, there are configuration costs in adapting the text- and data-mining algorithms, adapting the Bayesian nets for new applications, as well as changes to the user interface. This route could evolve into a home-based health care monitoring product line with variation points in selecting different text/data-mining algorithms, databases, diagnostic rules, and so on.

The third, most radical, route focuses on the generic SAAS architecture that could be applied to any domain where awareness monitoring is necessary with human-in-the-loop feedback-style adaptation. This route approaches component-based software engineering-style design for reuse, with a potentially vast exploitation target in many applications. Unfortunately, the development by reuse costs hinder such ambitions. New monitors, interpreters, and feedback interfaces need to analyzed and developed for each set of domains, and no standards or frameworks exist to guide such developments, although proposals for requirements patterns (Withall, 2007) and libraries of conceptual models (Sutcliffe, 2002) could provide the foundations for more systematic CBSE-matching requirements through abstract architectures to software components. De facto the current state of the art in the open-source/eclipse community (Sourceforge, 2012) is driven by more specialized objectives in middleware, while the applications level is dominated by the commercial business model perspectives of ERP providers (Moon, 2007). While exploitation of SAMS will concentrate on the first two routes, the architectural framework may have an indirect economic benefit in methodological terms, if system architects approach the design of awareness and adaptive systems in a more principled manner. Assessing the economic success of SAMS, as with most software architectures, poses many challenges for future research, as economic data are often difficult to collect and where it does exist is frequently commercially confidential.

4.6 Conclusions and discussion

The generic architecture described in this chapter extends the range of pragmatic system architectures produced in product lines and enterprise resource plans (Keller and Teufel, 1998; Moon, 2007). SAMS provides a reference architecture for user-centered awareness and adaptive systems, with a specific focus on health care management systems, while also contributing to research SAAS architecture more generally. While product lines have enjoyed considerable success in limited domains such as automotive engineering (Pohl et al., 2005), the approach of a relatively monolithic architecture with variation points has not evolved in more wide-ranging domains. ERP systems are closely related to the SAAS framework since ERPS provide reference architectures or frameworks (Scheer and Habermann, 2000; Moon, 2007) focused on particular generic problems, although the modular design of ERPs has been motivated by business process, whereas SAAS architectures are a wider-ranging abstraction applicable to a variety of domains (Cheng et al., 2009; Huebscher and McCann, 2008).

Orchestration in service-oriented architectures (Endrei et al., 2004) also addresses the concerns of modularity and reuse; however, the general approach of loose data coupling tends to limit service architectures to composition of transaction processing and information processing in business systems. The architecture framework we propose complements previous approaches (Salehie and Tahvildari, 2009; Huebscher and McCann, 2008) while raising the prospect of a more methodical means of reasoning about design of system architecture at the conceptual or user requirements level. The SAMS-SAAS architecture and design framework could be synthesized with architectural strategies (Bass et al., 2003) and tactics (Bachman et al., 2003), with the conceptual architecture providing the structural design as well as highlighting application domain concerns. The heuristics and metrics of design architecture strategies could refine conceptual architectures in trade-off analysis to deal with nonfunctional requirements.

Within the genre of SAAS architecture, the architecture we propose follows established models such as MAPEK (IBM, 2004) and CADA (Collect-Analyze-Decide-Act: Cheng et al., 2009), although our approach was oriented more closely to user-centered systems with a human in the loop, rather than robotic systems and autonomous driverless vehicles that have motivated research on autonomous systems (Huebscher and McCann, 2008). This perspective is reflected in taxonomies of sensors and interpreter components that draw new distinctions between hard and soft (human augmented) data collection, and interpreters where our contribution draws attention to more datacentric analysis of the system's environment. SAMS as a reference architecture therefore expands the concept of SAAS architectures toward different forms of adaptation and analysis, from a software to a systems architecture view where the loop of awareness to adaptation may include human agents. While we did not directly address the "self" properties of autonomic and adaptive systems (Kephart and Chess, 2003), we believe that the SAMS architecture has added a new view of "cooperative" to adaptation, healing, and protection. The RequMon toolkit (Robinson, 2006) is related to our work in that it provides a range of adaptable monitors and interpreters that can track system behavior against specific goals. RequMon has been applied to several domains in e-commerce, demonstrating its capability as a generic, adaptable architecture. The AI planner solver developed by Dalpiaz et al. (2013), based on the Tropos architecture, also implements monitors and interpreters that track compliance with goals (or requirements) in a monitor-diagnose- reconcile (goal check), compensate (adapt) cycle. Although components for monitoring and diagnosing changes in context, goal compliance, and time are implemented, their solution only provides a general modeling language for delivering specific applications built with Tropos and Belief-Decision-Intent (BDI) agent-based reasoning tools. Many other self-aware adaptive systems tools have been implemented (see reviews by Salehie and Tahvildari, 2009; Huebscher and McCann, 2008). However, none to our knowledge have included components oriented to datacentric analysis (i.e., data/text mining) and user interfaces for monitoring and adaptation/feedback.

The SAMS architecture framework did stand the test of application in design for reuse. Furthermore, it was produced by a systematic process based on expert knowledge of problem analogies coupled with scenario analysis of contextual variations. The process of goal-oriented segmentation coupled with scenario analysis at variation points within each component offers a new approach to architecture design. However, application in one case study does not provide sufficient evidence to validate the approach. Further research is necessary to apply the SAMS framework in more wide-ranging reuse domains (e.g., awareness monitoring and adaptation in training and educational applications). In addition, the framework needs the addition of more detail in model subfamilies as generic requirements and design issues, possibly linking these to architectural tactics and strategies.

The value of SAMS and other SAAS conceptual-level architectures may be realized in several ways. The first way is to use the route described in this chapter as a "tool for thought" and source of design knowledge that can be applied for designing generic systems for reuse as well as specific self-aware adaptive systems. The second route for SAAS architecture and the domain theory (Sutcliffe, 2002),is to index open-source components for matching to application requirements so that appropriate components can be found. Open-source components are currently classified by application domains (Wikipedia, 2013; Sourceforge, 2012), which can hinder reuse as many components are specialized with domains. Indexing could be extended to using conceptual architectures to reengineer components for more general and wide-ranging reuse. The third route may be to implement conceptual architectures as configurable application generators (Sutcliffe, 2008), so that the architecture drives an end-user design dialogue for acquiring sufficient detail to generate specific applications. Variants of this route are the autonomic software toolkits (IBM, 2004; Parekh et al., 2003), which might be applied to a variety of existing systems to augment them with self-awareness and adaptation and capabilities, although application of SAAS-autonomic toolkits has yet to be demonstrated on an industrial scale (Dobson et al., 2010). The potential economic rewards for the second and third routes are considerable, but further research on architectural modeling and abstraction is needed to realize such ambitions. Furthermore, economic benefits for component-based design of architectures depend on standardization and intercomponent compatibilities. Component standardization may be difficult to realize in the dynamic and rapidly evolving software marketplace.

Future research in systems architectures needs to develop the systematic approach to specification, which this chapter has taken as a small initial step. The grand challenge is to develop a theory of abstraction in architecture that defines the level of modularity, coupling, and generalization that may be desirable for design goals and nonfunctional requirements. Partitioning application problems into reusable modules and designing automated configuration tools present an enduring research challenge for software architecture.

References

Ananiadou, S., McNaught, J. (Eds.), 2006. Text Mining for Biology and Biomedicine. Artech House, Norwood, MA.

Arango, G., Schoen, E., Pettengill, R., 1993. Design as evolution and reuse. Proceedings: Secnd International Workshop on Software Reusability (Advances in Software Reuse). IEEE Computer Society Press, Los Alamitos, CA, pp. 9–18.

Bachman, F., Bass, L., Klein, M., 2003. Deriving architectural tactics: a step towards methodical architectural design. Carnegie Mellon University Software Engineering Institute Technical Report TR 2003-0044. Carnegie Mellon University, Pittsburgh.

Bass, L., Clements, P., Kazman, R., 2003. Software Architecture in Practice. Addison-Wesley, New York.

Buschman, F., Henney, K., Schmidt, D.C., 2007. Pattern Oriented Software Architecture: On Patterns and Pattern Languages, vol. 5. Wiley, Chichester, UK.

Cheng, B., De Lemos, R., Giese, H., et al., 2009. Software engineering for self-adaptive systems: a research roadmap. In: Cheng, B., et al., (Eds.), Software Engineering for Self Adaptive Systems (LINCS 5225). Springer Verlag, Berlin, pp. 1–26.

Clements, P., Northrop, L., 2001. Software Product Lines: Practices and Patterns. Addison-Wesley Professional, Reading, MA.

Dalpiaz, F., Giorgini, P., Mylopoulos, J., 2013. Adaptive socio-technical systems: a requirements-driven approach. Requir. Eng. 18, 1–24.

Dix, A., Rhodden, T., Davies, N., Trevor, J., Friday, A., Palfreyman, K., 2000. Exploitation space and location as a design framework for interactive mobile systems. ACM Trans. Comput. Hum. Interact. 7 (3), 285–321.

Dobson, S., Sterritt, R., Nixon, P., Hinchey, M., 2010. Fulfilling the vision of autonomic computing. Computer 43 (1), 35–41.

Endrei, M., et al., Patterns: Service-oriented Architecture and Web Services. IBM/Redbooks, New York.

Fayad, M.E., Johnson, R.E., 2000. Domain-specific Application Frameworks: Frameworks Experience by Industry. Wiley, New York.

Fickas, S., Feather, M.S., 1995. Requirements monitoring in dynamic environments. Proceedings, 1995 IEEE International Symposium on Requirements Engineering (RE-95). IEEE Computer Society Press, Los Alamitos, CA, pp. 140–147.

Fogg, B.J., 2003. Persuasive Technology: Using Computers to Change what we Think and Do. Morgan Kaufmann, San Francisco.

Fowler, M., 1997. Analysis Patterns: Reusable Object Models. Addison-Wesley, Reading, MA.

Gamma, E., Helm, R., Johnson, R., Vlissides, J., 1995. Design Patterns: Elements of Reusable Object-oriented Software. Addison-Wesley, Reading, MA.

Garland, D., Shaw, M., 1993. Software Architecture: Perspectives on an Emerging Discipline. Prentice Hall, Harlow, UK.

Ghezzi, C., Tamburrelli, G., 2009. Reasoning on non-functional requirements for integrated services. Proceedings, IEEE International Conference on Requirements Engineering, RE-09. IEEE Computer Society, Los Alamitos, CA, pp. 69–78.

Hollnagel, E., 1998. Cognitive Reliability and Error Analysis Method: CREAM. Elsevier, Oxford, UK.

Huebscher, M.C., McCann, J.A., 2008. A survey of autonomic computing: degrees, models, and applications. ACM Comput. Surv. 40 (3), 1–28.

IBM, 2004. An architectural blueprint for autonomic computing. Technical Report. <http://www.redbooks.ibm.com/abstracts/sg246635.html> (accessed 22.02.13.).

Jackson, M., 2001. Problem Frames: Analysing and Structuring Software Development Problems. Pearson Education, Harlow.

Keller, G., Teufel, T., 1998. SAP/R3 Process Oriented Implementation. Addison-Wesley-Longman, Reading, MA.

Kephart, J.O., Chess, D.M., 2003. The vision of autonomic computing. IEEE Comput. 36 (1), 41–50.

Krumbholz, M, Maiden, N.A.M., 2001. The implementation of ERP packages in different organisational and national cultures. Inf. Syst. 26, 185–204.

Maimon, O., Rokach, L., 2005. Data Mining and Knowledge Discovery Handbook. Springer, Berlin.

Moon, Y.B., 2007. Enterprise resource planning (ERP): a review of the literature. Int. J. Manag. Enterp. Dev. 4 (3), 235–264.

Norman, D.A., 1999. The Invisible Computer: Why Good products can Fail, the Personal Computer is so Complex, and Information Appliances are the Solution. MIT Press, Cambridge, MA.

Nuseibeh, B., 2006. Weaving together requirements and architecture. IEEE Softw. 34 (4), 115–117.

Parekh, J., Kaiser, G., Gross, P., Valetto, G., 2003. Retrofitting autonomic capabilities onto legacy systems. Technical Report, CUCS-026-03. Columbia University, New York.

Pohl, K., Böckle, G., van der Linden, F., 2005. Software product Line Engineering: Foundations, Principles, and Techniques. Springer, Berlin.

Ramos, I., Berry, D.M., 2005. Social construction of information technology supporting work. J. Cases Inf. Technol. L2, <http://hdl.handle.net/1822/4793>.

Rapanotti, L., Hall, J., Jackson, M., Nuseibeh, B., 2004. Architecture-driven problem decomposition. Proceedings: 12th IEEE International Requirements Engineering Conference. IEEE Computer Society Press, Los Alamitos, CA, pp. 80–89.

Reason, J., 1990. Human Error. Cambridge University Press, Cambridge, UK.

Reeves, B., Nass, C., 1996. The Media Equation: How People Treat Computers, Television and New Media like Real People and Places. CLSI/Cambridge University Press, Stanford CA/Cambridge.

Robinson, W.N., 2006. Requirements monitoring for enterprise systems. Requir. Eng. 11, 17−41.

Salehie, M., Tahvildari, L., 2009. Self-adaptive software: landscape and research challenges. ACM Trans. Auton. Adapt. Syst. 4 (2), 14.

Sawyer, P., Bencomo, N., Whittle, J., Letier, E., Finkelstein, A., 2010. Requirements-aware systems a research agenda for RE for self-adaptive systems. Proceedings, 18th IEEE International Conference on Requirements Engineering (RE-10). IEEE Computer Society Press, Los Alamitos CA, pp. 95−103.

Scheer, A.W., Habermann, F., 2000. Enterprise resource planning: making ERP a success. Commun. ACM. 43 (4), 57−61.

Simos, M., Anthony, J., 1998. Weaving the model web: a multi-modeling approach to concepts and features in domain engineering. In: Devanbu, P., Poulin, J. (Eds.), Proceedings: Fifth International Conference on Software Reuse. IEEE Computer Society Press, Los Alamitos, CA, pp. 94−102.

Sourceforge, 2012. <http://sourceforge.net/> (accessed 22.02.13.).

Souza, V.E., Lapouchnian, A., Robinson, W.S., Mylopoulos, J., 2011. Awareness requirements for adaptive systems. Proceedings of SEAMS-11, 6th International Symposium on Software Engineering for Adaptive and Self-Managing Systems. ACM Press, New York, pp. 60−69.

Sutcliffe, A.G., 2002. The Domain Theory: Patterns for Knowledge and Software Reuse. Lawrence Erlbaum Associates, Mahwah, NJ.

Sutcliffe, A.G., 2008. The socio-economics of software architecture. Autom. Softw. Eng. 15, 343−363.

Sutcliffe, A.G., 2009. On the inevitable intertwining of requirements and architecture. In: Lyytinen, K., Loucopoulos, P., Mylopoulos, J., Robinson, B. (Eds.), Design Requirements Engineering: A Multi-disciplinary Perspective for the Next Decade. Springer, Berlin.

Sutcliffe, A.G., Maiden, N.A.M., 1998. A theory of domain knowledge for requirements engineering. IEEE Trans. Softw. Eng. 24 (3), 174196.

Vici, A.D., Argentieri, N., Mansour, A., d'Alessandro, M., Favaro, J., 1998. FODAcom: an experience with domain analysis in the Italian telecom industry. In: Devanbu, P., Poulin, J. (Eds.), Proceedings: Fifth International Conference on Software Reuse, pp. 166−175.

Whittle, J., Sawyer, P., Bencomo, N., Cheng, B., Bruel, J-M., 2010. RELAX: a language to address uncertainty in self-adaptive systems requirements. Requir. Eng. 15 (2), 177−196.

Wikipedia, 2013. List of Free and Open-source Software Packages. <http://en.wikipedia.org/wiki/List_of_free_and_open-source_software_packages> (accessed 22.02.13.).

Withall, S., 2007. Software Requirement Patterns. Wiley/Microsoft, New York.

Zave, P.A., Jackson, M., 1997. Four dark corners of requirements engineering. ACM Trans. Softw. Eng. Method. 6, 1−30.

Economics-Driven Architecting: Design Mechanisms and Evaluation

Economics-Driven Software Architecting for Cloud

5

Funmilade Faniyi and Rami Bahsoon

University of Birmingham, Birmingham, UK

5.1 Introduction

Today's software systems are influenced by new trends such as social networking, as made popular by Facebook and Twitter among others; hence they have large user bases (usually in the tens of millions). These systems are orders of magnitude larger in size than conventional systems. They are often accessed over the Internet, in a very dynamic manner, subjecting them to the challenge of coping with a highly variable and unanticipated workload. At the heart of their design are diverse hardware and software components composed in new ways to provision services. Unlike their predecessors, usage of these services is charged on a pay-as-you-use or spot-market business model rather than shrinkwrap licensing.

These features are attributed to the Cloud computing paradigm and its disruptive impact on software engineering (Armbrust et al., 2010). From the perspective of an application owner, that is, the Cloud user, who deploys an application in the Cloud, it is possible to access an infinite pool of computational resources in a self-service style. Coupled with the attractive business model of making users commit to a manageable contract (i.e., hourly/weekly/monthly), adoption of the Cloud has been phenomenal. For security-savvy users who are constrained by law or corporate policies to protect customer data, they have the option of building a private Cloud on-premise. Thus they are able to enjoy the resource-provisioning flexibility offered by the Cloud paradigm, while incurring the management overhead that comes with such an investment.

In this chapter, we limit our discussion to public Clouds and the interesting challenges they pose to the economics-driven software engineering domain. Public Clouds, for example Amazon Web Services (AWS), are more suited to economics reasoning when compared with private and community Clouds, since they have a broader user base and a heterogeneous mix of computational resources.

Before delving deeper into the topic, it is important to identify the key characteristics of the Cloud that makes the economics analogy useful.

- Utility-based usage: By providing access to resources in a self-service style and paying for only what is needed, when it is needed, users are able to use computing resources as utility, just as they do with gas and electricity.
- Elastic scale: The illusion of infinite resources as perceived by the user is actually a constrained pool of resources offered in an elastic manner. Since many users access the Cloud from geographically distributed locations, efficient resource allocation is a challenging problem.

- Heterogeneity: In practice, users often have different (sometimes conflicting) objectives based on their resource needs. The managed resources, in the form of either software or hardware, also differ in computational capacities and the offered Quality of Service (QoS). It is therefore crucial to consider the likelihood of meeting a user's objectives, when allocating resources to that user.
- Unpredictability: With such a large mix of users, workload patterns may be hard to predict, for example, due to bursty web traffic. Furthermore, Cloud resources are not immune to failure, and sadly these failures may occur when least expected.

In general, to appreciate the relation between computing systems, such as Cloud, and economics, one will inevitably come across a variety of views, depending on the context of the computing problem. As it is known, economics is a broad field, with many interesting applications. In particular, the vision of applying principles from economics to control software-intensive systems is not new (Lai, 2005). This idea has been pursued in grid computing, service-oriented computing, and, more recently, in the Cloud (Buyya, 2009a).

In the Cloud context, a number of research questions lend themselves to economics reasoning. Concretely, this chapter takes the perspective of using *economics-inspired approaches*, which have their root in game theory, to architect Cloud software. Given the large pool of computational resources in the Cloud and the variability of stakeholder concerns, the key question is: How can the Cloud software architecture support efficient computational resource allocation in such a way that the objectives of Cloud users, vendors, and the overall Cloud ecosystem are satisfied?

As research into Cloud computing gains more attention, there have been conflicting views about the definition of the term *Cloud software architecture*. This is perhaps due to the various levels of abstractions from which the Cloud can be viewed, for example, in terms of service offered (see Figure 5.1) or locality of the Cloud (private or public). We clarify this ontology issue by providing the following interpretation of software architecture for different Cloud artifacts. Software architecture:

- *of the Cloud* refers to the software architecture of the Cloud itself, for example, the software architecture of AWS.
- *of a Cloud application* refers to the software architecture of an application deployed in the Cloud. The deployment could be
  - *full*, in which case all the application components are in the Cloud, for example, deploying an e-Commerce web application in the Cloud.
  - *partial*, in which case some application components are in the Cloud and others are in non-Cloud subsystems, for example, the Smart Bank case study in (Faniyi et al., 2011), where a subsystem stored the bank's regulated data in-house, and other nonregulated data were stored in the Cloud.
- *of a Cloud federation application* refers to an application that makes use of multiple Clouds, that is, in the form of a system of systems, perhaps using an Service Oriented Architecture (SOA) approach—for example, the BizInt system described in (Nallur and Bahsoon, 2012).

The software architecture of Cloud applications, deployed in the *full* sense, is the one considered in this work. We believe that software architecture is the right level of abstraction to reason about the concerns of Cloud users and vendors, since it offers separation of concerns and generality, and supports analysis and refinement using tools (Kramer and Magee, 2007).

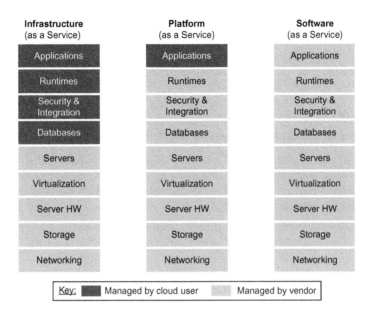

FIGURE 5.1

Cloud services at infrastructure, platform, and doftware layers.

This chapter focuses on the use of the retail-inspired posted offer market to improve the user's QoS satisfaction in the Cloud. Section 5.2 surveys the use of market-based approaches in Cloud architecting and defines relevant concepts and terminologies from the economics domain. Section 5.3 presents the dynamic resource allocation problem in Cloud services. In section 5.4, the process of applying market mechanism to design Cloud software architectures is demonstrated. A discussion of the open problems in economics-driven Cloud architecting is presented in section 5.5, while section 5.6 concludes the chapter.

5.2 **Background**

Cloud services, as illustrated in Figure 5.1, afford users different levels of freedom. This freedom translates to the space of dynamic configurations (i.e., combinations of applications, runtime settings, databases, etc.) that a user can compose and deploy to the Cloud. Markets have intrinsic properties that make them of interest in this setting, namely, decentralization, scalability, adaptiveness, and robustness.

Visualizing the Cloud as a market, we can utilize tools and techniques from economics and game theory to engineer economically and computationally efficient Cloud software architectures. Here, the architecture abstracts the concerns of Cloud users and vendors, and the complexity of their interaction (as realized by a market mechanism).

However, the differences between the human world and computing systems makes it impracticable to perform a one-to-one mapping in the application of economics principles to computing systems. Carefully crafting this analogy in such a way that it adds value to the computing problem under study is at the heart of the software architect's thinking.

5.2.1 Basic terms

Terminologies that will be used in the discussion that follows are defined here.

- Agents: "are computer systems [or architectural components] that are capable of independent, autonomous action in order to satisfy their design objectives. . . . As agents have control over their own behaviour, they must cooperate and negotiate with others in order to satisfy their goals" (Ciancarini and Wooldridge, 2000).
- Market: an institution that facilitates interaction (trading) among agents by exchanging currency and (re)distributing resources. In the computational sense, markets are mostly virtual rather than physical institutions. Also, the exchanged currency is usually artificial instead of real cash.
- Buyer: a market agent who requires some resources and is willing to acquire it in exchange for currency.
- Seller: a market agent who provides some resources and is willing to release it in exchange for currency.
- Market Mechanism: the rule that governs how market agents interact, that is, the interaction between forces of demand and supply, to determine prices and units of services sold in the market.
- Nonstrategic Market Agents: simply follow the rules defined by the market mechanism without adapting their behavior based on emergent scenarios.
- Strategic Market Agents: behave rationally, by adapting in way that gives them an advantage over other agents. Examples of such adaptation could be to reveal their true valuation, cheat, or collude with other agents.

In a market setting, buyers and sellers necessarily need to interact to carry out any trading. The field of mechanism design is dedicated to the problem of defining the rule of this interaction and aligning it with the behavior of interacting parties, in different contexts, to ensure that a desirable outcome emerges. Consequently, the choice of the market mechanism to be used for managing the interaction has a significant impact on the outcome.

A market mechanism can be evaluated in a number of ways, including social welfare, Pareto efficiency, individual rationality, stability, computational efficiency, and communication efficiency (Sandholm, 1999). An introductory survey of classic economic mechanisms for a computer scientist can be found in (Parsons et al., 2011).

5.2.2 Market-inspired approaches to Cloud architecture

Designers of market-based systems adhere to a centralized or decentralized approach depending on the goal of the system. In a centralized market system, a market marker or auctioneer collects bids and asks from buyers and sellers, respectively (see Figure 5.2). The auctioneer matches these bids and asks in some way (depending on the mechanism) to decide the pairing of buyers and sellers. A famous and

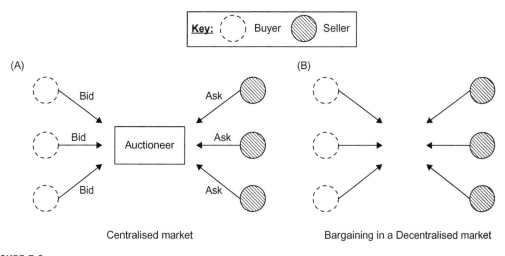

FIGURE 5.2

Centralized and decentralized market setup.

well-studied centralized market mechanism is the continuous double auction (CDA) (Klemperer, 1999). For large-scale systems, the auctioneer constitutes a bottleneck and therefore limits the scalability of the system. Also, failure of the auctioneer or delays in computing results could make the system unusable. To address these limitations, some market systems instantiate multiple auctioneers, either as a way of balancing the load or having specialist auctioneers for different concerns.

On the other hand, a decentralized market has no central entity. Instead, buyers and sellers are left to explore the market and bargain with one another to decide who to trade with, in a distributed manner. An example of a mechanism that follows this approach is the bilateral bargaining mechanism (Cliff and Bruten, 1997). While this approach is more scalable than its centralized counterpart, the search time to explore the market limits performance in a large system. Moreover, there is no guarantee that the resulting buyer−seller pairing is optimal. Optimality here implies that pairing gives the maximum utilities to the buyer and seller.

Both approaches have been used for resource allocation in distributed systems such as grid computing (Wolski et al., 2001; Ranjan et al., 2006). In the context of Cloud, the market analogy was first proposed by Buyya (2009a). The Cloud was envisioned as a global market where several customers (Cloud users) having various requirements meet sellers (Cloud vendors) possessing different capabilities to trade. In their vision, such trading could be achieved via a Cloud exchange in which brokers manage the selection of Cloud vendors on behalf of the users.

Following this proposal, researchers have pursued in-depth study of this market-oriented Cloud from various dimensions, including price modeling (Lee et al., 2010), resource sharing among service providers (Fujiwara et al., 2010; Song et al., 2010; Shang et al., 2010), and resource allocation at the hardware layer (You et al., 2009). These results mostly focus on the use of market mechanisms for selection of Clouds with specified QoS or price offer for service composition at the SaaS layer.

Other researchers have focused on Cloud services at the IaaS layer (Ardagna et al., 2011; Shi and Hong, 2010; Sun et al., 2010). The work of Ardagna et al. (2011) provided a game theoretic

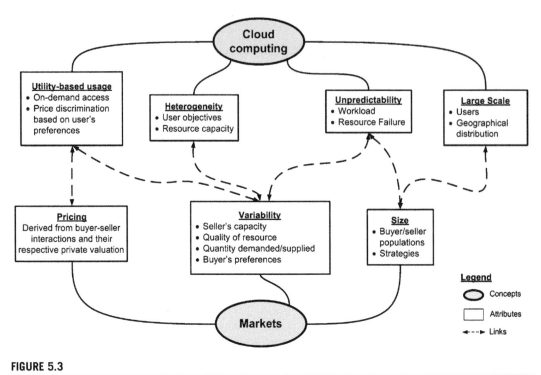

FIGURE 5.3

Conceptual relationship between cloud computing and Markets.

formulation of the service-provisioning problem in Cloud systems. Shi and Hong (2010) studied the problem of running independent equal-sized tasks on a Cloud infrastructure with a limited budget. They concluded that a constrained computing resource allocation scheme should be benefit-aware; that is, the heuristics for task allocation should incorporate the limited resource in supply within the system. Sun et al. (2010) proposed a Nash Equilibrium-based Continuous Double Auction (NECDA) Cloud resource allocation algorithm. They used the continuous double auction and a Nash Equilibrium solution concept to allocate resources in an M/M/1 queuing system, with the objectives of meeting performance and economics QoS.

The relation between Cloud computing and markets, as depicted in Figure 5.3, makes it possible to apply concepts from markets to computational resource allocation problems in the Cloud. The utility derived from consumption of Cloud resource determines the buyer's valuation of the resource and the price the buyer is willing to pay for it. The notion of variability in markets, in terms of seller's capacity and so on, can be used to model trends in the Cloud domain, such as heterogeneity and unpredictability of components in Cloud software architectures.

5.2.3 Stateless and state-based market agents

Another dimension for distinguishing between resource allocation in Cloud software architectures is to consider whether components are state-based or stateless, when allocating resources at runtime. Stateless approaches make allocation decisions based on predefined rules without consideration of the extent to which resource nodes are able to meet the expected QoS. In contrast, state-based approaches take into account QoS concerns before allocating resources.

One state-based approach for managing the behavior of resource nodes in a dynamic environment is the use of reputation metrics. This is especially true in multi-agent systems where the concept has been well researched and applied to problems of trust management in ad-hoc mobile networks (Buchegger and Le Boudec, 2003) and peer-to-peer computing (Rahbar and Yang, 2007). In these domains, the system designer defines what constitutes *acceptable* and *unacceptable* behavior. Consequently, an agent's reputation rating (or trust value) increases when it acts in an acceptable manner and decreases when it acts otherwise. Modern recommender systems also utilize this concept to elicit shopping trends, subsequently dispatching targeted marketing materials that best reflect the user's preferences.

Market designers leverage on the notion of reputation measurements to elicit the trustworthiness or dependability of market agents to ensure optimal resource allocation (Dash et al., 2004; Ramchurn et al., 2009). An agent's reputation ratings could then be used to make decisions about whether it is more likely to meet the service-level terms of jobs allocated to it.

This chapter adopts an agent-based reasoning in which software components in the Cloud are modeled as agents. Such agents vary in their roles, objectives, and capacity of their resources. For example, a job dispatcher software component may have the objective of ensuring that its decisions result in fewer service-level agreement (SLA) violations, while job-executing nodes seek to successfully execute as many jobs as possible. In both cases, the agent's reputation measurement is indicative of its accumulated performance. Weaving these agents as architectural components has the benefit of orchestrating component interaction, binding, and unbinding to arrive at efficient runtime architecture design decisions.

5.3 The dynamic resource allocation problem

As an example, consider services provided at each layer of a Cloud-based system as depicted in Figure 5.1.

For the Software-as-a-Service (SaaS), the vendor manages the entire stack of Cloud resources. However, the Platform-as-a-Service (PaaS) and Infrastructure-as-a-Service (IaaS) service types impose responsibilities on both the Cloud user and vendor. In the case of PaaS, the user's sole responsibility is to develop and deploy his or her application, while the Cloud vendor manages the rest of the stack. The IaaS Cloud somewhat shares responsibilities more evenly between Cloud user and vendor. In all cases, resources are demanded by, possibly, many Cloud users, and the vendor must have a way of sharing them among users to reach some objectives—for example, reduce violations of service-level agreements (Faniyi and Bahsoon, 2012a).

Suppose we draw an analogy between economics and Cloud services, specifically using the notion of a market-based controlled system (Clearwater, 1996). A market is a good example of a system, where interaction between self-interested parties (buyers and sellers), by optimizing their individual utilities, create a desirable overall utility for the system. The desirable outcome depends largely on the objective of the system designer (e.g., a balanced load, high utilization of servers, profitability, reduction of carbon footprint).

Cloud resources are the goods to be traded in this market, where the buyers are users and sellers are vendors. Since modern software systems place extensive demands on these resources, the goal of the seller at one point may be to satisfy as many requests as possible. If requests are homogeneous, that is, the same combination of resources and QoS expectation, then we can treat this as a classic scheduling problem. As pointed out earlier, this is unlikely to be so, as users care about different objectives at different times (heterogeneous demand). For example, the demand on a social networking service is likely to rise during holidays and festive periods, since friends and family tend to converse more and upload more pictures. In addition, the self-interested nature of users implies that they are likely to request more resources than they actually need and to hold on to it for longer periods than expected. Using a market-based analogy, this problem can be addressed by giving users an incentive to request the right amount of resources for the period that they actually need them.

From a software architecture point of view, the primitives of a market provide essential ingredients for controlling interaction between components in a software system. Given the dynamic nature of the interaction, a self-adaptive software architecture (Lemos et al., 2010) can be used to realize the objectives of Cloud users and vendors. Specifically, the goal of the adaptation is to allocate Cloud resources in such a way that the Cloud user's QoS expectations, as captured in SLAs, are not violated.

5.4 A software architecture for IaaS Cloud

In the previous section, the resource allocation problem at the SaaS, PaaS, and IaaS Cloud service layer was introduced. This section goes further to describe this problem at the IaaS layer, and proposes a market-based solution to address it. The solution concept discussed can be implemented as a middleware that manages the interaction of Cloud users and vendor's resources, toward reaching the objective of satisfying users' QoS expectations.

Faniyi and Bahsoon (2012a) proposed a generic decentralized Cloud Market Architecture, where the focus was to describe the elements of the architecture and demonstrate its feasibility using simulation studies. A refined version of the architecture is presented (see Figure 5.5), with the aim of showing the added value of state-based heuristics (i.e., reputation metrics), when trading in a Cloud resource market.

5.4.1 Illustrative scenario

The Cloud provider Y owns a massive infrastructure which it offers to the public over the Internet on a pay-as-you-use basis. The jobs submitted to the Cloud can be categorized as a combination of memory-intensive, CPU (central processing unit)-intensive, and bandwidth-intensive jobs. The resources nodes (servers) vary widely in their CPU, memory, and bandwidth capacities. The problem at hand is that customers are unsatisfied because their jobs seldom get executed as specified in the SLA. Cloud provider Y has traced the problem to unpredictable software trashing, network flooding, and inability to accurately predict workload.

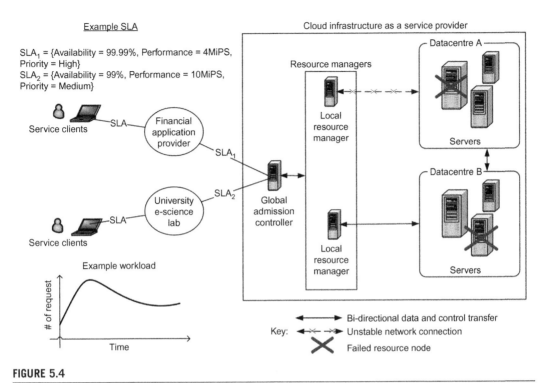

FIGURE 5.4

The Cloud service provision problem.

There are two data centers, each having different mixes of resources. Data centers are connected via a high-speed network that occasionally fluctuates due to traffic overloading. In this system, resource nodes could fail due to software/hardware failures, network fluctuation, or power outage. Thus, in this system, unreliability of resources is a norm, not an exception. In addition, the workload imposed on the system is unpredictable.

Figure 5.4 shows a snapshot of the request in flow and state of resource nodes and network at a time instance for two users: finance and e-Science applications. These conditions change over time, hence, a static solution approach may not be feasible due to the dynamic nature of the problem.

5.4.2 Analysis of market primitives

Computational systems that are controlled by market algorithms fundamentally rely on "price" as the tool for understanding the interaction among market agents, and it aids the system design in a way that ensures some desirable global properties are realized. However, price alone tells us little about whether or not agents are reliable. To elicit the reliability of agents, we model their behavior using price and reputation metrics that capture their trading capabilities and performance over time. Measuring both dimensions gives a holistic view to improve the efficiency of resource allocation.

5.4.3 Compute Cloud market model

As earlier stated, a self-adaptive architecture is able to incorporate the dynamics of the Cloud environment. Hence, we adopt a layered self-adaptive architecture model to capture the interaction between market agents (i.e., buyers and sellers); see Figure 5.5.

5.4.4 Self-adaptive Cloud software architecture

The goal management layer depicts the various jobs and associated SLA constraints as specified by Cloud users. Each Cloud user's request translates to a local objective that is managed on its behalf by a buyer agent. The objective is to maximize the SLA compliance level. The resource nodes (e.g., servers and clusters) owned by the Cloud provider are modeled as seller agents, who manage these resources to ensure that allocated jobs are successfully completed. The adaptation mechanism consists of a market algorithm that makes decisions about what resource node(s) to use for executing individual jobs submitted to the system. Due to the dynamics of the environment, resource nodes vary in their capability and reliability measures from time to time. Hence, the adaptation mechanism continuously senses the current state of resource nodes and uses the acquired knowledge to improve it allocation decisions.

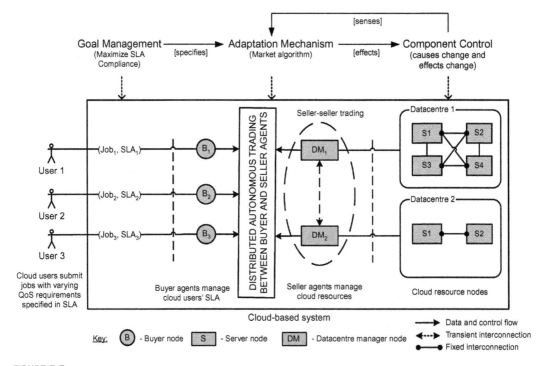

FIGURE 5.5

Cloud market architecture—Modeled on reference self-adaptive architecture (Kramer and Magee, 2007).

Basically, the solution strategy consists of the following steps:

1. Collect data on the performance of resource nodes (monitor, acquire knowledge).
2. Make decisions about job allocation to resource nodes (decide: reactive or anticipatory).
3. Optionally, migrate jobs across resource nodes.
4. Continuously adapt to changes in resource nodes' behavior and incoming jobs' SLA.

5.4.5 Market mechanism

The retail-inspired posted-offer market model (Ketcham et al., 1984) is used to coordinate agent interactions. Our motivation for using it follows from previous work (Lewis et al., 2010) where it was used for load-balancing in a decentralized computational market. Essentially, negotiation between agents in a posted-offer market is computationally inexpensive. Also, the model is highly scalable and robust to faulty nodes (Lewis et al., 2010).

To capture the dynamics of the Cloud provider's Y system, the following assumptions are made.

- A job's SLA captures its nonfunctional requirements.
- Buyer nodes act on behalf of Cloud users to find suitable resource nodes for their jobs.
- Seller nodes are computational resource nodes with finite capacity and varying reliability.
- Seller nodes have reputation ratings that indicate their accumulated performance.
- Buyer nodes keep track of seller nodes' performance via reputation ratings.

5.4.6 Experiments and results

In this section, we aim to evaluate the Cloud software architecture shown in Figure 5.5 under the following conditions.

1. The sensitivity of the market mechanism to failure of resource nodes (seller agents). This is shown by comparing the mechanism under two seller agent, S_{Agent}, configurations—low and high resilience.
2. The effect of the buyer agent's, B_{Agent}, strategies on the outcome allocation. Two representative trading strategies are defined and considered here.
3. The effect of scale on the mechanism's outcome allocation.

To ease the analysis of the mechanism, we define a simplistic SLA model for jobs submitted to the system. Three nonfunctional (NF) attributes (availability, performance, and security) are considered, along with a value for the SLA priority. The idea is to use the NF attributes to describe a job's computational requirement, while the priority captures the Cloud user's valuation of the job.

The SLA model is shown in Table 5.1. The table also defines boundary values for buyer and seller agents. These attribute values are randomly initialized for each job submitted to the system following a normal distribution. As can be observed from the table, we have deliberately set higher values for seller agents for all attribute values. This is because the primary objective of the experiment as defined above is to evaluate the mechanism's scalability and its resilience to failure, rather than the process of matching of buyers to sellers.

Table 5.1 SLA Model: Attribute-Metric-Value for Buyer and Seller Agents

Attribute	Metric	B_{Agent} Value	S_{Agent} Value
Availability	Uptime (%)	90–99.9999	100
Performance	Number of instructions per second	80–99.9999	100
Security	Encryption support	Yes (1) or No (0)	Yes (1)
Priority	Low, medium, high	Random	

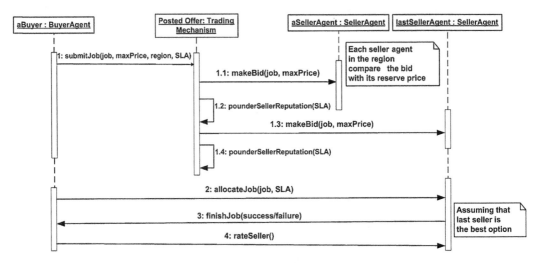

FIGURE 5.6

Posted-price offer market mechanism.

5.4.7 Reputation and pricing models

The two key ingredients of the posted offer mechanism (see Figure 5.6) are the reputation model used to assess the seller agents, and the utility functions of buyers and sellers. The models used to capture these properties of the mechanism for the experiments presented here are discussed below.

Reputation Model The reputation rating of a seller agent, S_{Agent}, is defined by an historic model as follows:

$$S_{Agent}^{Rep} = \frac{Request_{total} - Request_{failed}}{Request_{total}} \times 100\% \qquad (5.1)$$

In every trading round, buyer agents determine the value of the threshold reputation rating, T^{Rep}, which is the mean of all S_{Agent}^{Rep} in the market; that is

$$T^{Rep} = \frac{\sum_{i=1}^{\#S_{Agent}} S_{Agent_i}^{Rep}}{\#S_{Agent}} \qquad (5.2)$$

In the experiments that follow, buyer agents (regardless of the strategy in use), consider only sellers with $S_{Agent}^{Rep} > T^{Rep}$ in that trading round. The only exception is in the first trading round, since the value of T^{Rep} cannot be computed at this stage; nothing is known about the reputation of seller agents.

Utility Functions: Given an SLA, the buyer utility function is defined as

$$U_b(job) = w_b + (k \times \beta_{price}) \tag{5.3}$$

The value of w_b is initialized based on the job's priority. For results presented here, w_b is defined as

$$w_b = \begin{cases} 2, & priority = high \\ 1, & priority = medium \\ 0, & otherwise \end{cases} \tag{5.4}$$

SLA priorities are randomly assigned to jobs, following a normal distribution. k is a sensitivity factor for tuning the valuation of the buyer agent; $k = 0.1$ for all experiments considered here. The value of β_{price} is derived from the summation of NF attributes of the buyer agent.

Given a job request, the seller utility is defined as

$$U_s(job) = w_s \times \theta_{price} \tag{5.5}$$

The value of w_s is initialized based on the rule

$$w_s = \begin{cases} 0.1, & priority = high \\ 0.01, & priority = medium \\ 0.001, & otherwise \end{cases} \tag{5.6}$$

Similar to β_{price}, the value of θ_{price} is derived from summation of NF attributes of the seller agent.

This formulation ensures that when reasoning solely based on price, it is always possible to find a seller agent for a job request. However, there is no assurance that the chosen seller will successfully execute the job. It is this problem of failure of seller agents that the mechanism seeks to adapt to, by preferring higher reputable seller agents to less reputable ones.

5.4.8 Setup

The CloudSim toolkit (Buyya et al., 2009b) was used for evaluation purposes. In particular, the broker and scheduling classes were extended to incorporate the proposed market mechanism. The configuration of the experimental platform is a 6 GB RAM, 2.40 GHz, 64-bits Windows 7 machine. For all cases, results are averaged over 10 independent simulation runs to account for stochasticity.

5.4.9 Evaluation criteria

5.4.9.1 Sensitivity to resource node failure

Resilience is measured by the ability of the mechanism to filter out resource nodes that are unable to meet a job's SLA. In order to introduce faulty behavior into the system, we define the *Failure*

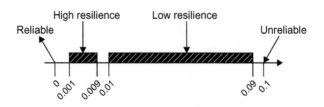

FIGURE 5.7

Failure rate interval.

Table 5.2 Resource Node Failure Scenarios

Scenario	Failure Rate	# B$_{Agent}$	# S$_{Agent}$
Low resilience (case A)	[0.01–0.09]	50	50
Low resilience (case B)	[0.01–0.09]	200	200
Low resilience (case C)	[0.01 –0.09]	500	50
High resilience (case A)	[0.001–0.009]	50	50
High resilience (case B)	[0.001–0.009]	200	200
High resilience (case C)	[0.001–0.009]	500	50

Rate of a resource node (seller agent) as the instantaneous probability of the node failing on demand. Therefore, a seller agent, S$_{Agent}$, has a failure rate in the bound [0, 0.1], where a value of 0 signifies maximum reliable behavior and a value of 0.1 denotes maximum unreliability. Two sub-intervals of the bound are compared (see Figure 5.7) across three scalability scenarios as shown in Table 5.2.

5.4.9.2 Effect of trading strategies

A market agent's trading strategy determines how the agent makes trading decisions (cf. section 5.2). Either buyer or seller agents can be equipped with trading strategies, ranging from very simple to complex strategies. We consider two buyer strategies here, to illustrate the impact of the applied strategy on the outcome allocation.

- Time Savers: purchase from any seller chosen at random, provided the price is acceptable, that is, selling price less or equal buyer's valuation.
- Bargain Hunters: are always in search of the seller with the best possible price. That is, the selling price must be the lowest among available sellers. If more than one seller offers the lowest price, then one is chosen at random.

Crucially, the significance of the impact of these strategies can be appreciated only when their benefits, in terms of number of failures recorded, and overhead are compared. Analyzing the strategies in isolation without having this big picture in mind provides limited insight for understanding the trade-off between their benefits and overhead.

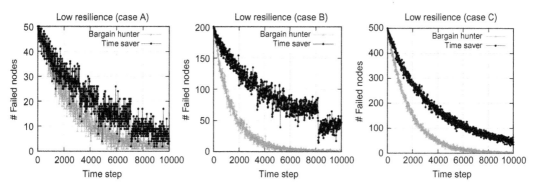

FIGURE 5.8

Low-resilience scenarios—Sensitivity to failure.

5.4.9.3 Effect of scaling jobs

Since buyer agents act on behalf of Cloud users for jobs submitted, increasing the number of buyer agents is equivalent to scaling out the jobs submitted to the system. Scenarios where buyer and seller populations are equal-sized are considered (case A and B in Table 5.2). Similarly, the opposite scenario, where the buyer population is larger than the seller population, is also studied (case C in Table 5.2).

For the low-resilient seller agent, Figure 5.8 indicates that *Time Savers* recorded higher failure than *Bargain Hunters* in all three cases. In case A, both strategies exhibit a lot of uncertainty in their ability to select reliable seller agents. In case B, *Bargain Hunters* were significantly more successful at distinguishing between reliable and unreliable sellers than *Time Savers*. Case C showed a close selection pattern between both strategies.

These results have a number of implications: (1) under low workload (case A), the system performed in an unpredictable manner; (2) under moderate workload (case B), where buyers and sellers are of equal population size, *Bargain Hunters* are the dominant strategy; (3) the impact of buyer strategy choice is least felt when the Cloud system is under heavy workload (case C). The third point is perhaps the most relevant to Cloud Y's (cf. section 5.4), as the job requests are characterized by heavy workload and the Cloud resources are of finite size.

Bargain Hunters and *Time Savers* in the high-resilience scenario (shown in Figure 5.9) exhibited more predictable behavior than the low-resilience scenario. The number of failures recorded is significantly smaller than the low-resilience cases, and convergence occurs at earlier time steps for both strategies.

The important lesson is that the mechanism was able to adapt to the failure distribution of resource nodes in all scenarios, with the record of failure recorded reflective of the resource node's resilience.

5.4.9.4 Overhead of the method

An additional evaluation criterion is to measure the overhead of using the mechanism. The overhead of each trading strategy is measured by the number of seller agents inspected before a trading decision is made.

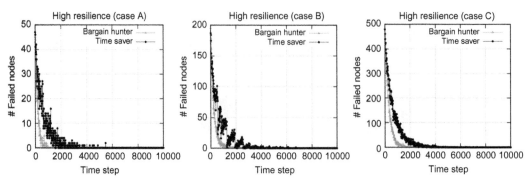

FIGURE 5.9

High-resilience scenarios—Sensitivity to failure.

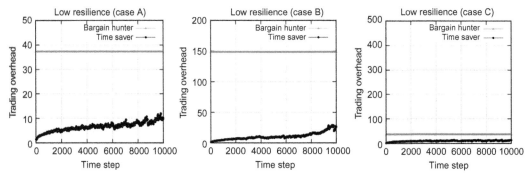

FIGURE 5.10

Low-resilience scenarios—Overhead of finding seller agent.

From Figures 5.10 and 5.11, it can be observed that in both scenarios *Time Savers* incurred a lower overhead when compared to *Bargain Hunters*. Therefore, *Time Savers* strictly dominate *Bargain Hunters* when timeliness is the critical factor. An interesting implication of the results is that regardless of the seller agents' resilience (low or high), the overhead incurred is very comparable. Furthermore, it was found that in the case of *Bargain Hunters*, the number of seller agents is the major determinant of the trading overhead. For example, as the number of sellers increased from case A (50) to case B (200), the trading overhead increased by a factor of 3. However, the reduction of seller agents from case B (200) to case C (50) reduced the trading overhead to a curve similar to that of case A.

Overall, we observe a trade-off between the sensitivity of the buyer strategies to failure and the overhead they incur. In practice, these results can guide the software architecture about how to resolve this trade-off space, that is, deciding which strategy to adopt for a job given its timeliness constraint and acceptable failure rate. Table 5.3 summarizes the SLA compliance, that is, percentage success, in the scenarios considered. Again, although *Bargain Hunters* strictly dominate *Time*

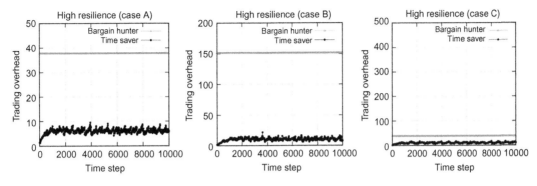

FIGURE 5.11

High-resilience scenarios—Overhead of finding seller agent.

Table 5.3 SLA Compliance by Trading Strategies

Scenario	SLA Compliance (%)	
	Time Saver	**Bargain Hunter**
Low resilience (case A)	51.73	69.68
Low resilience (case B)	51.02	80.52
Low resilience (case C)	52.61	76.19
High resilience (case A)	94.63	97.29
High resilience (case B)	94.66	97.48
High resilience (case C)	94.30	97.42

Savers in terms of SLA compliance, it should be noted that they incur a higher overhead than *Time Savers*.

5.5 Discussion

Some of the overarching issues and open research problems in the economics-driven domain, as it applies to market-based software architecting for Cloud, are discussed here.

5.5.1 Aligning market mechanisms to self-adaptive Cloud architectures

Self-adaptive software systems have matured significantly in recent times. Hence, experts believe it is now feasible to engineer systems using this paradigm (Serugendo et al., 2008). However, a number of challenges and open problems will have to be solved before true self-adaptive systems emerge. Two of the challenges posed are (1) to design control mechanisms which are capable of meeting changes in user requirements, system, and environmental conditions (Cheng et al., 2009), and (2) to gain assurance about the ability of the control mechanism to meet desirable goals at design time and eventually when the system is deployed (runtime). Therefore, a principled and systematic approach to mechanism design, verification, and validation is required.

Market-based approaches are promising to meet these objectives. However, it is not clear how to map these market mechanisms to specific Cloud software architectures. For example, five high-level architecture patterns for self-adaptive software systems were identified in Lemos et al. (2010), namely: hierarchical, master−slave, regional planner, fully decentralized, and information sharing. In this chapter, we have only considered the hierarchical pattern, and more so, applied it in a constrained Cloud IaaS architecture. The question of which market mechanism is suitable for other architecture patterns, and in what context, remains open.

5.5.2 Gaining assurance about market models

In order to demonstrate the feasibility of market-based approaches in general and to gain assurance about their behavior at runtime, it is important to evaluate representative architecture patterns that fit the design abstraction of the problem. This we have done using simulation studies. The extent to which this result holds in deployed systems can be argued. Kevin Lai (2005) suggests that the process of system design and market mechanism should be integrated, not disjoint. In this way, the software architect can align the underlying assumptions of the mechanism with those of the architecture at hand. Even at this, much is to be learned from a real deployed system, where some of the assumptions may fail or change in ways not anticipated at design time.

5.5.3 Applicability to Cloud federations

Architecting software in a Cloud federation, composed of multiple Cloud vendors, poses new challenges (Faniyi et al., 2012b). Unlike the architecture described in section 4, a Cloud federation is a more decentralized and open system. A decentralized architecture lends itself to achieving scalability, robustness, and resilience properties in such an environment. Typically, a challenge with such systems is that it is difficult for components to have a global view of the system. Hence, decisions are made based on available local information.

In addition, Clouds in the federation may define policies that constrain their participation in the market (e.g., share more resources during nonpeak times and less at peak times). Therefore, the market mechanism must be capable of providing incentives for Cloud vendors to share resources in the federation.

5.5.4 Other methods

Aside from markets, another approach is to reconfigure the software architecture based on constraints specified at the component level (Georgiadis et al., 2002). Here, no central configuration manager is present; rather, components autonomously steer the reconfiguration process by binding/unbinding based on local rules. Some of the open challenges raised by (Georgiadis et al., 2002) are also applicable to the use of market-based control in the Cloud: for example, the need for automated derivation of component selector functions (these are strategies in the market context), improved scalability (currently, the mechanism used to communicate among agents limits the scale of the system), and the need to evolve the architecture by adding new strategies, without making the system unstable.

5.6 Conclusion

In this chapter, we have drawn an analogy between economics and Cloud computing, and we have discussed the benefits of this analogy to the Cloud computing domain. Specifically, market-based control from microeconomics has been identified as a viable approach for addressing the problem of resource allocation in Cloud software architectures. The dynamic resource allocation problem at the infrastructure-as-a-service Cloud service layer has been used to demonstrate the value of this approach. Furthermore, open problems and issues that are promising to the field were discussed.

Research is ongoing in the area of applying other promising market mechanisms, aside from the posted-offer model, to realize architectural objectives in the Cloud (Nallur and Bahsoon, 2012). While the results presented here are based on simulations in the future, we plan to implement these ideas in a Cloud laboratory. The problem of guaranteeing QoS to users of an online video streaming service will be used to demonstrate the feasibility of the approach in a real Cloud. Finally, we hope to arrive at concrete metrics for quantifying the utility of the approach to Cloud users and vendors.

References

Ardagna, D., Panicucci, B., Passacantando, M., 2011. A game theoretic formulation of the service provisioning problem in Cloud systems. In: Proceedings of the 20th international Conference on World Wide Web, ACM Press, New York, pp. 177–186.

Armbrust, M., Fox, A., Griffith, R., Joseph, A.D., Katz, R., Konwinski, A., et al., 2010. A view of Cloud computing. Commun. ACM 53, 50–58.

Buchegger, S., Le Boudec, J., 2003. A robust reputation system for mobile ad-hoc (Tech. Rep.), EPFL-IC-LCA.

Buyya, R., 2009a. Market-oriented Cloud computing: vision, hype, and reality of delivering computing as the 5th utility. CCGRID '09: Proceedings of the 2009 9th IEEE/ACM International Symposium on Cluster Computing and the Grid. IEEE Computer Society, Washington, DC, p. 1.

Buyya, R., Ranjan, R., Calheiros, R., 2009b. Modeling and simulation of scalable Cloud computing environments and the Cloudsim toolkit: challenges and opportunities. In: International Conference on High Performance Computing Simulation, HPCS '09, pp. 1–11.

Cheng, B., et al., 2009. Software engineering for self-adaptive systems: a research roadmap. In: Cheng, B., de Lemos, R., Giese, H., Inverardi, P., Magee, J. (Eds.), Software Engineering for Self-Adaptive Systems. Springer, Berlin/Heidelberg, pp. 1–26. , Vol. 5525 of Lecture Notes in Computer Science.

Ciancarini, P., Wooldridge, M., 2000. Agent-oriented software engineering. In: Software Engineering, 2000. Proceedings of the 2000 International Conference, pp. 816–817.

Clearwater, S.H. (Ed.), 1996. Market-Based Control: A Paradigm for Distributed Resource Allocation. World Scientific Publishing Co., River Edge, NJ.

Cliff, D., Bruten, J., 1997. Minimal-Intelligence agents for Bargaining behaviors in Market-Based Environments (Tech. Rep.). HP Laboratories.

Dash, R.K., Ramchurn, S.D., Jennings, N.R., 2004. Trust-based mechanism design, Proceedings of the Third International Joint Conference on Autonomous agents and Multiagent Systems, vol. 2. IEEE Computer Society, Washington, DC, pp. 748–755.

Faniyi, F., Bahsoon, R., 2012a. Self-managing sla compliance in Cloud architectures: a market-based approach. Proceedings of the Third International ACM SIGSOFT Symposium on Architecting Critical Systems. ACM, New York, pp. 61–70.

Faniyi, F., Bahsoon, R., Evans, A., Kazman, R., 2011. Evaluating security properties of architectures in unpredictable environments: a case for Cloud. In: Proceedings of the Ninth Working IEEE/IFIP Conference on Software Architecture, WICSA, pp. 127–136.

Faniyi, F., Bahsoon, R., Theodoropoulos, G., 2012b. A dynamic data-driven simulation approach for preventing service level agreement violations in Cloud federation. *Procedia Computer Science*, 9 (0). Proceedings of the International Conference on Computational Science. ICCS, pp. 1167–1176.

Fujiwara, I., Aida, K., Ono, I., 2010. Applying double-sided combinational auctions to resource allocation in Cloud computing. Proceedings of the 2010 10th IEEE/IPSJ International Symposium on Applications and the Internet. IEEE Computer Society, Washington, DC, pp. 7–14.

Georgiadis, I., Magee, J., Kramer, J., 2002. Self-organising software architectures for distributed systems. Proceedings of the First Workshop on Self-healing Systems. ACM, New York, pp. 33–38.

Ketcham, J., Smith, V.L., Williams, A.W., 1984. A comparison of posted-offer and double-auction pricing institutions. Rev. Econ. Stud. 51 (4), 595–614.

Klemperer, P., 1999. Auction theory: a guide to the literature. J. Econo. Surv. 13 (3), 227–286.

Kramer, J., Magee, J., 2007. Self-managed systems: an architectural challenge. In 2007 Future of Software Engineering. IEEE Computer Society, Washington, DC, pp. 259–268.

Lai, K., 2005. Markets are dead, long live markets. SIGecom Exch. 5, 1–10.

Lee, Y.C., Wang, C., Zomaya, A.Y., Zhou, B.B., 2010. Profit-driven service request scheduling in Clouds. Proceedings of the 2010 10th IEEE/ACM International Conference on Cluster, Cloud and Grid Computing. IEEE Computer Society, Washington, DC, pp. 15–24.

Lemos, R., de Giese, H., Müller, A.H., Shaw, M., 2010. Software engineering for self-adaptive systems: a second research roadmap (draft version of May 20, 2011).

Lewis, P., Marrow, P., Yao, X., 2010. Resource allocation in decentralised computational systems: an evolutionary market-based approach. Auton. Agents Multi-Agent Syst. 21, 143–171.

Nallur, V., Bahsoon, R., 2012. A decentralized self-adaptation mechanism for service-based applications in the Cloud. IEEE Trans. Softw. Eng. .

Parsons, S., Rodriguez-Aguilar, J.A., Klein, M., 2011. Auctions and bidding: a guide for computer scientists. ACM Comput. Surv. 43 (2), 1–59.

Rahbar, A.G.P., Yang, O., 2007. Powertrust: a robust and scalable reputation system for trusted peer-to-peer computing. IEEE Trans. Para. Dist. Syst. 18 (4), 460–473.

Ramchurn, S.D., Mezzetti, C., Giovannucci, A., Rodriguez-Aguilar, J.A., Dash, R.K., Jennings, N.R., 2009. Trust-based mechanisms for robust and efficient task allocation in the presence of execution uncertainty. J. Artif. Int. Res. 35, 119–159.

Ranjan, R., Harwood, A., Buyya, R., 2006. Sla-based coordinated super-scheduling scheme for computational grids. In: 2006 IEEE International Conference on Cluster Computing, pp. 1–8.

Sandholm, T.W., 1999. Distributed rational decision making. In: Weiss, G. (Ed.), Multiagent systems: a modern approach to distributed artificial intelligence. MIT Press, Cambridge, MA, pp. 201–258.

Serugendo, G.D.M., Fiald, J., Romanovsky, A., Guelfi, N., 2008. A generic framework for the engineering of self-adaptive and self-organising systems. In: Bellman, K., Hinchey, M.G., Müller-Schloer, C., Schmeck,

H., Würtz, R. (Eds.), Organic computing—controlled self-organization. Dagstuhl, Germany: Schloss Dagstuhl—Leibniz-Zentrum fuer Informatik, Germany.

Shang, S., Jiang, J., Wu, Y., Yang, G., Zheng, W., 2010. A knowledge-based continuous double auction model for Cloud market. Proceedings of the 2010 Sixth International Conference on Semantics, Knowledge and Grids. IEEE Computer Society, Washington, DC, pp. 129–134.

Shi, W., Hong, B., 2010. Resource allocation with a budget constraint for computing independent tasks in the Cloud. In: 2010 IEEE Second International Conference on Cloud Computing Technology and Science (CloudCom), pp. 327–334.

Song, B., Hassan, M.M., Huh, E.-n, 2010. A novel heuristic-based task selection and allocation framework in dynamic collaborative Cloud service platform. Proceedings of the 2010 IEEE Second International Conference on Cloud Computing Technology and Science. IEEE Computer Society, Washington, DC, pp. 360–367.

Sun, D., Chang, G., Wang, C., Xiong, Y., Wang, X., 2010. Efficient nash equilibrium based cloud resource allocation by using a continuous double auction. In: 2010 International Conference on Computer Design and Applications (ICCDA), vol. 1, pp. V1-94–V1-99).

Wolski, R., Plank, J.S., Brevik, J., Bryan, T., 2001. Analyzing market-based resource allocation strategies for the computational grid. Int. J. High Perform. Comput. Appl. 15, 258–281.

You, X., Xu, X., Wan, J., Yu, D., 2009. Ras-m: resource allocation strategy based on market mechanism in Cloud computing. In: Fourth ChinaGrid Annual Conference, 2009, pp. 256–263.

A Decision-Support System Approach to Economics-Driven Modularity Evaluation

6

Yuanfang Cai[1], Rick Kazman[2], Carlos V.A. Silva[3], Lu Xiao[1], and Hong-Mei Chen[2]

[1]*Drexel University, Philadelphia, PA, USA*
[2]*University of Hawaii, Honolulu, HI, USA*
[3]*Federal University of Bahia, Bahia, Brazil*

6.1 Introduction

"As software matures, should we refactor or just keep adding features?" Such questions present a recurring dilemma to software practitioners. Refactoring is an activity that improves the modularization of a code base while leaving its functionality intact. Although it has been recognized that modularity has a significant impact on software maintainability and thus survivability, it has historically been difficult for software developers to justify modularization activities, in particular, refactoring, to their managers. And managers also have a difficult time understanding, analyzing, and predicting the costs and benefits of refactoring. The costs of refactoring activities are significant and immediate, but the effects—the benefits—of refactoring are largely invisible, intangible, and long term. Without a decision to refactor (e.g., to pay back the modularity debt), modularity decay can continue to cause huge losses in terms of reduced ability to provide new functionality and fix bugs, operational failures, and even canceled projects. Such a dilemma calls for effective methods and decision support for quantifying modularity debt and the long-term benefits of refactoring activities.

Modularity debt is the most difficult kind of technical debt to quantify and manage. It has been well established that more than half of the total development effort in software projects is spent on the maintenance phase (Lientz and Swanson, 1980). During the maintenance phase, software tends to age, and the code base gets cluttered by an accumulation of changes, often referred to as *technical debt* (Brown et al., 2010). Modularity debt is a specific kind of technical debt incurred by modularity decay.

If decision makers (e.g.. project managers) do not have good insight into modularity debt (e.g., does the debt exist? how much debt? how costly is this debt?) as well as the benefits of refactoring, it is difficult to know *when* to refactor, if at all. A number of prediction models have been proposed to identify components that are error-prone or to predict project development cost and effort. However, to our knowledge, no existing work directly supports a project's decision makers in answering the following question: *When is it worthwhile to refactor the software to reduce the complexity and make it better modularized?*

Answering this question is difficult first because there is no established quantitative association between modularity variation and maintenance effort variation. That is to say, there is no way for a decision maker to know, with confidence, if a project's modularity gets worse (or better) how much more (or less) it will cost to maintain and extend. Without such a foundation, it is difficult to predict the costs of the modularity debt incurred from a deterioration in a project's modularity. And it is equally difficult for decision makers to justify the potential cost-savings from a proposed refactoring activity.

Our research goal is to develop a decision-support system that would allow managers to play out various "what-if" scenarios to manage modularity debt and make informed decisions regarding refactoring. A decision-support system approach would appropriately address the need to simulate and visualize scenarios that include many different (current and future) factors under different assumptions that may affect the decision outcome. The DSS is composed of a data warehouse and a model base to support a variety of analyses needed by each scenario. Our proposed system is called the modularity debt management decision-support system (MDM-DSS).

Our MDM-DSS is built on a scientific foundation that we are constructing for explicitly manifesting the economic implications of software modularization activities, so that the costs *and* the benefits of such activities can be understood, analyzed, and predicted in a way that is amenable to both engineers and managers. The research questions being addressed include: how to manifest the costs and benefits of modularization activities as functions of modularity variations; how to locate the components with the most uncertainty and risk; how to determine that there is a *debt*; how to quantitatively account for the relation between modularization activities and their economic consequences; and, in particular, how to manifest the value of modularity as *options* so as to plan an optimal strategy of evolution based on viewing software as investment?

In addressing these research questions, we have developed an *integrated economics-driven modularization evaluation (IEDME) framework* that combines code-level analysis, design-level analysis, expert stakeholder elicitation, and history-based cost-benefit analysis. This framework links measures of modularity with quantified economic benefits—that is, maintenance cost-savings—to serve as the foundation of our target MDM-DSS

We believe that the DSS approach is most appropriate for resolving the refactoring dilemma facing software practitioners today. The IEDME framework has the potential to change the management of the software industry by providing a sound basis for the pricing and risk analysis of software development projects and practices. The IEDME framework, supported by interactive and user-friendly tools, forms the basis of our MDM-DSS, which will help architects and managers make more optimal, better informed, data-driven modularization decisions by focusing on their economic (and not just engineering) consequences, generating better modularized, higher quality, easier to maintain software systems that have lower lifetime maintenance costs. Business managers would be informed of the severity of modularity decay, in the form of maintenance cost numbers, making their investment opportunities explicit. These opportunities currently only exist as metaphors understood by software practitioners.

In what follows, we present the design considerations for the MDM-DSS. In section 6.3, we discuss the two key research results of the IEDME framework that are the underpinning foundation for the MDM-DSS. In section 6.4, we present the most recent progress on empirical validation of the key building blocks of the MDM-DSS system. Section 6.5 discusses our future work, and section 6.6 provides concluding remarks.

6.2 A decision-support system approach: design considerations

Modularity decisions are, in the end, economic decisions. These are decisions about when to incur and when to pay back technical debt (Cunningham, 1992; Brown et al., 2010). We incur technical debt through normal project activities, which primarily include bug-fixing and adding features. We pay back technical debt by refactoring—choosing to simplify the architecture and restore better modularity. A great many factors may contribute to this decision of if, when, and where to refactor.

We now present an overview of a set of requirements on decision-support capabilities for modularity debt management.

6.2.1 Modularity violations versus architecture complexity

One factor to be considered is the complexity of the architecture and the presence of modularity violations. Modularity violations make the architecture harder to understand, modify, debug, and perfect. However, perhaps just as important as the complexity of the architecture is the degree to which parts of it are anticipated to change. If some portion of the architecture is complex but it is stable, seldom changing or incurring bugs, then there is no reason to invest in repairing it (as the old saying goes "if it ain't broke, don't fix it"). The complexity of this portion of the architecture is simply not causing enough problems to warrant an investment (to improve its modularity and hence reduce its complexity).

6.2.2 Inherent complexity versus accidental complexity

Furthermore, not all complexity is bad complexity. Some complexity is simply necessary and warranted by the inherent nature of the task at hand—this is *inherent* complexity. But some complexity arises by accident, by the accumulation of many small, uncoordinated changes and bug fixes, by "hacks" implemented quickly due to schedule pressure, or by activities of the maintainer who did not understand the intent of the original architecture. All changes accumulate and create *accidental* complexity in a project. Because we want to create a system to aid project stakeholders in making economics-based modularity decisions, we must be able to distinguish between inherent and accidental complexity. There is nothing that we can do about inherent complexity, but we may choose to invest in the architecture and code to reduce accidental complexity.

6.2.3 Automated (Metrics-based) versus interactive decision support

Another important factor to consider in making economics-based modularity decisions is the stream of changes that are expected to affect each portion of the architecture. This might be determined from project history—all other things being equal, we would expect a highly changed portion of the architecture to continue to experience lots of change requests and a stable portion to continue to be stable. It might also be determined by corporate or project strategy: Perhaps a new marketing feature or marketplace demand will drive the architecture to evolve in new and unplanned ways. Or the impetus for changes might originate internally: Perhaps project staff members want to change the structure of some portion of the architecture.

To summarize, to aid stakeholders in making refactoring decisions, they need to be able to assess the accidental complexity of each part of the architecture. In addition, they need to assess the degree to which they believe that part of the architecture will undergo significant changes in the future (since accidental complexity in some portion of the architecture is only problematic if we want to maintain or evolve that portion).

What the stakeholders therefore require to help them make such choices is a *decision-support system (DSS)*. A DSS is any system that aids management in making decisions. Such systems may be fully computerized, fully manual, or (more commonly) a combination of both. They have existed for half a century and are most widely associated with executive information systems, process optimization, and management design (Sauter, 2011).

A simple, automatic (i.e., noninteractive) example configuration of such a DSS, showing the major data flows, is provided in Figure 6.1.

This simple DSS takes, as input, source code artifacts, the project's revision history, and the project's bug history. Based on these sources of information, such a DSS could determine likely "hot spots" in the architecture and could then propose potential sites for refactoring. This type of analysis is completely feasible today and can be fully automated, which makes it appealing. Systems based purely on metrics, for example, already work like this. They identify areas of the code that have unacceptable values of certain metrics, as a way of drawing attention to those areas. But metrics-based systems only consider the source code as input. Our claim is that such systems are far too simplistic and limited to be of great value to a project.

Why? Because the noninteractive system of Figure 6.1 does not account for the *costs* and the *benefits* of refactoring. To accomplish this more complex and holistic view of the problem and its solution, we need a more sophiscated, interactive DSS, one that takes into account concerns such as the future trends affecting the system, uncertainty in our measures and judgments, and the system's external context. For these additional kinds of inputs to the DSS, we need the expertise and judgment of a human—presumably a project manager or architect. This expert would be able to add information that could not be directly gleaned from an automated analysis of project artifacts.

For example, some expert such as a project manager or strategic planner would need to input information regarding the likely future direction of the project (expressed as a series of changes that affect source code modules). This information, along with the existing revision history of the project, provides a means of estimating the likely stream of changes that are predicted to affect a

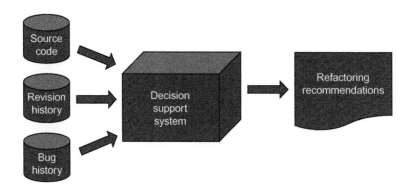

FIGURE 6.1

Simple, automated, noninteractive decision-support system for making refactoring decisions.

portion of the system in the future. This information is critical in estimating the potential *benefit* of any refactoring investment. Furthermore, a second human expert (likely the software architect) would need to provide cost estimates for the proposed refactorings. Each of these experts would be able to use the DSS to understand its existing state and to perform what-if analyses. In this way a complete economic model of modularization activities can be built and made usable.

The major components and interrelationships of this more sophisticated and more effective decision-support system are shown in Figure 6.2. In this figure the arrows represent data flow.

As with the noninteractive, metrics-based DSS, the more sophisticated, interactive MDM-DSS of Figure 6.2 takes, as input, source code artifacts, the project's revision history (patches and commits), the project's bug history, and project discussions. The project discussions could be gathered from an issue-tracking system, project mailing lists, blogs, or any other sources of textual communications. All of this information is loaded into a data warehouse. In addition to the project's own data, industrial or open-source data collected from many projects could also be loaded. This would be useful, for example, in a project that had not yet collected a substantial corpus of data of its own. Based on this data, potential sites for refactoring could be identified, and the costs and benefits of refactorings could be estimated.

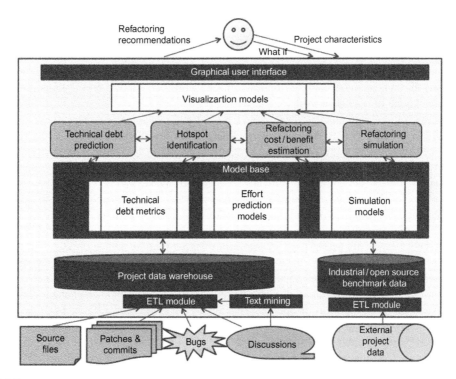

FIGURE 6.2

MDM-DSS: An interactive decision-support system for refactoring decisions, including cost and benefit estimates.

An expert could then interact with this MDM-DSS—examining the automatically generated refactoring recommendations, visualizing the project's characteristics along multiple dimensions and at varying levels of granularity, and exploring questions of interest by performing "what-if" analyses. An example of a what-if analysis is: "What would be the costs and benefits of refactoring the pricing logic in the system".

This envisioned usage of the proposed MDM-DSS in Figure 6.2 is consistent with typical uses of a DSS in businesses today in any domain: as a managerial "dashboard" for making strategic investment decisions.

6.2.4 Analysis via the theory of real options

Software projects have many dimensions of uncertainty. Application domains vary, team sizes vary, languages of implementation vary, the underlying tool infrastructure varies, and so forth. As a result, the cost and benefit estimates that emanate from any generic model of a software project are not going to be precise; they will vary according to the market, according to the skills of the developers, and perhaps a dozen other factors, some of which we may even be unaware of. So any estimates from such a model need to be *probabilistic*, with stated measures of uncertainty. This is standard practice in project management, where estimates of cost and schedule are generated using techniques such as Monte Carlo simulation, which generate a statistical distribution over possible outcome values.

In recent years, theories from financial economics have been applied to architectural decision making, such as simple cost-benefit analysis (Guo and Seaman, 2011), analytic hierarchical process (AHP), portfolio management, and real options. In our work, we use the real options model as the economic backbone of our framework.

The theory of real options has been noted by software engineering researchers (Erdogmus, 2002; Sullivan et al., 1999) to have an obvious analog to architectural design decisions. A real option is the right, but not the obligation, to take an action in the future—typically making an investment—when there is uncertainty. This theory, which originated in financial economics, has also been applied to the economics of software architectures. Ozkaya et al. (2007) created and demonstrated a method for using the binomial real options valuation approach to aid in architectural decision making. The rationale of applying real options theory is as follows.

Improving software architecture by refactoring can be seen as an investment decision because it incurs relatively certain short-term costs in the form of time, money, and/or resources in the pursuit of more uncertain longer-term benefits—in the form of maintenance cost-savings. The architecture after refactoring should have better modular structure where every module provides the right but not the symmetric obligation to be replaced with a better version to accommodate changes. The value of such an investment is in the form of options. This analogy accounts for differences in the timing of refactoring (i.e., when shall we refactor?), the timing of paying of the investment (when will the refactored part be used?), and the associated "risk" (i.e., how confident are we of the estimates?).

People have experimented with applying the Black–Scholes valuation formula (Sullivan et al., 1999) to value architectural investments (of which refactoring is a common example). The Black–Scholes formulation, however, is unfamiliar to most IT managers and requires the estimation of key parameters that are difficult to determine in practice, such as a "replicating portfolio" to estimate the future value of an asset, which does not exist for software modularization. Baldwin and Clark's Net Option technique (Baldwin and Clark, 2000; Sullivan et al., 2001) exploits the same idea but uses statistical methods to calculate options values. The key parameter is called the technical potential of a module, which measures how likely the module will be changed.

Given the empirical foundation and the detected refactoring candidates in our MDM-DSS, it becomes possible to value a refactoring activity using real options models. We believe that a good choice is to use the Datar–Mathews (Mathews and Datar, 2007) method for valuing real options, which was developed for practical industrial use and is more transparent and intuitive for managers to apply. This method uses Monte Carlo methods, which have a long history of usage in the financial world. Another advantage is that most of the inputs to this model can be inferred from the interest probability, interest amount, and principal associated with a refactoring activity.

We are experimenting with the use of the Datar–Mathews method for valuing real options (Mathews and Datar, 2007), which employs Monte Carlo simulation as a practical means of valuing modularization activities. The Datar–Mathews method was developed for practical industrial use (initially in the Boeing Corporation) and is more transparent and intuitive for managers to apply while being analytically equivalent to Black–Scholes. This method employs two discount rates that any manager should be able to estimate: a "hurdle" or risk rate for discounting projected project profits to today's dollars and an investment rate, for discounting project costs to today's dollars. Monte Carlo methods have a long history of usage in the financial world as a means of predicting the value of stock options. Monte Carlo techniques consist of a mathematical framework and an accompanying simulation tool suite and method, which we will adopt as a means of valuing proposed modularization activities, because the value is bound up in how the software will evolve in the future, which is in turn dependent on market forces. The real option value of an asset is calculated by simulating the following formula using a Monte Carlo simulation package, such as Oracle's Crystal Ball[1] or Palisade's @Risk[2]:

$$\text{Real option value} = \text{Average}[\text{MAX}(profit - cost, 0)] \tag{6.1}$$

where *profit* is a distribution—a random variable—of the discounted profits at time 0 and *cost* is the cost of implementing the modularization activity. The intuition is simple: The more often you change a particular piece of code, the more value you will reap by purchasing the option to make that code easier to modify. For example, if the pricing logic in an e-commerce site is frequently changed, then there is benefit in having this logic be "easy to modify." To precisely calculate the benefit of refactoring the pricing logic, stakeholders need to estimate the future volatility of that portion of the code: *How often is pricing logic expected to change, and in what ways?* The stakeholder can make estimations based on intuition or, hopefully, on project history. That is, the modules that are changed most frequently and most recently will be automatically suggested as candidates. The triangular distribution used in the Monte Carlo simulation simply requires that the stakeholder estimates an optimistic, pessimistic, and most likely value for any estimated parameter (such as the number of changes anticipated). Given the expected *number* of changes to the system, we need to multiply it by the *expected costs savings* (due to the modularization activity) per change to determine the benefits. The user can leverage the data collected from project history to estimate

---

[1]http://www.oracle.com/crystalball
[2]http://www.palisade.com/risk

cost saving based on modularity improvements the proposed refactoring may bring, and use the concrete target components identified as refactoring candidates to estimate the cost of refactoring.

Given the expected benefit that accrues to a change (as calculated above) along with the expected frequency of the change, we can now estimate, via Monte Carlo simulation, the modifiability benefits of the change at any time period in the future, using the Datar–Mathews method. Another benefit of refactoring is that better modularized code exhibits fewer bugs and those bugs are less expensive to resolve. To calculate the total benefit of a modularization effort, we consider both the modifiability and the debugging benefits.

An example of how this calculation would be formulated is shown in the Excel spreadsheet shown in Figure 6.3, where the Monte Carlo simulations are performed by the @Risk software add-in. In this example project, the current code structure complexity increase factor is 9% (a number of potential structural complexity metrics are presented in sections 3.1 and 3.2), and a proposed refactoring promises to bring the number back to 5%.

This structural code complexity factor is a formalization of Lehman's second law of software evolution *Increasing Complexity* (Lehman, 1980) and could be calculated, for example, by comparing *propagation cost* (MacCormack et al., 2006) increases across releases to determine the structural complexity increase rate, as a result of normal maintenance activities. In addition, the history data shows that the current code defect rate is 0.003, and the average defect fixing cost is $320,

Project Risk rate	Investment Rate	Inflation Rate	Code Complexity Adjustment	Ref'd Code Complexity Adjustment	Code Defect Rate	Refactored Code Defect Rate	Average Cost/ Defect	Average Refactored Cost/Defect	Code Size (KLOC)
15%	5%	3%	9%	5%	0.003	0.0026	$ 320	$ 250	$2000

Year	Operating profit NPV	Refactoring cost NPV	Expected	Cost/Change with refactoring			Expected	Cost/Change with refactoring			Defect reduction benefit
				Pessimistic	Most likely	Optimistic		Pessimistic	Most likely	Optimistic	
2010	$ -	$ 42,833									
2011	$ 9,412	$ -	$ 841	$ 1,300	$ 900	$ 700	$ 1,449	$ 2,300	$ 1,500	$ 1,200	5178
2012	$ 11,651	$ -	$ 811	$ 1,460	$ 973	$ 786	$ 1,415	$ 2,582	$ 1,684	$ 1,347	6022
2013	$ 13,880	$ -	$ 783	$ 1,639	$ 1,053	$ 882	$ 1,381	$ 2,899	$ 1,891	$ 1,531	6933
2014	$ 14,780	$ -	$ 756	$ 1,840	$ 1,138	$ 991	$ 1,348	$ 3,255	$ 2,123	$ 1,698	7444

Total $ 49,723 $ 42,833

ROV   6890

#Charges/ Year			#Defects Year				Refactoring Cost		
Pessimistic	Most Likely	Optimistic		Pessimistic	Most Likely	Optimistic	Pessimistic	Most Likely	Optimistic
8	12	7	5	155	180	156	130	$ 51,000	$ 42,500	$ 35,000
12	18	11	8	181	210	182	150			
18	28	14	11	208	240	204	180			
22	30	21	14	223	260	220	190			

FIGURE 6.3

An example spreadsheet realizing the Datar–Mathews model.

while the numbers were 0.0026 and $250 when the modularity measure was 5%. The benefit for year i is calculated as:

$$\text{Benefit}_i = \text{NPV}(E(\Delta\text{cost-per-change}_i) * E(\#\text{changes}_i) + \text{avg-cost-per-defect} * E(\Delta\#\text{defects}_i)) \quad (6.2)$$

That is, the benefit in any given time period i is the NPV (net present value) of the expected delta cost per change as reflected by modularity improvement, multiplied by the expected number of changes in time period i plus the average cost per defect in the refactored code multiplied by the expected number of defects in time period i. In our example, the chosen time period was a year, but making such estimates on a per-quarter basis is also common practice. Note that each component of Equation (6.2) is an *expected value*, which would be determined via simulation.

The costs per change and numbers of defects increase each year due to inflation and due to the ever-increasing size and complexity of the code base. The benefit calculation in Equation (6.2) is performed for each time period, for as many periods as is desired. According to the Datar-Mathews method, the real option value is equal to the average net profit—calculated as the benefits (discounted to present value using the project risk rate) minus the costs (discounted to present value using the investment rate)—contingent on terminating the project when a net loss is forecast, as is shown in Equation (6.1).

The costs of a proposed modularization activity could be estimated by a project manager or architect using existing cost estimation methods. Alternatively, these costs can be informed by the ranked modularization candidates, from the modularity violations detection approach that locates the components to be better modularized and hence targets the developers to be involved. The costs and benefits are appropriately risk-adjusted, discounting profits by the project risk rate and discounting costs by the investment rate.

In the spreadsheet shown in Figure 6.3, the yellow values would be entered by the users (typically a project manager or architect, in consultation with other key stakeholders such as a chief financial officer); the green values are calculated via Monte Carlo simulation; and the orange value is the final real option value. For this example, the value of the refactoring project in the following figure is $6890, indicating that it has a positive return on investment for the organization.

6.2.5 Options-based DSS components

Based on the previous discussion, to make the option-based decision-making system possible we need both estimations and predictions inferred from the project's historical data. In addition, we need input from project managers such as predicted refactoring costs and the expected frequency of future changes affecting the candidate components. The main elements that need to be inferred from history data include the candidate components that need to be refactored and—perhaps the most challenging aspect—the potential cost-savings that may be experienced by refactoring these components.

6.3 The IEDME framework

The MDM-DSS introduced in the previous section integrates a number of fields of research that we draw upon in performing economics-driven modularity evaluation. The main contributions of our

IEDME framework is manifested in the modularity debt prediction and refactoring cost/benefits estimation modules. Specifically, we have made advances on two research areas:

- Research on structural metrics—attempting to automatically correlate changes in architectural/ structural metrics with changes in maintenance effort
- Research on design violations—attempting to automatically determine when existing architectural design decisions are problematic

These research advances allow the MDM-DSS to: (1) predict maintenance effort variation based on file metrics variations; and (2) identify the parts of the system that need to be refactored.

6.3.1 Predicting maintenance effort variation based on file metrics variations

To begin our discussion of how we have related file metrics to maintenance effort, we will first review prior research on file metrics. We will then examine the state of the research on correlating file metrics to maintenance effort.

6.3.1.1 File metrics

Published source code metrics can be broadly divided into five categories, based on what they measure: size, complexity, coupling, cohesion, and inheritance. We provide a brief description of each category, along with some of the most influential publications on each of these categories of metrics.

Size is the most obvious metric for source code. The number of lines of code (LOC) is the simplest way of measuring size. But it has its drawbacks. For example, it is always possible to write the same functionality with fewer (or more) lines of code, while maintaining similar complexity. To address this problem, several other—more sophisticated—metrics have been proposed.

Measures of the complexity of a source file are postulated to affect modifiability and maintainability: lower complexity is better. While older metrics attempted to measure code complexity, newer metrics tend to be coupling-based. Coupling describes the number of connections a file or class has to other files or classes. The assumption is that lower coupling is better, indicating higher modularity. Another coupling metric is propagation cost, based on a design structure matrix (DSM) (Baldwin and Clark, 2000; Steward, 1981) representation of an architecture. This metric was first introduced by (MacCormack et al., 2006). We will discuss DSMs in greater detail later in this chapter.

Cohesion measures how strongly the responsibilities within a code unit are related. The rationale behind measuring cohesion is the belief that code units, such as source files or classes, should focus on just one thing, and that doing so will improve maintainability. Inheritance-based metrics only apply to object-oriented code. Less complex inheritance hierarchies are expected to be easier to understand and maintain. (Chidamber and Kemerer, 1994) developed the best known and most thoroughly validated metrics suite aimed at measuring object-oriented source code, including metrics for coupling, cohesion, and inheritance.

6.3.1.2 File metrics and maintenance effort

There has been substantial research attempting to correlate source code metrics to maintenance effort. Next we describe representative work in this field.

Welker et al. (1997) proposed a polynomial maintenance effort prediction model. This model automatically fitted the weights of multiple metrics so that the result matches expert judgment in eight systems. This polynomial model was presented as the *Maintainability Index*. Using this Maintenance Index, (Misra, 2005) and (Zhou and Xu, 2008) compared a number of complexity and inheritance metrics at the system level. In both papers, significant correlations to inheritance and complexity were reported. Alshayeb and Li (2003) studied the correlation between a number of well-known file metrics, modeled in a polynomial, with maintenance effort measured as lines of code added, deleted, and changed, in multiple iterations of projects. Their study showed that the constructed polynomial was limited to predicting effort between short-cycled changes, but not long-cycled evolution process.

Harrison et al. (1998) conducted a controlled experiment and compared file metrics against both expert judgment and maintenance measurements. Their result showed that complexity metrics were correlated with the expert judgment, and both complexity and cohesion metrics correlated with maintenance measures. Arisholm (2006) studied and recorded hours spent on making ten changes to an industrial software project and found no correlation between effort and file metrics. One possible reason could be the small data size. Li and Henry (1993) studied two projects and correlated a number of metrics to the change volumes of classes, and found that complexity, coupling, cohesion, and inheritance metrics are significantly correlated to change volumes. Binkley and Schach (1997) studied an industrial system and positively correlated change volume to coupling and complexity metrics, as well as one inheritance metric. Ware et al. (2007) also found significant correlations between complexity and coupling measures and the number of lines changes in files in a commercial application.

Different from the above work, (Anbalagan and Vouk, 2009) reported a significant correlation between time spent to fix a bug with the number of participants in the bug report. Although the number of participants is not an effort measure, it reflects the corresponding effort overhead and the organizational dimension of a software project.

6.3.1.3 *New proxy measures of maintenance effort*

As we discussed before, the most critical—but also the most challenging—part of the MDM-DSS is to estimate the potential cost-saving brought about by modularity improvement. More fundamentally, we need to estimate the maintenance cost at the level of *files*. Although numerous attempts have been made to find the correlation between file metrics and maintenance effort, there is a gap between correlations and actual effort, and hence cost, calculations that can be plugged into the proposed Datar–Mathews real option calculation model.

We lack an established quantitative association between the variation of structure measures of a file and the variation of the maintenance effort (measured quantitatively) spent on it. Without such an association, there is no way for decision makers to confidently estimate how much *more* or *less* it will cost to maintain a file when its structure measures get better or worse. Consequently, it becomes impossible either to calculate the amount of *technical debt* accumulated in a file due to its modularity deterioration or to justify the potential cost-savings from a refactoring proposal.

More fundamentally, the raw data needed to establish such an association is simply not available. For open-source projects, the vast majority of developers do not report their effort; for close-source software projects, effort data are usually not publicly available. Although in open data repositories, such as Promise,[3] we can find a few donated commercial software project data, the way

---
[3]https://code.google.com/p/promisedata/

effort data are recorded makes them unsuitable for our purpose. The reason is that effort is usually logged using person-hours, person-days, or person-months, spent on the overall system, subsystem, or task. What we need is effort spent on *files*, which is hard to infer from the effort data logged in these commercial projects. Time spent on maintaining individual files is just not recorded in practice. As a result, even if file metrics indicate structure deterioration of a file, the resulting extra maintenance effort/spent on it is hard to quantify and distinguish.

Later in this chapter we report our progress on the search of file-level proxy measures of effort that are applicable to both open-source and closed-source projects, and on the empirical foundation that correlates file metrics variation with variation in effort spent on maintaining file. Our analysis shows that the variation of the proposed proxy measures is significantly correlated with the variation of file metrics, and that these measures are complementary to each other.

6.3.1.4 File-level proxy measures of effort

Toward our goal of providing an empirical foundation to support decisions on modularization activities, we first propose and justify the adoption of three-dimensional *proxy* measures for effort: *actions*—the total number of patches and commits made to a file for the purpose of addressing issues; *churn*—the number of lines of code changed in a file for the purpose of addressing issues; and *discussions*—the number of textual comments made to address issues and related to a file. These measures can be obtained from both open-source and closed-source projects. We hypothesize that these proxy measures have the potential to bridge the gap between the variation of file metrics and file-level maintenance effort.

In our search for proper measures of effort, we considered various factors, including granularity and credentials. To fit the need of the envisioned DSS system, proper measures of effort should be at the *file* level because source files are the target of refactoring and manifest modularity decisions. The traditional measure of effort, in the unit of person-hours, person-days, or person-months, is associated with tasks or subsystems, and is too coarse-grained for file-level decisions and hard to attribute to files. We chose actions and churn based on the prior work on software cost estimation. The use of discussion as a measure of effort is supported by application of the grounded theory method to open-source software.

Churn. Lines of code represents probably the most widely and longest used measure of effort in software engineering. Although this measure of effort is not perfect, it has been the output of traditional software effort estimation models, such as the CoCoMo family of models (Boehm, 1981). We thus use the total lines of code added, deleted, or changed, commonly referred to as *churn*, as *one* type of effort measure. Recently, *churn* has been intensively investigated to predict error-proneness in source files (Giger et al., 2011).

Actions. Although code churn can be easily identified and counted, the change volume of a file from one version to the next does not always accurately represent the effort spent on the modification. It is possible that some lines of code require far more effort to create or understand than others. In open-source software (OSS) projects, in order to address an issue, contributors may propose many *patches*, each of which may change some code in some source files. Some of the patches may be accepted and others may be rejected. Simply counting the code churns between versions would not capture the full complexity of multiple patches, which also represent effort. Accordingly, we chose to use the number of patches and commits as another complementary measure of effort: the more patches/commits that are needed to address an issue, the greater the effort. We refer to this effort measure as *actions*.

Discussions. As we have discussed, not all lines of code are equal. There are times when programmers struggle over dozens of lines of code, or hundreds lines of code can be created relatively easily. This difference is partially caused by the inherent complexity of the issue being addressed. In an open-source project, such issues are often *discussed* among the developers. Accordingly, we consider that the amount of discussion associated with a file can be another useful measure of effort, which we call *discussions*.

Our reasoning is based on a grounded theory (GT) investigation. Grounded theory was first proposed by (Glaser and Strauss, 1967) as a methodology in the social sciences to discover theory by forming hypothesis and concepts from collected data. In OSS projects, development activities are usually logged in textual form via issue-tracking systems, commit messages, and mailing lists. These textual corpuses formed the dataset needed for GT methodology. We first investigated the discussions in Apache Lucene and then extended our dataset to include multiple Apache projects. The raw data for the analysis include commit titles, JIRA archives, IRC discussions, and mailing lists.

Using several GT analysis techniques, we first obtained groups of similar concepts needed to generate a theory. After that, we augmented the data and refined the derived concepts using additional projects. Using this method, a *core category* (theory)—*iterative informed consent* (IIC)—emerged. IIC identifies a behavior pattern of contributors: They iteratively discuss and provide solutions (tests and patches) to achieve consent. After the core category was identified, we observed many forms of supporting evidence in many OSS communities. For example, specific patches would show up as part of proposed implementation solutions, for the purpose of clarifying or strengthening the chances of consent. Although is not *always* the case since a solution can be directly submitted by developers with commit permission, it is the norm in OSS communities. We thus believe that the results of our GT analysis support the choice of *discussions* as another effort proxy.

We also considered other possible proxy measure of maintenance, including the time spent to resolve an issue and the number of bugs within a file. We decided not to use time as an effort measure first because the time elapsed during the life cycle of issues often reflect not only the actual effort caused by file complexity, but in most cases, the priority of a bug. For example, a ticket may remain open for a long time because of its low priority rather than inherent difficulty.

Unlike other work in the area of defect prediction (e.g., Hassan, 2009) we chose not to use defect rate as an effort proxy first because not all defects are addressed and bug reports may have duplications. Moreover, if a defect is fixed, then fix has to be manifested as changes in source file, patches, commits, and discussions, which will be captured by our three effort measures. On the other hand, if a defect is not fixed (no churn), or if no attempt is made to fix it (no actions and/or no discussions), then there is no evidence of any effort spent on fixing these bugs. Accordingly, only considering the number of bugs is not sufficient to capture the effort caused by source file complexity.

6.3.1.5 File metrics variation and file maintenance effort variation

In order to validate the proposed proxy measure of effort, we conducted an empirical study to investigate the behavior of the three proposed proxy effort measures, from the following aspects (Uunk et al., Valetto):

1. *What is the relation between these three proxy measures?* We would like to understand if there is any consistent relationship among these proxy measures. Intuitively, the three proxies should

complement each other because using only one or two of them does not seem to be sufficient to capture different manifestations of effort spent on file maintenance.

2. *Is the variation of file metrics icorrelated with the variation of these proxies?* If these proxy measures are valid, that is, if they truly reflect the effort caused by file complexity, then the variation of these measures should be consistent with the variation of file metrics that have long been recognized as the indicator of maintenance effort.

3. *Does the relation between file metrics and effort proxies differ in different projects?* We would like to understand if the best correlated effort proxy and file metrics are project-specific.

In our empirical study, we selected five Apache open-source projects containing between 8 and 18 releases as our experimental subjects. For each file of each project, we calculated its structural properties using a set of file metrics that are recognized to be significantly correlated with maintenance effort, and computed the delta of each metric between subsequent releases. We also extracted the three proxy measures of maintenance effort for each file, and their deltas between releases. After that, we analyzed the correlation between pairs of effort measure deltas and pairs of code metrics deltas and effort measure deltas to answer the aforementioned questions.

6.3.1.6 The selection of subject projects and metrics

In our search for subject projects, we attempted to obtain a diverse set of subjects that are heterogeneous in terms of application domain, source code size, team size, and project age. Currently, we restrict ourselves to Java projects so that the same metrics extraction process can be applied for all the subjects. Moreover, we only selected projects that employ version control and issue tracking systems so that we can extract the proxy measures of maintenance data. The five projects we selected all contain source code and revision history data for at least eight releases, and have more than 300 resolved issues. The five projects we selected are Derby,[4] Lucene,[5] PDFBox,[6] Ivy,[7] and FtpServer.[8] These projects are from different domains, with different team sizes and different project ages. The number of resolved issues ranges from 329 to 3058.

For file metrics, we selected the following nine file-level metrics that have been intensively studied in the past: Source Lines of Code (LOC)—the total lines of code in the file; Weighted Method Complexity (WMC)—the sum of method complexities in a class; Response for a Class (RFC)—the total number of methods that may be invoked due to the invocation of any method in a class; Coupling Between Objects (CBO)—the number of other classes that the class file is coupled with; Lack of Cohesion of Methods (LCOM)—the number of method pairs in the class that do not share the same attribute of the class; Depth in Tree (DIT)—the number of superclasses of the class in consideration; Number of Children (NOC)—the number of child classes of the class in consideration; Afferent Couplings (Ca)—the number of other classes that use the class in consideration; and Number of Public Methods (NPM)—the number of public methods in the class.

WMC, RFC, CBO, LCOM, DIT, and NOC have been proposed by (Chidamber and Kemerer, 1994), and their effectiveness of predicting software maintainability has been validated in many

---

[4]http://db.apache.org/derby/

[5]http://lucene.apache.org/core/

[6]http://pdfbox.apache.org/

[7]http://ant.apache.org/ivy/

[8]http://mina.apache.org/ftpserver/

studies (Misra, 2005; Harrison et al., 1998). In addition, we selected Propagation Cost (PC), a coupling-based metric first introduced by (MacCormack et al., 2006). We chose this metrics because of recent research that shows the promising predictive power of PC on maintenance effort (Carriere et al., 2010; MacCormack et al., 2006).

PC is calculated on a binary visibility matrix, where a project's files are labeled on the rows and columns, and dependencies between the files are the values in the cells. The dependency values are calculated using the length of dependency chain, L, for a file A to be dependent on a file B path. For example, a path of length of 1 models direct dependency. The propagation cost is calculated as the total number of dependencies, divided by the total number of possible dependencies in the visibility matrix. We compute the incoming propagation cost of a file by taking the total number of its incoming dependencies (the sum of dependencies in the column of the file) divided by the total number of possible dependencies. Similarly, we calculate the outgoing dependency of a file by taking the sum of the row representing the file and dividing the sum by the length of the row.

In this research, we studied both incoming and outgoing propagation costs with path lengths of 1, 3, 5, 10, and 20, with and without decay rate (e.g., the rate that reduces the strength of indirect dependencies by a factor for each additional step of the dependency path). For example, we use PROP-OUT-10-N to model outgoing propagation cost with path length 10 and without decay. Considering all combinations, there are 18 propagation cost metrics to consider. These 18 propagation cost metrics, plus the aforementioned 9 metrics, gave us a total of 27 metrics that we use to measure each file of each release of each project.

6.3.1.7 Correlation analysis

Our objective is to investigate the *relationship* between the variation of effort measures and the variation of file metrics. We transform the selected file metrics and the three proxy measures to reflect the *change* in value from one release to the next. For each metric value of each file, we divide it by the equivalent metric in the previous release. If the quotient is greater than 1, it means the value has increased; otherwise, if the quotient is less than 1, it has decreased; if it equals 1, the value is unchanged. We calculate effort variations in the similar way. This way, we obtained a dataset, each representing a change in file metrics or effort measure between two consecutive versions of a file.

After that, we performed a Spearman analysis on a set of 81 (27×3) file metrics and effort proxy data. We have run a total of 729 Spearman tests and thus obtained 729 p and rho values. We filter the results with a maximum p-value of 0.01 to ensure significance. We now explain the results, along with the aforementioned research questions.

1. What is the relation between these three proxy measures?

   From the aggregated data of all the five projects, the Spearman correlation analysis shows that the variation of churn and discussion are often correlated, but the variations of churn and actions are, surprisingly, never correlated. Analyzing each project separately, we only observed one significant correlation between action and churn in Derby. In most cases, churn and actions do not appear to be significantly correlated in most cases. More interestingly, churn is often significantly correlated with discussions, and discussions are somewhat correlated with actions.

   The correlation between churn/action and discussion supports the *iterative informed consent* theory: More actions and more churn are the result of more discussions. The result indicates that the effort spent on discussions should not be neglected. The fact that actions and churns are rarely correlated is unexpected: Intuitively, more actions should have resulted in more changes in LOC. But the analysis result implies that in many cases, one commit may change a large number of lines of code; on the other hand, more patches to an issue may end up just changing a small amount of code. In other words, small code churn may require more effort in the form of multiple attempts. These results support our suspicions that using just one measure, for example, churn, is not sufficient to capture the maintenance effort caused by file complexity.

2. Is the variation of file metrics correlated with the variation of the proxies?

We applied Spearman analysis both on the aggregated dataset of all the five projects and on each individual project dataset. We picked significant correlations with $p < .01$, rho $> = .3$ and a sample size of at least 15. The most significant results reveal a strong correlation between file metrics with just two effort proxies: actions and churn. Moreover, 7 out of the top 10 results show a strong correlation between coupling-based metrics and maintenance effort: variants of propagation cost and 3 C&K metrics: Ca, CBO, and RFC. Previous research has shown that these file metrics are good predictors of maintenance effort (Li and Henry, 1993; Binkley and Schach, 1997; Basili et al., 1996). The fact that the variations of the proposed proxy effort measures are significantly correlated with the variation of these files metrics provides evidence that these effort proxies are valid.

The results also showed that the rho value tends to increase as the release number increases. This result is encouraging first because a good predictive model should improve as more data are accumulated. Second, if the measure of maintenance effort is accurate, it should increase over time as maintenance issues and technical debt accumulate during evolution.

3. Does the relation between file metrics and effort proxies differ in different projects?

The Spearman analysis results on individual project data suggest that indeed the file metrics significantly correlated with effort proxies differ in different projects. In all five projects, actions and churn are strongly correlated with the C&K and PC metrics; discussion is observed to be significantly correlated with PC in Derby and is strongly correlated with LCOM in PDFBox. The results of both aggregated and project-specific data show that coupling-based metrics are significantly correlated with effort proxies in most of the cases. Recent research (Menzies et al., 2011) already showed that predictions based on data from only one project usually are not generalizable to other projects, which is consistent with the result of our study.

In summary, this empirical study shows that coupling-based file metrics are often directly correlated with churn and actions, but usually do not have strong correlation with discussions. Churn and actions, in turn, are frequently and significantly correlated with discussions. This result implies that file metrics and discussions impact each other in an indirect manner. We conclude that the three effort proxy measures are complementary to each other, each measuring maintenance effort from related but different perspectives.

6.3.2 Detecting refactoring candidates

Another key element of the proposed decision-support styem is to identify the *part* of the system that needs to be refactored. Using the file metrics and the proposed effort measures, project managers will only be alerted when modularity decay accumulates to the extent that software quality and productivity are negatively impacted. The probem is as follows: How can we detect modularity *debts* as soon as they occur? Detecting which part of the software needs to be refactored is different from detecting which part of the software has bugs because a software system that has a poor structure may still function correctly. There is a growing body of work that detects source code problems that are not directly related to bugs. For example, (Fowler et al., 1999) describes the concept of *bad smells* as a heuristic for identifying redesign and refactoring opportunities. Example bad smells include "code clone" and "feature envy." There is substantial research on automatically detecting these bad smells. Syntactical problems such as dependency violation or tight coupling can also be revealed by reverse-engineering from source code.

The problem is that, in a large system, the number of files with *bad smalls* or dependency violations can be very large. For example, in one system Dr. MacCormack studied, 7245 out of 18,612 files had high visibility before refactoring. Which files are incurring the severest *penalty* and need to be addressed first? Is it possible to detect these modularity debts uniformly? How can we detect dependecy violations that are *not* in the form of syntactical violations? We propose two approaches to detect refactoring candidates, *modularity violation detection* and *rare class analysis*.

6.3.2.1 Modularity violation detection

The rationale is that the essence of software modularity is to allow for independent module-wise evolution and independent task assignment. When decomposing a software into modules, choosing an architectural style, or applying a design pattern, designers make implicit assumptions about which modules should be independent from each other and which parts should remain stable. During software evolution, if two components always change together to accommodate modification requests but they belong to two separate modules that are designed to evolve independently, then there is a discrepancy. This discrepancy may be caused by side effects of a quick and dirty implementation, or requirements may have changed such that the original designed architecture could not easily adapt. When such discrepancies exist, the software will deviate from its designed modular structure, which we call a *modularity violation*.

Wong et al. (2011) presented a tool called *Clio* to detect modularity violation. The basic idea is as follows: Given a set of files that are changed first (which we call the *starting change set*), Clio first predicts their change scope based on the dependency structure of the system. That is, all other files that either depend on the starting change set or belong to the same module of the set should be within the change scope. In the meanwhile, Clio examines change coupling from revision history by checking which other files often change together with the starting change set, and predict associated change scope based on this information. Finally, Clio calculates the differences between the two change scopes and count only the discrepancies that happen frequently enough as potential *violations* (modularity *debts*) that deserve further investigation.

To assess if modularity violations indeed manifest design problem, Wong et al. (2011) have evaluated and demonstrated the effectiveness of Clio using several open-source projects. For example, in Hadoop, Clio identified 231 modularity violations from 490 modification requests, of which 152 (65%) were conservatively confirmed by the fact that they were either indeed addressed in later versions or were recognized as problems in the developers' subsequent comments. Their study showed that heterogeneous symptoms (bad smells) that previously needed multiple tools to detect (i.e., code clones, indirect cyclic dependencies, and problematic inheritance hierarchy) are instances of modularity violations and can all be uniformly detected using their approach. Moreover, the preliminary results showed that 40% of the confirmed violations in Hadoop were not defined as bad smells and are not detectable using existing approaches.

Given a set of detected violations, we can rank them according to their frequency and recency. The rationale is that the most frequently and recently changed modules have higher probabilities to be changed again, and will remain the most active parts for modification in the near future. Those components possess the most uncertainty, deserve more experiments, and can be refactoring candidates.

6.3.2.2 Rare class analysis

Thus far we have discussed using source code metrics and architectural (module) analysis as techniques for locating likely trouble spots in a code base. But there are other potential sources of evidence as well that we can bring to bear on the problem of finding the locations of modularity debt. One approach that we have experimented with is to use a history-based data-mining approach to assess likely sites of future bugs. These sites will incur (potentially heavy) costs in the future.

To do this, we use a rare class classifier (RUSBoost Seiffert et al., 2008) to classify risky files that contain high-priority bugs. To understand how the method works, we must discuss (1) what data is provided to the classifier, (2) how we characterize a risky file, and (3) what it means to use a *rare classifier*. To understand (1) consider that the classifier must first learn from the data. Then it can subsequently make classifications. Here, the data on which the classifier is trained is information regarding the issue priority from a project's JIRA (issue tracking) archive. Issue priorities in the archive may be classified as: Trivial, Minor, Major, Critical and Blocker. The development team uses these priorities to manage the issues.

Since in JIRA an issue can mean adding a new feature, fixing a bug, and so on, we filter our training data to only contain information about bugs. The resulting dataset therefore contains only issues that are related to bug fixes. For every issue in JIRA that is a (resolved) bug, files are submitted by developers that change the code (patches) and the bug is eventually fixed by commits containing some set of patches. In other words, a commit to fix a bug contains a set of one or more files, and one or more commits can be sent to fix an issue. If a commit is labeled with the issue code (e.g., PDFBOX-033), then we can map which files were submitted to fix an issue.

Our input data for classification therefore contains all the files that were submitted to fix each issue, along with their associated bug priority. For instance, if files A, B, and C were submitted to fix an issue of bug priority *Critical*, then we say that the *risk* associated with files A, B, and C is critical. If files A, B, and C are then modified to address another issue of risk *Trivial*, then we will have the case that files A, B, and C are associated with both the risk *Critical* and the risk *Trivial*.

Finally, if we know the risk of each file, we can extract metrics from these files. Following this example, if files A, B, and C were *modified* to address an issue of priority *Critical*, then any significant change will be captured by one of the metrics (e.g., added or removed LOC). The same occurs when the files A, B, and C were modified to address the issue of priority *Trivial*. Note that at this point the metrics that we capture on the modifications of the files take into account the succession of changes that the file was affected. If, for example, file A had initially 10 LOC, then say when addressing the issue *Critical* 5 LOC is added to it, this results in 15 LOC. If, on addressing the issue of priority *Trivial*, a patch removes 2 LOC, then the final LOC value for file A will be 13. This is important to note because it means that the data being used as input to the rare classifier takes into account the *evolution* of the file by capturing each metric value change that is registered on the dataset.

One can then view the classifier as an "expert" who attempts to observe what is the *state* of the file (captured across different file metrics) and compare this state against the risk associated with each change. The expert, after looking at many such states, should be able to notice patterns of risky files. As a result, the expert should be able to determine, by examining the state history, the *risk* of a given file.

Imagine that an expert observes a huge amount of bugs for all but the most important classes (Critical and Blocker). It is reasonable to assume that this expert can properly classify all but those two categories. In fact, the expert might be tempted to consider a Critical and a Blocker risk an accident of data entry. However, in reality it was simply that the occurrence of such files (that is, the occurrence of issues of priority Critical and Blocker) is unbalanced.

In the project dataset described in section 3.1, we observed that on all five of the projects, Critical and Blocker issues together constitute only 3% of all issues that were linked to files. A rare classifier must then be used to account for such a problem. Otherwise the classifier would perform poorly precisely when we need it most: when a file's risk is Critical or Blocker.

In our analysis of these five projects we have observed that 36% to 64% of the Critical and Blocker issues can be correctly predicted using this method. One may find it strange that the prediction accuracy varies. This is because of the nature of the rare classifier algorithm we employed (RUSBooost). Part of the algorithm (RUS) stands for Random Under Sampling. This means that the algorithm, before learning, randomly removes dat points (e.g., file A, its metrics, and its associated risk in one of the logged changes) from any but the rare priority (that is, Trivial, Minor, and Major) randomly. Since, by randomly removing, it can remove datapoints that improve or bias the algorithm, the accuracy then can vary. We are considering as future work employing other rare classes of algorithms and making improvements with other types of data (e.g., text mining).

6.4 Pilot industrial case studies

In this section, we briefly present two pilot case studies in industrial settings where several elements of the proposed MDM-DSS have been prototyped and subsequently improved.

6.4.1 VistaPrint corporation

Our prior work (described in Carriere et al., 2010) applied in VistaPrint Corporation in Boston, Massachusetts, provides an early example of the feasibility of our decision-support approach to making modularity and refactoring decisions. In this prior research, we devised a model to estimate the modifiability benefits of refactoring. We first *trained* the model as follows: We categorized the *tickets* (change requests) extracted from the organization's revision history, and we determined the set of components associated with each ticket. Then we measured these components using the *propagation cost* metric (MacCormack et al., 2006), calculated on DSM models both before and after the architectural change. We also captured the historical cost associated with resolving tickets, both before and after an architectural change. The final step of the training phase was to correlate these two sets of measures, which allowed us to predict, per ticket category, how much benefit—in terms of reduced coupling and effort—we can expect from a future architectural change. For example, in one refactoring activity at VistaPrint, when propagation cost in the Pricing subsystem went from 15% to 6%, the average time to resolve a ticket improved by 69%.

6.4.2 Siemens corporate research

Recently, we applied a revised modularity violation technique to a real industrial project at Siemens Corporate Research (SCR) (Schwanke et al., 2013). Based on the research results, the development team was able to identify a set of files that needed to be refactored and the refactoring proposal was successfully approved. Two challenges are involved in applying the Clio tool directly for modularity violation detection. First, the original Clio (Wong et al., 2011) algorithm assumes that a change originated in a "starting change set" and propagated to others. In reality, from revision history, it is hard to tell which files are the "starting change set." Even if it exists, it was only in the developer's mind and it is impossible to determine what it was. Second, in industrial settings, there is no uniformly agreed-to definition of "module." Different developers have different understandings about a system's module architecture, and their definition of "modules" differs from the concept used in the original Clio algorithm. In order to detect modularity violation, we should first agree on what a *module* is.

To overcome these challenges, we revised the original modularity violation detection algorithm as follows: First, the revised algorithm only counted the frequency of pairs of files changed together, and ranked the pairs according to the frequency, without considering which set of files "caused" the change. Second, a Java package, according to the project's own definition, is considered a "module." We then defined "expected" and "unexpected" changes as follows: If class A depends directly on class B, or A and B are in the same Java package, we consider them "expected" to change together; otherwise they are "unexpected" to change together. This definition can be adjusted in later research, for example, to adjust the concept of "same package" to include "closely related packages."

Based on these two modifications, we used a clustering algorithm to group files that unexpectedly and frequently changed together. We first rank the unexpected file pairs according to their change frequency, and we put the two files from the most frequent pair into the first cluster, *C1*. For the next pair of files, if one of them is already in *C1*, then the other is added to *C1*. Otherwise, a new cluster, *C2*, is created to contain both files from the second pair. Repeat these steps until all the unexpected, frequently changed pairs are in clusters.

We then assign the "expected" change pairs to the existing clusters in a similar manner. After generating those clusters, we generate a structure diagram for each cluster that contains only the cluster elements and elements that are immediate neighbors of at least two cluster elements. These diagrams convey the role that those frequently co-changed classes play in the overall architecture, and why they are frequently changed together even though they neither directly depend on each other nor are in the same package.

Using these diagrams, we observed many design problems. For example, a class in the infrastructure layer that is supposed to be stable is changing frequently together with several files in the data layer that also are supposed to be stable. At the same time, this file was ranked number one in terms of its fan-out. Our analysis shows not only that this architecturally critical file has a lot of illegal dependencies, but also that these dependencies made it change very frequently, making the most critical architectural interfaces unstable.

We also examined the most frequent change pairs in order to investigate why they changed together frequently. The reasons we found include code clone and moving functions from one file to the other. A more interesting reason was that these files often depended on the same set of other classes, so that when changes were necessary to those shared classes, both files changed. These classes shared "design secrets" about how the classes should be used.

A more intriguing observation is that these shared "design secrets" were not explicit in the code. One example was the knowledge about the granularity of time (which became 10,000 times finer partway through Release 1). Another was the knowledge about open and closed ends of time intervals, which followed different standards in different external partner systems. Because these design decisions were not made explicit in the interface specifications, they later required many changes to remove inconsistencies.

These problematic files were reported to the developers. The developers were convinced that these files are problematic because MDM-DSS shows not only that, for example, a file has a high coupling, but also that couplings are illegal. Furthermore, MDM-DSS shows that the consequences of these high couplings are frequent co-changes, which, in turn, imply high maintenance costs.

6.5 Discussion and future work

As discussed in section 2, the execution of the option-based decision-making framework requires not only the data that can be inferred from evolution history, but also the prediction of future changes and cost estimations made by software architects. Our immediate future work is continuing the implementation of the MDM-DSS.

The MDM-DSS includes a data warehouse that stores the structural metrics, effort measures, and evolutionary history of all the files of all the versions of a system. The MDM-DSS will provide a graphical user interface that reveals "hot spots"—areas that are predicted to be likely carriers of high modularity debt—as refactoring candidates. The MDM-DSS will reveal the architectural importance of these hot spots together with their structure and history measures. More importantly, the MDM-DSS will allow the users to input their estimation of future change frequency and refactoring costs of these candidates. Combining the information from history, structure, and future, the MDM-DSS will calculate the option value of refactoring these candidates.

The MDM-DSS is unique because it combines history mining, architecture structure, and future estimation to support modularization decision making. The integrated information is used both to automatically identify refactoring candidates and to infer the cost and benefits of a refactoring activity.

6.6 Conclusions

In this chapter, we have presented an options-based decision-support system to help manage modularity debt and to help resolve the refactoring decision dilemma faced by software practitioners today. Using the Datar−Mathews real-options valuation technique as our core economic model, our proposed MDM-DSS allows for what-if analysis, integrating history-based analysis, text mining, and input from the project manager to identify "hot spots" and to calculate the value of refactoring activities interactively.

We have advanced existing research in two specific areas to enable the realization of the MDM-DSS: (1) the introduction of three new proxy measures of effort and (2) the automated identification of refactoring candidates. These research advances allow the MDM-DSS to: (1) predict maintenance effort variation based on file metrics variations and (2) identify the parts of the system that need to be refactored. We also presented two pilot industrial case studies where refactoring decisions are supported based on the key modules of our MDM-DSS. The case studies served to improve our MDM-DSS prototype and to give them a solid empirical basis for finding potential modularity "hot spots" in an existing code base. These hot spots are the likely sites of future complexity, high risk, high cost, high number of bugs, and difficulty in finding and fixing these bugs.

The MDM-DSS vision is ambitious. It is inherently multidisciplinary. We have articulated the difficulty of managing modularity debt and the uncertainty it involves. We have presented two key economics-driven modularity evaluation research results underpinning the key modules of the MDM-DSS. The MDM-DSS is, of course, open to other kinds of metrics and analyses, and we expect to be continually incorporating new research results to the MDM-DSS through our own research and the research of others.

6.7 Acknowledgments

This work was supported in part by the National Science Foundation under grants CCF-0916891, CCF-1065189, and CCF-1116980. It is also supported in part by work funded and supported by the Department of Defense under Contract No. FA8721-05-C-0003 with Carnegie Mellon University for the operation of the Software Engineering Institute, a federally funded research and development center.

References

Alshayeb, M., Li, W., 2003. An empirical validation of object-oriented metrics in two different iterative software processes. IEEE Trans. Softw. Eng. 29 (11), 1043–1049.

Anbalagan, P., Vouk, M., 2009. On predicting the time taken to correct bug reports in open source projects. IEEE International Conference on Software Maintenance, pp. 523–526.

Arisholm, E., 2006. Empirical assessment of the impact of structural properties on the changeability of object-oriented software. Inf. Softw. Technol. 48 (11), 1046–1055.

Baldwin, C.Y., Clark, K.B., 2000. Design Rules, Vol. 1: The Power of Modularity. MIT Press, Cambridge, MA.

Basili, V., Briand, L., Melo, L., 1996. A validation of object-oriented design metrics as quality indicators. IEEE Trans. Softw. Eng. 22 (10), 751–761.

Binkley, A.B., Schach, S.R., 1997. Inheritance-based metrics for predicting maintenance effort: an empirical study. Computer Science Department, Vanderbilt University, Tech. Rep. TR 9705.

Boehm, B.W., 1981. Software Engineering Economics. first ed. Prentice Hall, Upper Saddle River, NJ.

Brown, N., Cai, Y., Guo, Y., Kazman, R., Kim, M., Kruchten, P., et al., 2010. Managing technical debt in software-reliant systems. Proceedings of the FSE/SDP Workshop on Future of Software Engineering Research, pp. 47–52.

Carriere, J., Kazman, R., Ozkaya, I., 2010. A cost-benefit framework for making architectural decisions in a business context. Proc. International Conference on Software Engineering.

Chidamber, S.R., Kemerer, C.F., 1994. A metrics suite for object oriented design. IEEE Trans. Softw. Eng. 20 (6), 476−493.

Cunningham, W., 1992. The WyCash portfolio management system. In: Addendum to the Proc. Object-Oriented Programming Systems, Languages, and Applications (Addendum), New York, pp. 29−30.

Erdogmus, H., 2002. Valuation of learning options in software development under private and market risk, pp. 503−552. The Engineering Economist. Addison-Wesley, Boston, MA

Fowler, M., Beck, K., Brant, J., Opdyke, W., Roberts, D., 1999. Refactoring: Improving the Design of Existing Code. first ed. Addison-Wesley Professional, Reading, MA.

Glaser, B.G., Strauss, A.L., 1967. The Discovery of Grounded Theory: Strategies for Qualitative Research. Aldine de Gruyter, NewYork.

Giger, E., Pinzger, M., Gall, H.C., 2011. Comparing fine-grained source code changes and code churn for bug prediction, pp. 83−92. Proceedings of the 8th Working Conference on Mining Software Repositories. ACM Press, New York

Guo, Y., Seaman, C., 2011. A portfolio approach to technical debt management. Proceedings of the 2nd Workshop on Managing Technical Debt, pp. 31−34.

Harrison, R., Counsell, S.J., Nithi, R.V., 1998. An investigation into the applicability and validity of object-oriented design metrics. Empirical Softw. Eng. 3 (3), 255−273.

Hassan, A.E., 2009. Predicting faults using the complexity of code changes. In: Proceedings of the 31st International Conference on Software Engineering, ser. ICSE '09, Washington, DC, pp. 78−88.

Lehman, M., 1980. On understanding laws, evolution, and conservation in the large program life cycle. J. Syst. Soft. 1, 213−221.

Li, W., Henry, S., 1993. Object-oriented metrics that predict maintainability. J. Syst. Soft. 23 (2), 111−122.

Lientz, B.P., Swanson, E.B., 1980. Software Maintenance Management. Addison-Wesley, Reading, MA.

MacCormack, A., Rusnak, J., Baldwin, C.Y., 2006. Exploring the structure of complex software designs: an empirical study of open source and proprietary code." Manag. Sci. 52 (7), 1015−1030.

Mathews, S., Datar, V., 2007. A practical method for valuing real options: the Boeing approach. J. Appl. Corp. Financ. 19 (2), 95−104.

Menzies, T., Butcher, A., Marcus, A., Zimmermann, T., Cok, D., 2011. Local vs global models for effort estimation and defect prediction. Proceedings of ASE 2011: 26th IEEE/ACM International Conference on Automated Software Engineering.

Misra, S.C., 2005. Modeling design/coding factors that drive maintainability of software systems. Softw. Qual. Control 13 (3), 297−320.

Ozkaya, I., Kazman, R., Klein, M., 2007. Quality-attribute based economic valuation of architectural patterns. Software Engineering Institute Technical Report CMU/SEI-2007-TR-003, Pittsburgh, PA.

Sauter, V., 2011. Decision Support Systems for Business Intelligence. second ed. Wiley, Hoboken, NJ.

Schwanke, R., Xiao, L., Cai, Y., 2013. Measuring architecture quality by structure plus history analysis. Proceedings of the 2013 International Conference on Software Engineering, pp. 891−900.

Seiffert, C., Khoshgoftaar, T., Hulse, J., Napolitano, A., 2008. RUSBoost: improving classification performance when training data is skewed. 19th International Conference on Pattern Recognition, 1−4.

Steward, D.V., 1981. The design structure system: a method for managing the design of complex systems. IEEE Trans. Eng. Manage. 28 (3), 71−84.

Sullivan, K.J., Chalasani, P., Jha, S., Sazawal, V., 1999. Software design as an investment activity: a real options perspective. Real Options and Business Strategy: Applications to Decision Making. Risk Books, London, UK.

Uunk, F., Kazman, R., Cai, Y., Black, N., Silva, C., Valetto, G., et al., On the search for proxy measures of effort. Drexel University Technical Report: DU-CS-13-01.

Ware, M.P., Wilkie, F.G., Shapcott, M., 2007. The application of product measures in directing software maintenance activity. J. Softw. Maint. Evol. 19 (2), 133−154.

Welker, K.D., Oman, P.W., Atkinson, G.G., 1997. Development and application of an automated source code maintainability index. J. Softw. Maint. Res. Pract. 9 (3), 127–159.

Wong, S., Cai, Y., Kim, M., Dalton, M., 2011. Detecting software modularity violations. Proc. 33th International Conference on Software Engineering, pp. 411–420.

Zhou, Y., Xu, B., 2008. Predicting the maintainability of open source software using design metrics. Wuhan Univ. J. Nat. Sci. 13, 14–20.

Practices of Software Architects in Business and Strategy—An Industry Experience Report

7

Michael Stal

University of Groningen, Groningen, The Netherlands

"If you think, good architecture is expensive, try bad architecture"
—**Joseph Yoder and Brian Foote**

7.1 Introduction

The product portfolio of Siemens, a company with over 400,000 employees worldwide, is quite diverse. It includes trains, railway control systems, health care systems, factory automation, power transmission and distribution, among many other products. These products represent embedded systems. In recent years, they moved from isolated islands to connected distributed real-time and embedded (DRE) systems that were integrated with an increasing amount of software tools and enterprise applications.

Only a few decades ago, software was considered a low value add-on to the hardware. Today, over two-thirds of all Siemens revenues depend on software. As a consequence, software development has become an important economic factor for embedded systems. Any failure or delay in software development does imply significant financial liabilities. Consequently, the success of mission-critical system development projects is essential for economic success. As software architects are responsible for designing the strategic backbone of such systems, they must be aware of economic constraints and business goals and take these factors into account in all their decisions.

Some organizations consider software architects as advanced software engineers with a high-technology bias. From their perspective, architects do not require expertise in business and strategy. Even software architects themselves tend to believe they are only responsible for technology and design decisions, but not for economic aspects. This attitude leads to solutions that are technically sound but fail to deliver the expected return on investment. If software architects do not understand economics and the business, they cannot come up with economic solutions that support the business case and business strategy. This is why mission-critical projects often do not achieve their business goals, thus incurring high additional costs. Although this holds for other engineering disciplines as well, the high flexibility expectations regarding software and its creation increases the economic risks.

This chapter provides war stories and practices for coping with the economic challenge software architects face. It is not based on empirical scientific studies or conceptual research, but on experiences of our company. The experiences were systematically analyzed and collected from existing and historical projects to identify common causes of failure and to extract guidelines for software architects to learn from failure and avoid it in their own projects. Being used for several years now, a framework of practices comprises the recommended process and collaboration patterns for architects to help them ensure economic success.

7.2 Identifying economic guidance for software architects

Within Siemens a team evaluated mission-critical software development projects to understand the responsibilities of software architects in development projects to achieve business and technology goals in an efficient and effective way. The analysis was the first step in setting up a companywide senior software architects certification program (Paulisch and Zimmerer, 2010). Afterward the evaluation guidelines were defined to clarify the role of software architects in business and strategy. These guidelines introduce the responsibilities, interactions, and activities of architects in the different project phases that are considered essential for project success. In additional workshops, the guidelines are also taught to managers such as heads of R&D and product (life-cycle) managers.

The project evaluation phase revealed that some of the software architects did not know the relevant business context of their projects, at least not in sufficient depth. Many software architects assumed they knew it, but actually they only understood it vaguely.

As a consequence, some large and mission-critical projects failed to achieve business and strategy goals and could not deliver on time and on budget. In a postmortem analysis, communication between software architects and product, project, and senior management often turned out to be inefficient, insufficient, and ineffective. However, mutual interaction between stakeholders is the prerequisite for creating economic and sustainable solutions that fit into the business and strategy goals of an organization. From this perspective, insufficient communication is the root of almost all technical and economic problems. Software architects need to know the economic constraints and forces in order to come up with architectural decisions that are in sync with the business case.

7.3 Structure of the chapter

In the first section, we introduce some considerations on economics-driven software before addressing the software architect's perspective. Succeeding sections in the first part of the chapter cover general facets architects should be knowledgeable about such as business context understanding and business strategy and planning. Succeeding sections address the involvement of architects in product and technology planning, cost estimations, and the treatment of legal issues and regulatory bodies.

In the middle part of the chapter, we show the responsibilities and activities of software architects during system development. This includes not only design activities, but also responsibilities in requirements engineering, testing, implementing, and integration. A coarse outline of a systematic process for architecture design is also introduced. The next sections emphasize specific development contexts such as software product lines and embedded systems.

In the last part, the chapter explains why communication among stakeholders is a success factor for development projects and provides some final conclusions.

7.4 Considerations on economics-driven software architecture

Software architecture is the main step in mapping the problem space to the solution space as it covers strategic aspects such as Quality of Service as well as major tactical aspects such as reuse and modifiability. Tactical design, that is, fine-grained design, depends on this architectural backbone. As a consequence, each architectural decision has an impact on costs. To enable economic system development, architects must explicitly consider economic issues in all process phases and disciplines.

For driving economic system design, software architects should be actively involved in requirements engineering. In particular, they need to elaborate the economic soundness of the specification. Some requirements might stay in conflict with each other or might be economically unfeasible. For example, if many quality attributes or functional requirements are rated highly, it is difficult or even impossible to come up with economic software architecture. Quality attributes such as efficiency and exchangeability lead to trade-offs between minimizing and maximizing the number of indirection layers, which results in complex systems that are hard and expensive to maintain or evolve.

At Siemens, software architects are required to enforce a unique prioritization of requirements jointly with product managers or customers to avoid such problems.

Unit costs are another economic aspect we encountered in projects. If an embedded operating system license costs $50 per device, it is impossible to achieve a unit price less than $50. Thus, technical decisions such as the integration of third-party (Common-Off-The-Shelf (COTS)) must take care about economic implications. For this reason, architects are involved in make-or-buy decisions as well as outsourcing or offshoring considerations. Availability of a second source for most COTS components is important to minimize dependence on suppliers. Likewise, architects are in charge of deciding whether inner or outer open-source components might offer economic benefits such as cost reduction. On the other hand, open source bears the risk of hidden patent violations and licensing models that would require a company to reveal some of its business secrets. In a value-based software development, organization architects need to address these risks.

War Story: In a project for developing a medical therapy system, the integration into the medical information systems had to be accomplished using software from a specific vendor due to a mandatory customer requirement. However, the supplier was also a competitor. All adaptations of the software took months and millions of euros even for simple changes.

Software patents are of crucial value in the industry. They help to protect the business of a company, and they are important assets when negotiating cross-licensing contracts. Patent portfolios can reach values of millions or even billions of U.S. dollars. Software architects are responsible for recognizimg innovative concepts early in their projects, especially those that should be subject to intellectual property rights.

To mitigate risk early and to obtain early feedback, architects at Siemens create the architecture using a piecemeal approach, starting with the most important use cases and quality attribute scenarios. An incremental and iterative approach ensures that in case of budget cuts or time delays the system can meet important requirements but leave out less important features and qualities. Providing early feedback also helps check the economic feasibility of the project. For example, if the first increment takes much more time than estimated, then it is very likely that the succeeding increments were also subject to wrong cost and time estimations.

Strategic design, that is, functional design and design of operational quality attributes such as safety or efficiency, should always precede tactical design, which comprises developmental qualities such as modifiability or reusability. This is because in order to modify a system or reuse components, the availability of the artifact to be modified or reused is necessary. Extensibility has no meaning without precisely knowing what to extend and for what purpose. Some systems that did not follow these rules were subject to overuse of patterns such as strategy, which made the systems slow and hard to maintain. If the engineers don't know what should be flexible, they might become cautious and introduce variability in many parts of the project, even where it is not beneficial. Binding of variability and configuration in such systems tend to be complex, tedious, and error prone.

Since quality attributes are essential for a product and hence an important cost factor, architects and product management should cooperatively define the quality scenarios, derive the quality tree, and estimate the economic impact as well as the technical complexity of each quality attribute scenario (Bass et al., 2013). Qualities with high economic impact should have higher priorities than those with less economic impact. If two quality attribute scenarios have the same economic value, the one with higher technical complexity is assigned a higher priority. Thus, the order of design and implementation can be driven by economic value and technical risk. Prioritization is also useful for setting up economic risk-based test strategies and test plans. Using a risk-based strategy, testing can focus on the most critical artifacts with adequate tests. By balancing economic and risk constraints, test managers and software architects determine the right amount of testing, and an appropriate test exit strategy.

One constituent of tactical design is to come up with a systematic reuse strategy. Different projects reveal that components that are hard to use are even harder to reuse because the costs for making them usable and reusable might outweigh the reuse benefits. In the most extreme cases, usage of components with bad design for reuse turned out to be much more expensive than design from scratch. Thus, architects need to provide an economically feasible reuse infrastructure. Systematic commonality/variability analysis helps to identify potential reuse candidates as well as their cost. This is an essential activity in all software applications and is of high economic importance in product line engineering.

Reuse within Siemens projects is not constrained to organizational units, but might even be applied in a cross-organization manner. For example, control systems in energy or automation domains are enforced to use the same control systems platform that has eventually become a high economic value. Furthermore, business groups use and reuse the same engineering tools.

Reuse is not constrained to implementation artifacts. Design reuse turned out to be much more important than code reuse in several projects. Within Siemens, certified architects leverage software patterns to re-use general and domain-specific design. Patterns include architecture, design, analysis s, domain-specific s, and refactoring patterns. This pattern-based architecture approach could save up to 40% costs in some previous and current company projects.

To avoid accidental complexity, each design decision must be rooted in an economic or a business reason and abide to the "keep-it-simple" principle. Otherwise, architects might introduce unnecessary design pearls that introduce accidental complexity, that is, oversophisticated design. Oversophisticated design is an important cost factor because it causes unexpressive, complex systems that are difficult to understand, to maintain, and to use.

In order to circumvent the economic pitfalls caused by inadequate design decisions, architects are supposed to conduct an architectural analysis after each increment. The earlier the design problems are detected and resolved, the less expensive is their treatment.

Design problems are resolved by refactoring and restructuring activities before succeeding with the next increment. Sometimes, refactoring of design problems cannot be conducted because of an upcoming product release. In this case, architects should explicitly document the findings, also known as design debt, report these findings and their consequences to the management, and plan later treatment of design debt.

Design debt leads to economic implications such as higher costs when untreated or resolved in a later increment. But it might also be the case that for some minor design problems it is cheaper to keep them unresolved. For most architecture problems, early feedback by architecture analysis and immediate treatment of identified design smells often proved to be much more economic than deferring refactoring to a later increment. If bad design decisions in a top-down architecture design are not resolved, fine-grained design and evolution adds more components and dependencies to these architectural locations. After a while, any refactoring will need to consider all those additional components and dependencies that might increase development costs significantly.

In the implementation phase, architects should also implement but not on the critical path. By participating in this phase, they can encounter problems in the architecture and prevent an architectural shift caused by developers who do not understand or follow the architectural design. Otherwise, architecture shift may have a major economic impact, especially when it is discovered late in the project.

For economic reasons, developer habitability should be a major concern in architecture creation. The better the habitability of a system, the easier developers can understand and use the architecture and the less development costs will be. At Siemens, strategic architecture documents must cover different stakeholder perspectives and be written from their viewpoint and needs in a systematic, prescribed way. Additional project diaries turned out to be useful to document the rationale of decisions that could not have been documented otherwise. Whenever new ineffective and time-consuming discussions pop up in meetings that cover previous decisions, the project diary reveals why a particular path has been taken. A project diary does not need to be a formal document but may be an informal Wiki site.

7.5 **The business context of software architecture**

If development and product management are strictly separated, this leads to unwanted effects. Literally speaking, product managers may "throw a specification over the fence," and software engineers may "throw their architectural specification or software release back." Each role makes assumptions about their own specifications, respectively, the specifications, responsibilities, and activities of the other roles. Some of these assumptions turn out to be wrong, incomplete, or ambiguous. When stakeholders do not practice regular and frequent communication and cooperation, there is a good chance for misunderstanding and thus for failure.

War Story: In a telecommunications project, architects thought that high flexibility was the key requirement, while in fact efficiency had the highest priority. After the first version of the base station was released, beta customers complained about the poor performance of the system. Architects and management figured out that the system architects did not regularly communicate with other roles so that nobody recognized the divergence between the specification and the actual design. It took the development team more than one year to solve the problem.

Hence, the prerequisite for architects in a development project is *to know the economic and the technical context of software architecture*, that is, the products an organization is going to build, the intended markets and customers, the business strategy of the organization, as well as the competitors (see Architects, 2008). To retrieve this knowledge, architects must communicate tightly with business roles.

Product management (see Geracie, 2010 and Mironov, 2008) should actively involve software architects in the fundamental process steps of business and strategy planning to avoid such problems. If they don't, architects should feel responsible to proactively obtain this information. Passively waiting for this information is not a viable option.

7.6 Business strategy and planning

Architects need to understand the business strategy of their organization. As a first step in software development, a SWOT analysis (Strength, Weaknesses, Opportunities, and Threats) (wikipedia.org) provides an overview of the *company's current position.*

- *Strengths* comprise various aspects, for example, the leadership position of the organization in the market, the completeness and focus of the existing product portfolio, and the availability of skilled personnel.
- *Weaknesses* may include factors such as the pricing model, lack of market awareness, lack of innovation, and inferior quality of products.
- *Opportunities* such as change of the legal environment, cost pressure of customers, standardization, compliance and conformance requirements, or outsourcing necessities lead to new or improved solutions that address these challenges.
- *Threats* put the market position of the organization at risk. For instance, when new competitors with innovative and cheap products appear, the market volume and, as a direct consequence, the profitability decreases.

From the SWOT analysis management derives improvement measures and actions. One sample measure could be to develop innovative products that attract new customer. A possible action is the search for "excitement features" that help achieve a competitive edge in the market.

Software architects should be knowledgeable about the capabilities of their company, in particular its strengths and weaknesses. They typically are not responsible for finding new opportunities or for defining measures. However, responsible management should involve them intensively in these activities to obtain valuable feedback and ideas. Eventually, the architects are responsible for creating concrete products from business goals and requirements.

Architects support the definition of a product roadmap (see McGrath, 2000) for information on product strategies) that captures the milestones and steps required to reach a midterm or long-term vision. This comprises the evolution of current products or product releases as well as the creation of new products that are intended to complete or enhance the product portfolio. All new services and features essential for the implementation of the product roadmap are subject to R&D planning (Matheson, 1997). In this context, architects are supposed to provide their technology knowledge by analyzing relevant technology trends and determining possible implications on the architecture caused by new technologies. They should also contribute to effort and cost estimations.

An important deliverable of this activity is *a technology roadmap* (Moehrle et al., 2013) (see Figure 7.1) that synchronizes and coordinates product management with development. The purpose of a technology roadmap is to identify the technologies required for specific product releases.

War Story: In a medical product development, architects did not receive sufficient information on the product roadmap from product management. Creation of the technology roadmap was assigned to product managers as well. When development of the second version started, it turned out that some architecture and technical decisions during version one development had to be completely refactored or modified for version two. Had the architects known the product roadmap a priori, development of version two could have been completed in a much more economic way.

These technologies might be developed by the organization itself, obtained through outsourcing from other companies, based on an open-source software product, or bought from leading technology vendors. Outsourcing activities require architects to cooperate with other cultures. They need training and experience to accomplish this task. Otherwise, lack of coordination and communication may result in delayed and inadequate deliveries and in increased costs.

Which of the technology options are more beneficial depends mostly on economic and strategic aspects. Issues such as the following should be addressed in this context:

- What effort in terms of time and budget is required to develop the specific technology or service?
- Does the component contain innovations or business secrets that provide a competitive advantage, and, therefore, should not be made available to external organizations?
- Does the market provide an existing technology or service that could be easily integrated into own products?
- Is there any open-source software solution available that could be reused to implement the technology and, if yes, are there any obstacles with respect to legal issues?
- In large companies the question could even be: Is there another company that provides the required technology and could be subject to Mergers and Acquisitions? This might be a viable alternative if the technology contains business secrets or innovations.

Software architects are prepared to help answer such questions due to their technology and architecture expertise. They can estimate efforts required for the development and integration of technology as well as its impact on the software architecture. In addition, they can serve as valuable partners for due diligence activities related to technologies and services.

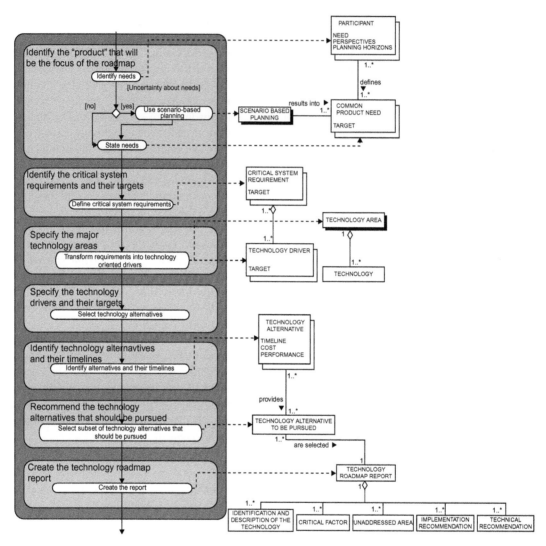

FIGURE 7.1

Extract from the process of technology roadmap creation.

For this reason, software architects should be actively involved in technology vendor assessment and management. Architects help to decide which vendors should become strategic suppliers. They make sure that technology deliveries abide by the expectations and necessities of product development. Their assessment includes the conformance of external deliveries to legal issues and relevant standards. If possible, architects should help identify a second source to decrease dependence on certain suppliers.

7.7 Products—definition and development

Architects are in charge of strategic design for products and solutions. But they also ought to participate in the product or solution definition phase.

For understanding customer expectations, architects and management leverage methods and tools such as KANO analysis (Kano et al., 1984). A KANO diagram (see Figure 7.2) illustrates the basic requirements the overall system must meet. It also identifies the additional excitement features that are not expected by customers, but provide a competitive advantage.[1]

Although KANO analysis focuses mainly on functional aspects such as features, one of the most critical and important facets relates to the definition, implementation, and validation of quality attributes. A product that meets all functional requirements but fails to deliver sufficient performance or robustness may result in customer dissatisfaction. For example, long interruptions of a mail system or website can incur millions of losses. And even worse, a medical device that causes lethal injuries becomes a major hazard for health care providers, patients, and the vendor.

Defining quality requirements and assigning unique priorities to these qualities requires close interaction between architects and business stakeholders. Within projects, stakeholders leverage utility trees and scenario diagrams (Bass et al., 2013) to achieve this goal.

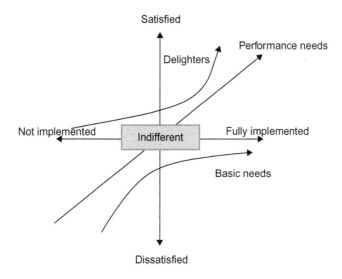

FIGURE 7.2

The Kano model is a theory of product development and customer satisfaction developed in the 1980s by Professor Noriaki Kano. It defines how a product addresses basic needs of users and usage efficiency, as well as the delighters it provides, i.e. properties user do not expect but that delight them.

© *Wikipedia. Used under Creative Commons.*

---

[1]A well-known example for an excitement feature is the touch-based UI of the first iPhone.

War Story: Product managers of a business application defined flexibility to be one of the key requirements. In addition, they rated almost all other quality attributes as high-priority requirements as well. Two problems emerged: First, the managers had completely different definitions in mind when discussing flexibility, but no stakeholder was aware of the problem. Second, all quality attributes were defined very vaguely, and some of them even conflicted with each other. In the project, the architects hold full responsibility for technical aspects of quality attributes, and product managers were responsible for business aspects. Thus, the product managers did not know the technical aspects, while the architects did not know the business aspects. The resulting system was overly complex and could not meet some important customer requirements. It had to be completely reengineered.

Operational and developmental quality attributes are specified with this kind of diagram by product managers and architects—which additionally fosters common understanding of the business case and the development challenges. The interaction also reduces the risk of incompleteness or inconsistence of the requirements specification. In a further step, architects estimate the complexity and efforts for implementing each scenario, while business stakeholders define the economic relevance of the scenarios. Scenarios with high business relevance and high implementation complexity are then developed first. From an economic viewpoint, design and implementation can focus on most business-relevant and risky scenarios, which helps mitigate risks and reduce costs.

7.8 Cost and effort estimations

Architects are important partners for project and product management with respect to cost and effort estimations. In the Siemens software architect certification program, estimation methods such as COCOMO (Steece et al., 2000) are introduced, including their pros and cons. However, the main focus is on the planning poker (Steece et al., 2000) (see Figure 7.3), a method provided by Scrum. Multiple business units are using Scrum as their preferred process model, or at least they mix-in some Scrum ingredients in their existing development process. Appropriate cost and effort estimations turned out to be of crucial importance in many projects. Because of work package dependencies, a delay in one milestone might cause delays in multiple dependent milestones and work packages.

Architects are supposed to leverage methods like the planning poker to come up with more realistic effort estimations. This method does not calculate costs, but rather combines different cost estimations to a joint and more realistic estimation by different stakeholders and persons.

War Story: In an automotive project for developing an entertainment system, management decided to use Windows CE as the underlying operating system. To increase the development team, they hired developers experienced in the development environment Visual Studio, most of whom had no knowledge of embedded systems development. Management's basic assumption upon cost and time estimation was that Visual Studio developers would be as productive in developing embedded apps as they were in building desktop applications. Eventually, the developers needed unplanned competence ramp-up for embedded development, which caused significant delays in the project.

FIGURE 7.3

In planning poker, cards with Fibonacci numbers are used to estimate efforts.

Specific cost analysis methods are not prescribed, but methods such as CBAM (cost-benefit analysis method) (Nord et al., 2013) provide guidance to software architects and software engineers. Architects typically ask product managers or customers about their requirements and the value they assign to the quality attributes and features. This information helps select appropriate design tactics and software patterns from various alternatives. Each selection must also take economic aspects into account. Technology and solution selection then serve as the base for detailed cost and effort estimations. This approach connects features and quality attributes with business value and costs so that software architects can consider the economic consequences of their decisions.

7.9 Legal environment

Whenever software architects are in charge of software design and implementation, they generally need to cope with legal issues as well. A legal services unit can offer sophisticated support, but is seldom knowledgeable about technical aspects. Various opportunities in software development projects require specific care. Without thorough considerations, some pitfalls may lead to economic risks.

War Story: During the development of a communication middleware, architects designed new means for efficient message-based communication. After project completion, it was detected that some of the open-source components used in the system would have required the organization to provide its source code publicly according to the open-source license models, thus revealing business secrets. Another problem was the use of a smart component loading/unloading mechanism that turned out to be already patented by another company. The legal services organization had to prove that this prior patent was invalid due to prior use, causing a delay of the project.

Licensing models for open-source software (Lindberg, 2008) may force an organization to publish its own source code. If the internal code contains sensitive information such as innovations or business secrets, this can cause significant reengineering or rewriting efforts to get rid of the open-source components. The economic impact of licensing models might be huge, especially if inappropriate licensing models are used. Thus, architects are required to closely interact with legal experts before using open-source software components and to make sure their organization can live with the specific constraints of the license models.

Patents (Blind et al., 2005; Cleland-Huang et al., 2013; Hahn, 2005; Hall et al., 2006; Lundberg et al., 2011; Rosenberg and Apley, 2012; Stobbs and Kluwer Law International (Firm), 2008) may become another trap. If an open-source component, a commercial COTS product, or an internal code artifact violates existing patents of competitors or suppliers, then costs for dealing with the patent violations will emerge. This subsumes costs for substituting the respective code with new implementations, costs for identifying and proving the invalidity of patents due to prior art, or costs for paying license fees to the patent owners. If competitors are among the patent owners, licensing may become quite challenging, if possible at all. Utilizing software such as Black Duck is helpful to identify possible patent violations in company-internal code and lead to large cost savings in some projects.

The other side of the coin is *securing intellectual property rights.* New solutions or products typically contain innovative ideas that qualify for becoming valuable patents. This might be even more important for products in markets with many competitors. Architects are responsible for identifying, leveraging and harvesting these patent opportunities in their projects (Knight, 2013). As large companies mostly have organizational units that support patenting, architects should communicate with patent lawyers very early about securing new inventions. In the industry, patent portfolios can have an economic value of several millions or even billions of U.S. dollars. Patent portfolios are also helpful in cross-license negotiations with other companies. The economic value and impact of patents should not be underestimated. Creativity and innovation workshops educate project participants as to how to find and create patents in a systematic way.

7.10 Standards and regulations

Safety- and security-critical systems, as well as enterprise and other systems, are often subject to standardization *conformance and regulations.* A medical device, a weapon, or a railway control system needs to be certified by national organizations such as the the United States' FDA (Food and Drug Administration) or Germany's TÜV (Technischer Überwachungs Verein). Otherwise, these products must not be sold in some target markets. The time period needed for certification, however, can span several months or even years. An organization has to explicitly consider such constraints and necessities in product planning. Software architects are responsible for the conformant design and implementation of the architecture. For example, they define concepts of how to integrate specific safety measurements where required. They, together with certification experts, also need to make sure that there are no violations of standards or legal regulations such as DiCOM or SIL in the product.

Not only the parts produced by an organization, but also deliveries from third-party suppliers need to undergo certification. This could be one of the criteria for vendor selection and for the creation of a technology roadmap. It is a core responsibility of architects to check third-party COTS components, implementation artifacts, and tools for possible conformance issues.

War Story: In developing medical products, safety is the most critical concern. In a project based on Microsoft Windows 7, architects only checked their own components for safety, but were asked later in the project to ensure the safety of the underlying operating system. Among many other efforts, developers had to provide additional layers on top of the Windows communication stack to provide checksums and other safety mechanisms. These activities had not been anticipated in the project plan.

Organizations have to keep in mind that regulation and standardization efforts might be huge, especially when different markets and thus different regulation bodies are addressed.

But it is not only mandatory regulation and standardization that are important. Sometimes customers expect products to implement specific standards (see Figure 7.4). One driver for this requirement is the interest of customers in not depending on a single vendor. Other facets may include the extensibility, customizability, compatibility, or configurability of products. An example is the availability of a REST-based API that allows easy product integration into customer environments. Software architects are in charge of evaluating and meeting these requirements.

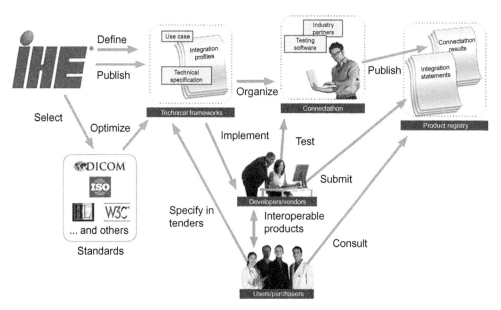

FIGURE 7.4

Health care modalities such as the MRI (magnetic resonance imaging) must undergo certification by the United States' FDA. In addition, they must adhere to standards such as IHE (Integrating the Healthcare Enterprise), DiCOM (Digital Imaging and Communication in Medicine) and HL/7 (Health Level 7).

7.11 **Project management**

The roles of software architects and project managers differ but complement each other. One key learning from projects is that these roles should be strictly separated. Only in very small projects nay an engineer wear both hats. If a software architect is also responsible for project management (Jones, 2010; Pries and Quigley, 2011; Whitaker, 2010), she cannot cover all software architecture-related responsibilities as well, at least not with the necessary depth. In such situations, either project management or software architecture will suffer, both of which may cause economic liabilities, for example, delay of development.

War Story: The project manager of a communication middleware system had to estimate the development efforts. She just reused the experiences from earlier projects for this purpose. However, all former products had been developed with C++, while the new product was supposed to be the first Java-based middleware. After the project started. it became clear that developers required competence ramp-up and that the work packages would take longer development time than expected.

The tight interaction between those roles respectively persons turned out to be one of the main success factors within Siemens. Architects need project management so that they can focus on the technical and economic aspects of software, while project managers are in charge of the logistics and planning aspects. Project managers need a close interaction with architects for making effort and cost estimates, for defining the project plan, for increasing the skill level of the staff, and for coping with problems in the project such as the delay of hardware development in an embedded systems environment. It is beneficial if software architects have some experience with project management, and, of course, if project managers have some experience in software engineering.

7.12 **Economic considerations in the development process**

7.12.1 **Requirements engineering**

In requirements engineering, architects interact with requirements engineers, customers (in solution organizations), and product managers (in product organizations) to support the definition of a system architecture (Berenbach and ebrary Inc., 2009; Broy and Rumpe, 1998; Chemuturi, 2013; Dorfman, 1994). Many of the activities are related to business aspects. KANO analysis and scenario diagrams are essential tools for this activity (see also Products—Definition and Development).

A very common challenge is the lack of a domain language for stakeholder communication. The same terminology may mean different things to different persons or roles, which often leads to wrong design decisions due to false interpretation of requirements. This problem typically becomes a critical economic factor when it remains untreated. Consequently, the establishment of a common language must be the first step in the requirements engineering phase. Domain languages range from informal glossaries to full-blown formal languages. They introduce a common understanding between stakeholders regarding the problem domain and the requirements. Domain analysis and domain-driven design (Evans, 2003) provide the basis for creating a domain language.

Another challenge arises from the *validation of the software requirements*. Is the quality of the requirements specification sufficient? For instance, are requirements consistent, unambiguous and complete? In other words, could they be an adequate basis for designing and implementing the system. Architects will also need to prove software feasibility. Is it possible to design and implement the system with reasonable time and budget, so that the result can meet the business goals? Requirements such as "product should use expensive DBMS system from vendor A" and "unit costs should not exceed X US-$" may be conflicting requirements that cannot be resolved. Architects must be aware of all such sensitivity and trade-off points in the architecture and inform management about problems.

War Story: In a large-scale product line development several business units were supposed to base their products on the same product line platform. The domain development team asked the two largest business units to provide their requirements and derived the reference architecture from these requirements. The first version of the platform failed because the other business units not involved in requirements analysis had different requirements with different priorities. Thus, they could not use the product line. Product line development had to be restarted.

To come up with reasonable decisions, a unique requirements prioritization is necessary. This prioritization captures the business value of requirements as well as technical complexity. If architects encounter conflicts in the specification such as trade-off points, they can take the prioritization as a base for their decisions. Of course, the prioritization must be sound. Sometimes there are requirements specifications in which high priority is assigned to almost all requirements. If this is the case, architects must address requirements engineering and ask for a finer-grained prioritization. A viable strategy for architects is to make assumptions about the prioritization, document them, and ask requirements engineering to provide feedback.

For quality attributes such as performance or modifiability, the usage of scenario diagrams and utility trees (see Figure 7.5) (Bass et al., 2013) helps in efficiently setting up a joint prioritization.

As Frederick P. Brooks has pointed out (Brooks, 2010), *in many cases it is not useful to perform architecture design and requirements engineering independently or by a fixed time sequence.* The reason for this is uncertainty. Initially, architects have insufficient understanding and knowledge of the requirements, while the stakeholders in charge of requirements have insufficient information about the feasibility and technical implications of their specification. An additional issue is that new technologies, services, or products may not be fully understood by project participants, which further increases uncertainty. From an economic viewpoint, this phase of uncertainty should be addressed by parallelizing and coordinating requirements specification and architecture design, at least at project start. The Twin Peaks model (Cleland-Huang et al., 2013) recommends and promotes such "parallelism." Prototypes and technology evaluations should be conducted in this phase, for example, the creation of prototypes that support assessment of technical and economic feasibility. If the organization enforces a strict waterfall model, requirements and architecture will be separately and sequentially conducted. All problems in the requirements specifications as well as insufficient technology knowledge will cause significant economic implications. The later a design problem is detected, the more expensive it is to solve it, if it is solvable at all.

A further deliverable of requirements engineering is the implementation and control of an IPR (intellectual property rights) strategy. Architects may even already identify and create patents in this phase.

Technical feasibility might be checked by implementing feasibility prototypes during the requirements engineering phase and architecture design. This helps rule out technologies that cannot meet technical and economic goals.

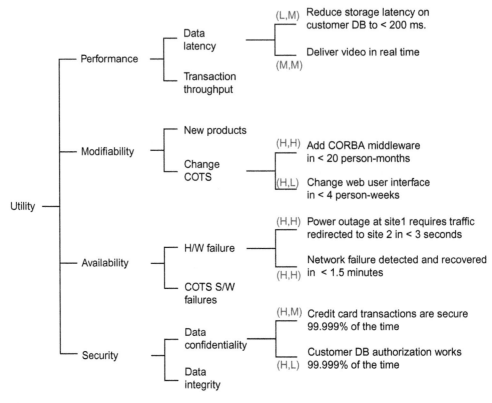

FIGURE 7.5

Utility trees are commonly used to prioritize quality attribute scenarios. Business decides on the business relevance of each scenario (left in tuple: High, Medium, Low), while development prioritizes according to development complexity (right in tuple: High, Medium, Low).

In some projects, delays emerged from the "uncertainty principle." Architects thought they needed a requirements specification where 100% of all requirements were fully specified in order to start with strategic design. Of course, all other information should be available as well. Although this completeness would never happen, architects were caught in an idle loop waiting for all information to flow in. Such behavior causes economic penalties, as it results in budget problems and time delays. Software architects should accept the idea that they live in a space of uncertainty— they won't be capable of creating a perfect design because requirements keep changing or growing in all projects. However, it is sufficient if at least the most important of the requirements are available at project start. Highly prioritized strategic requirements affect the architecture more than less important strategic or tactical requirements. Thus, it is possible to start with a sound but incomplete conceptual design that will be continuously refactored and refined during the project.

Together with test managers, architects will also participate in defining a (risk-based) test strategy during or after the requirements engineering phase. Without an adequate test strategy (Patton,

2005), testing activities may cover the wrong and less important things, while neglecting risky and important issues. The responsibility of testing (Veenendaal et al., 2006) is to provide sufficient information to architects and developers (and management) for efficient and successful quality control. With an appropriate test strategy in place, testing efforts can be minimized and focused on the risks. Testing activities such as integration testing also serve as a safety net for architects when they design the architecture. In addition, the overall test strategy includes a test exit strategy, which determines when the quality is considered high enough for product release.

7.12.2 Design and implementation

In the design phase (Bass et al., 2013) the main focus of architects is, of course, the architecture design itself. But additional activities have an economic impact, such as establishing the integration sequence and integration concepts (Summers, 2013), or setting up supplier agreements and reviewing development partnerships. These activities are fundamental for solution or product development in that errors in this phase mostly have a significant financial impact.

This is especially true for system development projects with various disciplines such as mechatronics, electronics, electrics, mechanics, and sometimes even including building construction (Blanchard, 2008)

War Story I: In an engineering project, the different disciplines were not synchronized because project management failed to take care of this responsibility, and lead system or software architects had not been established. The engineers at the construction site were forced to wait for deliveries from the development sites, and the development sites could not check for integration issues in an appropriate time frame. All this resulted in large delays that caused the customer to stop the project and to demand high penalty payments from the product organization. Eventually, even the product organization itself was closed.

War Story II: Architects responsible for the development of a credit card production system focused primarily on flexibility. The main objective of the project had been to quickly set up a configuration for banks ordering new credit cards. Eventually, the system was highly configurable, but it took experts several weeks to prepare the production. The system could not be refactored. Instead, a new development project had to be started from scratch.

Architects mainly deal with strategic design such as defining the technical architecture and defining the main architecture principles that should govern the implementation. They are also in charge of preventing architecture shift. Without establishing and enforcing such principles, the implementation will suffer from structural and operational quality issues as well as unnecessary efforts for reinventing the wheel multiple times. An example is the usage of different patterns or solutions to solve identical problems in the same problem context. Allowing multiple solution strategies for recurring problems produces systems that are hard to understand, assess, change, extend and maintain because reviewers, architects, and developers will need to deal with several approaches instead of one. For economic and technical reasons, the enforcement of software pattern usage and of quality indicators and architecture metrics should be mandatory in order to increase the overall quality.

It is mandatory that software architects relate all of their design or technology decisions to the business case as well as to business goals and business strategy. Each decision must have a concrete economic rationale. Otherwise, software engineers may create complex design pearls without economic value. As a consequence, the probability of accidental complexity will increase, which has a direct and negative impact on costs for maintenance, testing, bug tracking, or refactoring. In addition, oversophisticated designs may reduce the overall quality by making the architecture more complex than is necessary instead of following the KiSS principle (Keep it stupid simple). Hence, quality control should be a permanent activity of architects to detect and avoid design flaws early.

Suitable instruments for ensuring quality are the following:

- Architecture governance for continuous architecture enforcement
- Regular code, design, and architecture assessments
- Testing

Architecture and design are not constrained to construction-oriented activities, building feature after feature but also for early refactoring. At each development cycle, architects are supposed to analyze the system for possible architecture or implementation problems such as wrong design decisions, design errors, or problems with structural and operational quality properties. Especially in architecture and design, problems that are detected and eliminated early reduce costs, since architecture is the backbone of software systems and hence provides a high economic value.

Software architects not only design the architecture, but they are in charge of conducting regular qualitative and quantitative architecture assessments that might be based on Architecture Tradeoff Analysis Method (ATAM) or a company-internal method, for example, an experience-based approach. Quantitative methods comprise prototyping or benchmarking.

If risks are detected such as design flaws in strategic aspects, measures are derived for eliminating these problems. Architecture refactoring helps to systematically get rid of problems in the architecture design. If architecture deficiencies are neglected, the architecture may grow and grow, continuously introducing new artifacts and dependencies. In a later stage, solving architecture problems might become very expensive or even impossible because the sum of deficiencies often leads to design erosion. If an architecture component with flawed design gets further refined and extended, dependencies between the component and its environment increase. To remove such flaws would consequently lead to huge efforts because many parts of the architecture and implementation have to be changed. Tight coupling between architecture components negatively affects structural and operational qualities of the system, thus increasing maintenance costs and service costs. Even a sound architecture design may turn into a serious bottleneck, when it is changed or developed in an unsystematic and wrong way. This is a main issue for product lines and platforms on which not one but many products depend. Such problems may cause huge maintenance costs, especially when the system is supposed to run for many years or even decades, which is a common challenge in industries like railway control, trains, or power plants.

These are the reasons why architects are responsible for taking the right actions. They design the architecture, conduct regular architecture assessments, obtain testing information, and improve the architecture before continuing their design activities.

Design and technical debt denote critical issues in this context. Shortly before product release, architects should not refactor the architecture or implementation if possible. They need to defer modifications and improvements to the next development cycle. Very critical and hence unacceptable problems are the only exception to this rule. However, a development organization increases design debt and technical debt whenever it postpones refactoring activities. It is essential that an organization keeps track of design and technical debt, that is, by managing a database with unresolved architecture problems and their criticality and priority. When the implementation of the next release starts, architects must resolve critical issues first before further extending the architecture. Design debt must be paid soon, not ignored.

7.13 Implementation and integration

In the implementation and integration phase, architects need to frequently join the development teams to prevent design problems and to obtain valuable feedback. If possible, projects must follow the "architect always implements" mantra to ensure that architects are actively involved in implementation and architecture enforcement activities. They review the fine-grained design and its conformance to design guidelines, check the deliveries of external suppliers, establish an open-source strategy, and control software integration. All these responsibilities include economic considerations such as cost estimations, or validating the fulfillment of business goals. By preventing drift between architecture and design, architects can control implementation and integration costs.

War Story: In a project for managing prepaid mobile phone cards, the architects created a "beautiful" architecture design document that they provided to the development teams. One of the key design principles the architects used was strict layering. When implementation was completed, it turned out that each change of the database schemas led to a crash of the presentation clients. In an architecture review, the UI client architect confessed that he had intentionally ignored the strict layering and accessed the lower layers from the client; his management had told him to do so for performance reasons. This resulted in a direct dependency between persistence layer and UI layer and caused huge restructuring costs. Other developers told us that they just ignored the details of the architecture document.

After roll-out, the responsibilities of architects do not end. They must continuously manage the architecture, monitor quality indicators and metrics, and identify needs for refactoring, restructuring, or re-implementing.

7.14 Development process for architecture design

On one hand, using a strict waterfall model in design is neither effective nor efficient, as the previous sections illustrate, because they often turn later modifications into high economic risks.. On the other hand, projects might require models such as the V-Model, because of customer requirements, which is very common in government projects, safety-critical system development, and infrastructure projects. In the last-named case, an iterative waterfall model is recommendable which allows iterating through phases and returning to earlier development phases whenever required.

War Story: For the development of an innovative control system, the organization strictly followed the V-Model. However, during development, the requirements specification used to change frequently. In addition, unexpected issues were encountered upon implementation of some innovative new patterns and algorithms. Late changes caused substantial modification efforts. Most of the errors and change requests emerged only after release of the first product version. Those modifications led to an overly complex architecture and other indicators for design erosion.

As illustrated in figure 7.6, architects should use an agile model for their design activities. In each increment they focus on one or a few use cases or scenarios, starting with the ones of highest priority. The existing base-line architecture keeps growing with each architecture extension or refinement. After the design activity, architects invite stakeholders and other architects to conduct an assessment of the current state of the base-line architecture (Clements et al., 2001). These reviews help identify design flaws, bugs, inefficient design decisions, quality defects, and other issues. Before continuing with fine design or the next increment, the detected issues are prioritized and, if possible, eliminated by architecture refactoring. Some refactoring necessities can be postponed for economic reasons to the next increments if the issues are less critical and require substantial rework shortly before important events such as product release. However, all postponed issues should be documented as design debt (Sterling, 2010) that must be paid back later in the project.

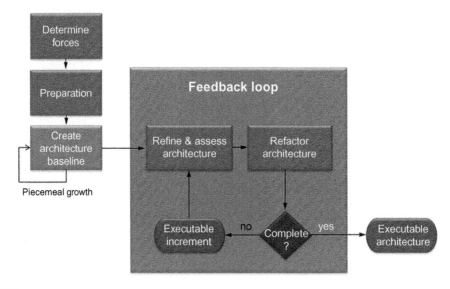

FIGURE 7.6

Architecture creation should follow a feedback loop that includes not only architecture refinement, but also architecture assessments and refactoring activities.

7.15 Product line organizations and re-use

Economic considerations are particularly essential in the context of developing and evolving product families and platforms. While evolution of a single product is typically constrained to the product itself, the evolution of a product line platform (see Figure 7.7) directly affects all members of the product family. One wrong decision harms all family members. In a product line organization, additional efforts are required to synchronize platform development with product development in a seamless and effective way (Bosch, 2000; Linden, et al., 2007; Pohl et al., 2005; Weiss and Lai,

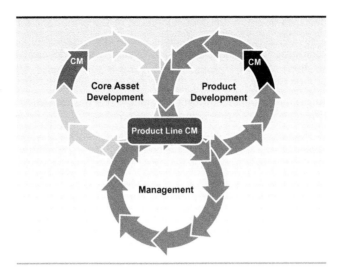

FIGURE 7.7

Product line engineering requires the management of multiple software development activities, in particular those for creating the product line assets common for all products as well as the individual products.

© *Software Engineering Institute at Carnegie-Mellon University. Used with permission.*

1999). Architects of products and the product line platform, together with business-oriented stake-holders, should jointly define the product line roadmap. One of the many challenges is the decision of whether a new asset should be integrated in the product line itself or provided by the minority of product organizations that require the asset. It is in the responsibility of architects to analyze all alternatives and rate their impact on complexity, costs, and sustainability.

Even more critical, architects are involved in the initial decision of whether a product line approach is feasible from a technical and an economic viewpoint. For this purpose, the organization should conduct a commonality/variability analysis (Authors, 2013) and, if required, further activities of domain engineering and application engineering such as constructing a conceptual architecture. If the overlap of various one-off products is significant in terms of commonalities and if, at the same time, variability is not too complex to implement, then a product line may turn out to be the best economic choice. In a joint activity, software architects and management then derive an effort and cost estimation from the preceding C/V analysis to calculate the return on investment of the software line approach compared to the current approach. For instance, one fundamental question is: How many products or product releases are needed until the expected revenues cover the additional estimated costs of a product line?

Success Story: At Siemens a product line platform called syngo was developed in the 1990s as a base for all modalities such as computed tomography (CT), magnetic resonance tomography (MRT), ultrasound, angiography, and positron emission tomography (PET). Previously, each modality used its own implementation. Thus, the various development teams had developed their own version of the same functionality. Some of the issues with this approach were that modalities could not connect with each other, and that customers complained about the different UIs offered for the different products. In addition, the redevelopment of the same functionality proved to be a great time and cost issue. By establishing a domain architecture organization, they came up with their common syngo platform, which made Siemens a leading vendor for health care products.

But also in organizations without a product line approach a more basic, albeit *systematic reuse strategy* (Dusink et al., 1991), helps in saving costs. Re-using functionality that would otherwise be implemented many times can become a strategic advantage. Not only software might be reused, but also design solutions for recurring problems that are documented as software patterns (Buschmann et al., 1996) or design tactics (Bass et al., 2013). In addition to pattern catalogs and systems for common problems, organizations may document and apply domain-specific patterns (Fowler, 1996) or use a DSL (domain-specific language) (Voelter, 2013) for generating at least parts of the implementation (Parr, 2010). Architects are responsible for fostering reuse whenever it makes sense, but also for figuring out whether the benefits of reusing a particular component outweigh the liabilities (e.g., by conducting a cost-benefit analysis). It requires some efforts to make components usable and also reusable. These efforts might be substantial—for example, when extracting a reusable functionality from an existing system that was not built with reusability in mind. Another question is who should be responsible for maintaining reusable functionality. If this question remains unanswered, reuse will not work in an economic way. In product line organizations, a clear separation between the domain engineering organization and the various product organizations is introduced to foster systematic reuse.

7.16 Embedded systems development

In business units that develop embedded systems, some additional challenges must be addressed by systems and software architects (Balarin, 1997; Domeika & Books24 × 7 Inc., 2008; Gupta, 1995). One general issue we observed is that in the area of embedded systems development the BoM (bill of material) (Haik and Shahin, 2011) and the unit costs can become economic obstacles for software engineering. If the product represents a mass product, then each economic decision regarding hardware and unit costs can also affect software development.

War Story: The decision to reduce the amount of memory in a car entertainment system forced software developers to introduce compression algorithms. However, the usage of these algorithms implied unacceptable performance penalties. A possible solution was to use a faster CPU, but then the unit costs would have been much higher than in the original design, that is, the design without memory reduction. Key learning:saving hardware costs may affect the efforts of software development as well as software architecture.

Higher customer expectations denote a further challenge in embedded systems development. When using embedded systems, customers will not accept large response or start-up times or instabilities of the system. Thus, an extended focus on quality control is inevitable, not only for technical but also for economic reasons. This includes effective Q&A and testing, in addition to frequent code and design reviews as well as regular quantitative and qualitative architecture assessments.

For mobile systems that are distributed with thousands of units across the planet, tracking down software defects, patches, and their reasons is difficult. On one hand, over the air or online updates can be an appropriate solution for quick and easy problem fixes, but on the other hand, these systems might contain different hardware and software versions or have a different patch state. (Software and system-) architects are responsible for coming up with an economic update concept that is reasonable and acceptable for the service organization and for customers.

In terms of development processes, there are additional phases relevant for systems engineering, for example, the production phase, the commissioning phase, and the maintenance and service phase. Extra requirements for software emerge in these phases from hardware and system infrastructure properties. For example, during assembly of a stepper motor, lubricant is applied as a lump on the winding. In order to distribute it evenly, the motor must be driven full cycles back and forth several times, slowly so as to not jerk the lubricant away. This "slow mode" is only needed when first used and never again. In production, it is necessary to move gauges to defined positions, turn on all light-emitting diodes, and display test patterns for automated "calibration" of gauges, especially gas and speed.

Systems and software architects have to know and consider such efforts. Ignoring these requirements leads to unplanned efforts and time delays (Maier, 2009). Regular communication and cooperation with systems engineers are essential to be prepared for utility software requirements.

Another common property of embedded systems development projects stems from the necessity to integrate different disciplines (see Figure 7.8) such as hardware, firmware, and software. Software development typically comprises significantly more development cycles than hardware development. Thus, integration of the individual artifacts to a complete product is one of the most critical steps. These integration steps need to be planned in advance with the help of system and software architects. Otherwise, integration tests cannot be executed at predefined milestones. Delay of one discipline causes other disciplines to remain idle due to their mutual (complex)

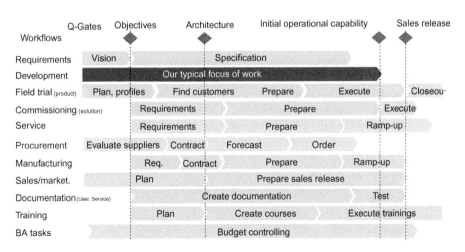

FIGURE 7.8

In systems engineering, multiple disciplines cooperate, for example, electronics and software development. Software development for embedded systems must be integrated into the systems engineering context such as synchronizing and integrating developments at quality gates.

dependencies, which in turn increases costs. Thus, project management and architects must thoroughly plan these milestones and continuously control progress. As the development cycles are different and integration tests occur less often, hardware and software integration requires all disciplines to deliver the best possible quality (Duvall et al., 2007).

A number of challenges present themselves when two low-quality artifacts are combined in a big bang approach. To reduce quality problems, software development adds more tooling to compensate for the slower hardware development. One common tool is model-based simulation of the target hardware, which enables software testing in the absence of hardware. In some industries automotive tools such as MATLAB/SimuLink help create simulations (Klee and Allen, 2011). With this approach the problem of different development cycles can be addressed. There is a caveat, however. Sometimes simulation can be more expensive than the delays between disciplines. And, of course, a simulator can only model the hardware but is not a full surrogate. In certain scenarios, simulation might behave differently than the real-world system, especially when timing is subtle and critical. Hence, simulators are very helpful but cannot substitute testing with the real target hardware. The rule here is to test on the target hardware as soon as possible.

7.17 Communication

As the chapter illustrated, communication is one of the most essential prerequisites for the economic success of software development. Alistair Cockburn's observation, "software engineering is a collaborative game" (Cockburn, 2006), is exactly what project experiences show. Architects need to communicate frequently and effectively with other stakeholders. They do not present the only communication hub, but they have an important role (see Figure 7.9).

In detail, architects communicate with

- systems architects to create a sustainable system architecture as well as to coordinate software development and system integration with other disciplines.
- software developers to enforce the architectural vision, obtain feedback, and prevent a drift between architecture and implementation.
- test managers to help create an appropriate test strategy and test plans.
- requirements engineers (i.e., the persons in charge of requirements engineering) to understand the requirements and ensure the quality of the requirements specification as a basis for architecture development. These stakeholders include requirements engineers, product (life-cycle) managers, and customers.
- project managers to achieve proper cost and effort estimations as well as to support project planning.
- heads of R&D to understand the business strategy and business goals of the organization.

Architects spend up to 40% of their time for communication, at least in large projects. It is obvious that communication must be effective. Tom DeMarco (DeMarco and Lister, 1999) once consulted two printer companies in the United States about how to improve their productivity. As it turned out, the company with fewer meetings and better meeting culture was much more productive than its meeting-addicted competitor. This is what industry projects show as well. Constant creation

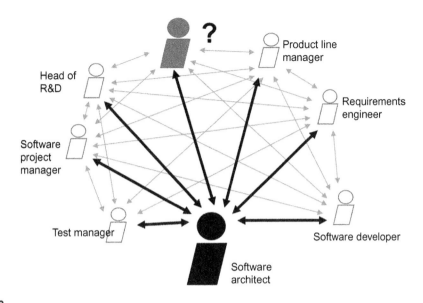

FIGURE 7.9

Architects need to interact with many other roles in a project to develop an economic solution. The figure shows product organizations as an example. In solution organizations, other roles such as the customer are essential.

of new task forces, frequent mandatory and long-lasting meetings without agenda and goals, combined with other unplanned ad-hoc activities, significantly reduce productivity. E-mail-centric communication is mostly very ineffective, especially if the amount of mail exceeds the limits persons can handle. Tom DeMarco calls this kind of mail overload "Corporate Spam." In turn, face-to-face communication is often the only effective option.

It is the responsibility of architects to demand but also to apply effective communication patterns. If they spend more than 40 to 50% of their time on communication, this might be an indication either of ineffective personal communication habits or of organizational communication overload. In the latter case, architects should escalate to management, while in the former case they should obtain feedback from colleagues, reflect, and then change and improve their habits.

7.18 Conclusions

In large industry companies such as Siemens, more than 50% of revenues depend on software. Since software architecture builds the backbone of each software system, the business value of software architecture represents a substantial economic and strategic factor. Conversely, problems in software architecture design lead to increased development costs. Software architects must understand and consider the economic impact of their design decisions, instead of focusing merely on technical aspects. They should be well educated, experienced and trained in software architecture as well as other related aspects such as business and strategy, quality assurance, requirements engineering, or soft skills.

Siemens has established an internal (Senior) Software Architect Certification curriculum to address this problem. The curriculum intends to increase the economic awareness and responsibility of software architects and to foster networking between architects and business units. It was built on experiences from success stories and war stories in former projects. In the last five years, the CEOs of various Siemens businesses have returned positive feedback regarding the actual value of the curriculum. We were told that senior architects began to intensively participate in business, product, and strategy planning. They closely follow the guidelines that were illustrated in this chapter to relate business goals and business plans with design decisions. They feel responsible for requirements engineering and testing as well because both activities establish the fundamentals for economic and sustainable design. It has become obvious that software architects have a huge impact on economic aspects, especially when so many embedded products depend on software. Perhaps Grady Booch perfectly explains the economic value of software architecture when he states: "Software architecture is about everything that is costly to change".

References

Architects, A.I.O., 2008. The Architect's Handbook of Professional Practice. fourteenth ed. Wiley, Hoboken, NJ.

Authors, V., 2013. Systems and Software Variability Management: Concepts, Tools and Experiences. Springer, New York.

Balarin, F., 1997. Hardware-Software Co-Design of Embedded Systems: The POLIS Approach. Kluwer Academic Publishers, Boston.

Bass, L., Clements, P., Kazman, R., 2013. Software Architecture in Practice. third ed. Addison-Wesley, Upper Saddle River, NJ.

Berenbach, B., Ebrary Inc., 2009. Software and systems requirements engineering in practice. Retrieved from <http://site.ebrary.com/lib/alltitles/docDetail.action?docID=10286222>.

Blanchard, B.S., 2008. *System Engineering Management* (Wiley Series in Systems Engineering and Management). Wiley, Hoboken, NJ.

Blind, K., Edler, J., Friedewald, M., 2005. Software Patents: Economic Impacts and Policy Implications. Edward Elgar, Cheltenham, UK.

Boehm, B., Abts, C., Brown, A.W., Chulani, S., Clark, B.K., Horowitz, E., et al., 2000. Software Cost Estimation with Cocomo II. Prentice Hall, New Jersey, USA.

Bosch, J., 2000. Design and Use of Software Architectures: Adopting and Evolving a Product-line Approach. Addison-Wesley, Reading, MA.

Brooks, F.P., 2010. The Design of Design: Essays from a Computer Scientist. Addison-Wesley, Upper Saddle River, NJ.

Broy, M., Rumpe, B., 1998. Requirements Targeting Software and Systems Engineering International Workshop RTSE '97, Bernried, Germany, October 12−14, 1997 Lecture Notes in Computer Science 1526. Retrieved from <http://dx.doi.org/10.1007/b71630>.

Buschmann, F., Meunier, R., Rohner, H., Sommerlad, P., Stal, M., 1996. Pattern-Oriented Software Architecture. Volume 1: A System of Patterns. Wiley, New York.

Chemuturi, M., 2013. Requirements Engineering and Management for Software Development Projects. Retrieved from <http://site.ebrary.com/lib/alltitles/docDetail.action?docID=10607533>.

Cleland-Huang, J., Mirakhorli, M., Supakkul, S., Hanmer, R.S., 2013. The Twin Peaks of Requirements and Architecture. IEEE (IEEE Software Magazine), Available from http://dx.doi.org/10.1109/MS.2013.39.

Clements, P., Kazman, R., Klein, M., 2001. Evaluating Software Architectures: Methods and Case Studies. Addison-Wesley Professional, Reading, MA.

Cockburn, A., 2006. Agile Software Development: The Cooperative Game. second ed. Addison-Wesley Professional, Reading, MA.

DeMarco, T., Lister, T., 1999. Peopleware: Productive Projects and Teams, second ed. Dorset House, New York, USA.

Domeika, M., Books24x7 Inc., 2008. Software development for embedded multi-core systems a practical guide using embedded Intel architecture. Newnes; 1st edition Boston, USA.

Dorfman, M., 1994. Standards, Guidelines, and Examples on System and Software Requirements Engineering. IEEE Computer Society Press, Los Alamitos, CA.

Dusink, L., Hall, P.A.V., British Computer Society, 1991. Software re-use, Utrecht 1989: Proceedings of the Software Re-use Workshop, November 23−24, 1989. Springer-Verlag, Utrecht, The Netherlands. London.

Duvall, P.M., Matyas, S., Glover, A., 2007. Continuous Integration: Improving Software Quality and Reducing Risk. Addison-Wesley Professional, Reading, MA.

Evans, E., 2003. Domain-Driven Design: Tackling Complexity in the Heart of Software. Addison-Wesley Professional, Reading, MA.

Fowler, M., 1996. Analysis Patterns: Reusable Object Models. Addison-Wesley Professional, Reading, MA.

Geracie, G., 2010. Take Charge Product Management: Take Charge of Your Product Management Development; Tips, Tactics, and Tools to Increase Your Effectiveness as a Product Manager. Actuation Press, Santa Clara, CA, USA.

Gupta, R.K., 1995. Co-synthesis of Hardware and Software for Digital Embedded Systems. Kluwer Academic Publishers, Boston.

Hahn, R.W., 2005. Intellectual Property Rights in Frontier Industries: Software and Biotechnology. AEI Press, Washington, DC.

Haik, Y., Shahin, T.M.M., 2011. Engineering Design Process. second ed. Cengage Learning, Stamford, CT.

Hall, B.H., MacGarvie, M., National Bureau of Economic Research, 2006. The private value of software patents NBER working paper series working paper 12195. Retrieved from <http://papers.nber.org/papers/w12195>.

Jones, C., 2010. Software Engineering Best Practices: Lessons from Successful Projects in the Top Companies. McGraw-Hill, New York.

Klee, H., Allen, R., 2011. Simulation of Dynamic Systems with MATLAB and Simulink. second ed. CRC Press, Boca Raton, FL.

Knight, H.J., 2013. Patent Strategy for Researchers and Research Managers. Wiley, Hoboken, NJ.

Lindberg, V., 2008. Intellectual Property and Open Source. O'Reilly, Sebastopol, CA.

Linden, F.V.D., Schmid, K., Rommes, E., 2007. Software Product Lines in Action : The Best Industrial Practice in Product Line Engineering. Springer, New York.

Lundberg, S.W., Durant, S.C., McCrackin, A.M., American Intellectual Property Law Association, 2011. Electronic and Software Patents: Law and Practice. third ed. Bureau of National Affairs, Arlington, VA.

Maier, M.W., 2009. The Art of Systems Architecting. third ed. CRC Press, Boca Raton, FL (Systems Engineering).

Matheson, D.M.J.E., 1997. The Smart Organization: Creating Value Through Strategic R&D. Harvard Business Review Press, Boston, MA, USA.

McGrath, M., 2000. Product Strategy for High Technology Companies. McGraw-Hill, New York.

Mironov, R., 2008. The Art of Product Management: Lessons from a Silicon Valley Innovator. BookSurge Publishing, Charleston, SC, USA.

Moehrle, M., Isenmann, R., Phaal, R., 2013. Technology Roadmapping for Strategy and Innovation: Charting the Route to Success. Springer, New York.

Nord, R., Barbacci, M.R., Clements, P.C., Kazman, R., Klein, M.H., Tomayko, J.E., 2013. Integrating the Architecture Tradeoff Analysis Method (ATAM) with the Cost Benefit Analysis Method (CBAM). Software Engineering Institute Pittsburgh, PA, USA.

Noriaki, S., Tsuji, S., Seraku, N., Takerhashi, F., 1984. Attractive Quality and Must-Be Quality, in: Hinshitsu Quality. The Journal of the Japanese Society for Quality Control Vol. 14 (No. 2), S39–S48.

Parr, T., 2010. Language Implementation Patterns: Create Your Own Domain-Specific and General Programming Languages (Pragmatic Programmers). Pragmatic Bookshelf, Frisco, TX, Raleigh, NC.

Patton, R., 2005. Software Testing. second ed. Sams Publishing, Indianapolis, IN, USA.

Paulisch, F., Zimmerer, P., 2010, May 2–8. A role-based qualification and certification program for software architects: An experience report from Siemens Paper presented at the Software Engineering, 2010 ACM/IEEE 32nd International Conference on Software Engineering.

Pohl, K., Böckle, G.N., Linden, F.V.D., 2005. Software Product Line Engineering : Foundations, Principles, and Techniques. first ed. Springer, New York.

Pries, K.H., Quigley, J.M., 2011. Scrum Project Management. CRC Press, Boca Raton, FL.

Rosenberg, M.D., Apley, R.J., 2012. Business Method and Software Patents: A Practical Guide. Oxford University Press, Oxford, UK.

Sterling, C., 2010. Managing Software Debt: Building for Inevitable Change (Agile Software Development Series). Addison-Wesley Professional, Reading, MA.

Stobbs, G.A., Kluwer Law International (Firm), 2008. Software Patents Worldwide. Wolters KluwerFirm), 2008, Alphen aan den Rijn, The Netherlands, Frederick, MD, Sold and distributed in North, Central, and South America by Aspen Publishers.

Summers, B.L., 2013. Effective methods for software and systems integration (p. 1 online resource (xix, 163 p.)). Retrieved from <http://www.crcnetbase.com/isbn/978-1-4398-7662-6>.

Veenendaal, I.P., Bob van de, B., Dennis, J., Erik, V., 2006. Successful Test Management: An Integral Approach. Springer, New York.

Voelter, M., 2013. DSL Engineering: Designing, Implementing and Using Domain-Specific Languages. CreateSpace Independent Publishing Platform, Hamburg, Germany.

Weiss, D.M., Lai, C.T.R., 1999. Software Product-Line Engineering : A Family-based Software Development Process. Addison-Wesley, Reading, MA.

Whitaker, K., 2010. Principles of Software Development Leadership: Applying Project Management Principles to Agile Software Development Leadership. Charles River Media/Course Technology, Cengage Learning, Boston, MA.

wikipedia.org. SWOT Analysis. from <http://en.wikipedia.org/wiki/SWOT_analysis>.

Managing Architectural Economics

Toward Collaborative Software Engineering Leveraging the Crowd

Benjamin Satzger[1], Rostyslav Zabolotnyi[1], Schahram Dustdar[1], Stefan Wild[2], Martin Gaedke[2], Steffen Göbel[3], and Tobias Nestler[3]

[1]*Vienna University of Technology, Vienna, Austria*
[2]*Technische Universität Chemnitz, Chemnitz, Germany*
[3]*SAP AG, Dresden, Germany*

8.1 Introduction

Short, unpredictable business cycles and fluctuations, rapidly emerging technologies and trends, globalization, and the global interconnectedness provided by the Internet have increased the world's economical clock speed and competition among companies. IT has always been a spearhead industry and is influenced by changing circumstances sooner than other industries. Competition in software engineering is high because of low market-entry barriers. IT companies, start-ups, and freelancers are competing against each other for market share. The professional development of software requires technology expertise and knowledge about the application domain, and must be inexpensive and agile to bring the company in a strong position. As technologies evolve constantly and new trends appear in very short time frames, the knowledge and competence of development teams have to be kept up to date accordingly. Time-consuming staffing periods causing long development cycles are not acceptable. However, many applications must follow strict guidelines to ensure both security and high quality.

In the event specific competences are not available within a team, external knowledge has to be included. The hiring of new employees with the right skill set is the traditional instrument to enhance the development unit's competence and capacity. However, it is too slow and inflexible for modern rapidly developed projects, as traditional hiring binds additional resources for assessing the job applicants. Not only Human Resources personnel are involved, but also domain experts to test the technical know-how of job applications. All of this is a rather time-consuming process. Recent developments in IT, like the rise of social networks, Cloud computing, global software development, and the emergence of crowdsourcing services, promise to help companies to cope with the new requirements they are facing. Social networks can be leveraged to support people in loosely coupled and open team structures to efficiently collaborate; Web-based crowdsourcing allows outsourcing tasks by broadcasting to a large network of people, the crowd, via an open call.

The IT industry giants also are considering this trend; for example, Microsoft outsources key parts of its IT operations for cost minimization and business simplification (Computerworld, 2012).

According to an internal strategy document that leaked out in early 2012, IBM plans to employ a radically new business model (Spiegel, 2012). It involves letting the company run by a small number of core workers. A dedicated Web-based platform is used to attract specialists and to create a virtual "cloud" of contributors. Similar to Cloud computing, where computing power is provided on demand, IBM's people Cloud would allow leveraging a flexible, scalable workforce.

However, usage of external workers entails new challenges compared to classical in-house software development. The distributed, dynamic nature of the crowd has to be considered in the whole software development process. As crowd-conducted and agile software projects share some common characteristics such as focusing on individuals (Beck, 2001), we argue that success factors in agile software projects (Chow and Cao, 2008)—namely, project, organizational, people, process, and technical factors—are also significant in crowd-conducted ones. Solving the following questions is a key to enabling professional software development conducted by a flexible workforce, as described above:

1. How to manage and organize software projects that are conducted, at least in part, by the crowd?

   A new management methodology must be developed with support to leverage the collective intelligence of the crowd and, at the same time, assure quality. It allows monitoring and guiding agile crowd development teams. Involved crowd members are able to discuss the goal of their task with the team and are integrated in planning the current development tact. Ongoing development activities are observable, which allows product owners to control and guide the distributed, remote software development process.

2. How to create virtual teams consisting of suitable experts and delegate tasks (semi-) automatically?

   Building and managing a platform that helps companies maintain a flexible workforce is of paramount importance for leveraging the crowd in software development. Worker profiles based on their interests and observed performance/behavior in past projects are important for making informed decisions regarding quality assurance and team creation. The platform must enable and assist project managers to map tasks to suitable developers or virtual teams, which may be established on demand. Reliable workers providing good quality need to be fairly rewarded, to feel gratified and motivated (Ramlall, 2004; Bruce et al., 1999). It is important not only to find suitable workers/teams for tasks and to provide the customer with satisfying quality, but also to maintain a motivated base of IT experts and provide stimulus for learning required, but underrepresented, skills. Only a recurring, satisfied crowd staff is able to ensure high long-term quality and to avoid thebrain drain of high potential crowd developers or affected in-house software developers.

3. How to improve cooperation of developers within loosely coupled teams?

   Distributed development is already a reality in several industries. Within large IT companies, today development teams are often distributed (DiMicco et al., 2008; Damian et al., 2007; Sengupta et al., 2006; Rodriguez et al., 2010). Management can be located in one country while the main development workforce is spread over several locations. Communication barriers, cultural differences, and different time zones hinder efficient collaboration and teamwork. Furthermore, keeping track and understanding what developers have produced becomes complicated if they are located in different offices. Team members have to take over code written by others or start a new project by reusing existing artifacts from other developers. Problems grow in projects that forward tasks to external developers and freelancers, especially if they do not know each other.

Today, crowdsourcing platforms and Internet-based tools for collaborative working are available, and some popular software is being developed based only on a remote workforce. In this work we investigate current solutions, their limitations, and point to new developments that help to realize crowd-enabled software engineering.

8.2 State of the art

Software engineering involves quite a number of people in various roles (Carmel and Agarwal, 2001). Many circumstances influence the way developers create the components of the software. If the whole team is at the same location, the collaboration is not very difficult to organize (Noll et al., 2010). Nonetheless, more and more software development teams are distributed all over the world. In particular, open-source communities are loosely coupled and need a platform to organize their workflows and the entire development process (da Silva et al., 2010; Koch, 2009; Robles and Gonzalez-Barahona, 2006).

A couple of platforms are established and used by IT experts for global software development (Lanubile et al., 2010; Dabbish et al., 2012). On the one hand, several cloud platforms are focused on open-source software, for instance, SourceForge (SourceForge, 2012) or BerliOS (BerliOS, 2012). On the other hand, platforms such as GitHub (GitHub, 2012) or Assembla (The Next Generation, 2012) support private projects as well (Walsh, 2009). SourceForge provides tools such as version control systems for source code, a bug tracker, a wiki system, forums, and an infrastructure for downloads. BerliOS uses a similar approach but also takes also different interest groups in the area of open-source software into account. Their aim is to fulfill a neutral mediator function. GitHub has a more social-driven approach with activity streams and additional visualization features to show the activities of the community. Assembla goes even further and integrates project management tools, agile development techniques, and scrum boards (Assembla, Kanban/Scrum Task Board, 2012).

In addition to platforms that focus on software development, a couple of generic systems simplify collaboration and are used in distributed software development. Social networks play an important role for Internet society and are actively used for advertising and business activities (Bosari, 2012). Even though social networks usually are not designed for distributed software development, they still are actively used for communication (Madey et al., 2002). Web-based office suites such as Google Docs (Google, 2012), the Zoho office suite (Zoho, 2012), Adobe Buzzword (Adobe, 2012) or Microsoft Office 365 (Microsoft, Microsoft Office, 2012) are replacing more and more classical document flows and provide concurrent, distributed editing. Another interesting example is Apache Wave (formerly Google Wave) (Apache, Apache Wave, 2012): In 2009 it was announced as novel social collaboration portal, but it did not gain much popularity. However, the wave idea received positive feedback in business and development environments, and is being used (Fidelman, 2010) even though Google discontinued the original project.

One of the most famous software development projects, built by a community, is Linux. Instead of assigning particular people to do different parts of the software development, anyone who wants to add or change any part of the software is able to do so (Malone et al., 2010). It is common that the crowd not only develops, but also decides about new features to add and when they are ready for integration. Sometimes, however, a project coordinator or a team of core developers makes this decision (Leo Kelion, 2012).

Today, some steps of development can already be explicitly crowdsourced to specific platforms. Crowdsourcing design portals (99designs, 2012) allow leveraging the crowd to retrieve UI design concepts. Particular coding tasks can also be crowdsourced. Sites such as TopCoder (TopCoder, 2012) conduct challenges that developers try to solve in code. Software testing is another sphere where crowdsourcing is very beneficial and efficient (uTest, 2012): Crowdsourcing allows testing applications or systems in different operation system configurations, different usage plans, and different types of users, involving many people with low effort. Additionally, virtually any tasks can be submitted to generic crowdsourcing platforms—for example, Mechanical Turk (Amazon, 2012) which Amazon Web Services provides as part of their cloud computing platform. However, these platforms do not consider complex tasks,such as software development, or collaborative task processing.

Service-oriented architecture (SOA) and, in particular, web services that enable cloud computing play a fundamental role in supporting flexible, cross-enterprise collaboration scenarios. In addition, several standards, specifications, and models render web services a convenient foundation for designing and deploying, but also monitoring and adapting dynamic service-oriented environments. For example, the Human-Provided Services (HPS) model (Dustdar and Bhattacharya, 2011) enhances the traditional SOA-based systems by enabling people to provide services with the very same technology used by implementations of traditional software-based services. An HPS interface allows humans to define and provide their services in a transparent way. Across this particular interface, they are able to participate in ad hoc as well as process-centric collaborations. Specifications such as WS-HumanTask (Agrawal et al., 2007) and BPEL4 People (Kloppmann et al., 2005), and additional extensions (e.g., (Schall et al., 2012), have been defined to address the lack of human interactions in service-oriented businesses.

All these tools and concepts pave the way for a global software development with distributed teams and demonstrate how to build a piece of software within a connected community. They simplify and improve distributed project development. However, there is no consistent solution integrating project management, crowd management, and collaboration support for general software development projects. In the next section we sketch a scenario to demonstrate the opportunities such an integrated approach would have to offer.

8.3 Benefits of software engineering from crowdsourcing

While the platforms and approaches mentioned above provide a good starting point, an automated environment for complex software engineering projects leveraging the crowd is still far in the future. An intelligent marketplace for development tasks is needed that binds social web technologies to existing development and project management platforms in order to foster a seamless crowd-enabled software engineering process. It supports all kinds of software development tasks (e.g., design, program, test, maintain) and incentive mechanisms to engage, motivate, and honor software developers to work on available tasks. Thus, companies are able to leverage the collective intelligence of developers from all over the world (external) or within large IT departments (internal) by platform-provided delegation mechanisms that are able to (semi-) automatically map tasks to solution capabilities, ranging from single individuals to the crowd. Developers and further stakeholders are supported to jointly work on open issues or unsolved problems, follow activities of

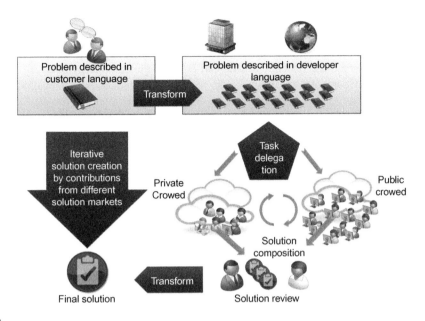

FIGURE 8.1

A crowd-enabled software development environment.

others, and share development results using communication paradigms known from social networks. Appropriate management instruments are provided to involve crowd members in ongoing development processes, to monitor their development progress, and to establish adequate quality assurance mechanisms for the integration of externally developed software fragments.

Figure 8.1 presents a scenario that exemplifies how crowd-enabled software engineering supports seamless integration of the crowd in the development process:

- **Domain-specific problem description:** A customer requests a solution to a problem via the crowd marketplace. Therefore, he or she needs to formalize the problem using a task-specification language, a nontechnical language to specify software development tasks, and their functional and nonfunctional properties. The project manager of an interested IT company gets in touch with the customer to specify the problem description further. Tools help to collaboratively define the requirements and the scope of the software.
- **Software architecture and development task definition:** The project manager translates the customer problem into a list of development tasks for functional and nonfunctional requirements and starts a new project. The software must be split up into components and services that need to be developed. Each of these components and services has a description that is typically quite informal at the beginning and will be refined into more formal definitions (e.g., interface descriptions) over time.
- **Task delegation:** Development tasks and related component and service definitions are the starting point for breaking work down into smaller pieces or tasks, which are then submitted via the crowd marketplace to a private or public crowd. The private crowd consists of employees,

organized or classified by organizational rules, while the public crowd consists of people outside the company, for example, specialized small companies or people in domain-specific communities, such as developers and testers on programming language-dedicated networks. Experts who understand the system and who can estimate the complexity of a task and its required prior knowledge and expertise should perform task creation and delegation. If a task requires deep background knowledge, it can be delegated to the internal crowd or to a person with a high level of expertise. If some required modules are highly interconnected, they can be offered as a combined task to a single person.

Based on the task and its constraints, different incentives are applied to motivate people to start creating a solution to the given problem. Tasks contain a description of work and of task execution environment (such as compiler, editor, testing software), criteria for testing the successful implementation of a solution, and general aspects regarding the task (e.g., milestones, due dates, rewards). It is possible that different people worldwide will compete on the same task, and the best solution wins; the discovery of people suitable for a task is performed by the platform.

In complex environments it is vital to consider the worker's expertise for task delegation. Lacking domain knowledge of software developers who are new to an area is a major source of misunderstandings and bugs in a traditional development and might be more pronounced in a crowd-sourced development. This problem is mitigated by deep integration of testing and by ensuring that developed code is actually working correctly. Such software testing results and votes of reviewers may provide feedback used by the platform to better estimate the capabilities of its members.

- **Iterative and collaborative software development:** Individual components and the resulting final solutions are developed in an iterative and evolutionary way, allowing early feedback from the customer regarding different stages of development. A notification engine informs developers about changes done by other developers and thus improves awareness and collaboration. Activity feeds, user-defined filters, and integrated development environment (IDE) integration allow developers to better understand the environment of their components and to monitor development progress in the context of such highly distributed projects. For example, developers can follow certain Java classes to get notification of changes made by other developers. Additionally, related information from social networks (e.g., Twitter, forums, or corporate-internal networks) is also made available in the activity feeds to the developers.

The whole approach is recursive; that is, every member of the crowd can also act as a customer—in other words accepting a request for work and delegating it to the private/public crowd.

In the next section we describe academia and industry efforts to tackle the three challenges identified in the Introduction and can help to realize crowd-enabled platforms aiming at professional software engineering.

8.4 Toward crowd-enabled software engineering

To implement crowd-enabled software engineering supporting introduced use cases, a number of research challenges, as discussed before, must be addressed. In the following we focus on approaches that, at least partially, try to solve the challenges identified in the Introduction.

8.4.1 Challenge 1: How to manage and organize software projects that are conducted, at least in part, by the crowd

While well-established methodologies and tools are typically used for managing traditional software projects (Institute, 2009), crowdsourced projects require different approaches. In addition to common project management challenges (Charette, 2005), managers of crowdsourced projects have to cope with issues such as a partially unknown workforce, fluctuating development practices, and communication barriers. The following subsections detail these problems and present ideas to solve them.

8.4.1.1 Project staffing

In traditional software projects conducted in small and consolidated companies, project managers usually know potential developers prior to the project setup. As a consequence, managers have at least an impression of each developer's skill set and performance when staffing the project. Using external workers such as freelancers is only considered if certain skills are rare or missing within one's own workforce. Large IT companies such as IBM and Microsoft employ thousands of developers distributed over many locations and product groups. A distributed workforce of this kind can be considered as an internal community or almost as a crowd. In crowd-conducted software projects, the workforce is only partially known to managers prior to the project setup because the staff is composed anew and dynamically, depending on the skills required to achieve the project goals. This carries many risks for project managers who have to manage their budgets, predict the project duration, estimate work performance, and, hence, determine the number of workers required to be involved and paid in the project.

Suitable tools have to support managers in their efforts to staff projects with qualified personnel by enabling them to express their needs for certain skills and qualifications in a simple and objective way. Today's professional network services such as LinkedIn (LinkedIn, 2012) and XING (Xing, 2012) allow searching for keywords in a person's online profile, retrieve short CVs, and show skills endorsed by other professional contacts. However, they do not offer facilities that go beyond these functions.

We propose a system that enables comparing potential staff members by their skill set, experience, and rating by former team members, managers, and customers. This system provides capabilities to organize and present the qualities of crowd workers on the one hand and to offer facilities to define project and job advertisements of the crowdsourcers on the other hand. In addition, the system allows project managers to define budget and time constraints in order to check the cost and availability of potential staff members. An approach to technically realize parts of this system is presented in section 4.2.1.

8.4.1.2 Project monitoring and controlling

In recent years, agile project management and development methodologies have found their way more and more into the software engineering process. Focusing on principles such as individuals, working software, customer collaboration, and change management (Beck, 2001), they are most suitable for crowdsourced software projects. Both in traditional and in crowd-conducted software projects that gather customer needs, setting goals and scope and defining tasks are critical success factors. Solely applying traditional development approaches to crowd-conducted projects, however, is insufficient and dangerous. For instance, as crowdsourced projects are typically characterized by their dynamic and flexible nature, the problem of managing changes while using static, preplanned, and long-ranging tasks and resource allocations would be even more prominent. Compared to traditional software projects in crowdsourced ones, definitions of tasks have to be even more precise and expressive. While employees for in-house undertakings undergo a number of training sessions in order to share the same work principles, speech, and standards, in crowdsourced projects this common understanding, knowledge basis, and working behavior cannot be assumed and is probably missing. In addition to expressive tasks descriptions, the tasks themselves must be small in size and self-contained that is, they cannot depend on other tasks. This allows re-delegating incompletely or incorrectly implemented tasks to other developers without heavily impacting the project schedule and related components. Project managers are enabled to easily replace crowd workers who do not seek to accomplish their tasks within the parameters they have agreed to. To ensure the completion of mission-critical tasks, project managers can assign such tasks to more than one crowd worker and use the best or fastest result. By applying agile methodologies in crowdsourced projects, fluctuating development practices of crowd workers and risks such as poor quality, bad reusability, or missing extensibility of results can be reduced to the size of a single work unit when adequate monitoring and controlling is in place.

Organizational network analysis as an agile software engineering modeling method allows managers to monitor and measure collaborative efforts across teams (Carroll et al., 2013). Well-established agile project management software such as Rational Team Concert (IBM, 2012), VersionOne (VersionOne, 2012) and TeamPulse (Telerik, 2012) allow managing human resources and work units. Those software products support project managers and developers in their daily work. They enable project managers to plan, organize, monitor, control, and review tasks as well as measure the project progress and team performance, and to generate charts and reports for the upper management. However, they are not enabled for crowdsourcing.

In order to assist project managers in crowdsourcing projects, we propose a toolkit extending today's agile project management software by (1) facilitating the preselection of suitable crowd workers, (2) applying a test-driven model to ensure the functionality and quality of work units and (3) providing semiautomatic feedback on the crowd workers' performance. Automatically detecting relevant keywords from task descriptions written by the project manager, as briefly described in Dustdar and Gaedke, 2011), helps to preselect suitable crowd worker candidates based on their matching skills. Such a method implicitly ensures the precise definition of tasks by the project manager and the expressive description of crowd workers' profiles (cf. the previous section on project staffing'). In case Scrum, as an agile project management approach, is applied and a new Sprint is to be planned, the tool supports project managers in that relevant tasks are preassigned with the best-fitting crowd workers and in accordance with budget and availability constraint settings as described above. Although tasks can be semiautomatically assigned to the most promising crowd worker, the quality of their solutions cannot be anticipated with certainty. Hence, we suggest implementing unit tests for each work item before dealing with the actual work item. Depending on the type and complexity of the crowdsourced project, the unit tests are created in-house or by the crowd. Quality of task implementations interfaces and the entire project's reusability and extensibility can be increased using a test-driven approach, that is, through detecting incorrect results by associated unit tests. Furthermore, the tool assists project managers in identifying crowd workers having low working standards, fluctuating development practices, or poor performance. This in turn provides feedback on crowd workers, allowing assessment of their suitability in future projects (cf. Figure 8.2).

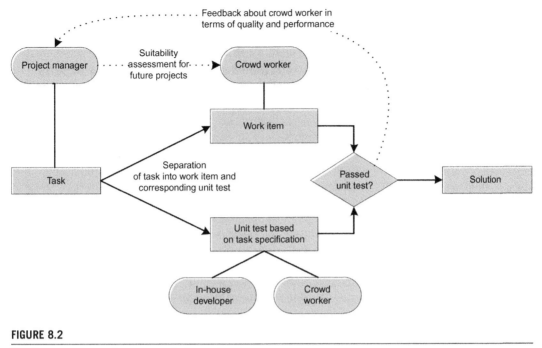

FIGURE 8.2

Quality assurance and assessment of crowd workers.

8.4.1.3 Project communication and documentation

Addressing the individual information needs of people involved in projects is typically implemented by means of a plan managing type, matter, and frequency of communication. Regular team meetings, status reporting, or review sessions are essential parts of a communication plan in traditional projects. In crowdsourced projects, however, such conventional communication methods are of limited usefulness as the staff is distributed, loosely coupled, and generally not continuously available over the entire project duration. For instance, team meetings do not make that much sense because external staff members—the crowd workers—are dynamically employed on a task basis. In line with the employment, we recommend communication on a task basis. As an example, when crowd workers need to discuss organizational issues in the context of their tasks, they have to contact the project manager using one of the preferred communication channels listed in the related profiles on the crowdsourcing platform. Different cultures and time zones can cause communication problems, which hinder an efficient collaboration. Technical issues requiring no special project knowledge can be raised by the crowd worker in a public, language-independent, collaboratively edited question and answer service such as the Stack Overflow (StackExchange, 2012). Although no direct communication between the crowd workers of a single project is needed (cf. section 4.1.3), we recommend that the project manager set up a wiki in the project preparation phase. Based on the flexible and evolving nature of a wiki, it is well suited to store the crowd-conducted documentation of the project. Besides the source code annotations of the crowd worker solving the assigned task, more comprehensive documentation is beneficial for the project manager to understand and evaluate the solution.

8.4.2 Challenge 2: How to create virtual teams consisting of suitable experts and delegate tasks (semi-)automatically?

Crowdsourcing platforms are still relatively rudimentary and lack automated rewarding and task matching. Crowdsourcing of complex, collaborative tasks, such as software development, is not supported. Amazon Mechanical Turk (AMT) (Amazon, 2012) is a prominent representative for a generic crowdsourcing platform, which allows processing of tasks by crowd workers. Employers on the AMT, so-called *requesters* (service consumers), are encouraged to submit tasks, so-called *human intelligence tasks* (HITs), to the system. Those HITs mostly require minor effort (most of them can be processed in a few seconds up to few minutes), but they still need human intelligence, notably, transcription, classification, and categorization. The crowd of contributors, so-called *workers*, picks up these HITs, completes them, and gets a monetary reward (normally a few cents per HIT) if the quality of the requester accepts their solution (Ipeirotis et al., 2010).

In order to achieve Challenge 2, crowdsourcing platforms must be able to also support complex, cooperative software development tasks. Crowdsourcing capabilities must be seamlessly integrated into software management approaches and collaborative software development tools.

8.4.2.1 Auction-based crowdsourcing

Satzger et al. (2011, 2013) propose using auctions for task matching in crowdsourcing. Auctions are a popular way of trading goods on the Internet. Market laws achieve price discovery automatically. However, they are not used in current task-based crowdsourcing systems. The big advantage is that rewards for tasks are based on supply and demand; moreover, requesters do not have to "guess" a fair, competitive reward as with current platforms such as MTurk, but they may still define a maximum amount of money they are willing to pay. This prevents overpaying or underpaying; underpaying may be as bad as overpaying and result in "nonsellers" with the potential to cause delays, for example, in the context of business process execution.

Figure 8.3 illustrates how requesters and workers interact with such an auction-based marketplace. At first, a requester submits a new task to the platform. The requester provides a description of the task and the maximum amount of money (reward) he or she is willing to pay. The marketplace then creates an auction for this task, inviting only those workers to the auction whose skills match those specified by the requester. Workers interested in processing the task can place their bids in the auction. After a predefined amount of time the auction closes, determines a winner, and informs the worker about winning the auction. It is now the job of the worker to process the task in time and to submit the result to the platform. Assuming the task has been processed in time, the marketplace informs the requester, who in turn provides a rating for the worker based on the quality of the processed task. If the quality conforms to the predefined agreement, the requester transfers a defined amount of money, based on the outcome of the auction and on a possible fee for using the crowdsourcing platform, to the marketplace. Considering the requester's feedback, the marketplace updates the skill profile of the worker and finally pays the worker for his or her effort.

The auctioning mechanism can be extended so that it does not blindly look solely at prices but instead also includes bid re-ranking techniques to ensure quality. In addition to the pure mapping

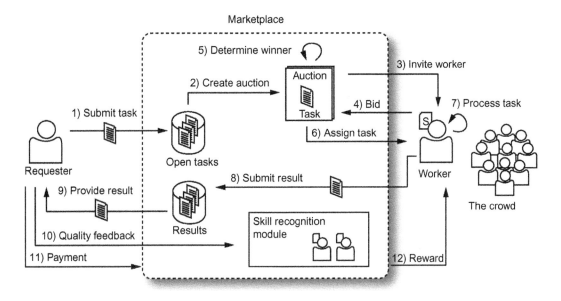

FIGURE 8.3

Auction-based crowdsourcing process.

of tasks to workers, also addressed is the issue of how to build and manage an automated crowd-sourcing platform. For establishing a successful crowdsourcing environment, it is important to maintain a motivated base of crowd members and provide the stimulus for learning required skills. Only a recurring, satisfied crowd staff is able to ensure high quality and high output. We propose a skill evolution model that encourages new and existing crowd workers in developing capabilities and knowledge needed by requesters. All standard processes in the crowdsourcing platform are automated and free from intervention, which allows handling a vast amount of tasks and makes it compatible with a SOA approach. To ensure sustainability, the model is designed not only to maximize the benefit of requesters, but also to take the welfare of workers into account.

8.4.2.2 Crowdsourcing of workflows
In the future, companies will increasingly use crowdsourcing to address a flexible workforce. However, how to carry out business processes leveraging crowdsourcing remains an open issue. Most task-based crowdsourcing platforms simply provide requesters the possibility to publish simple task descriptions into a database to which all workers have access. A task description in AMT, for instance, consists of a title, textual description, expiration date, time allotted, keywords, required qualifications, and monetary reward. Business processes or workflows, on the other hand, describe a logical structure between tasks that crowdsourcing platforms cannot handle. The main problem is, however, that people book tasks voluntarily in crowdsourcing, which means the only way to influence the booking and execution times of single tasks is either to change incentives or to modify other aspects of a task, for example, define a later deadline.

Khazankin et al. (2012) describe an enterprise crowdsourcing approach that executes business processes on top of a crowdsourcing platform. For each single task in the business process, we reason about the optimal values for incentives (typically monetary reward) when crowdsourcing them. The goal is to carry out the business process with minimal investments before the deadline. During execution of the business process, we constantly monitor the progress and adjust incentives for tasks that a worker has not yet booked. Our approach for calculating optimal values is based on mining historical data about task executions, which influence higher rewards have on the booking time, analyzing the current status of the business process, and quadratic programming, which is a mathematical optimization formulation that can be solved efficiently.

The main goal is to ensure the timely execution of business processes that contain crowdsourced tasks while minimizing the expenses associated with crowdsourcing rewards. Expenses can be reduced by setting lower rewards for tasks, but if the reward is too low, a task might remain not booked for too long, if booked at all. Such situations can significantly affect the execution of the process, and become a reason for missed deadlines. The main idea of our approach is to find a most beneficial trade-off between rewards and booking/processing times for crowdsourced tasks within a business process.

Figure 8.4 shows a framework for deadline-driven reward optimization for processes containing crowdsourced tasks. The estimator collects statistical data from platform logs and estimates the functional dependency between incentives and booking/processing times for each type of task ①. The optimizer retrieves structure and state of processes ③, booking state of already published tasks ④ and functional dependencies ②, and determines optimal values, mainly for setting monetary rewards. These values are further used by the publisher, ⑤ which announces tasks to the platform at an appropriate time and updates them if needed ⑥. The optimization and publisher are activated periodically, thus realizing the adaptive behavior.

8.4.2.3 Games with a purpose

Some software development tasks do not require special education and can be solved by almost anyone, at least if they are presented accordingly. Such tasks could be distributed with existing crowdsourcing platforms. However, alternatives are available that promise to get solutions cheaper, faster, and sometimes even with better quality. An interesting crowdsourcing approach based on different forms of incentives is games with a purpose, that is, human-based computation games that outsource certain computation logic to human players in an entertaining way (von Ahn, 2006). Note that this idea is somehow different from the idea of "serious gaming" that describes games whose main purpose is to educate or improve some skill, instead of entertaining (Johnson, 2007).

This niche is actively being developed and focuses on possibilities to wrap crowdsourcing tasks into a game that presents computational challenges to humans in an entertaining way. Workers are motivated and interested in the task-solving process because it is fun. Especially if played within a community, it is often additionally motivating to get the highest score, which commonly represents the best solution for the stated problem. Foldit (2012), a set of online challenges, but also GWAP (2012) and Phylo (McGillUniversity, 2012) belong to this category.

We propose reorganizing the game with a purposed approach by giving game developers more control over tasks that can be integrated into games, which can result in fun-to-play, state-of-the-art games that elegantly disguise tasks by sophisticated in-game challenges. If the crowdsourcing task

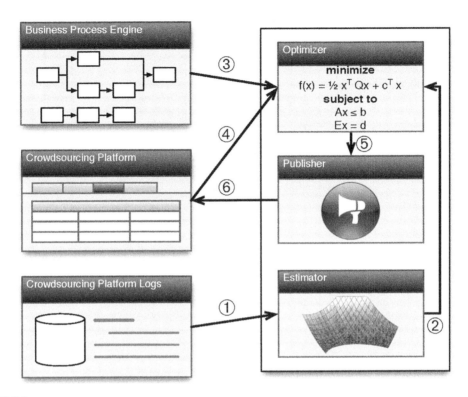

FIGURE 8.4

Architecture of the crowd-enabled workflow engine.

is to detect the location of a specific object on an image, the player can be told that pointing the correct object will open a secret door. If the crowdsourcing task is to classify the content of a photo, it could be presented simply as enemy, and observing which weapon, spell, or potion a player picks for attacking or defending would allow learning about the image category.

The main idea is to split today's unnatural merger between the institution that creates the crowdsourcing task and the game developers. Professional game studios and indie game creators would benefit from the cooperation with institutions that need to process human-only solvable puzzles. On the other hand, having experts embed tasks into games greatly increase chances of acceptance.

As shown in Figure 8.5, at the core of the idea is the mediator, a puzzle broker that mediates typical crowdsourcing puzzles to game developers of high-quality games. In contrast to paid crowd workers, a crowd of players solves the tasks transparently in the context of the game. The puzzle broker can offer better reliability and throughput to its customers because of a big player base. This helps game developers to provide cheaper or even free games to its customers. Additionally, developers and players benefit as the game content is highly varying and new puzzles must be solved each time even for the same level or quest.

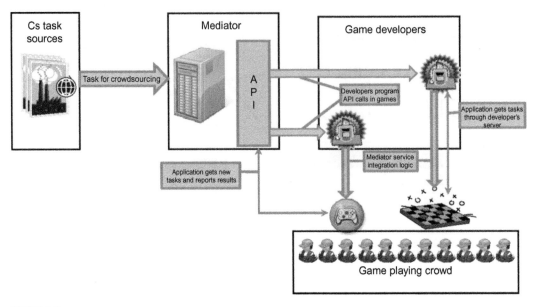

FIGURE 8.5

Better integration of crowdsourcing tasks into games with a purpose.

8.4.3 Challenge 3: How to improve cooperation of developers within loosely coupled teams?

The development of high-quality software products in a loosely coupled, web-based, collaborative setting, as we envision it for crowd developed, leads to a range of new requirements that existing development tools can only partly fulfill. Agile development typically requires the co-location of all involved stakeholders. Within crowd development setups, this constraint cannot be fulfilled due to the distribution of the crowd developers. Indeed, the actual source code development does not necessarily require the presence of all developers in one physical room. However, the early phases of a software development project are characterized by discussions and brainstorming in order to define the scope, functionality, and quality of the product. These meetings require the attendance and active participation of all stakeholders (e.g., back-end developer, quality engineer, UI designer, mobile app expert) in order to create a common understanding within the development team. During the development phase, distributed co-development between people who may not be part of the same company or organization increases the need for sophisticated update and notification mechanisms in order to follow the latest development and understand the full context. The following subsections discuss potential ways of cooperation and highlight our research and development results that promise to improve the collaboration within such distributed work environments.

8.4.3.1 Crowd-enabled collaboration

Unlike in traditional projects, where common procedures, routines, and practices such as regular team meetings, brainstorming sessions, or assisting co-workers are essential parts of the daily business, in crowdsourced projects the workers do their job in a decoupled manner. As a result of such loosely coupled and distributed team structures, it is difficult to implement measures that will enable collaboration between team members and strengthen a team's cohesiveness, identity, and work principles (Kittur et al., 2013; Reason and Andersen, 1991). Company policies rigidly defining labor standards, security guidelines, or the tool chain are unsuitable for crowd-enabled undertakings. This is because sufficient compliance implementation and control are difficult to realize because of the diversity of the work environments of the crowd workers. While in-house project developers can share data via dedicated servers, in crowd-conducted software development data have to be managed differently in order to cope with restrictions in terms of accessibility and exchangeability.

Because of these facts, a flexible collaboration environment for facilitating discussion, decision making, and data management is required. Going beyond the capabilities of established social collaboration platforms such as Jive (Jive, 2012) or Yammer (Microsoft, 2012), we recommend an environment that enables crowdworkers in the creation of highly customizable and tailored workspaces. Workspaces are individual compositions of predefined components serving specific purposes. This includes traditional collaboration and communication capabilities (e.g., telephony services, instant messaging, voting, whiteboard, document upload) as well as specific services tailored to meet the need in distributed development projects (e.g., task overview, access to documentation material, knowledge database). Crowd workers temporarily integrated into development projects are able to join the collaboration platform and design their individual workspaces out of these components. In this way, they include components that are only valuable for them as well as shared components that foster collaboration and awareness between co-workers. As an example, a crowd worker could see other developers currently working on the same project or area and ask for support via a component offered by the crowdsourcer.

The technical foundation for such a collaboration environment has been developed within the OMELETTE research project (Chudnovskyy et al., 2012a). Based on sound technologies provided by the open-source projects Apache Rave (Apache, Apache Rave, 2012) and Apache Wookie (Apache, Apache Wookie Project, 2012), a collaboration platform as described above has been developed. The platform enables users to create, customize, and share workspaces out of OpenSocial (2012) and W3C (2012). In order to offer crowd workers these forms of advanced communication and collaboration capabilities, a comprehensive set of widgets ranging from video chats, conference calls, and screen-sharing solutions over shared text-editors, collaborative whiteboards to calendars and contact lists have been developed. Workspace descriptions can be exported using Open Mashup Description Language (OMDL) (2012), which allows it to be used as the basis for other workspaces or as a workspace template. As a data management platform, we recommend an extensible and flexible system, such as the WebComposition/Data Grid Service (DGS) (Chudnovskyy et al., 2012b). The DGS facilitates, for instance, the handling of heterogeneous data by dedicated and specialized data storage engines as well as the definition of fine-grained access control rights for crowd workers using the emerging WebID (W3C, WebID 1.0—W3C, 2005) standard. The combination of both platforms constitutes a solid foundation for crowd-enabled collaboration.

8.4.3.2 Collaborative requirements engineering

Requirements engineering is a crucial phase at the beginning of every product development to define the scope of development together with customers. As mentioned in the introduction of this section, the early phases of a software development project and in particular the requirements engineering are characterized by discussions and brainstorming in order to define the scope, functionality, and quality of the product. Therefore it is essential to support active collaboration between all co-workers in order to establish a common understanding of the envisioned product. In the traditional waterfall model, requirements engineering is only executed in the first phase of development, followed by analysis, design, and the actual software development. Many existing solutions (e.g., Briggs and Grünbacher, 2002; Davis, 2010) focus on rather complex (nonagile) methodologies for requirements engineering that have not been widely adopted in the software industry. These existing solutions do not seem to be feasible for crowd development because they are quite inflexible. Instead, agile methods such as User Story Mapping (Maurer and Hellmann, 2013) together with agile development approaches such as SCRUM or Kanban (Leffingwell, 2010) have been established in the software industry in recent years. They repeat requirements engineering techniques in several iterations during the whole software development process. This way findings and customer feedback from the ongoing project can be used for further planning. The result of the requirements engineering process is captured in a so-called Prioritized Product Backlog. The product backlog contains a set of user stories that describe the product features from a user's perspective. The individual user stories can be used as a means to distribute development tasks to the crowd if they have the right granularity.

Based on this general overview of requirements engineering for crowd development, we can identify three main challenges:

Defining a set of user stories with the right granularity: User stories should be ideally self-contained without dependencies on other user stories. Then development can be done in parallel by different developers with low interference and communication demand. However, this ideal is often difficult to achieve in practice.

Supporting collaboration of remote teams: Agile techniques for requirements engineering typically advocate co-located teams for most efficient work and make heavy use of paper, whiteboards, blackboards, sticky notes, and the like. However, crowd development is fundamentally distributed in nature. Thus, tools fostering communication and collaboration between remote developers are required. The kind of tools ranges from general-purpose tools such as videoconferences, online chats, wikis, and forums to specially tailored tools for specific collaboration or communication tasks.

Supporting iterative refinement of prioritized product backlogs: At any point in time during product development, it must be easily possible to refine and change existing requirements in the form of the prioritized product backlog.

While the aforementioned OMELETTE collaboration environment addresses the second challenge, dedicated tool support is required to address the other two. The following examples constitute the results of our real-time collaboration research in the context of agile techniques. Both applications share a collaborative character, meaning that they enable multiple distributed web users to work on a shared content in real time.

The *affinity diagram* (Holtzblatt and Beyer, 1993) is a well-known technique for gathering and structuring large amounts of data or ideas by a group of people. For example, results from customer interviews can be captured to derive key results from it. In the context of requirements engineering, affinity diagrams can be used in early phases to obtain more insights into the new product and, thus, prepare the definition of the product backlog. The actual process behind affinity diagrams is quite simple:

1. Record each idea or whatever data on a card. All involved people can do this in parallel.
2. Put all cards on a wall and group related cards to clusters. People can discuss the clustering.
3. Find names for clusters.

In order to leverage this well-known technique for crowd development, we have developed a web-based collaboration tool (see Figure 8.6) that allows distributed teams to follow the same process with virtual cards. The focus of the tool development is on usability to support an easy, intuitive, and fast-working mode that tries to come close to the work with physical cards, pens, and walls. Users are able to add or remove cards, edit the content of cards, and group related cards in clusters.

User story mapping (Patton, 2009) is an established agile technique used to define the scope of an envisioned product. It involves the whole team, including internal and external stakeholders, and its goals are to produce a common understanding of the product, create user stories, and visualize the backlog as a structured map.

Similar to the presented affinity diagram tool, we have developed a web-based tool (Figure 8.7) that supports creating and editing user story maps. Most operations can be performed through drag and drop, similar to the working mode with physical cards. By also supporting tablet computers-such as the iPad, user interactions become even more intuitive and close to the physical model.

Although agile techniques such as user story mapping or affinity diagrams are usually done with pen and paper, dedicated (web-based) tools offer several advantages:

- Results are available in electronic form and can easily be archived.
- Results can be exported to other tools. For example, we have developed an interface to the popular backlog management tool JIRA (Atlassian, 2012) for the user story mapping tool, which allows exporting user stories into JIRA.

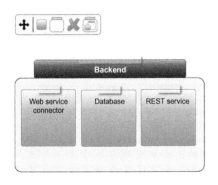
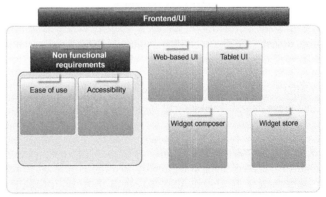

FIGURE 8.6

Affinity diagram tool.

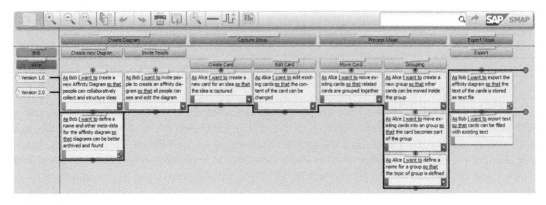

FIGURE 8.7

User story mapping tool.

- Data can be changed more easily. There is no need for striking through or writing text to a new card. Additionally, a virtual wall has no size limitation that one would face using a real wall.

However, these general advantages apply for almost all virtualized tasks and do not sufficiently differentiate our work from existing web applications that cover the same functionality (e.g., SilverSories (Agile Story Mapping Tool | Silver Stories, 2011) or CardMapping (Jeremy Lightsmith, 2011) for user story mapping). As signaled in the introduction of the tools, we advanced the state of the art by adding real-time collaboration support for multiple distributed users. As crowd workers by definition cannot physically be present in workshops or brainstorming sessions, tools must eliminate this limitation as much as possible. Therefore, the presented tools utilize real-time collaboration based on operational transformation mechanisms (Ellis and Gibbs, 1989). This technology allows multiple crowd workers to interact on shared artifacts such as a user story or a single sticky note in real time. All changes are immediately synchronized and propagated to all active participants of a session. Errors are resolved automatically in order to secure one consistent state. Furthermore, the tools visually create awareness of users' interactions. In order to support developers in the implementation of this kind of collaborative applications, we have created two different development approaches. While the first one allows the transformation of existing single-user web applications into collaborative multiuser applications (Heinrich et al., 2012), the second approach enables developers to build new collaborative applications from scratch using an annotation-based development framework (Heinrich, 2013).

8.4.3.3 Social development

One of the challenges for globally distributed crowd developers is to follow the mutual development progress. Everyone involved needs to be up to date regarding changes done by others in order to (1) ensure the transparency of work, (2) improve the awareness of the actual situation, and (3) ease collaboration among all involved people. Currently, following the mutual development progress works at the level of file changes being committed to a version control system such as

GIT or SVN. Developers need to scan through all changes and manually find the relevant ones, which is time consuming and might miss important changes.

Therefore, we propose a social layer on top of traditional Version Control Systems (VCS). Transferring established concepts from social networks, such as activity feeds, gives crowd developers a better understanding of the work others do and helps them monitor development progress in the context of such highly distributed projects. Using sophisticated subscription and filtering mechanisms, the amount of relevant information for the developer can be minimized and the developer does not need to check all changed files of a commit. Moreover, it is beneficial to connect data from social networks and dedicated developer communities with the actual development activities or even particular code changes in order to get context-sensitive, helpful information. Finally, all involved developers need to be able to exchange ideas and share information within the public or private cloud using feed update mechanisms.

In order to receive notifications about all changes done by others, crowd developers can "follow" (as in Twitter) not only their peers but also artifacts of the source code such as a certain Java class or even single methods within Java classes. Compared to change sets in traditional VCSs that are only based on line numbers in text files, the system reports software changes at the level of known programming language concepts (e.g., classes, methods, member variables) in the form of activity feeds.

These feeds can be enriched with additional information from social networks (e.g., Twitter, forums, corporate-internal networks, online communities). Developers discussing issues and trying to understand error messages and exceptions frequently use these information sources. Linking this information with a specific change set helps other developers of the crowd to understand the background and context of the change. Consider, for example, a solution to a specific problem posted in online communities that can now be easily linked to a dedicated code snipped in order to give other developers the necessary background information to understand the actual implementation.

Indeed, following code artifacts and ongoing tasks of developers creates a huge amount of activity feeds. The question that arises is how a single developer can consume this flood of information in a nondisruptive manner. Integration into the actual development environment in a tight and context-sensitive way significantly reduces the disruption caused by switching tools (e.g., IDE, browser) or even devices. Features to summarize retrieved information as well as the ability to explore the repository structures and code evolution (submitted change sets) using easy navigation, search and filtering capabilities (e.g., only changes from last week, only changes from developer X) are considered in the proposed social layer created on the following components:

VCS Connector: The notification system requires a generic interface and specific adapters for selected VCSs (e.g., SVN, GIT, Perforce) in order to gather information about ongoing development activities. These VCSs serve as one primary source for the update and notification mechanism.

Program Language Analyzer: The classification of programming languages (e.g., statically/dynamically typed, OO, functional) constitutes the foundation for a generic programming language model (class, method, interface, member variables). This leads to a set of sophisticated analyzer components for specific programming languages (e.g., Java, C#) by using and extending available open-source frameworks. The result can be used to monitor ongoing development activities, create (semi-) automatic status updates, and follow code artifacts.

Artifact Linking and Notification Mechanism: A linking mechanism between code artifacts, developers, and additional information sources (e.g., Wiki, discussion, Twitter) is required in order to realize the traceability of development changes and connect the actual code with external information. Therefore, connectors to suitable social networks have to be created that enable developers to either retrieve relevant information from dedicated communities or publish status updates and information related to their current development tasks. Furthermore, each developer needs to have a profile that links to his or her social network profiles.

IDE Integration: Additional side panels, plug-ins, or entries in context menus enrich the existing development environment with new capabilities in an integrated manner. For staying focused on their actual implementation tasks, developers can apply filters and use search tools to decide what information is propagated in which way. Without leaving the work environment, they also can reach out to their peers in the crowd or consume the content of community pages using integrated browser views.

In summary, crowd development requires new ways of collaboration in order to ensure the time and quality of a product. The efficient usage of the combined intelligence of a large group of developers, the seamless integration of knowledge stored in social communities, the required tool-supported awareness of actions and changes done by others, as well as the general form of social interaction during the development phase are the key differentiators in traditional software development.

8.5 Conclusion

Within the current trends toward cloud computing, many IT companies are interested in new ways of dealing with the workforce. Inspired by emerging success stories of crowdsourcing, IT companies are trying to improve their business processes with the help of this new paradigm. However, applying crowdsourcing comes with a set of new challenges that are gaining the attention of research and development.

The distributed nature of crowdsourcing requires new methodologies for project management. This problem is partially solvable by adapting agile development techniques using existing social collaboration approaches, but as of today, no complete solution is available.

Another challenge is how to distribute tasks, motivate workers, and set up team structures dynamically in order to produce high-quality software. Existing platforms, such as Amazon Mechanical Turk (Amazon, 2012), provide fundamental features for task delegation, but they leave issues such as task generation, worker evaluation, and motivation unsolved. We present possibilities to automate the crowdsourcing of business processes and different ways to motivate workers through auction-based or entertainment-based task distribution.

In crowd-enabled software development, workers typically have to collaborate remotely during various development steps. Web-based social collaboration tools, for example, forums, instant messaging platforms, online office suites, or social networks, provide rudimentary features for collaborative software development. However, new collaboration tools are emerging that can be used to create crowd-enabled IDEs and management tools.

However, this chapter does not claim to present a complete list of the challenges that face companies trying to apply crowdsourcing technologies. As is true of any new technology, crowdsourcing comes with other challenges that are not directly related to the development process. For example, it is an open research topic how companies have to handle legal issues such as intellectual property rights, payment of rewards, taxation, and business secret protection. Even though all of these and further issues are very important and vital for a company's adoption of crowdsourcing , they are out of the scope of this chapter, which, rather, focuses on the core challenges.

Overall, the benefits of crowd-enabled software engineering are beginning to be acknowledged, and to some degree similar concepts are already in use. However, there is no holistic approach allowing crowd-enabled project management, crowd management, and integrated tool support. The concepts presented in this chapter try to solve these problems and show the current research efforts that can help to improve today's experience with crowd-enabled software engineering.

References

99designs, 2012. Logo Design, Web Design and More. |. Retrieved from 99designs. <http://99designs.com/>.

Adobe, 2012. Adobe Buzzword. Retrieved from Adobe Buzzword. <http://www.adobe.com/uk/acom/buzzword/>.

Agile Story Mapping Tool | Silver Stories, 2011. Retrieved from Silver Stripe Software. <http://toolsforagile.com/silverstories/>.

Agrawal, A., Amend, M., Das, M., Ford, M., Keller, C., Kloppmann, M., et al., 2007. Web Services Human Task (WS-HumanTask), Version 1.0. Available at: <http://incubator.apache.org/hise/WS-HumanTask_v1.pdf>.

Amazon, 2012. Amazon Mechanical Turk. Retrieved from: <https://www.mturk.com/>.

Apache, 2012. Apache Rave—The Apache Software Foundation! Retrieved from Apache Rave: <rave.apache.org/>.

Apache, 2012. Apache Wave—Welcome to Apache Wave (incubating). Retrieved from Apache Wave: <http://incubator.apache.org/wave/>.

Apache, 2012. Apache Wookie Project. Retrieved from Apache Wookie: <wookie.apache.org/>.

Assembla, 2012. Kanban/Scrum Task Board with Collaboration Tools Configuration. Retrieved from Assembla: <https://www.assembla.com/catalog/101-kanban-scrum-task-board-with-collaboration-tools-package>.

Assembla, 2012. The Next Generation Agile Project Management Tools | Assembla. Retrieved from Assembla: <https://www.assembla.com>.

Atlassian, 2012. Issue and Project Tracking Software | Atlassian. Retrieved from Atlassian JIRA: <http://www.atlassian.com/software/jira>.

Beck, K.A., 2001. Manifesto for Agile Software Development. Retrieved from Manifesto for Agile Software Development: <http://agilemanifesto.org>.

BerliOS, 2012. BerliOS: The Open Source Mediator. Retrieved from BerliOS: <http://www.berlios.de/>.

Bosari, J., 2012. The developing role of social media in the modern business world. <http://www.forbes.com/sites/moneywisewomen/2012/08/08/the-developing-role-of-social-media-in-the-modern-business-world>.

Briggs, R., Grünbacher, P., 2002. Easywinwin: managing complexity in requirements negotiation with GSS. Proceedings of the 35th Annual Hawaii International Conference on System Sciences (HICSS'02)—Volume 1. IEEE Computer Society, Washington, DC, pp. 21.1. < http://dl.acm.org/citation.cfm?id=820887 >.

Bruce, A., Pepitone, J.S., Formisano, R.A., Peitone, J.S., 1999. Motivating Employees. McGraw-Hill, New York.

Carmel, E., Agarwal, R., 2001. Tactical approaches for alleviating distance in global software development. Softw. IEEE 18 (2), 22−29.

Carroll, N., Richardson, I., Whelan, E., 2013. Service science: exploring complex agile service networks through organisational network analysis. In: Wang, X., Ali, N., Ramos, I., Vidgen, R. (Eds.), Agile and Lean Service-Oriented Development: Foundations, Theory, and Practice. Information Science Reference, Hershey, PA, pp. 156−172. Available from: http://dx.doi.org/doi:10.4018/978-1-4666-2503-7.ch008.

Charette, R., 2005. Why software fails. IEEE Spectr. 42−49.

Chow, T., Cao, D.-B., 2008. A survey study of critical success factors in agile software projects. J. Syst. Softw. 81 (6), 961−971.

Chudnovskyy, O., Nestler, T., Gaedke, M., Daniel, F., Fernández-Villamor, J.I., Chepegin, V., et al., 2012a. End-user-oriented telco mashups: the omelette approach. Proceedings of the 21st International Conference Companion on World Wide Web. ACM, New York, pp. 235−238.

Chudnovskyy, O., Wild, S., Gebhardt, H., Gaedke, M., 2012b. Data portability using web composition/data grid service. Int. J. Adv. Internet Technol. 4 (3 and 4), 123−132.

Computerworld, P.T., 2012. Microsoft signs outsourcing pact with Indian giant Infosys. Microsoft Signs Outsourcing Pact with Indian Giant Infosys. <http://www.computerworld.com/s/article/9175442/Microsoft_signs_outsourcing_pact_with_Indian_giant_Infosys>.

da Silva, F., Costa, C., Franca, A., Prikladinicki, R., 2010. Challenges and solutions in distributed software development project management: a systematic literature review. 2010 5th IEEE International Conference on, Global Software Engineering (ICGSE), pp. 87−96.

Dabbish, L., Stuart, C., Tsay, J., Herbsleb, J., 2012. Social coding in github: transparency and collaboration in an open software repository. Proceedings of the ACM 2012 Conference on Computer Supported Cooperative Work, pp. 1277−1286.

Damian, D., Izquierdo, L., Singer, J., Kwan, I., 2007. Awareness in the wild: why communication breakdowns occur. Second IEEE International Conference on Global Software Engineering, 2007. ICGSE 2007, pp. 81−90.

Davis, A., 2010. Requirements Bibliography. Retrieved from: <http://www.reqbib.com/>.

DiMicco, J., Millen, D.R., Geyer, W., Dugan, C., Brownholtz, B., Muller, M., 2008. Motivations for social networking at work. Proceedings of the 2008 ACM conference on Computer Supported Cooperative Work, pp. 711−720.

Dustdar, S., Bhattacharya, K., 2011. The social compute unit. Internet Comput. IEEE 15 (3), 64−69.

Dustdar, S., Gaedke, M., 2011. The social routing principle. Internet Comput. 15 (4), 80−83.

Ellis, C.A., Gibbs, S.J., 1989. Concurrency control in groupware systems. Proceedings of the 1989 ACM SIGMOD International Conference on Management of Data. ACM, New York, pp. 399−407.

Fidelman, M., 2010. 5 Powerful Project Management Features You can only do on UnaWave (Google Wave).

Foldit, 2012. Solve Puzzles for Science | Foldit. Retrieved from Foldit: <http://fold.it/>.

GitHub, 2012. GitHub. Retrieved from: <https://github.com/>.

Google, 2012. Google Docs—Online documents, spreadsheets, presentations, surveys, file storage and more. Retrieved from Google Docs: <http://docs.google.com>.

GWAP, 2012. gwap.com—Home. Retrieved from GWAP: <http://www.gwap.com/gwap/>.

Heinrich, M.G., 2013. Exploiting annotations for the rapid development of collaborative web applications. Proceedings of the 22nd International Conference on World Wide Web. International World Wide Web Conferences Steering Committee, pp. 551−560.

Heinrich, M., Lehmann, F., Springer, T., Gaedke, M., 2012. Exploiting single-user web applications for shared editing: a generic transformation approach. Proceedings of the 21st International Conference on World Wide Web. ACM, New York, pp. 1057−1066.

Holtzblatt, K., Beyer, H., 1993. Making customer-centered design work for teams. Commun. ACM 36 (10), 92−103.

IBM, 2012. IBM—Rational Team Concert. Retrieved from IBM - Rational Team Concert: <http://www-03. ibm.com/software/products/us/en/rtc/>.

Institute, P.M., 2009. A guide to the project management body of knowledge (PMBOK Guides). Project Management Institute.

Ipeirotis, P., Provost, F., Wang, J., 2010. Quality management on amazon mechanical turk. Proceedings of the ACM SIGKDD Workshop on Human Computation, pp. 64−67.

Jeremy Lightsmith, J.P., 2011. Card Mapping. Retrieved from Card Mapping: <http://cardmapping.com/>.

Jive, 2012. Social Collaboration for Social Business. Retrieved from Jive Software: <www.jivesoftware.com/>.

Johnson, W.L., 2007. Serious use of a serious game for language learning. Front. Artif. Intell. Appl. 158, 67.

Khazankin, R., Satzger, B., Dustdar, S., 2012. Optimized execution of business processes on crowdsourcing platforms. 8th International Conference on Collaborative Computing: Networking, Applications and Worksharing (CollaborateCom '12). IEEE, pp. 443−451.

Kittur, A., Nickerson, J.V., Bernstein, M., Gerber, E., Shaw, A., Zimmerman, J., et al., 2013. The future of crowd work. Proceedings of the 2013 conference on Computer Supported Cooperative Work, pp. 1301−1318.

Kloppmann, M., Koenig, D., Leymann, F., Pfau, G., Rickayzen, A., von Riegen, C., et al., 2005. Ws-bpel extension for people—bpel4people. Joint white paper, IBM and SAP.

Koch, S., 2009. Exploring the effects of SourceForge. net coordination and communication tools on the efficiency of open source projects using data envelopment analysis. Empirical Softw. Eng. 14 (4), 397−417.

Lanubile, F., Ebert, C., Prikladnicki, R., Vizcaino, A., 2010. Collaboration tools for global software engineering. Softw. IEEE 27 (2), 52−55.

Leffingwell, D., 2010. Agile software Requirements: Lean Requirements practices for teams, Programs, and the Enterprise. Addison-Wesley, Boston, MA.

Leo Kelion, B.N., 2012. Linus Torvalds: Linux succeeded thanks to selfishness and trust. Retrieved from BBC News: <http://www.bbc.co.uk/news/technology-18419231>.

LinkedIn, 2012. LinkedIn. Retrieved from LinkedIn: <http://www.linkedin.com/>.

Madey, G., Freeh, V., Tynan, R., 2002. The open source software development phenomenon: an analysis based on social network theory. Proc. Am. Conf. Inf. Syst. 1806−1813, Dallas, Texas.

Malone, T., Laubacher, R., Dellarocas, C., 2010. The collective intelligence genome. IEEE Eng. Manage. Rev. 38 (3), 38.

Maurer, F., Hellmann, T.D., 2013. People-centered software development: An overview of agile methodologies. Softw. Eng.. Springer, New York, 185−215.

McGillUniversity, 2012. PHYLO | DNA Puzzles. Retrieved from PHYLO: <http://phylo.cs.mcgill.ca/>.

Microsoft, 2012. Microsoft Office—Microsoft Word, Outlook & Excel—Office.com. Retrieved from Microsoft Office 365: <http://office.microsoft.com>.

Microsoft, 2012. Yammer: The Enterprise Social Network. Retrieved from Yammer: <https://www.yammer. com/>.

Noll, J., Beecham, S., Richardson, I., 2010. Global software development and collaboration: barriers and solutions. ACM Inroads 1 (3), 66−78.

OMDL, 2012. Open Mashup Description Language. Retrieved from Open Mashup Description Language: <omdl.org/>.

OpenSocial, 2012. OpenSocial Specification. Retrieved from OpenSocial | OpenSocial Foundation: <http:// opensocial.org/>.

Patton, J., 2009. User Story Mapping. Retrieved from User Story Mapping. <http://www.agileproductdesign. com/presentations/user_story_mapping>.

Ramlall, S., 2004. A review of employee motivation theories and their implications for employee retention within organizations. J. Am. Acad. Bus. 5 (1/2), 52−63.

Reason, J., Andersen, H., 1991. Errors in a team context. Draft Paper for Mohawk Stresa Workshop.

Robles, G., Gonzalez-Barahona, J., 2006. Geographic location of developers at SourceForge. Proceedings of the 2006 International Workshop on Mining Software Repositories, pp. 144−150.

Rodriguez, J.P., Ebert, C., Vizcaino, A., 2010. Technologies and tools for distributed teams. Softw. IEEE 27 (5), 10−14.

Satzger, B., Psaier, H., Schall, D., Dustdar, S., 2013. Auction-based crowdsourcing supporting skill management. Information Systems Journal (IS), Elsevier 38 (4), 547−560.

Satzger, B., Psaier, H., Schall, D., Dustdar, S., 2011. Stimulating skill evolution in market-based crowdsourcing. 9th International Conference on Business Process Management (BPM '11). Springer, New York, pp. 66−82.

Schall, D., Satzger, B., Psaier, H., 2012. Crowdsourcing tasks to social networks in BPEL4People. World Wide Web. Springer.

Sengupta, B., Chandra, S., Sinha, V., 2006. A research agenda for distributed software development. Proceedings of the 28th International Conference on Software Engineering, pp. 731−740.

SourceForge, 2012. SourceForge—Download, Develop and Publish Free Open Source Software. Retrieved from SourceForge: <http://sourceforge.net/>.

Spiegel, D., 2012. Frei schwebend in der Wolke. Frei schwebend in der Wolke.

StackExchange, 2012. Stack Overflow. Retrieved from Stack Overflow: <http://stackoverflow.com/>.

Telerik, 2012. TeamPulse—Telerik. Retrieved from TeamPulse: <www.telerik.com/agile-project-management-tools>.

TopCoder, I., 2012. Home of the World's Largest Development Community. Retrieved from TopCoder: <http://www.topcoder.com/>.

uTest, 2012. Software Testing | uTest. Retrieved from uTest: <http://www.utest.com/>.

VersionOne, 2012. Agile Project Management Software, Agile Tools, Scrum Tools, Agile Software, Scrum Software | VersionOne. Retrieved from VersionOne: <http://www.versionone.com/>.

von Ahn, L., 2006. Games with a purpose. Computer 39 (6), 92−94.

W3C, 2012. Packaged Web Apps (Widgets) - Packaging and XML Configuration, second ed. Retrieved from W3C Widgets Specification: <http://www.w3.org/TR/widgets/>.

W3C. 2005. WebID 1.0 - W3C. Retrieved from WebID 1.0: <www.w3.org/2005/Incubator/webid/spec/>.

Walsh, R., 2009. The web startup success guide. Apress.

Xing, 2012. XING - The professional network | XING. Retrieved from XING: <http://www.xing.com/>.

Zoho, 2012. Zoho Office Suite. Retrieved from Zoho Office Suite: <http://www.zoho.com/>.

Architectural Debt Management in Value-Oriented Architecting

Zengyang Li[1], Peng Liang[2], and Paris Avgeriou[1]
[1]University of Groningen, Groningen, The Netherlands
[2]Wuhan University, Wuhan, China

9.1 Introduction

In the field of software architecture (SA), there has been a paradigm shift from describing the outcome of the architecting process to documenting architectural knowledge (AK), such as architecture decisions and rationale, which are considered as first-class entities of a software architecture (ISO/IEC/IEEE, 2011). Architecture decisions often involve trade-offs made between a number of stakeholder concerns. In particular, technical concerns (e.g., system quality attributes) are often compromised to meet business concerns (e.g., development cost or time to market). For example, poorly designed legacy components may be reused instead of implementing their functionality from scratch, in order to achieve fast product delivery. Such trade-offs made in architecture design may lead to **architectural technical debt** (ATD, or shortly *architectural debt*).

In a broader scope, technical debt (TD) refers to immature software artifacts that fail to meet the required level of quality (Cunningham, 1992; Seaman and Guo, 2011). Accordingly, ATD refers to immature architecture design artifacts that compromise systemwide quality attributes (QAs), particularly maintainability and evolvability. On the one hand, TD needs to be repaid sooner or later, as it may have grave consequences for future software development cycles; on the other hand, TD (and ATD as a type of TD) is not necessarily a "bad thing," but rather something that can be leveraged for business advantage when incurred with full knowledge of the consequences, that is being explicitly managed (Kruchten et al., 2012).

Although many approaches have been proposed to document architecture decisions in the architecting process (e.g., decision views in architecture design; see van Heesch et al., 2012a, 2012b), the ATD caused by decisions is still not effectively managed. In most cases, ATD is not made explicit, and architecture decision making does not take into account the ATD that will be incurred by the different design options. This may cause problems particularly during system maintenance and evolution, when ATD is accumulated and difficult to repay. In this chapter, we present an initial attempt to tackle this problem through the following: (1) an ATD conceptual model; and (2) an architectural technical debt management (ATDM) process applying the proposed conceptual model, and aligned with a general architecting process. Our contribution to this end can facilitate optimal decision making in architecture design and achieve a controllable and predictable balance between the value and cost of architecture design in the long term.

The rest of this chapter is organized as follows: Section 9.2 discusses architectural technical debt, while section 9.3 proposes an ATD conceptual model. Section 9.4 presents an ATDM process integrating the proposed conceptual model and the application of the ATDM process in value-oriented architecting. Section 9.5 describes an industrial example to demonstrate how value-oriented architecting with ATDM works in real-life projects. Section 9.6 discusses work related to the topic of this chapter, and Section 9.7 concludes this chapter with future research directions.

9.2 Architectural technical debt

Technical debt in software development has attracted increasing interest from practitioners and researchers in the software engineering community. Technical debt is a metaphor, coined by Ward Cunningham in 1992, for the trade-off between writing "clean" code at higher cost and delayed delivery, and writing "dirty" code cheaper and faster by making shortcuts resulting in higher maintenance cost once it is shipped (Buschmann, 2011; Cunningham, 1992). This metaphor was initially proposed and concerned with software coding. Currently, the concept of technical debt is extended to other phases in the software development life cycle, such as software architecture design, detailed design, and even software documentation and testing (Brown et al., 2010; Ozkaya et al., 2011).

TD is essentially invisible to users because they cannot witness the existence of TD when they are using a software system that works well. Conceptually, technical debt concerns the technological gaps between the current solutions and the optimal solutions, which may have a negative impact on system quality, especially the maintainability and evolvability of a software system (Kruchten et al., 2012). Architectural technical debt (ATD) is a type of TD at the architectural level. It is caused mainly by architecture design decisions that compromise the maintainability and evolvability of a software system. In contrast, code-level technical debt is concerned with the quality of the code and is usually incurred by the poor structure of the code and disobedience of coding rules and best practices (i.e., bad code smells).

Maintainability and evolvability are the two main system quality attributes that are compromised when incurring ATD. According to the ISO/IEC FDIS 25010 standard (ISO/IEC, 2011), maintainability includes the following subcharacteristics (i.e., quality attributes): modularity, reusability, analyzability, modifiability, and testability. Evolvability is not defined in either ISO 9126 or ISO/IEC FDIS 25010. We define software evolvability as the ease of adding new or changing existing requirements (functional and nonfunctional). As an example of ATD, consider an architecture decision, which uses a legacy component implemented with an obsolete technology to speed up development. This may make it hard to add new functionalities with new technologies that are incompatible with the obsolete technology. In summary, ATD essentially results from the compromise of modularity, reusability, analyzability, modifiability, testability, or evolvability during architecting. In this chapter, we only consider the quality attributes (QAs) maintainability and evolvability, while other QAs are out of scope of ATD (Kruchten et al., 2012).

ATD, as a kind of TD, can be seen as an important type of risk for a software project in the long term (Seaman and Guo, 2011), but the architecture and management teams often ignore ATD. The main reason is that ATD concerns the cost of the long-term maintenance and evolution of a software system instead of the visible short-term business value. Furthermore, ATD is not easy to identify and measure since it is invisible until the following cases happen: Maintenance tasks are hard to conduct, new features are difficult to introduce, and system quality attributes are challenging to meet. This chapter helps solve this problem by making ATD explicit through a conceptual model and by offering a process to manage ATD through explicit cost-benefit trade-offs.

ATD is incurred by either explicit or implicit architecture decisions. ATD can be managed in two ways: When architecture decisions are being made and after decisions have been made. The former aims at dealing with ATD before it is incurred by an explicit architecture decision, whereas the latter focuses on handling ATD after it has been incurred by an existing explicit or implicit architecture decision. Both ATD management approaches are presented in section 9.4.

9.3 ATD conceptual model and template

This section proposes an ATD conceptual model for capturing and using ATD in the architecting process.

9.3.1 Conceptual model

We constructed an ATD conceptual model that is depicted in Figure 9.1 using UML notation, based on our understanding of ATD and TD literature (Brown et al., 2010; Kruchten et al., 2012). The gray part of this model (*Architecture rationale*, *Architecture decision*, and *Concern*) represents the concepts

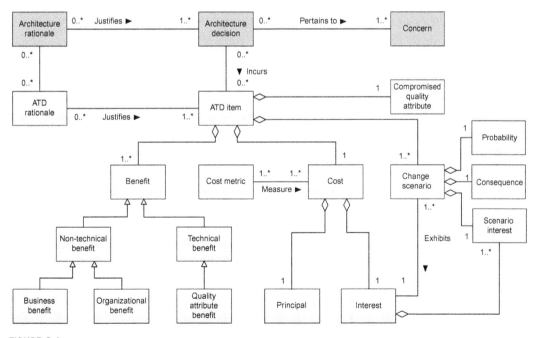

FIGURE 9.1

ATD Conceptual model.

adopted from the conceptual model of architecture decisions and rationale in ISO 42010:2011 (ISO/IEC/IEEE, 2011). In this conceptual model, the core concept is the ATD item, which acts as the basic unit to record ATD. An example of an ATD item is presented in section 9.3.2. Note that in the rest of this chapter, the phrases "resolve an ATD item" and "repay ATD" will be used interchangeably.

- An **ATD item** is a basic unit of ATD that is incurred by an architecture decision that compromises a system quality attribute: evolvability or maintainability. The detailed representation and description of this concept with a template are presented in section 9.3.2.
- **ATD rationale** justifies why an ATD item is incurred, and it records explanation, justification, or reasoning about an ATD item incurred. The ATD rationale for an ATD item may partially use the architecture rationale for the architecture decision that incurs the ATD item, when the architecture rationale explains trade-offs between maintainability or evolvability and other system quality attributes.
- A **compromised quality attribute** refers to the QA that is sacrificed to meet other concerns (e.g., business benefit). A compromised QA concerning an ATD item can only be either maintainability (which includes the following sub-QAs: modularity, reusability, analyzability, modifiability, and testability (ISO/IEC, 2011) or evolvability according to the clarification of why TD is incurred (Kruchten et al., 2012).
- **Cost** refers to the sum of the effort (e.g., person-day, time, or money) that is needed to resolve an ATD item and the added effort spent on maintenance and evolution tasks.
- A **cost metric** is used to measure the cost to resolve an ATD item in a quantitative way, and it can be person-days, calendar days, monetary units (e.g., U.S. dollar), or others.
- **Principal** refers to the cost if an ATD item is being resolved at the time the ATD item is identified, that is, according to the architecture design at that time.
- **Interest** refers to the extra cost due to maintenance or evolution work if an ATD item is not resolved. The interest of an ATD item may increase when related changes take place in the part of the software architecture that contains the ATD item. For instance, the principal of an ATD item is five person-days for the current release of the system, while the interest will be another three person-days when the ATD item is left unresolved in the next release of the system. The interest of an ATD item consists of the scenario interests caused by a set of relevant change scenarios, which are explained in the next bullet.
- A **change scenario** describes a possible change (an evolution or a maintenance task) that influences an ATD item and the consequence of this change. A change scenario can be used to calculate the interest of an ATD item. Typical change scenarios include: (1) the unimplemented features that are planned in the roadmap of the software system, but difficult to introduce without modifying the architecture; and (2) the maintenance tasks that improve certain QAs (except maintainability and evolvability which have been compromised in ATD) of the implemented software architecture. Each scenario consists of three elements: consequence, scenario interest, and probability.
- **Consequence** refers to extra work resulting from a change scenario when the related ATD item is unresolved.
- **Scenario interest** refers to the interest of a change scenario related to an ATD item.
- **Probability** refers to the likelihood a change scenario will actually happen in the next release.
- **Benefit** refers to the positive impact on the system when an ATD item is incurred, for example, shorter time to market or improved system quality.

- **Technical benefit** refers to the benefit gained in terms of design-time or runtime quality attributes of the software system, when an ATD item is incurred.
- **Nontechnical benefit** refers to the benefit gained in terms of business and organizational aspects when an ATD item is incurred.
- **Business benefit** refers to the benefit gained in business aspects when an ATD item is incurred, such as shorter time to market or decreased development cost.
- **Organizational benefit** refers to the benefit gained to the organization that develops the software system (i.e., the benefit to the organization instead of the software system itself) when an ATD item is incurred. As an example, consider an organization that chooses to reuse in a new system existing components developed in other projects, though these components do not fit the software architecture perfectly. As a result, the organization does not need to maintain various components with similar functionalities.
- **Quality attribute benefit** refers to the benefit gained in terms of improvement of a specific quality attribute of the software system when an ATD item is incurred. The improved quality attribute can be any type except maintainability and evolvability. Here is an example: A software system adopts the relaxed layered pattern instead of the strict layered pattern to achieve higher performance at the cost of lower maintainability.

Note that the interest of an ATD item will increase as changes occur in the part of the architecture that influences the ATD item; we propose to measure the interest of an ATD item using software release as the time unit. The time length within which one can predict possible change scenarios, influences the amount and accuracy of the estimated interest of ATD items. The longer time length one adopts, the more change scenarios one will get but with less accuracy. We argue that architects can predict change scenarios in the next release of a software system more reasonably since they are more certain about what changes will occur in the next release than in the next two or more releases.

9.3.2 **ATD item**

As shown in Table 9.1, the ATD item template provides detailed information needed to document an ATD item. This template is based on the ATD conceptual model, so most of the elements in this template are adopted from the model. The explanation of each element is briefly described in the template. We provide more detailed description about some key elements in the template. *ID* is the unique identification number of the ATD item, so that an ATD item can be referred to within the architecture description of a software system by using this ID. The *Name* of an ATD item reflects the essence of the ATD item. The *Status* of an ATD item can be unresolved or resolved. Resolved ATD items of a software architecture are a type of architectural knowledge (AK) of the software system. This type of AK shows how the ATD of a software system was managed; therefore, it can benefit future decision making of this system, or it can be reused in similar systems. The unresolved ATD items of a software system should be monitored. An ATD item is *Incurred by* an architecture decision. In order to keep the scope of an ATD item manageable, if ATD is incurred by a group of architecture decisions, we decompose it into several ATD items so that each item is caused by an individual architecture decision. *Change scenarios* are used to measure the interest of an ATD item. Each scenario with a *scenario number (#)* consists of *scenario description*, *consequence*, *scenario interest*, and *probability*. The *interest* of an ATD item is the

Table 9.1 Template for Documenting an ATD Item

ID	An Unique Identification Number of the ATD Item
Name	The name of this ATD item
Date	The date when this ATD item was generated or changed
Status	Resolved or unresolved
Incurred by	The decision incurs this ATD item
Responsible	The name of the person or team responsible for managing this ATD item
Compromised QA	The QA(s) that are compromised, from modularity, reusability, analyzability, modifiability, testability, or evolvability
Rationale	The reason the ATD item is incurred
Benefit	The value gained when this ATD item is incurred
Cost	The cost suffered by incurring this ATD item, which is the sum of principal and interest below.
Principal	The cost if this ATD item is resolved at the time when the ATD item is identified
Interest	The interest that this ATD item accumulates (the interest is calculated based on the predicted change scenarios described below)

Change Scenarios	#	Scenario description	Consequence	Scenario interest	Prob.
	1	Scenario 1	consequence of scenario 1	I_1	P_1
	2	Scenario 2	consequence of scenario 2	I_2	P_2
	...	...	...	...	...
	n	Scenario n	consequence of scenario n	I_n	P_n
	The interest of this ATD item (total interest) $= \sum_{k=1}^{n} I_k \times P_k$				
Architecture Diagram	A diagram or model that illustrates the concerned part in the architecture design				
History	Change history of this ATD item				

sum of the product of the *scenario interest* of each scenario and its *probability* as calculated by the formula in Table 9.1.

To explain the use of this template to document ATD items, a concrete example of an ATD item is presented in Table 9.2. This ATD item is from an architecture design of an industrial information system with which users can query product test results and customize reports on product test results. The test results of various products, which are generated by external automatic test systems, are stored in a remote database. There are also some pictures and text files as the test results of some types of tests and these files are stored in file servers. The current architecture is made up of four layers as shown in Table 9.2. The User Interface layer handles users' events. The Algorithm layer is responsible for generating product quality reports. The Test Result File Management layer is responsible for getting test result files from right server and parsing test results files into specific forms. The Data Access layer provides services to store and query the data in the database.

Table 9.2 An Example ATD Item

ID	ATD-6
Name	Compromised modifiability due to relaxed layered pattern
Date	26-10-2012
Status	Unresolved
Incurred by	Decision-6: Using relaxed layered architectural pattern to speed up development
Responsible	Zengyang
Compromised QA	Modifiability
Rationale	From a technical perspective, the strict layered pattern is a more appropriate solution. We decided to employ the relaxed layered architectural pattern to allow invocations to go across layers. Compared with the strict layered pattern, it is not necessary to encapsulate everything within the upper layers from the lower layers. Thus, we can save development time by skipping the effort of encapsulating every service of a layer from the layer below. Meanwhile, the performance of this software system is improved since invocations can go across layers in the relaxed layered pattern. But this solution will have a negative impact on modifiability of the system when the predicted change scenarios happen since a change in a lower layer may cause modifications of all upper layers that directly depend on the lower layer.
Benefit	i. 11 person-days of development time are saved by implementing the relaxed layered pattern compared to implementing the layered pattern in the system. ii. The performance of the software system is improved.
Cost	Principal + Interest = 10 + 15.2 = 25.2 person-days
Principal	10 person-days (if we use the layered pattern to resolve this ATD item at the time when the ATD item is identified)
Interest	$12 \times 0.6 + 10 \times 0.8 = 15.2$ person-days

Change Scenarios	#	Scenario description	Consequence	Scenario interest	Prob.
	1	Change file transfer method in layer 1	Both layer 2 and layer 3 are influenced and must be modified accordingly.	12 person-days	0.6
	2	Replace the data access method of the lowest layer (DB Access) because a new technology is adopted	All the upper layers need to be modified accordingly.	10 person-days	0.8

Architecture Diagram

History	Created: 18-07-2012 by Zengyang Updated: 26-10-2012 by Zengyang, revised the probability of change scenario 1 from 0.5 to 0.6.

9.4 Method

This section proposes a decision-based ATDM (DATDM) approach. To derive the process, we collected activities for technical debt management from a number of publications surveyed in (Li et al., 2013), and we combined these activities to form an ATDM process (i.e., the DATDM approach) that is based on architecture decisions and integrates the proposed ATD conceptual model. The DATDM approach is introduced and employed in the architecting process to facilitate various architecting activities.

9.4.1 ATDM process

We surveyed publications on technical debt management and identified a number of activities for managing TD (Li et al., 2013). These activities have been adapted from TD to ATD. ATD identification, measurement, and monitoring are adopted from Brown et al. (2010). ATD prioritization is selected from Zazworka et al. (2011). ATD repayment is introduced in Brown et al. (2010). The details of each ATDM activity as well as their input and output in the architecting process are as follows.

1. **ATD identification** detects ATD items during or after the architecting process. An ATD item is incurred by an architecture decision; thus, one can investigate an architecture decision and its rationale to identify an ATD item by considering whether the maintainability or evolvability of the software architecture is compromised.
2. **ATD measurement** analyzes the cost and benefit associated with an ATD item and estimates them, including the prediction of change scenarios influencing this ATD item for interest measurement. For interest measurement, three types of change scenarios are considered: (1) the planned new features according to the release plan of the software project; (2) the already-known maintenance tasks that enhance specific QAs (except maintainability and evolvability) of the implemented software architecture; and (3) the emerging requirements. The first two types of change scenarios can be predicted, while the third is unforeseeable. For some complex software systems (e.g., operating systems), the time interval between two releases can be very long. For instance, Microsoft Windows 7 Service Package 1 was released 16 months after the first release of Microsoft Windows 7. For such kind of software system, it is inevitable that new requirements emerge during the development of a new release. Some of these new requirements need to be implemented in the release. Thus, in such cases, to ensure a reasonable accuracy of interest measurement, the interest of related ATD items should be re-measured at different times during the development of the release.
3. **ATD prioritization** sorts all the identified ATD items in a software system using a number of criteria. The aim of this activity is to identify which ATD items should be resolved first and which can be resolved later depending on the system's business goals and preferences. There are a number of ATD items in a software system, and not all the ATD items will be resolved at one time owing to their costs or technical issues. The ATD items have different financial and technical impacts on the system. Consequently, it is wise to choose the items with higher priorities to be resolved first. Software projects have different contexts, and there are no standard criteria to decide the priority of an ATD item in a project. However, the following factors need to be taken into account in ATD prioritization: (1) the total cost of resolving an

ATD item; (2) the cost/benefit ratio of the ATD item; (3) the interest rate of the ATD item; (4) how long the ATD item has been incurred; and (5) the complexity (e.g., the number of involved components of an ATD item) of resolving an ATD item. Since not all types of benefits can be measured in a unified metric, it is hard to automatically prioritize the ATD items by tooling. However, an appropriate tool, which reasonably deals with the factors described above, can facilitate ATD prioritization.

4. **ATD repayment** concerns making new or changing existing architecture decisions in order to eliminate or mitigate the negative influences of an ATD item. An ATD item is not necessarily resolved at once. In certain situations, only part of an ATD item is resolved, because it could be too expensive to resolve the entire ATD item, and resolving part of the ATD item can make the ATD item under control with an acceptable cost. When an ATD item is partially resolved, the ATD item will be revised and split into two parts: the part that is resolved and the part that is not.

5. **ATD monitoring** watches the changes of the costs and benefits of unresolved ATD items over time. When an architectural change occurs in the part of architecture design containing an unresolved ATD item or when one ATD item is partially resolved, the affected ATD item will be recognized as a changed ATD item. All the changed ATD items will be measured in the next ATDM iteration. This ATDM activity makes ATD changes explicitly and consequently keeps all the ATD items of the system under control.

Figure 9.2 shows the process of ATDM with the inputs and outputs of each ATDM activity. In a software project, the ATDM process is generally performed multiple times during the life cycle of the project. An ATDM iteration is defined as a period in which the ATDM process goes through all possible ATDM activities. For instance, an ATDM iteration can be a release, an increment development period, or a Sprint in Scrum. The time when an ATDM iteration will happen depends on the actual necessity of performing ATDM activities. The activities in the ATDM process can be revisited when necessary. In addition, it is not mandatory that all ATDM activities should be performed in every iteration of the ATDM process. In the rest of this section, we discuss how this ATDM process deals with ATD items. The detailed ATDM process is presented as follows:

1. When a new architecture decision made results in compromising maintainability or evolvability, the architect identifies a new ATD item. If an architecture decision is reconsidered, there are two options: If it already compromised maintainability or evolvability, then the existing ATD item is revised; if it did not previously compromise maintainability or evolvability, then a new ATD item is created. First, the architect identifies which QA is compromised by this decision by analyzing the documented architecture decision and its rationale. Then, taking the compromised QA as the basis of the *ATD identification*, the architect further identifies the ATD item and rationale.

2. The ATDM process moves to the *ATD measurement*. After change scenarios related to the architecture decision are predicted, the architect estimates the interest of this ATD item based on these change scenarios. With the ATD rationale, the architect also estimates the principal and the benefit of the ATD item.

3. The ATDM process continues with *ATD prioritization*. ATD prioritization sorts all the identified ATD items according to specific criteria (e.g., the ATD item with higher cost gets a higher priority to be resolved) when a new ATD item is introduced or any existing ATD item is changed. The criteria are defined by architects according to the concrete architecting context

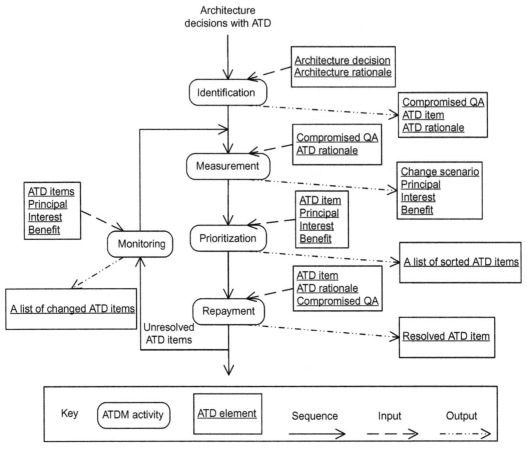

FIGURE 9.2

ATDM process with inputs and outputs of ATDM activities.

since there is no uniform unit to compare all the costs and benefits of ATD items. The architect then browses the prioritized ATD items and decides the ATD items that should be resolved.

4. If there are ATD items that should be resolved, the ATDM process moves to *ATD repayment.* Otherwise, the ATDM process moves to *ATD monitoring* of existing ATD items. *When any change occurs with the monitored ATD items, the ATDM* process will repeat the following activities sequentially: *ATD measurement, ATD prioritization,* and *ATD repayment.*

9.4.2 ATDM within the architecting process

Hofmeister et al. proposed an architectural design model that consists of three core architecting activities: architectural analysis, synthesis, and evaluation (Hofmeister et al., 2007). Architectural analysis "examines, filters, and/or reformulates architectural concerns and context in order to come

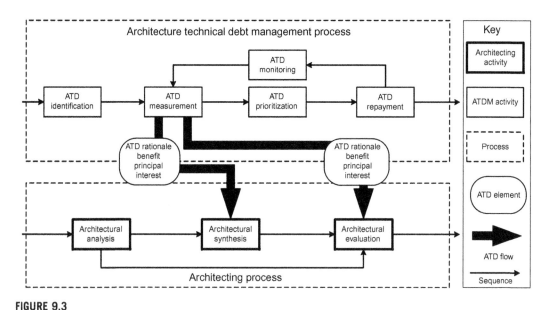

FIGURE 9.3

ATDM in architecting process with ATD flow.

up with a set of architecturally significant requirements (ASRs)" (Hofmeister et al., 2007, p. 113). Architectural synthesis proposes a collection of architecture solutions to address the ASRs identified during architectural analysis (Hofmeister et al., 2007). Architectural evaluation evaluates the candidate architectural solutions that are proposed during architectural synthesis against the ASRs (Hofmeister et al., 2007). These architecting activities are not performed sequentially but are iterated during architecture design. Furthermore, these activities are also performed during software maintenance and evolution in order to maintain the consistency and correctness of the architecture.

In this work we apply the proposed ATDM process (i.e., DATDM approach) to managing ATD within the general architecting process in Hofmeister et al. (2007). A software architecture can be considered as a set of architecture decisions (Jansen and Bosch, 2005). Therefore, the architecting process can be regarded as a decision-making process. The objective of this approach is to facilitate the architecture decision-making process by managing ATD and, consequently to assist architects in making appropriate and well-founded decisions and to ensure that the ATD of a system remains controllable.

Figure 9.3 shows ATDM within the architecting process and focuses on how the ATD flow can facilitate the architecting activities. The ATD flow refers to a kind of data (artifacts) flow from the ATDM process to the architecting process. The ATD flow, consisting of instances of ATD concepts, bridges the gap between the ATDM process and the value-oriented architecting process. ATDM can facilitate both architectural synthesis and evaluation. In particular, measured ATD items can be used as input for architectural synthesis and evaluation activities: (1) In architectural synthesis, an architect can reflect on the design options for a decision topic in terms of ATD, and particularly in terms of the costs and benefits of the identified ATD items. (2) In architectural evaluation, the evaluator assesses the architecture decisions made (either implemented into code or not) against the related architecturally significant requirements (ASRs), for example, scenarios pertaining to a certain quality attribute. The identified and measured ATD items can be used as inputs and outputs of architectural evaluation. The existing architectural evaluation methods tend to assess to what extent the architecture design meets the existing requirements. ATDM is concerned with the balance of cost and benefit of a software system from an ATD perspective. Thus, ATDM provides a complementary perspective on the costs and benefits of architecture decisions caused by ATD to existing evaluation methods.

ATDM can be used to facilitate decision making in architectural synthesis (i.e., make architecture decisions for decision topics) and to evaluate architecture decisions that have been made. ATDM activities can be triggered in the following situations: (1) maintenance tasks are hard to complete, or new functionalities are difficult to add and implement in an existing architecture; (2) there is a need to update the information of existing ATD items of an architecture due to changes of this architecture; and (3) there is a need to evaluate the existing decisions at any point of time.

In architectural synthesis, for each decision topic, the main steps in using the DATDM approach are:

1. Proposing design options for the decision topic.
2. Identifying ATD items. The architect identifies the ATD items incurred by each design option for the decision topic by analyzing each design option.
3. Measuring ATD items. For each ATD item identified in Step 2, the cost and benefit are estimated.
4. Making the architecture decision with consideration of ATD items. The ATD items are also recorded as part of the rationale of the architecture decision.

In architectural evaluation, the main steps in using the DATDM approach are:

1. Collecting architecture decisions of those types: (i) that have not incurred ATD; (ii) that are related to architectural maintenance tasks hard to conduct; (iii) that are related to new requirements difficult to introduce; and (iv) that are related to changes of the existing architecture design. Architecture decisions with their rationales are the inputs for the next step.
2. Identifying ATD items. For each architecture decision collected in Step 1, identify the ATD items incurred by the architecture decision through analyzing the decision and its rationale.
3. Measuring ATD items. For each architecture decision, estimate the costs and benefits of the ATD items (including the newly identified ATD items in Step 2 and the ATD items already identified in architectural synthesis and previous architectural evaluations).
4. Evaluating architecture decisions with consideration of ATD items, more specifically the costs and benefits of ATD items.

After architectural evaluation, all the identified ATD items will be prioritized and the ATD items with the higher priorities will be the candidate ATD items to be resolved first. Then, the ATDM process moves to ATD repayment. To resolve an ATD item, the architecting process revisits architectural synthesis activity with this ATD item as an input.

9.5 Case study

This section presents an industrial example to demonstrate how the proposed ATD conceptual model and process for ATDM can support reaching a balanced architecture design in terms of value and cost in the long term. The software system used in this example is a system for automatic testing of hardware products with embedded systems running on them—Automatic Test System (ATS)—which is a real-life project developed by a leading telecommunications equipment manufacturer in China. The rest of this section introduces the background of the ATS, the architecture design of the ATS, and the use of decision-based ATDM in the architecting process.

9.5.1 Background

ATS aims to automatically test hardware products. Typical tested hardware products by ATS are mainboards of high-performance routers and base stations of wireless telecommunications. Generally speaking, two kinds of tests need to be performed on the products before delivery: functional test and performance test. The functional test is used to ensure that the functionalities of the tested products work in various conditions (e.g., high-temperature and low-temperature environments), while the performance test is to make sure the tested products satisfy the minimal performance requirements (e.g., a specific radio frequency sensitivity of telecommunication base stations) in different conditions. The ATS in this example is dedicated to performing functional tests of base stations.

Typically, an ATS is a combination of hardware and software subsystems. The hardware subsystem is used as a test environment. The software subsystem is responsible for communicating with the Unit Under Test (UUT), perform the test, and generate the test results in various forms. In this example, the ATS refers to the software subsystem in a typical ATS. In this case study, the ATS provides features, such as test automation, test results visualization, and test results persistence (i.e., storing test results to a database).

9.5.2 Architecture design

Figure 9.4 shows the main components in the software architecture of the ATS. ATS Controller handles the commands from the GUI component. The typical test process is described as follows: (1) A user logs in to the ATS through the *GUI* component, and *ATS Controller* deals with the user login in *User Management*. (2) The user configures the current test through *GUI* component, and the *ATS Controller* deals with the test configuration in *Test Settings*. (3) The user starts an automatic test in the *GUI* component, and the *ATS Controller* starts the *Test Engine* that is the most important component and responsible for executing the *Test Item Flow*. (4) The *Test Engine* loads the test configuration data for the current test, requests the *Test Item List Parser* to parse all the test items of this test, and loads the specific *Test Item Flow* for test items. *Test Item Flow* implements the concrete test execution flow for all test items of a specific test. (5) The *Test Engine* executes each test item and generates test results. The *Test Engine* updates these test results to the *GUI* component and *Test Result Saver*, so that the user can see the real-time test results in the *GUI* component and the test results can be collected and stored in right time. (6) *Test Result Saver* stores test results to the database (*MS SQL Server*) through *DB Handler*, which provides services to store data to and query data from the *MS SQL Server*. (7) If any fault or exception happens during the test, the *Logger* records the fault or exception information in a log file to assist problem tracing and fixing.

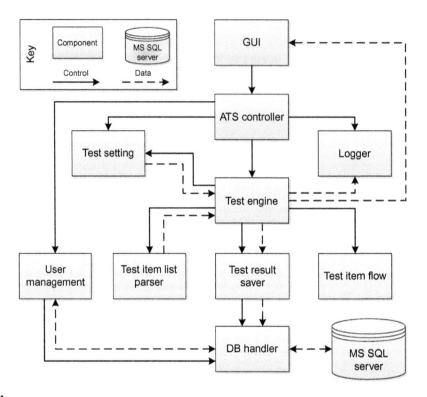

FIGURE 9.4

Component diagram of ATS software architecture.

9.5.3 Using DATDM in architecting activities

This subsection illustrates two concrete examples using DATDM in architectural synthesis and evaluation, respectively, in the context of the ATS architecture design.

9.5.3.1 ATDM in architectural synthesis

In architectural synthesis, the architect proposes design options for each architecture decision topic and then chooses the more appropriate one that addresses the decision topic according to the pros and cons of the design options.

To improve the reliability of the test results persistence and to keep the ATS running uninterruptedly when the remote database server (MS SQL Server) is inaccessible, a decision topic arises (of AD-12): how to store test results locally in a "cache" when the remote database server is inaccessible. The architect proposes two design options for this decision topic: storing test results in XML files (design option 1) and storing test results in MS Access (design option 2). Since the test results are stored in a remote database and a local database (or file), any change to the table design in the remote database needs to be updated to the local one. Otherwise the test results cannot be stored correctly. In addition, the test results in the local database (or file) need to be synchronized to the remote database. Therefore, the two design options will incur ATD. The ATD items ATD-10 and ATD-11 that are incurred by the two design options are presented in Table 9.3 and Table 9.4, respectively.

After comparing the ATD items with their costs and benefits, the architect chooses design option 2 as the solution (design decision) to address the decision topic, since the cost of ATD-11 (incurred by option 2) is less than ATD-10 (incurred by option 1) and the benefit of ATD-11 is more valuable for the project currently in the current release.

9.5.3.2 ATDM in architectural evaluation

Suppose that the first release of the ATS product has been delivered; the architecture of ATS needs an architectural evaluation since the first delivery was developed in a tight schedule and its architecture design did not receive a serious external evaluation by an independent party. As an example, architecture decision AD-8 was evaluated using the DATDM approach. The architecture decision is described below:

AD-8: The Test Engine updates test results to the GUI component and Test Result Saver. This architecture decision is adopted from a previous automatic test application, so that some legacy components can be reused in this ATS.

According to the DATDM approach to architectural evaluation described in section 9.4.2, the following steps are performed:

1. Architecture decision AD-8 with its rationale is used as the input of the architectural evaluation.
2. An ATD item (i.e., ATD-3) is identified using the ATD item template as shown in Table 9.5.
3. Two change scenarios are predicted. These scenarios are negatively influenced by AD-8, and they are used to measure the cost of ATD-3. The benefit of ATD-3 is estimated according to the decision and its rationale. The benefit and cost of ATD-3 are analyzed and described in Table 9.5.
4. ATD-3 is considered as part of output of this architectural evaluation.

In addition, suppose that a number of ATD items are identified and measured in the ATS architecture design in the architectural evaluation using DATDM. After analyzing and comparing the benefits and costs of these ATD items, ATD-3 is prioritized as the most critical ATD item, and the architect decides that this ATD item should be resolved urgently since it negatively influences the evolution of the ATS. Therefore, the ATD-3 enters the ATD repayment activity in the DATDM process. The root reason resulting in ATD-3 is that the generation of test results is not transparent to use of the test results. If the architect adds a *Test Result Repository* as an intermediate component between *Test Engine* and *GUI component* with *Test Result Saver*, the *Test Engine* is then free from direct uses of test results. Consequently, adding a new functionality that uses the test results will not result in the modification and testing cost to the *Test Engine*. Therefore, a solution to resolving architectural technical debt ATD-3 is to add a *Test Result Repository* that stores the test results temporarily, as shown in Table 9.6. The *Test Engine* updates the latest test results to the *Test Result Repository*, and all the components that use test results will request the test results from the *Test Result Repository* instead of the *Test Engine*. The resolved ATD item ATD-3 is shown in Table 9.6, which only depicts the updated elements comparing with the ATD-3 in Table 9.5.

Table 9.3 An ATD Item Identified from Design Option 1 of Architecture Decision AD-12

ID	ATD-10
Name	Compromised modifiability due to using XML files to store test results
Date	10-11-2012
Status	Unresolved
Incurred by	AD-12: storing test results in XML files (design option 1)
Responsible	Tom
Compromised QA	Modifiability
Rationale	If XML is used to store test results temporarily when the remote database server is inaccessible, extra functions to store and read the test results to and from XML files are needed. In addition, any new table added in the remote database requires a new XML schema.
Benefit	i. XML files are platform-independent, and they can be reused in the ATS when running in other operating systems. ii. The developers are experienced in developing and testing with XML, so that they do not need additional training, which saves time and cost.
Cost	$1 + 8.1 = 9.1$ person-days
Principal	1 person-day (this is the architecture redesign cost to resolving this ATD item, and there is no implementation cost of a design change during architecture design phase)
Interest	$5 \times 0.9 + 4 \times 0.9 = 8.1$ person-days

Change Scenarios	#	Scenario description	Consequence	Scenario interest	Prob.
	1	Synchronize the data in local storage files to the remote database server	Add functions to read the test results from XML files and store the test results to MS SQL Server	5 person-days	0.9
	2	Add new tables (around 10) to record the new test results in MS SQL Server	Design XML schemas and add functions to store the test results to XML files	4 person-days	0.9
Architecture Diagram					

History	Created: 10-11-2012 by Tom

Table 9.4 An ATD Item Identified from Design Option 2 of Architecture Decision AD-12

ID	ATD-11
Name	Compromised modifiability due to using MS Access to store test results
Date	10-11-2012
Status	Unresolved
Incurred by	AD-12: storing test results temporarily in local MS Access database (design option 2)
Responsible	Tom
Compromised QA	Modifiability
Rationale	If MS Access as a local database is used to store test results temporarily when the remote database server is inaccessible, any change of the table design in the remote database requires the according modification to the tables in MS Access. In addition, data in the local MS Access database need to be uploaded and synchronized to the remote database.
Benefit	i. DB Handler can be reused to store data to the MS SQL Server since both MS SQL Server and MS Access support the SQL standard.
	ii. The performance of MS Access is better than file-based storage methods (e.g., XML).
	iii. This design option can enrich the development team with the experience of using MS Access as a database, which may be helpful to other ATS projects.
Cost	$1 + 2.25 = 3.25$ person-days
Principal	1 person-day (same reason as described in Table 9.3)
Interest	$2 \times 0.9 + 0.5 \times 0.9 = 2.25$ person-days

Change Scenarios	#	Scenario description	Consequence	Scenario interest	Prob.
	1	Synchronize the data in local storage files to the remote database server	Develop functions to query test results from MS Access and test the functions	2 person-days	0.9
	2	Add new tables (around 10) to record the new test results in MS SQL Server	Add the new tables in MS Access and test them	0.5 person-days	0.9
Architecture Diagram					

History	Created: 10-11-2012 by Tom

Table 9.5 An ATD Item Identified from Architecture Decision AD-8

ID	ATD-3
Name	Compromised evolvability due to dealing with test results in the *Test Engine*
Date	26-10-2012
Status	Unresolved
Caused by	AD-8: The Test Engine updates test results to *GUI component* and *Test Result Saver*
Responsible	Zengyang
Compromised QA	Evolvability
Rationale	The use of test results is heavily related to the most important component—*Test Engine*. Adding any new functionality that needs to use test results will result in modification and testing of the *Test Engine* and any functionality depending on the *Test Engine*.
Benefit	i. The reliability of test result persistence of the ATS is good since the test results are updated to the *GUI component* and the *Test Result Saver* immediately when the results are generated. ii. The performance of updating test results to the *GUI component* and *Test Result Saver* is good since the test results are updated directly to these two components without crossing intermediate components. iii. The ATS can reuse a component of a legacy system that employs a similar strategy to the *Test Engine* in the ATS; therefore, 6 person-days are saved.
Cost	8 + 14.4 = 22.4 person-days
Principal	8 person-days
Interest	$10 \times 0.9 + 6 \times 0.9 = 14.4$ person-days

Change Scenarios	#	Scenario description	Consequence	Scenario interest	Prob.
	1	Add a Unit Under Test (UUT) visualization component	Have to modify the code in the *Test Engine* and test all functionalities depending on the *Test Engine*	10 person-days	0.9
	2	Generate a report for the just-finished test	Have to store the test results somewhere, such as a buffer	6 person-days	0.9

Architecture Diagram

History	Created: 26-10-2012 by Zengyang

Table 9.6 Resolved ATD Item ATD-3

ID	ATD-3
Date	26-11-2012
Status	Resolved
Responsible	Zengyang
Rationale	The solution to resolving ATD-3 is to add a *Test Result Repository* that stores the test results temporarily, as shown in the following architecture diagram. The *Test Engine* updates the latest test results to the *Test Result Repository*, and all the components that use test results will request the test results from the *Test Result Repository* instead of the *Test Engine*. In this way, the *Test Engine* is free from the direct uses of test results.
Architecture Diagram	

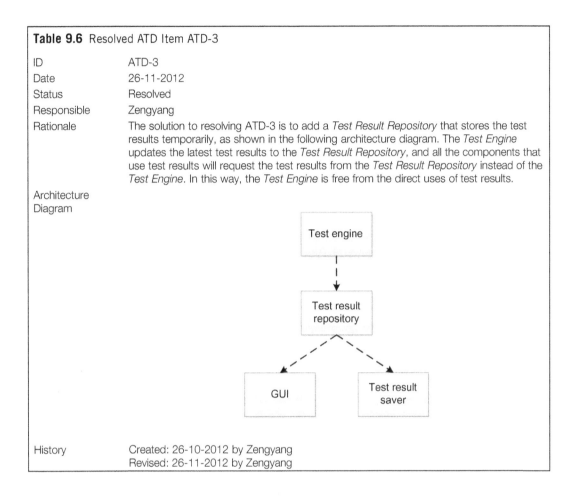

History	Created: 26-10-2012 by Zengyang Revised: 26-11-2012 by Zengyang

9.6 Related work

Value-oriented software architecting is an important area in value-based software engineering (Boehm, 2006), especially for architecture practitioners, since it explicitly considers economic aspects as a driven factor within the whole architecting process. Practitioners and researchers in the software architecture community have already put considerable effort into this area and have investigated value and economic impact in architecture design. Kazman et al. proposed the Cost-Benefit Analysis Method (CBAM) for architecture evaluation (Kazman et al., 2001), which models and calculates the costs and benefits of architecture decisions to assist architecture evaluation in a cost and benefit perspective. Both CBAM and architecture evaluation with DATDM evaluate architectural strategies from a cost-benefit perspective based on scenarios. The major differences between CBAM and architecture evaluation with DATDM are as follows: (1) CBAM evaluates the quality attribute benefit of an architectural strategy, while our approach evaluates both the nontechnical benefit (e.g., organizational benefit) and the quality attribute benefit of an architecture decision; (2) CBAM estimates the cost of implementing an architectural strategy, but our approach estimates the future cost of maintenance and evolution tasks, plus the implementation cost of an architecture decision; and (3) our approach considers the probability of a change scenario in the next release as a parameter when estimating the cost of an ATD item. Martínez-Fernández et al. presented a reuse-based economic model for software reference architectures (Martínez-Fernández et al., 2012). This economic model provides a cost-benefit analysis for the adoption of reference architectures to optimize architectural decision making. This model also estimates the development and maintenance benefits and costs of a specific product based on reuse of a candidate reference architecture, and the reference architecture with highest ROI (return on investment) is selected. With this model, the benefits and costs of a software architecture as a whole are calculated, while in our DATDM approach, benefits and costs are measured based on architecture decisions and incurred ATD items.

Architectural technical debt management is an emerging research area in software architecture. To date, little research has been conducted on technical debt management at the architecture level, and the scope of architectural technical debt is not clear (Kruchten et al., 2012). Nord et al. employed an architecture-focused and measurement-based approach to develop a metric to quantify and manage architectural technical debt (Nord et al., 2012). In their approach, architectural technical debt is modeled as rework, and the amount of rework caused by a suboptimal architecture design strategy is considered as the metric for architectural technical debt measurement. This approach "can be used to optimize the cost of development over time while continuing to deliver value to the customer" (Nord et al., 2012, p. 91). Measuring ATD incurred by different design paths in this approach provides a good way to estimate the ATD incurred by a group of architecture decisions.

9.7 Conclusions and future work

Architectural technical debt is an important element that needs to be considered in the architecting process, especially for value-oriented architecting, but currently it is seldom addressed. This chapter proposes an ATD conceptual model with an ATD item template for ATD management and integrates this conceptual model into the ATDM process in order to facilitate decision making and decision evaluation in a value-oriented perspective in architecture design. Working examples with a template in using ATDM in architecture synthesis and evaluation also provides architecture practitioners a ready-made solution for managing ATD in their architecting contexts. In a methodology perspective, the contribution of this work provides a controllable and predictable balance between the value and cost of architecture design in the long term.

Using ATDM in value-oriented architecting is a new research area, and the following directions need further exploration:

1. *ATDM theory*. A number of research questions remain: How to measure quantitatively the benefits of an ATD item? Is it possible to measure the benefits of an ATD item in a uniform metric, or is measuring ATD items necessary and helpful for architects to make decisions? How to define the criteria used to decide whether a specific ATD item should be resolved intermediately or left unresolved until later releases? Besides the cost of resolving an ATD item

and its interest related to change scenarios, how do other value considerations such as aesthetics, social, societal, and governance concerns influence the cost of an ATD item? What is the correlation between the metrics of ATD and risk, such as cost for ATD items and impact for risk?

2. *ATDM tool support.* What features should an ideal ATDM tool have? For example, an ATDM tool may better support architects with ATD item documentation, ATD monitoring in a dashboard, and visualization of the relationships between incurred ATD items and architecture decisions.

3. *Evidence.* We currently lack scientific evidence (e.g., academic or industrial studies through controlled experiments) on how ATDM can facilitate architecting. Empirical studies on using ATDM in architecting activities are needed.

Acknowledgments

This work is partially supported by AFR-Luxembourg under the contract No. 895528 and the NSFC under the grant No. 61170025. We would like to thank the anonymous reviewers for their valuable comments on the earlier version of this chapter.

References

Boehm, B., 2006. Value-based doftware rngineering: overview and sgenda. In: Biffl, S., Aurum, A., Boehm, B., Erdogmus, H., Grünbacher, P. (Eds.), Value-nased Doftware Rngineering. Springer, Berlin, pp. 3−14.

Brown, N., Cai, Y., Guo, Y., Kazman, R., Kim, M., Kruchten, P., et al., 2010. Managing technical debt in software-reliant systems. Paper presented at the Proceedings of the FSE/SDP Workshop on Future of Software Engineering Research (FoSER'10), Santa Fe, New Mexico.

Buschmann, F., 2011. To pay or not to pay technical debt. IEEE Softw. 28 (6), 29−31.

Cunningham, W., 1992. The WyCash portfolio management system. Paper presented at the Addendum to the Proceedings on Object-oriented Programming Systems, Languages, and Applications (Addendum). Vancouver, British Columbia, Canada.

Hofmeister, C., Kruchten, P., Nord, R.L., Obbink, H., Ran, A., America, P., 2007. A general model of software architecture design derived from five industrial approaches. J. Syst. Softw. 80 (1), 106−126.

ISO/IEC, 2011. Systems and Software Engineering—Systems and Software Quality Requirements and Evaluation (SQuaRE)—System and Software Quality Models. ISO/IEC FDIS 25010:2011, pp. 1−34.

ISO/IEC/IEEE, 2011. Systems and software engineering—Architecture description. ISO/IEC/IEEE 42010:2011 (E) (Revision of ISO/IEC 42010:2007 and IEEE Std 1471−2000), 1−46.

Jansen, A., Bosch, J., 2005. Software architecture as a set of architectural design decisions. Paper presented at the Proceedings of the 5th Working IEEE/IFIP Conference on Software Architecture (WICSA'05), Pittsburgh, Pennsylvania.

Kazman, R., Asundi, J., Klein, M., 2001. Quantifying the costs and benefits of architectural decisions. Paper presented at the Proceedings of the 23rd International Conference on Software Engineering (ICSE'01), Toronto, Ontario, Canada.

Kruchten, P., Nord, R.L., Ozkaya, I., 2012. Technical debt: from metaphor to theory and practice. IEEE Softw. 29 (6), 18−21.

Li, Z., Liang, P., Avgeriou, P., 2013. A systematic mapping study on technical debt. Under submission.

Martínez-Fernández, S., Ayala, C., Franch, X., 2012. A reuse-based economic model for software reference architectures. Departament d'Enginyeria de Serveis i Sistemes d'Informació, Universitat Politècnica de Catalunya, Barcelona, Spain.

Nord, R.L., Ozkaya, I., Kruchten, P., Gonzalez-Rojas, M., 2012. In search of a metric for managing architectural technical debt. Paper presented at the Proceedings of the 10th Working IEEE/IFIP Conference on Software Architecture (WICSA '12), Helsinki, Finland.

Ozkaya, I., Kruchten, P., Nord, R.L., Brown, N., 2011. Managing technical debt in software development: report on the 2nd international workshop on managing technical debt, held at ICSE 2011. SIGSOFT Softw. Eng. Notes 36 (5), 33−35.

Seaman, C., Guo, Y., 2011. Measuring and monitoring technical debt. In: Zelkowitz, M. (Ed.), *Advances in Computers*, vol. 82. Elsevier Science, London, UK, pp. 25−45.

van Heesch, U., Avgeriou, P., Hilliard, R., 2012a. A documentation framework for architecture decisions. J. Syst. Softw. 85 (4), 795−820.

van Heesch, U., Avgeriou, P., Hilliard, R., 2012b. Forces on architecture decisions—a viewpoint. Paper presented at the 2012 Joint Working IEEE/IFIP Conference on Software Architecture and European Conference on Software Architecture (WICSA/ECSA '12).

Zazworka, N., Seaman, C., Shull, F., 2011. Prioritizing design debt investment opportunities. Paper presented at the Proceedings of the 2nd International Workshop on Managing Technical Debt (MTD '11), Waikiki, Honolulu, Hawaii.

Value Matrix: From Value to Quality and Architecture

Anand Kumar, Kesav Vithal Nori, Swaminathan Natarajan, and Doji Samson Lokku

Tata Consultancy Services, Pune, MH, India

10.1 Introduction

Software systems are increasingly complex, multidimensional, multidisciplinary, and evolving in nature. They involve several stakeholders and multiple organizations and purposes. They are governed by various factors with intricate interrelationships that impinge on the characteristics of the software system as a whole. In order to cope with such myriad factors and interrelationships, software architects put together multiple structures in terms of interacting software components, their composition, their interrelationships with each other and the surrounding environment, control structures, protocols, roles, interfaces, properties, data structures, design patterns, and so on (Faisandier, 2012) to conceive the software system.

Traditionally, such organizational structures of software systems are referred to as software architectures. These structures, when expressed as software architecture descriptions, aid in intellectual reasoning, analysis, and satisfaction of the key software system requirements, espoused by various stakeholders, and key properties pertaining to its behavior (ISO/IEC, 42010, 2011). Software architecture descriptions present software systems at a level of abstraction that helps us understand the whole system (Garlan and Shaw, 1994; Perry and Wolf, 1992).

Software architecture is the fundamental organizational scheme of a software system relative to the purpose that the system is trying to accomplish (Ring, 1998). In other words, a software architect's schema of software elements for achieving the software system's purpose is the software architecture. It is the responsibility of the software architect to define what the software system does (behavior) to achieve this purpose and how the software system achieves it (structure, function) (Maier and Rechtin, 2009; Ring, 1998) in a specific situation (context). In order to create this definition, a software architect arrives at a set of desired quality characteristics that should exist in the software system (including both functional and nonfunctional qualities) and creates an appropriate scheme/organization structure of software elements. This structure, when realized and used, will enable the desired quality characteristics to be experienced.

The definition of a specific software system in terms of its architecture and constituent elements depends on stakeholders' interests and responsibilities. It includes assessments and decisions (in terms of rationale) to select the elements that compose the system, models, properties of discourse, operational concepts, principles and guidelines. Once the software system is realized and put to use, users (or customers) and other stakeholders observe the effects of the system on the problem area that is addressed by the software system (Ring, 1998). These effects occur because of the quality characteristics of the various software systems, as a result of which users and other stakeholders experience benefits.

By ensuring that the desired quality characteristics are present in the software system; stakeholder satisfaction, with respect to the accrued benefits, becomes possible (Kano, 1996). In other words, in order to achieve stakeholder satisfaction, it is necessary for the software system to have qualities that meet stakeholders' requirements (Kano, 1996). It becomes the responsibility of the software architect to ensure that the desired quality characteristics are induced into the software system by design (quality should not be incidental). While software architects create the software architecture so as to achieve certain qualities, the ultimate goal is to deliver satisfaction to all stakeholders. This means that the architect should not only determine the sources of satisfaction for each stakeholder, but should also identify and embed necessary software elements and appropriate processes by which the software system produces or influences the stakeholder's satisfaction. For this to happen, it is necessary to reconcile the system objectives with stakeholder satisfaction considerations (Boehm).

Value matrix enables software architects to look beyond requirements (Ring, 1998). It is based on identifying the set of concerns a software architect needs to consider and address in order to deliver value to stakeholders (Anand et al., 2008; Anand et al., 2012). It proposes that software architects should:

1. Move from addressing requirements to delivering value to stakeholders
2. Shift their priorities from performing a series of activities to achieving qualities
3. Concern themselves with the character of the system which is above and beyond its common use
4. Understand what is beneficial to stakeholders in tackling a specific problem/problem situation
5. Go beyond benefits and look at net benefits to stakeholders
6. Work toward delivering these net benefits

The value matrix approach is based on the premises that the purpose of the software system is to deliver value to stakeholders and that the responsibility of software architects is to ensure that this purpose is achieved. It provides a set of guidelines that aids a software architect to:

- Identify value to stakeholders
- Identify value that needs to be delivered for a specific problem/problem situation
- Identify quality characteristics that can deliver this value
- Correlate identified value with the quality characteristics
- Use these quality characteristics to propose a concept that has necessary architectural properties
- Create descriptions of the resultant architecture, including traceability of how the architecture achieves the desired quality

The subsequent sections will discuss the conceptual foundations and various perspectives that this approach brings to the fore.

10.2 Underlying themes

The outcome of software architecting is software architecture. Traditionally, this process provides general guidance to the software architect and utilizes an envelope of practices and design patterns that govern the software architecture creation (IEEE Computer Society, 2004). Its purpose is to aid the software architect to synthesize a solution that satisfies the requirements (ISO/IEC, 15288, 2008), and it is the responsibility of the software architect to identify the right practices/patterns necessary for creating an appropriate solution. Its outcome is a set of manageable, conceptual, and realizable solutions. While most of the standards and guidelines state that the objective of software architecture is to meet requirements (IEEE Computer Society, 2004), the value matrix approach is based on the premise that the objective of software architecture is to ensure that the software system has enough qualities built into it such that it delivers value to its stakeholders.

10.2.1 Value creation cycle

The objective of the value creation cycle illustrated in Figure 10.1 is to transition a software architect from focusing on the software system to focusing on the stakeholders' value that is created by using the software system. Accordingly, the value expected by stakeholders in their value creation context serves as the starting point.

Note: According to Womack's lean principles, for creating value without waste, in order to promote a robust process of establishing the value of the end product or system to the customer with crystal clarity early in the program, the process should be customer-focused, involving the customer frequently and aligning accordingly (Womack and Jones, 1996).

Software architects then identify the desired quality characteristics of the proposed software system and induce them into the software architecture. Once the software architecture is realized, it exhibits quality characteristics that are in line with the desired quality characteristics. If this

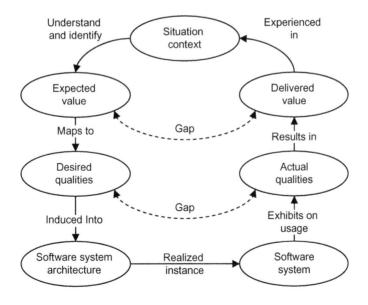

FIGURE 10.1

Value creation cycle.

realized system is put to use, it is perceived that it will result in value delivery in the stakeholders' value context. By design, the value creation process is iterative, with the gap between actual qualities and desired qualities bridged by successive refinements of the realization of the software system and the gap between actual value and expected value bridged by successive refinements of the quality characteristics induced into the software system.

10.2.2 Software architecting

Software architecting is iterative and requires the participation of several stakeholders along with relevant domain experts. It results in a possible space of solutions, which are predominantly architectural possibilities, with appropriate quality goals. Its purpose is to synthesize a solution that satisfies the value requirements. It involves generation of the proposed form to cater to the desired function and prediction of the form's properties before its embodiment. It involves understanding how resources necessary for creating this form are organized formally and semantically, as well as how they are represented and how these representations can be acted upon to produce effective transformations from value to quality to architecture. Figure 10.2 is the context diagram for software architecting.

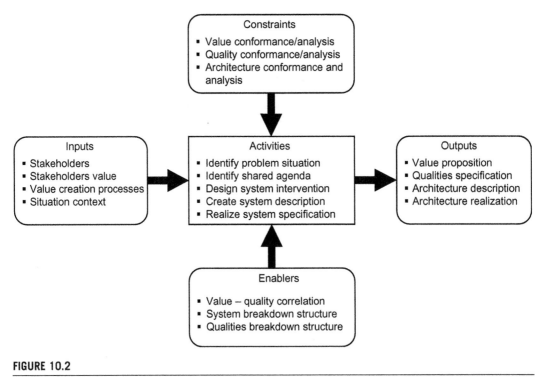

FIGURE 10.2

Context diagram for software architecting.

10.2.2.1 *Inputs to software architecting*

Software architecture provides conceptual integrity in achieving the software system's purpose and arises from the necessity of delivering value to customers. The purpose of the software system is to deliver value to stakeholders (Ring, 1998). In such a case, the input to the software architecting is the context in which value is to be delivered to stakeholders. This input is based on:

- The complete understanding of requirements gathered from various stakeholders
- Software architects' knowledge of the problem domain
- Usage model/processes by which user stakeholders add value to their customers
- Software architects' responsibilities in inducing value
- Software users' responsibilities in delivering value
- Various constraints from the situation context and the situation environment
- Various realization and design constraints in the developer stakeholders' premises

10.2.2.2 *Constraints for software architecting*

Stakeholder value serves as the basis for arriving at the fundamental quality characteristics that must exist in the software system, and the different parts of the software system must be coordinated and manifest these quality characteristics. Together, these quality characteristics and the system usage processes enable the software system to fulfill its purpose. In such a case, the constraints for software architecting are stakeholder's value, deliverable qualities, and realized architecture. These constraints can be summarized as:

- Conformance to the stakeholder value requirements (asserted by value analysis)
- Conformance to the qualities that correlate to the stakeholder's value requirements (asserted by qualities analysis)
- Conformance of the architecture description to the architecture that is envisaged by the software architect (asserted by architecture analysis)

10.2.2.3 *Enablers for software architecting*

The architectural design decisions necessary to arrive at the software architecture must be made within the specific context in which value is to be delivered to the stakeholders. As a result, the software system's architectural elements or properties, their relationships, principles, and guidelines that govern their design and evolution are bound to the specific context. Possible changes/variations in the context must be factored into the appropriate architectural elements/properties. The various competing/conflicting factors that arise in the specific context become constraints on the software architecture and assert the correctness, completeness, and validity of the functional, behavioral, and social obligations of the system.

- Quality characteristics that will improve on or detract from the overall value of the software system (Reekie and McAdam, 2006)
- Value to quality mapping within the particular context for which it is created and used (Reekie and McAdam, 2006)
- Architectural abstractions expressed as models through which architects can structure, identify, analyze, and synthesize design

- Hierarchical decomposition of software system configurations (parts and interconnections), with desired qualities embodied in the elements (system breakdown structure, layered systems)
- Separation of layers of understanding, with each layer representing a closed world of discourse (Anand et al., 2008)
- Delineation of quality characteristics by localizing their discussion within a specified layer (the qualities' breakdown structure, separation of concerns) (Zachman, 1987)

10.2.2.4 Outputs of software architecting

The output is a possible space of solutions that are predominantly architectural possibilities with appropriate quality goals. From these sets of solutions, the choice of a specific architecture is based on the ability to achieve the quality goals of the solution within the architectural constraints imposed on the software architect. The typical outputs could be:

- Usage processes using which software users can utilize the software system and obtain value
- Processes that aid stakeholders in meeting their real world responsibilities
- Principles, guidelines, properties, and interfaces of software system elements
- Traceability of the software system elements to quality characteristics and value
- Software system architecture description using any architecture description language
- Traceability of software system description, with system expectations (in terms of value and quality)

Note: While choosing a particular software system configuration, complex factors arise that govern a specific architectural configuration. These factors arise as responses to stakeholder requirements and constrain the way the interactions in an architectural configuration can exist. They are always competing, and conflicting, and it is the software architect's responsibility to establish a dynamic equilibrium between the various factors and choose the configuration that best achieves the desired quality goals.

10.2.2.5 Software architecting activities

The purpose of software architecting is to define, select, and synthesize a software system's architecture and enable it to satisfy and trade off with the quality requirements. The software system will have specific properties designed to deliver value to its stakeholders. Because of the evolution of the context of use or other technological possibilities, the software architecture composed of software system elements will change along the life cycle of the system so that it can continue to satisfy its stated purpose. Because of the iterative nature of software architecting, inputs and outputs evolve incrementally throughout the process. Major activities and tasks performed during software architecting include the following:

- Identify all of those stakeholders who get affected by the system.
- Understand the value creation processes of stakeholders.
- Understand how stakeholders perform their work processes to deliver outcomes.
- Work out the underlying purpose and agree on problem abstractions.
- Analyze the situation context and work out a collection of feasible solution concepts.
- Analyze solution value creation processes and identify what value delivery is possible.
- Redefine what value the software system creates for its stakeholders.

- Establish what software architecture needs to deliver. Define capabilities of the system.
- Identify essential and distinguishing attributes that deliver the intended value.
- Prioritize, delineate and segregate quality characteristics across different levels of understanding.
- Create a form based on layered abstractions, with each layer chosen based on the knowledge domains involved.

10.3 Value matrix framework

Software systems are technical works that involve the participation of many stakeholders (developer side stakeholders, user stakeholders, product marketing stakeholders, customer stakeholders, etc.) in ways that dictate and constrain the purpose and architecture of the software system as a whole. A software system has to accommodate all the affected stakeholders' needs, perceptions, own goals, and measures of value, which are often diverse and incompatible. One way to ease such a situation is through economics. The value matrix framework is based on insights arrived at by asking four different questions that need to be answered for the software system to succeed economically:

1. What are the benefits and who are the beneficiaries of the software system?

   Anyone who gets affected by a software system or participates in it in any way is a beneficiary. For the software to be beneficial to someone, it is necessary to figure out the benefits in terms of (1) usefulness in satisfying a customer need, (2) relative importance of the need being satisfied, (3) availability relative to when it is needed, and (4) the cost of ownership. These economic considerations dictate customer satisfaction and customer ability to satisfy their purposes.

2. How are these benefits realized, and what are the enablers for achieving these benefits?

   For the software system to live-up to the expectations in terms of delivering benefits, it should exhibit the appropriate software quality characteristics. Quality characteristics determine how well a software system is able to deliver benefits, and it defines how the system behaves in a given scenario. They differentiate one system from another and measure excellence in a chosen dimension (Kano, 1996). Quality attributes are generally considered important for obtaining a software design of good quality—various "ilities" (maintainability, portability, testability, traceability), various "nesses" (correctness, robustness), including "fitness of purpose." (IEEE Computer Society, 2012)

3. What is the underlying form of the software system that enables benefits achievement, and how does one comprehend it?

   Software architecture deals with the design and implementation of the software system structure and is the assembly of a number of architectural elements in some well-chosen forms to satisfy the functional and nonfunctional quality characteristics of the software system. The process of creating the form (software architecture) starts with understanding the quality characteristics, value creation context, and specific situation; diagnosing it using archetypes, patterns, and existing models; and synthesizing an approximate symbolic (or) mathematical (or) conceptual (or) physical representation (Meredith et al., 1973). In summary, a software architecture description is a multifaceted artifact produced by the architecture design process and composed of relatively independent and orthogonal facets/models of the software system.

4. How does one realize the benefits of the delivering system, and how does one use it to enjoy the benefits?

Essentially, architecture description is used during implementation to create software system elements and during integration to provide plans and criteria for combining these elements. The value and quality requirements are used to verify and validate the various software system elements and their interconnections. This feedback is then used in the next iteration of the system design cycle, particularly when problems or challenges are identified (IEEE Computer Society, 2012). The software system is the output that is created by the software realization process, which transforms design inputs into an acceptable output. This system is characterized by quality attributes that are of value to its users. When this system is put to use, it creates value and related experience to the users (IEEE Computer Society, 2012).

10.3.1 Exemplar problem

For illustration purposes, we consider the problem that every manager in an information technology-enabled environment faces when he or she sets out to figure out how much time an individual spends on various day-to-day IT tasks. Even though the outcome of different individuals performing similar work is acceptable to the organization, all individuals have their own notion of how to perform their work and how to sequence their work activities in information systems. This individuality stems from their differing perceptions and interpretations of work, differences in usage of enterprise information systems, speed of movement, effort, dexterity, consistency, and so on. For easy reference in later sections of this chapter, we label this scenario the Time Study scenario. The problem under consideration is as follows:

In an IT-enabled environment, business users use workstations as the single interface point to access all enterprise IT systems. They perform their work activities in this environment by interacting with enterprise information systems and play different roles throughout their working period to discharge their responsibilities. They perform IT tasks in their workstations, which straddle across multiple IT systems, in different permutations and combinations to complete their work. In this environment, time is money; time is opportunity; resources are allocated for time; individuals' productivity is measured against time; costing is based on time; budgets are proposed for time; schedule slippage is measured by time.

Understanding time spent on work activities gives an insight into the direction of work efforts and is an essential link between the individuals' effort and the organization's goals. Therefore, obtaining accurate information of time spent by individuals in performing their work activities is of utmost importance. Currently, time measurement is approximate, time consuming, and subjective as there are no standard methodologies available for measuring work done in IT systems. Our objective is to create the architecture of a system that can aid in time study of an individual and make it possible to measure time and effort expended by individuals on work activities in information systems.

The technology needs for time study in IT-enabled environments presents both an opportunity for users and a challenge for software architects. For users, a wealth of computing, informational, and communication resources are available everywhere, and they should be in a position to accomplish their work tasks using any of these resources with very less effort to track the various work activities they perform. For architects, the challenge is to harness these resources without burdening users with management of the activities that are performed, underlying technologies that are used, and infrastructure support that is necessary.

In the area of time study, the focus, so far, has been primarily on two areas. One is the problem of dealing with **sensors everywhere** issues: given a highly instrumented environment containing various kinds of information-gathering devices, how to use this information effectively. Key subproblems are information gathering, filtering, fusion, and abstraction. The second problem is that of **seamless access** issues: given a dedicated set of devices and services that track an individual profile and access across the organization resources, how to draw meaningful interpretations out of this information effectively. Key subproblems are tracking, querying, allowing access, auditing, storing, and retrieving. In subsequent sections we present an alternate set of solutions and adopt the value matrix approach to create the solution architecture.

10.3.2 The four perspectives

The insights obtained from answering the four different questions serve as four different interrelated perspectives as shown in Figure 10.3. While two perspectives focus on stakeholder world concerns, the remaining two focus on system world concerns. The two stakeholder perspectives are *value proposition* (Q1 in the figure) that is delivered by the software system when put to use and *qualities specification* (Q2) that are built into the software system so as to deliver the desired value. The two system perspectives are the *architecture description* (Q3), which is the specification of the software system, and the *architecture instance* (Q4), which is the instantiated architecture for the particular situation context. Together, these four perspectives and their interrelationships provide a structure that enables the architect to comprehend the dynamics of value-based software architecting. These four perspectives, as illustrated in Figure 10.3, address the issue of how value to stakeholders can be traced from its conception as value proposition; transformation as quality characteristics; specification as architecture descriptions; and realization as a software system.

The following sections provide some initial steps that can be taken for each of the four perspectives of the value matrix approach. They are fairly compatible and can be used in various combinations. While discussing each of these perspectives, a few guidelines are introduced. These guidelines are categorized under appropriate metaphors (McConnell, 2004) (heuristics Maier and Rechtin, 2009) in order to enable better understanding, decision making, value judgment, and assessment (Maier and Rechtin, 2009). They provide successive transitions from qualitative, provisional needs to descriptive and prescriptive guidelines and, hence, to rational approaches and methods (Maier and Rechtin, 2009).

10.3.3 Value proposition

Value is a measure of worth (e.g., benefit divided by cost) of a specific product or service by a customer, and potentially by other stakeholders, and is a function of (1) the product's usefulness in satisfying a customer need, (2) the relative importance of the need being satisfied, (3) the availability of the product relative to when it is needed, and (4) the cost of ownership to the customer (SE Handbook Working Group, INCOSE, 2011). Additionally, all the things that contribute

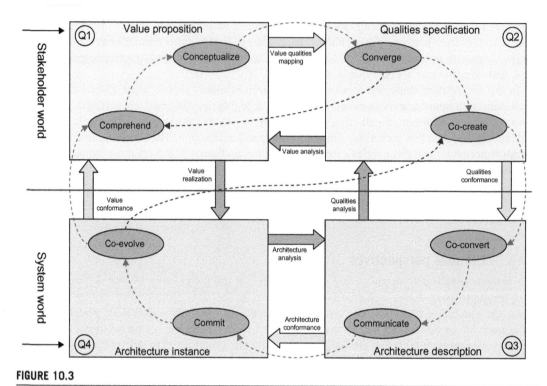

FIGURE 10.3

Value matrix framework.

significantly to stakeholders in terms of achieving their goals, plans, improvements, developments needed for growth, and so on, are considered as appealing to a stakeholder serves as perceived/possible value.

For a system to succeed in creating value for any one stakeholder, it must create value for all whose contributions are critical to systems success. The failure to satisfy any one critical stakeholder creates risks of compensatory actions that may lead to value delivery failure, thus satisfying no one. Ensuring a credible value proposition for each stakeholder at each point in time is an essential part of design (Boehm and Sullivan). In the value proposition perspective, since value is the goal, the key question is, "How is one to discern value, not only after the software system becomes operational but before the software system is created, and especially when value changes (Ring, 1998)?" The answer is to understand stakeholder value in a given value creation context, explicate this context to define a set of possible solutions, abstract and identify the purpose of the system, and explicate this to quality specifications.

Table 10.1 lists the metaphors/heuristics to follow for the value proposition perspective, along with a set of guidelines to consider. For ease of use, these guidelines are grouped under appropriate metaphors/heuristics. Figure 10.3 illustrates the relationships between these heuristics; the following sections elaborate and provide details about these guidelines.

Table 10.1 Metaphors and Guidelines for value Propositions

Comprehend {Meaningful reflection of the problem situation}

- Identify Stakeholders.
  - Identify all of those stakeholders who get affected by the system.
- Understand Stakeholders' Value Creation Context.
  - Understand the value creation processes of stakeholders.
- Understand Situation Context.
  - Understand how stakeholders perform their work processes to deliver outcomes.

Conceptualize {Meaningful reflection of the common shared agenda}

- Define Problem Space.
  - Work out the underlying purpose. Agree on problem abstractions.
- Define Solution Space.
  - Analyze the situation context and work out a collection of feasible solution concepts.
- Define Solution Value Creation Context.
  - Analyze the solution value creation processes and identify what value delivery is possible.

10.3.3.1 Identify stakeholders

Anyone who is affected by the system or participates in the system in any way is a stakeholder. This association can occur anytime during the lifetime of the system. Such stakeholders can be individuals, groups, agencies, regulatory bodies, providers, developers, consumers, customers, and so on, and their importance in creating value dictates the priority of the requirements expressed by them and its eventual satisfaction. These identified stakeholders can be expressed as a list or as an organizational structure; what is important, however, is the identification of all stakeholders affected by the system. For the time study illustration, some of the probable stakeholders are:

- Business users, as they perform the work activities
- Business managers, as they dictate the work goals for the business user
- Project team, as team members share the work agenda with the business user
- Developers, as they create the time study system.

10.3.3.2 Understand stakeholder requirements

Requirements identify the current needs of stakeholders in terms of functional and nonfunctional attributes. Certain constraints within the operating environment inhibit some of the stakeholders' needs from being satisfied. It is necessary for the architect to consider these inhibiting factors along with the requirements. While requirements are often collected from customer stakeholders, architects are expected to take into account requirements of developer stakeholders, customers' customers, vendors, regulatory bodies, and so on. In other words, the requirements of all stakeholders affected by the system need to be taken into consideration, and an appropriate balance should be worked out among the overlapping/conflicting needs. These identified needs can be expressed as a simple list or as a hierarchical structure; it can be elicited using any approach; however, what is important is the identification of all the stakeholder requirements. For the time study illustration, some of the probable requirements are:

- Business users would need the ability to specify tasks and associate them with software artifacts.
- Business users would need the ability to prioritize tasks and manipulate their attributes.
- Business users would need the ability to manipulate captured time spent on various tasks.
- Business managers would need the ability to generate dashboards and timesheet reports.
- Project teams would need the ability to customize rules governing the tracking of tasks and the gathering of time against these tasks.
- Developers would need the ability to represent the timesheet in multiple data formats.

10.3.3.3 Understand stakeholder value

In economics, value is regarded as a principle, standard, or quality that is worthwhile or desirable. Such value can be tangible benefits, profits, savings, social value, feeling, experience, resiliency, innovativeness, and so on, and their importance to the stakeholder dictates his or her satisfaction. Value is measured by its desirability in respect to some property and is the quality (positive or negative) that renders the entity of interest desirable or valuable. Generally, value to user is the worth of a software system to a user's problem from the user's point of view at the time of usage. This value should exist over the software system's lifetime for it to remain satisfactorily in use. Every stakeholder has a different notion of what is of value. Based on an understanding of the stakeholders and their requirements, different interpretations of what is of value to them can arise.

One such value of interest is the *value* that is appropriated by the stakeholder when the proposed software system is put into use. In order to deliver minimal/must-have value, a comprehensive understanding of various aspects of stakeholder requirements is necessary. In order to enhance delivered value, understanding the stakeholders' roles, their goals and responsibilities, their purposes and work processes, their quality and value concerns, and the work constraints that exist in the specific context is necessary. In order to deliver delightful/exciting value, understanding stakeholders' customers, stakeholders' obligations to their customers, and any other factors that benefit stakeholders' customers is also necessary. For the time study illustration, stakeholder value includes:

- Reduce effort and time spent in tracking various IT tasks performed for the business user.
- Reduce effort and time spent in tracking work performance for the business manager.
- Reduce effort and time spent in non value adding activities for projects.
- Enhance value by segregating value adding and non-value-adding activities for projects.
- Enhance value by reconfiguring work tasks to be tracked for a business user.
- Enhance value with ability to predict work completion for a business manager.

10.3.3.4 Understand the situation context

Context models are abstractions of a situation context. They can be used to structure, identify, analyze, and synthesize a situation wherein the model commutes with the situation and relates to it. As the understanding of the situation improves, its codification, interpretation, and representation as model evolves. Such models are approximations. The various entities in the model are manipulated

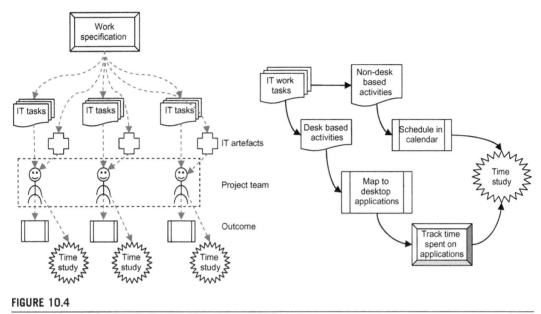

FIGURE 10.4

Context model for rime study in IT-enabled environment.

to create a formal or logical structure. These structures serve as the basis for understanding and interpreting abstractions in the situation. The act of context modeling starts with understanding the situation to be modeled by reductionism, diagnosing it using archetypes, processes, patterns, and existing models, and finally synthesizing an approximate symbolic/mathematical/conceptual/physical representation. Context modeling involves identifying the characteristics of the situation and expressing it as a model so that the situation can be understood. It also allows visualization of information about the situation represented by the model. For the time study illustration, the context model is illustrated in Figure 10.4.

10.3.3.5 Define the problem space

Once stakeholder need, value drivers, and situation context are well understood, it is necessary to identify the set of problems that have to be addressed by the proposed software system (problem formulation—what is it an architect is trying to solve). Ideally, this problem formulation should cover functional and nonfunctional aspects; evolution and variation scenarios; constraints imposed by the operating environment; initial and evolved requirements; common structures and design patterns; desired customization; possible configuration changes; and the like.

A key step in formulating the problem is the creation of abstractions of the problem concepts and associated laws without tying down to unnecessary details. Abstractions conform to these laws through the problem formulation. They are developed from an understanding of the situation context; they are an approximation; they capture different properties of the problem understanding; and they contain the essential details. The purpose of abstractions is to introduce simplicity, nonarbitrariness, and clear organization in problem formulation. For the time study illustration, the problem formulation and corresponding abstractions could be as follows:

10.3.3.5.1 Problem
Facilitate personal time study for individuals working in an information system's reliant environment so that they can manage their time better.

10.3.3.5.2 Abstractions
- Work activities are performed in the desktop using some application.
- Any activities done outside the desktop are scheduled in the calendar.
- Work time is the time expended in performing a work activity.
- Nonwork time is the time expended in any other activities that cannot be accounted for.

10.3.3.6 Define the solution space
Designing a solution to a problem involves solving many subproblems by creating corresponding solution fragments that are then composed to create the larger solution to the actual problem (Hillier and Leaman, 1974). There could be multiple such solution fragments for each subproblem that arises based on design patterns, opportunities, operational concepts, technological concepts, formal structures, and the like. Similarly, there could be multiple ways of combining solution fragments to create the larger solution. A solution would then be a configuration of solution fragments.

Accordingly, a solution space comprises a collection of solution configurations. The result of architectural design activity is the creation of many candidate solution configurations that correspond to different ways of solving the problem of interest. Each solution configuration presents a perspective on addressing the problem and a set of related concerns. Each perspective is different, but not necessarily independent, and if semantically motivated asserts how the problem is understood, analyzed, and solved. Different perspectives allow architects to look at different details of the problem and permit different solution configurations to be created.

The conditions that lead to the creation of a specific perspective make the corresponding solution configuration capable of addressing the problem from that perspective. This helps the architect to reframe the problem-in-focus into a more general form. Such a reframing enables various stakeholders to step back and take another look at the problem and its solution in its entirety. For the time study illustration, the various solution concepts could be:

- Personal time study → Time study of work activities performed by an individual.
- Team time study → Time study of work activities performed by a team having a shared agenda.

For the time study illustration, the various solution fragments could be:

10.3.3.6.1 Solution fragment 1
Define a simple structure for representing work activities based on the ETVX model as illustrated in Figure 10.5. Here, entry criteria would signify the condition that need to exist in workstations when a specific work activity is started. Tasks to perform would be the series of interactions performed in the workstation as part of the work activity. Validation would be to check if the work is complete, and exit criteria would signify the condition that would exist to indicate the end of the

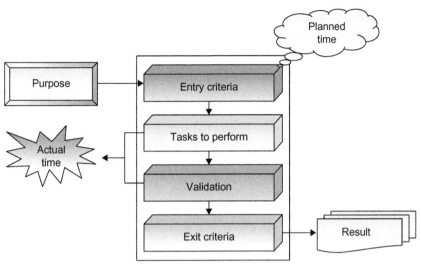

FIGURE 10.5

ETVX model.

work activity. For example, we can consider the entry criteria for documentation would be when the document editor is in the foreground; tasks to perform would be interactions with the editor and utilization of its document editing functionalities; validation that the work is complete would be when the various sections of the document are completely written; and the exit criteria would be when the document editor is closed or sent to background. Create an event that would signal when the entry criteria are reached and another event that would signal when the exit criteria are reached. The time difference between these two signals would result in the time spent on a specific activity.

10.3.3.6.2 Solution fragment 2

In an IT-enabled environment, work takes place in workstations. Individuals use software applications while they work at their workstations; this is the first computing resource that needs to be tracked. While working in thick client applications, individuals work on files and folders (aka file system) when they use software applications; this is the second computing resource that needs to be tracked. While working in thin client applications, individuals access websites and URLs from browsers (yet another software application); this is the third computing resource that needs to be tracked. There could be other computing resources that need to be identified for tracking as well. By establishing a correlation between the usage of computing resources and work activities performed by an individual, and creating appropriate rules, time study of individual activities is possible.

For example, we can consider documentation as the activity performed when individuals use Microsoft Word or Microsoft Excel; we can consider literature review as the activity performed when individuals search in Google or read pdf files; we can consider programming as the activity performed when individuals work on files with the extension .cpp or .c

Table 10.2 Personal Time Study—Value Creation Context

Value Creation Process	Predicted Value
Specify tasks, associate tasks to computer system resources, and track tasks to create timesheets	Reduces effort by creating accurate timesheets to business user
Time study to identify effort expended on various tasks	Enhances value by identifying non-value-adding activities to business user
Time management by planning, tracking, and analyzing time expended on various tasks	Enhances value by better work management to business user

10.3.3.7 Define the solution value creation context

While the act of architectural design unravels a set of solution possibilities, architecting translates these solution possibilities into solution specifics. It is through this translation that the correlation between solution space and problem space is established. The critical factor that governs this translation is the ability of a particular solution to deliver desired value to its stakeholders. For each of the solution configurations worked out earlier, it is necessary to identify the value creation processes and the corresponding value that they can provide to various stakeholders. Performing value analysis would then establish the gap between the predicted value and the desired value. Any value that is over and above the desired value would make the solution more appealing to stakeholders. For the time study illustration, some of the value creation processes and predicted value are covered in Table 10.2.

10.3.4 Qualities specification

The quality of a software system lies in the degree to which the system satisfies the stated and implied needs of its various stakeholders and thus provides value. It is a characterization of the software behavior and is a function of (1) outcomes of the software system, (2) impact of the software system on its stakeholders, (3) measure of the degree of satisfaction of customer needs, and (4) measure of the capabilities of the software system to allow users to accomplish tasks in the real world. All the things that exist in the software system that contribute to the creation of value to stakeholders and are the carriers of value are considered as the various qualities of the system. It measures the excellence of the software system in a chosen dimension and is the basis for satisfying its stated purpose.

By constructively resolving the value requirements through quality characteristics the system must possess; we can arrive at the architecture of the solution without any recourse to technical artifices, wherein it is evident that the stakeholder value concerns have been addressed. As a result, we can perceive the suitability and adequacy of the functionality and appreciate the capacity of the resources needed to cater to the demands of all the nonfunctional quality characteristics. The key question is; "How to establish the quality characteristics that the system must have in order to be acceptable to all of its stakeholders?" The solution is to establish mappings between the benefits (value) desired by the various stakeholders and the proposed quality characteristics of the product, discerning priorities to resolve conflicts between stakeholder desires.

Table 10.3 Metaphors and guidelines for qualities specification
Converge {Meaningful reflection of specific interests and values}

• Redefine Stakeholders Value Requirements.
  ◦ Redefine what value the software system creates for its stakeholders.
• Define System Configuration.
  ◦ Establish what software architecture needs to deliver. Define capabilities of the system.
• Define System Quality characteristics and Its Correlation to Value.
  ◦ Identify essential and distinguishing attributes that deliver the intended value.

Co-Create {Meaningful reflection of the system intervention}

• Create System Breakdown Structure.
  ◦ Create a form based on layered abstractions, with each layer chosen based on knowledge domains involved.
• Create Quality Breakdown Structure.
  ◦ Prioritize, delineate, and segregate quality characteristics across different levels of understanding.
• Create Usage Processes.
  ◦ Create stakeholders' responsibility satisfaction processes and associated management processes in the system with respect to achieving the identified purpose.

Table 10.3 lists the metaphors/heuristics to follow for the qualities specification perspective, along with a set of guidelines to consider. For ease of use, these guidelines are grouped under appropriate metaphors/heuristics. Figure 10.4 illustrates the relationships between these heuristics. The following sections elaborate and provide details about these guidelines.

10.3.4.1 Redefine stakeholders' value requirements

For the identified set of solution concepts, value analysis can help bridge the gap between desired value and predicted value. Value creation factors such as cost to deliver value; value creation dynamics; resources involved; and value indicators can help identify the solution concept that is best suited to satisfy the stakeholders' value requirements. However, value cannot be an afterthought, and it should be engineered into the solution by intent. An understanding of what value is feasible and which solution concepts can deliver this value would serve as a valid input to the architectural design process in achieving this intent. Such an input would lead to the redefinition of stakeholders' value requirements and the constraints that govern their eventual satisfaction. This would then establish what the architecture needs to deliver. For the time study illustration, some of the redefined requirements are:

• Create definitions of what it means to perform work, when the work begins, and when it ends.
• Establish the correlation between computing resources and work activities performed by an individual.
• Anonymize data collected from individuals so as to address their privacy concerns.
• Accommodate variability in work processes.

10.3.4.2 Define system configuration

Based on the identified solution concept and the redefined stakeholders' value requirements, the software system configuration needs to be worked out. Creating this configuration deals with creating form/structure that caters to desired function and involves specification of mechanisms that effect changes in form/function of the system to consummate with changes in the environment. The very center of this activity is the bringing together of parts to form a whole and involves carrying out a simple set of operations on parts and interconnections. If the elemental structure of parts is different, then composing or performing operations on these parts becomes difficult, necessitating the need for the existence of a common elemental structure among different parts as well as the whole. The key to understanding the creation of such a configuration depends on the logical structure of the combination of different parts, and it could be spatial, behavioral, or a mapping between spatial and behavioral. This structure can be expressed using simple entity relationship diagrams or SysML diagrams. What should effectively come out of this diagram are the various components, relationships, interfaces, information flow, and roles. For the time study illustration, the system configuration for personal time study solution concept is illustrated in Figure 10.6.

10.3.4.3 Establish value to qualities correlation/translation

Software architects need a handle on value. Generally, among a set of similar software systems, a software system of higher quality is found to be of more value. We can safely state that *quality* is a key for better software. Traditionally, software quality is the degree to which the system satisfies the stated and implied needs of its various stakeholders; we extend its meaning to state that

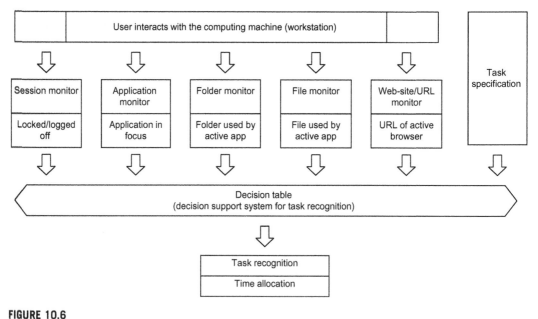

FIGURE 10.6

Personal time study solution concept.

software quality is the degree to which the system is able to deliver value to its stakeholders. In this case, it is the responsibility of software architects to identify those qualities that are of value and to infuse them into the software system by design. When quality software systems are deployed and used by customers, they will then *appropriate* value. Therefore, architects need to establish quality characteristics that the system should have in order to be acceptable to all its stakeholders and also establish the correlation between value desired by the various stakeholders and the proposed quality characteristics of the software system. There may be many-to-many relationships between qualities and value, and satisfaction of these relationships during realization asserts that the solution delivers desired value. For the time study illustration, Table 10.4 lists the value quality correlation.

10.3.4.4 *Establish quality characteristics*

As stated earlier, stakeholders' value arises from a set of qualities of the solution, such as functionality, integration, performance, security, usability, business continuity, response time, regulatory compliance, and reusability. There may be multiple instances of the quality in the system (e.g., response time for different transactions, different aspects of security), and each of the instances needs to be identified separately. In essence, all the quality characteristics critical for the solution need to be identified and their interrelationships worked out. For each of these qualities, there must be a way of asserting its design. However, not all of the qualities might be of value from the customer's point of view, some of them might be trivial, some of them noninteresting, and others delightful. Therefore, it is necessary to find appropriate qualities which, when present in the software system, will deliver the desired value to stakeholders when the software system is put to use. As reference quality characteristics, either the ISO 9126 or the subsequent ISO 25010 product quality characteristics can be considered. For the time study illustration, the quality characteristics could be:

10.3.4.4.1 Functional quality characteristics

- Specify desk-based tasks and relate them to computing system resources.
- Specify desk-based task tracking rules and exceptions.
- Track desk-based tasks and time spent by individuals on these tasks based on these rules.
- Specify non-desk-based tasks and relate them to calendar entries.
- Generate time study reports and time expended on different tasks.

Table 10.4 Value Quality Correlation for Time Study Illustration

Desired Stakeholders Value	Quality Characteristics That Can Deliver This Value
Reduces effort (Savings)	Task specification, configuration, and tracking Rule-based task tracking and time capture Automated timesheet generation
Enhanced value (Feelings)	Nonintrusive 24 × 7 tracking Small size, highly confidential, user customizable Ability to modify gathered information
Elimination of waste	Separates value adding from non-value-adding tasks Facilitates better time management

10.3.4.4.2 Nonfunctional quality characteristics

- Should run as a background service (nonintrusive tracking of task and time).
- Should consume very less computing resources and runs 24×7.
- Should be simple to use, and the information collected should be of 9×5 levels of accuracy.
- Privacy of individuals should be protected; data confidentiality should be at 9×5 levels.
- Appropriate fail-safe mechanisms should be included.
- The disk and image size of the software system should be much less.
- The software system should be portable across multiple operating systems.

10.3.4.5 Create system breakdown structure

A software system is made up of a set of interconnected components coherently organized in such a way that when the software system is put to use, these components work together seamlessly to deliver the desired functionalities that enable stakeholders' appropriate value. There are two kinds of components: primary components, which are mainly responsible for the overall function and value delivery; and secondary components, which interface the primary components and assert that the interconnected primary components work seamlessly. These secondary components work through a flow of information, which determines how the software system operates.

Depending on the size and complexity of the software system, it is designed recursively as a hierarchical structure of levels of stable intermediate forms of components (components made up of subcomponents; subcomponents made up of sub-subcomponents, and so on) (Hitchins, 2008). This hierarchical structure organization is based around the desired quality characteristics of the software system. Techniques like adapting design patterns, following architectural styles, and utilizing third-party components introduce a systematic approach for the form/structure creation. It is left to the architect's discretion to adapt appropriate practices for creating this form/structure; what we express here is the need for creating the structure. For the time study illustration, the system breakdown structure is given in Figure 10.7.

10.3.4.6 Create qualities breakdown structure

Quality characteristics need to be engineered into the software system configuration by design. Our approach to induce qualities is based on a framework as illustrated in Table 10.5 that separates levels of understanding of quality characteristics based on the different knowledge domains involved (Nori and Swaminathan, 2006). The layers of understanding are a useful artifice for delineating quality characteristics by localizing their discussion within a specified layer. At each layer, a subset of the quality characteristics is addressed, and the remaining quality characteristics are passed on to the next layer. The decisions taken at higher layers should not be violated by lower layers. The layers illustrated in Table 10.5 are a useful delineation.

Problem Space Layer: In this layer, the quality characteristics that the system must have in order to be acceptable to all of its stakeholders are established. These quality characteristics are arrived at by establishing the correlation between the benefits (value) desired by the various stakeholders and the proposed quality characteristics of the software system.

Architecture Layer: In this layer, functional and nonfunctional quality characteristics that are feasible in solution space are established, without any reference to technical artifices, keeping in mind the expressed stakeholders' concerns and the overall quality characteristics of the software system.

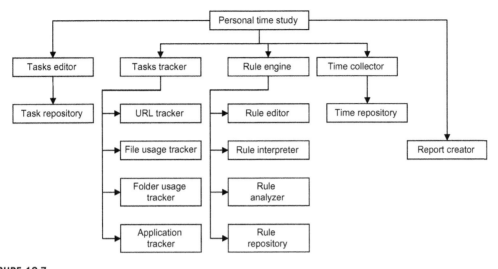

FIGURE 10.7

System breakdown structure for time study illustration.

Table 10.5 Levels of Understanding—Qualities Delineation

Levels of Understanding	Quality Characteristics		
Problem Space		Desired Quality Characteristics	
Architecture		All functional quality characteristics addressed	Nonfunctional qualities that do not include functional qualities are passed on
Computing		Information system quality characteristics addressed	Noncomputing-related qualities are passed on
Engineering		Engineering quality characteristics addressed	Nonengineering-related qualities are passed on
Construction		Implementing technologies/platforms-related quality characteristics addressed	Nonconstruction -related qualities are passed on
Deployment		Infrastructurerelated deployment quality characteristics addressed	Nondeployment-related qualities are passed on
Operating Environment		Usage qualities addressed	

Features of the Software System

Computing Layer: In this layer, the correlation between the solution quality characteristics and the information system characteristics are established, with a specific binding to computing resources needed to satisfy the nonfunctional needs.

Engineering Layer: In this layer, the capabilities of the computing resources that need to be utilized are established, so that the quality characteristics established in the computing layer can be addressed.

Construction Layer: In this layer, the correlation between the computing resources and the implementing platforms/technologies are established.

Deployment Layer: In this layer, the correlation between the quality characteristics of the stakeholders' infrastructure environment and the software system's computing resources are established.

Operating Layer: In this layer, the correlation between the stakeholders' operating environment and the software system's working environment are established.

Quality characteristics are segregated into different layers with the belief that they are not backward or upward influences. Trade-offs deal with cross influences between quality characteristics within a layer of discourse. If cross-layer influences between quality characteristics are discerned, then the independence of the layers is no longer valid. In that event, a design step may have to iterate over the layers, or worse still, the design step will have to coalesce all the intervening layers into a single layer and deal with the problem as one would deal with trade-offs. Here again, the practitioner's experience comes to the fore, and a series of preconditions can be placed on each layer so that the independence of each layer is warranted.

Each layer represents a closed world of discourse; localizes quality discussions to within the layer; and at each level a subset of quality characteristics is induced into the system configuration. The problem domain layer induces qualities that must be acceptable to all stakeholders; the architecture layer induces functional qualities that relate to problem domain; the computing layer induces the qualities related to computing technologies and structures; the engineering layer ensures that the computing qualities referred to above are satisfied; the construction layer focuses on effective use of implementation technologies; and the deployment layer establishes a match between the solution and its operational environment. For the time study illustration, the qualities breakdown structure is illustrated in Table 10.6.

10.3.4.7 Create usage processes

Software systems employ the capabilities of the computing system as a means of allowing users to accomplish one or more specific tasks that benefit them in the real world. They are made up of a collection of components that provide the desired functionality needed by users. Each component internally supports the necessary transactions and housekeeping processes to realize this functionality. These processes are a set of tasks/activities to be performed both inside and outside the software system.

A software system is executed through usage processes. While the actual action is performed inside the machine, the sequence of steps to be invoked by the user are the software usage processes. These processes are designed so that the different software components are coordinated and manifest the desired functionality. Since the purpose of a software system is to deliver value to its stakeholders, the architect's responsibility then is to design usage processes with quality so that it will deliver this value. While system design attends to the systems purpose that makes it desirable, usage process design ensures that these purposes are met. For the time study illustration, some usage processes are illustrated in Figure 10.8.

Table 10.6 Qualities Breakdown Structure for Time Study		
Levels of Discourse	**Functional Qualities**	**Nonfunctional Qualities**
Problem Domain	Specify tasks	Reduce time and effort
	Specify rules for tracking tasks	Increase productivity
	Track tasks performed by user	Increase effectiveness
	Generate reports	Eradicate bottlenecks and inefficiencies
Architecture	Categorize tasks as desk-based/non-desk-based	Small, light, and powerful
		Eliminate wasted effort
	Create a model of how task is performed in the machine (ETVX)	Scalability and speed
		Extensibility
	Correlate task with computing resources	Reusability of task/rule specifications
	Confidentiality of gathered data	
	Traceablity of tasks performance	
Computing	Connectivity to multiple IT systems	Simple to use
	Interface with multiple IT systems	User assistance
	Interface with report generators	Background task monitoring
	Restricted access to collected data	
Engineering	Unattended 24 × 7 hours tracking	Graceful exit
	9 × 4 levels of connectivity	Unlimited data storage
	9 × 5 levels of accuracy	Low CPU time
	9 × 4 levels of data protection	Low memory and storage requirements
	9 × 4 levels of fault tolerance	
Construction	GUI events tracking	Standardization
	Screen scrapping	Resource consumption
	Active application tracking	Customizability
	Active URL tracking	
Deployment	Adaptability to user environment	Portability
	Migrate-ability	User assistance
	Package-ability	Fitness for use
	Ready to use	
Operating Environment	Simplicity in use	Cope with change
	Compliance to user environment	Consistency and unsurprising
	Responsive to user actions	Visual indicators

Note: The discussion to this point might seem to be a discussion on the architecture phases, but that is not the case. All that we have accomplished so far is to identify a set of solutions; relevant software elements and quality characteristics; and segregation of these software elements and quality characteristics. We also have a layered understanding of the quality characteristics and the system structure.

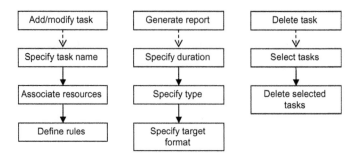

FIGURE 10.8

Some usage processes for the time study.

10.3.5 Architecture description

Architecture descriptions define a collection of characteristics of the software system and other elements of interest. These may include both structural and behavioral aspects, such as properties, properties, software elements, components, and their interrelationships, to represent the state and behavior of the software system. Architecture descriptions provide a general-purpose capability to express software systems as a hierarchy of relevant structures (OMG) (Hitchins, 2008). It is used by various stakeholders who create, utilize, and manage modern systems to improve communication and cooperation, enabling them to work in an integrated, coherent fashion (ISO/IEC, 42010, 2011). Architecture descriptions are expressed using an architecture description language that provides the conceptual framework and the vocabulary necessary for specifying the architecture.

Creating the architecture descriptions involves stating the purpose of the architecture; providing the desired value-adding qualities from an understanding of the user's needs; naming the architectural elements that comprise the design; identifying architectural styles to be used; planning and preparing the design methodology to be adopted; stating the parts and interconnections, creating spatial structures that represent these parts; and representing these structures as architecture views. The key question is; "How do architects formulate their architecture specification? How do they establish the link between architecture abstractions and architecture description that is to be created?"

The answer is to express the architectural abstractions as models and transform the models to multiple layers of understanding based on the knowledge domain and architectures involved (e.g., logical architecture, physical architecture, deployment architecture, infrastructure architecture), which are essentially different perspectives/views in understanding software. Table 10.7 lists the metaphors/heuristics to follow for the architecture description perspective, along with a set of guidelines to consider. For ease of use, these guidelines are grouped under appropriate metaphors/heuristics. Figure 10.4 illustrates the relationships between these heuristics. The following sections elaborate and provide details about these guidelines.

10.3.5.1 Identify architecture styles

Software is a configuration of configuration items, and it is as a configuration that it works and is experienced. Each configuration is semantically motivated and explains why it adds up and how it

Table 10.7 Metaphors and Guidelines for Architecture Description

Co-Convert {Meaningful translation of architectural abstractions}

- Identify Architecture Styles.
  - Identify common patterns that characterize the system as a whole.
- Define architecture rationales.
  - State the reasons for the choices made.
- Define architectural models.
  - Models can be used to structure, identify, analyze, and synthesize design.

Communicate {Meaningful reflection of software architecture}

- Create architectural views and viewpoints.
  - Frame specific system concerns; establish conventions for realization.
- Translate to architecture description.
  - Utilize architecture frameworks (adopt standardized (agreed-upon) definitions and perspectives to describe the system).
  - Express identified system structure, usage processes, qualities decomposition using architecture description languages.
- Qualities Conformance
  - Trace identified qualities; expected value to architecture description.

addresses the problem. Each of these configuration items has a variety of attributes that are implicitly, behaviorally, and physically necessary for its description. Thereby, every software system's behavior is constrained by its individual configuration item's behavior. The act of architecting creates complex configurations from the basic elements. There exist commonalities in the way the different elements are organized. Such common patterns characterize the software as a whole and also syntactically carry a signature of style. Some of these patterns govern the overall style that organizes the software elements; others identify the character of an interface or an abstraction for interaction (Shaw, 1994). It is through these patterns that software acquires the potential to satisfy the desired properties. For the time study illustration, some of the architecture styles are:

- Client–server system (client collects data related to tasks and transfers to server; server stores data and generates appropriate reports) (Garlan and Shaw, 1994)
- Table-driven interpretation (decisions tables are interpreted for identifying tasks/activities performed by the user) (Garlan and Shaw, 1994)
- Event-based system (change in activity performed by an individual is an event) (Garlan and Shaw, 1994)
- Instrumentation-based system (soft sensors track user activity) (Garlan and Shaw, 1994)

10.3.5.2 Define architecture rationales

Architecture rationales play a significant role in architectural design and realization (Maier and Rechtin, 2009). They serve as guidelines for treating complex situations and ill-structured problems, and they are used as aids in decision making, value judgments, and assessments. A good rationale is simple, relates well to other relevant rationales, and explains much of the experimental evidence and other observed phenomena. Rationales are used to give insight into the problem and correlate it with the identified solution fragment. The first step in creating a set of decision rationales for software architecture is to determine the criteria for selection. Some of the criteria are:

1. The rationale must make sense in its original domain or context. To be accepted, a strong correlation, if not a direct cause and effect, must be apparent between the rationale and the successes or failures of specific systems, products, or processes. Maier and Rechtin (2009)
2. The general sense, if not the specific words, of the rationale should apply beyond the original context. That is, the rationale should be useful in solving or explaining more than the original problem from which it arose. Maier and Rechtin (2009)
3. The rationale should not be wrong or contradictory in other domains because it could lead to serious misunderstanding and error. Maier and Rechtin (2009)
4. The rationale should be easily analyzable (i.e., it should be obvious).

For the time study illustration, some of the architecture rationales are:

- Work happens in desktop:
  - Work activities are performed in the desktop using some application.
  - Any activities done outside the desktop are scheduled in the calendar.
- Work time is categorized into two parts:
  - Work time is the time expended in performing a work activity.
  - Nonwork time is the time expended in any other activities that cannot be accounted.
- Tracking is enabled by in-direct inference:
  - Structure exists inside the desktop to recognize any work performed by individual.
  - The correlation between computing resources and work activities is established to facilitate tracking.
  - The appropriate task is decided upon based on a predefined task rule table.

10.3.5.3 Define architecture models

An architecture model is a partial abstraction of a system. It is an approximation, and it captures the different properties of the system. It is a scaled-down version and is built with all the essential details of the system. Architecture modeling involves identifying the characteristics of the system and expressing it as models so that the system can be understood. Architecture models allow visualization of information about the system represented by the model. The modeling process can be bottom up/inside out, by which details of the system are built utilizing knowledge about components and interconnections and how they compose together to realize the characteristics of the system. Alternatively, it can be top-down/outside in, by which details of the components and interconnections are extracted from knowledge of the whole. For the time study illustration, an architecture model is illustrated in Figure 10.9.

10.3.5.4 Create architecture views and viewpoints

In order to represent and understand the system as a whole, multiple views are necessary (e.g., functional view, semantic view, dynamic view IEEE Computer Society, 2004), with each view

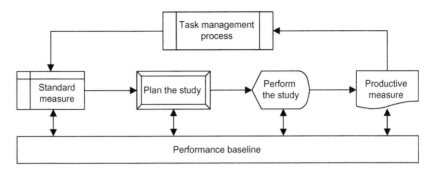

FIGURE 10.9

Architecture model for time study (ISO/IEC).

defining a set of properties corresponding to respective concerns (Kruchten, 1995; Systems Engineering and Cybernetics Centre, 1999). Each view is a different perspective in representing the system and if semantically motivated explains how the system is understood, analyzed, and synthesized.

Creating views and viewpoints is predominantly an act of identifying a configuration that satisfies stated constraints and formulating it as a mutual relationship of configuration items (Hallier). It is also the process of developing an analogical system of relations, catering to a predefined form and convention, comprised of entities and relationships between them (Hallier). For time study illustration, the first viewpoint, as shown in Figure 10.10, is a representation of various components that provide desired functionality to the software system and their interrelationships expressed as provided and required interfaces. For our illustration purposes, it is expressed using SysML Block definition diagrams.

The second viewpoint, as shown in Figure 10.11, is a representation of the usage processes that facilitate the functionalities provided by various components to be utilized to perform tasks in the real world. SysML Use case diagram has been used to represent these usage processes.

10.3.5.5 Translate to architecture descriptions

The end result of software architecting is the creation of the architecture. Software architecture descriptions are the work products of software architecting (Kruchten, 1995). They are used to express software architectures of the software system of interest. While software architecture is an abstraction of concepts, principles, guidelines, and so on, architecture descriptions use architectural elements including components, connectors, relationships, properties, styles, roles, and interfaces to express software architectures.

In the value matrix approach, value and qualities serve as the concepts; qualities prioritizations, quality breakdown, and value quality translation are the principles that are manifest in software architecture.

Along with these principles, architecture models, architecture views and architecture view points allow stakeholders to understand the structure of the system. Additionally, quality characteristics, intended use, limitations, design decisions and design rationales allow stakeholders to understand

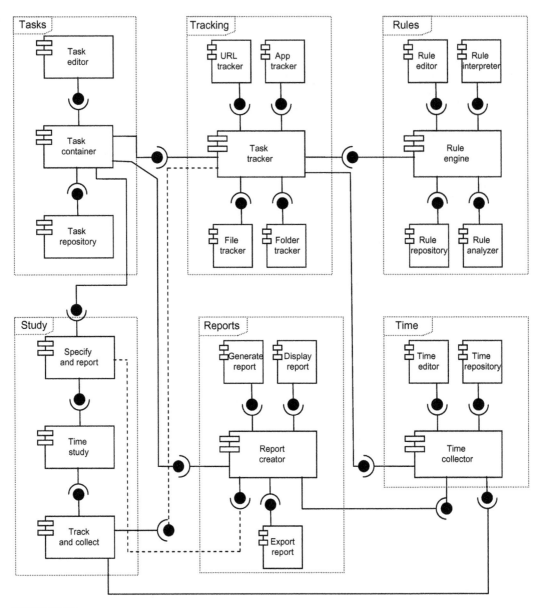

FIGURE 10.10

Personal time study components and interfaces using SysML block diagrams.

the behavior of the system. The translation to architecture description depends on both the architecture framework that is of interest and the architecture description language that is adopted. This translation is constrained by the need to conserve the meaning originally specified and is designed for evolution and propagation of change.

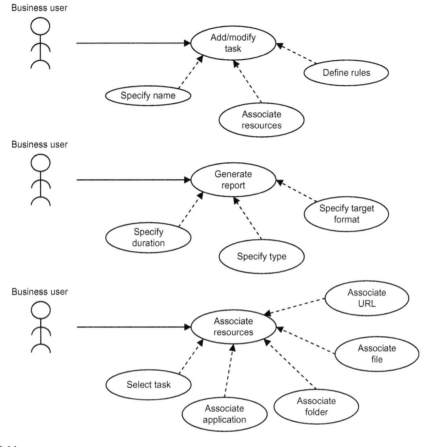

FIGURE 10.11

Usage processes using SysML use case diagram.

10.3.5.6 Qualities conformance

Qualities conformance refers to the degree to which an envisaged architecture meets its architecture description. Its focus is on the internal operating view of the quality characteristics of the software system. A conformance analysis would enable an architect to establish the level of conformance of an architecture description against the envisaged architecture. These levels are: irrelevant (no common quality characteristics exist), consistent (some common quality characteristics exist), compliant (some of the specified quality characteristics are expressed), conformant (all the specified quality characteristics are expressed, and some unspecified quality characteristics exist), fully conformant (there is full correspondence between architecture and its description), and nonconformant (full or partial mismatch). A conformance analysis serves as the basis for improving the architecture description. It is necessary to ensure conformance between the architecture and its description for a successful implementation (ISO/IEC).

10.3.6 Architecture instance

The purpose of the architecture instance is to instantiate architecture for a specific situation. It transforms specified behavior, interfaces, and implementation constraints into fabrication actions that create a software system according to the practices of the selected implementation technology. The software system is constructed or adapted by processing the information appropriate to the selected implementation technology and by employing appropriate technical specialties or disciplines. This process results in the satisfaction of specified structural/behavioral requirements through verification and stakeholder requirements through validation. In short, the architecture instantiation designs, creates, or fabricates a software system conforming to the architecture description. It is constructed by employing appropriate technology and industry practices (SE Handbook Working Group, INCOSE, 2011).

For the instantiation to succeed, it is necessary to address the system design requirements of all stakeholders. The failure to satisfy any one critical stakeholder creates risks of compensatory actions that lead to value delivery failure. In the architecture instance perspective, since system creation is the goal, the key question is; "How to utilize computational and technology resources in such a way so as to conform to the architecture description of the software system and provide an intervention in a specific situation considered as the architecture instance?"

Table 10.8 lists the metaphors/heuristics to follow for the architecture instance perspective, along with a set of guidelines. For ease of use, these guidelines are grouped under appropriate metaphors/heuristics. In Figure 10.4 the relationships between these heuristics is illustrated. The following sections elaborate and provide details about these guidelines.

10.3.6.1 Architecture realization

Architecture description is a conceptualization of the architecture. Its usefulness is in conceiving and expressing the functional and nonfunctional quality characteristics along with the proposed form/structure of the software system. This artifact is still an idea that needs to be realized through construction with available technologies so that value can be delivered to various stakeholders. Since the specification is predominantly in terms of building qualities into the software system, one approach for realization would be to create appropriate production processes that identify the

---

Table 10.8 Metaphors and Guidelines for Architecture Instance

Commit {Meaningful reflection of realization}

- Architecture Realization
  - Instantiate the architecture for a specific instance and realize the system.
- Architecture Analysis and Improvement
  - Trace architecture description to its realization.

Co-Evolve {Meaningful reflection of operation, existence, and growth}

- Qualities Analysis and Improvement
  - Analysis of delivered qualities against desired qualities and appropriate improvement
- Value Analysis and Improvement
  - Analysis of delivered value against desired value and appropriate improvement

outcomes, activities, tasks, and deliverables necessary for delivering the quality goals expressed in the architecture description. The specific processes to achieve qualities come from different knowledge domains that provide knowledge bases on how to achieve performance, security, data integrity, and the like. They also provide process steps for achieving the qualities that can be fitted into the framework. The architect's responsibility in this case is more that of an observer in order to gain knowledge about the pitfalls the developers face with regard to realization of the architecture specification.

10.3.6.2 Architecture analysis and improvement

One reason for making the software architecture of a system explicit is to allow for early analysis of decisions made in it. This is the area of software architecture analysis (Abowd et al., 1997). Architecture analysis measures the degree to which a software system realization meets its architecture description and is worked out based on quality characteristics. It enables an architect to establish the level of conformance of an architecture description against the implementation and thereby serves as the basis for filling the gap between an architecture specification and its implementation. The various conformance levels are: irrelevant (no common quality characteristics exist), consistent (some common quality characteristics exist), compliant (some of the specified quality characteristics are expressed), conformant (all the specified quality characteristics exist, and some unspecified quality characteristics also exist), fully conformant (there is full correspondence between architecture description and its implementation), and nonconformant (full or partial mismatch) (ISO/IEC).

There are a number of approaches to architecture analysis, and they can be classified based on (1) the software architecting process and (2) software architecture artifacts. These methods are predominantly scenario based and can evaluate quantitative as well as qualitative attributes. The key point to remember is that the results of the analysis are only as good as the assumptions that are made and the inputs that are given. The purpose of architectural analysis is to achieve reasonable confidence that the desired qualities are achieved, but it does not guarantee quality achievement. Architectural analysis can be done at every stage of software architecting, and its purpose is to understand the pressure points/trade-off early so that the analyzed information can produce an understanding that supplements intuitive and experimental decision making. An overview of architectural analysis techniques is given by Abowd et al., (Abowd et al., 1997) and it can be adapted for our purposes.

10.3.6.3 Quality analysis and improvement

Stakeholders appropriate value due to quality characteristics of software system. However, because of the intractability of the methods used to realize these quality characteristics and nonavailability of appropriate computing technologies, realization of quality characteristics is an approximation, and there is always a gap between desired quality characteristics and delivered quality characteristics. This necessitates the need for continuous refinement. It is therefore necessary to ensure that there is enough feedback from design cycle into the realization process so as to ensure that approximation is minimal. This is the first qualities analysis and improvement that needs to be taken care of.

Not every stakeholder has the same perception of value. Although functional quality characteristics serve as the initial source of value (as users employ these features to perform tasks); unmet and unarticulated needs pave the way for new features and serve as the source for future value; unused and evolving features pave the way for more value to users during usage.

Over time, these functional quality characteristics lose their ability to deliver value to stakeholders as they become the standard across similar systems. However, nonfunctional characteristics determine the excellence of features and hence serve as the differentiator between various software system providing similar features. Hence, they also serve as a last source of value. In order to improve the nonfunctional qualities, it is necessary to ensure that there is enough feedback from the stakeholders to the design/realization cycle. This is the second qualities analysis and improvement that needs to be taken care of. For the time study illustration, the probable qualities improvements could be:

10.3.6.3.1 Functional quality characteristics
- Track work-related tasks performed on the mobile/communication device.
- Upload timesheet reports into the enterprise project management systems.
- Download tasks from the enterprise project management systems.

10.3.6.3.2 Nonfunctional quality characteristics
- The software system should be portable across multiple computing devices.
- Individuals should be able to work with multiple task configurations.
- The software system should be location aware and should reconfigure based on the location.

10.3.6.4 Value analysis and improvement
Once the software system is realized and put to use, various stakeholders appropriate value. However, the relationship between value and qualities is not straightforward. In the stakeholders' world, it is a function of many variables such as processes, interactions, knowledge, maturity, usage model, performance, planning, and management. As a result, a gap always exists between the delivered stakeholders' value and the desired stakeholders' value. This gap needs to be addressed, resulting in continuous refinement of the software system. There should be enough feedback from the design cycle into the realization process so as to ensure that this gap is minimal. Techniques such as the Cost-Benefit Analysis Method (CBAM) can be used to make decisions with regard to value achievement (Kazman et al., 2002). Although the consensus basis of the CBAM method allows for active discussion and clarification among stakeholders, the traceability basis of this method permits iterative improvement for value achievement (Kazman et al., 2002).

The stakeholder's perception of value keeps changing over time. If this change is not taken into consideration, then the software system will diminish in the eyes of various stakeholders. Value is the single most important contributing factor impacting the software system. One way to address this issue is to create value snapshots over multiple periods of time (e.g., before system intervention; after system intervention; after the system is put to regular use) and perform value analysis over the various snapshots to figure out the lacunae in value and propagate the identified change to the design cycle. For the time study illustration, the value improvements could be:

- Reduce the complexity of work done by business users
- Increase the throughput and productivity of business users
- Increase the operational effectiveness of business users in their work environment

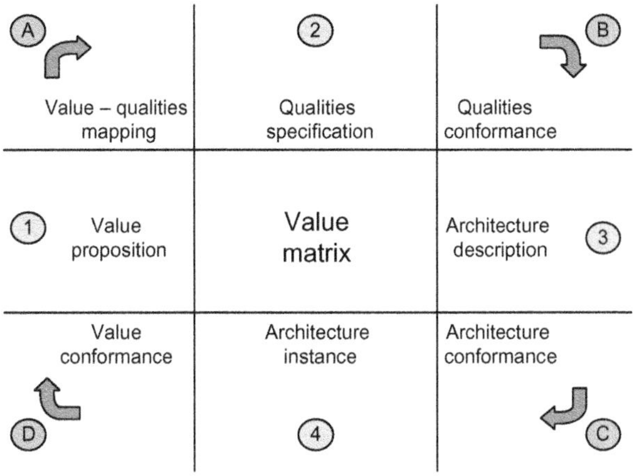

FIGURE 10.12

X-matrix representation of the value matrix framework.

10.4 Value matrix representation

The representation of the value matrix framework is based on the X matrix as shown in Figure 10.12 (Lokku, 2011). An X matrix has four dimensions and four linkages, as shown in the figure. The four dimensions are:

- *Value to stakeholders* (1) that is delivered by the software system when put to use
- *Quality characteristics* (2) that are built into the software system so as to deliver the desired value
- *Architecture description* (3), which is the specification of the software system
- *Architecture instance* (4), which is the instantiated architecture for the particular situation context

The interrelationships between the various dimensions are expressed as linkages, and they are:

- *Value—Qualities Mapping* (A) is the translation from value to quality characteristics
- *Qualities Conformance* (B) is degree to which an envisaged architecture meets its architecture description
- *Architecture Conformance* (C) is degree to which architecture description meets implementation
- *Value Conformance* (D) is degree to which delivered value relates to proposed value

10.5 Summary

The basis of the value matrix framework is the **values viewpoint** for creating and describing software architectures. It includes identifying the need for architects to understand value creation processes, creating a separation of value and quality concerns across levels, creating appropriate

Table 10.9 Summary of the value Matrix Framework

Perspective	Metaphors	Guidelines
Value Proposition	Comprehend	Identify stakeholders
		Understand stakeholders value creation context
		Understand situation context
	Conceptualize	Define problem space
		Define solution space
		Define solution value creation context
Qualities Specification	Converge	Redefine stakeholders value requirements
		Define system configuration
		Define system quality characteristics and their correlation to value
	Co-create	Create system breakdown structure
		Create quality breakdown structure
		Create usage processes
Architecture Description	Co-convert	Identify architecture styles
		Define architecture rationales
		Define architectural models
	Communicate	Create architectural views and viewpoints
		Translate to architecture description
		Qualities conformance
Architecture Instance	Commit	Architecture realization
		Architecture analysis and improvement
	Co-evolve	Qualities analysis and improvement
		Value analysis and improvement

form/structures for realizing value, and establishing traceability among value, quality, and architecture. While the architecture of a solution creates the framework for achieving qualities, the ultimate goal of architecture is to deliver value to all the stakeholders.

Accordingly, the architect should determine not only the sources of value for each stakeholder, but also the processes by which the offering produces or influences their value. In the value matrix framework, we discuss the role of architects with respect to value and qualities, techniques for modeling the context and value influences, and use of the models to establish the relationship between value and qualities. We also propose a separation of qualities and value delivery concerns among software engineering life-cycle activities, and we use it to identify the responsibilities of the architect. We use the X-matrix representation to capture the traceability from stakeholder value to offering features and quality attributes to architectural decisions.

The core ideas behind the value matrix, as illustrated in Table 10.9, are the four different perspectives that are substantiated by the use of corresponding metaphors for each perspective. Its scope includes improving stakeholder value, solution lifetime, and consistency with the environments of the solution. The critical concerns that need to be tackled are (1) dialog with stakeholders in terms of desired benefits, (2) translating benefits to solution qualities, (3) defining the solution profile in terms of qualities, (4) defining the architecture in terms of architecture descriptions, and (5) realizing the architecture description and validating it for value and quality delivery.

Acknowledgments

Our thanks to colleagues of Tata Consultancy Services and members of the ISO study group on architecture (WG42) who helped us refine our understanding of software architecture.

References

Abowd, G., Bass, L., Clements, P., Kazman, R., Northrop, L., Zaremski, A., 1997. Recommended Best Industrial Practice for Software Architecture Evaluation (CMU/SEI-96-TR-025). Software Engineering Institute, Carnegie Mellon University, <http://www.sei.cmu.edu/library/abstracts/reports/96tr025.cfm>.

Anand, K., Nori, K.V., Reddy, N.K., Raman, A., 2008. User value driven software development. Information Systems 2008. Barcelona, Spain.

Anand K., Samson D., Zope, N., 2012. Value driven approach for services design, 56th Conference of International Society of Systems Science, San Jose, California.

Boehm, B., Value based software engineering, ACM Sigsoft, Softw. Eng. Notes 28 (2), 1–12.

Boehm, B., Sullivan, K., Software economics: a roadmap. The Future of Software Engineering. <http://www.cs.ucl.ac.uk/staff/A.Finkelstein/fose/finalboehm.pdf>.

Faisandier, A., 2012. Systems Architecture and Design, vol. 3, Sinergy' Com.

Garlan, D., Shaw, M., 1994. An Introduction to Soft-Ware Architecture, Advances in Software Engineering and Knowledge Engineering. World Scientific Publishing Company, New Jersey, USA.

Hallier, B., Space is the Machine. A Configurational Theory on Architecture. eBook.

Hillier, B., Leaman, A., 1974. How is design possible. J. Arch. Plan. Res. 4–11.

Hitchins, D., 2008. Emergence, hierarchy, complexity, architecture: how do they all fit together? A Guide for Seekers after Enlightenment. Self-published white paper. Available at: <http://www.hitchins.net/EmergenceEtc.pdf> (accessed 4.09.12.).

IEEE Computer Society, 2004. Guide to software engineering body of knowledge, SWEBOK.

IEEE Computer Society, 2012. Guide to software engineering body of knowledge. Softw. Design.

IEEE Computer Society, 2012. Guide to software engineering body of knowledge. Softw. Eng. Econ.

ISO/IEC, ISO—25010, Systems and software engineering—Systems and software quality requirements and evaluation (SQuaRE) system and software quality models, ISO and IEC.

ISO/IEC, ISO— 42030—Architecture evaluation, ISO and IEC (Working Draft).

ISO/IEC, ISO—15939, Systems and software engineering—Measurement Process, ISO and IEC.

ISO/IEC, 15288, 2008. Systems engineering—System life cycle processes, ISO and IEC.

ISO/IEC, 42010, 2011. Systems and Software Engineering—Architecture Description.

Kano, N., 1996. Guide to TQM in Service Industries. Asian Productivity Organization, Tokyo.

Kazman, R., Asundi, J., Klein, M., 2002. Making architecture design decisions: An economic approach, Technical Report, CMU/SEI-2002-TR-035, ESC-TR-2002-035.

Kruchten, P., 1995. Architectural—Blueprints, The 4 + 1 view model of software architecture. IEEE Softw. 12 (6), 42–50.

Lokku, D.S., 2011. Value distilled: a framework based approach to establish the trace of technology value in the context of engineering management, Eurocon.

Maier, M., Rechtin, E., 2009. The Art of Architecting. third ed. CRC Press, Boca Raton, FL.

McConnell, S., 2004. Code Complete. Microsoft Press, Redmond, WA, USA.

Meredith, D.D., Wong, K.W., Woodhead, R.W., Wortman, R.H., 1973. Design and Planning of Engineering Systems, Prentice Hall, University of California.

Nori, K.V., Swaminathan, N., 2006. A framework for software product engineering. Asia-Pacific Software Engineering Conference. Bangalore.

OMG, OMG Systems Modeling Language Version 1.3. <http://www.omg.org/spec/SysML/20120401>.

Perry, D.E., Wolf, A., 1992. Foundations for the study of software architecture. ACM SigSoft Softw. Eng. Notes 17 (4), 40−51.

Reekie, J., McAdam, R., 2006. A Software Architecture Primer, Angophora Press.

Ring, J., 1998. Value seeking approach for systems engineering. IEEE-SMC, Conference Proceedings.

SE Handbook Working Group, INCOSE, 2011. Syst. Eng. Handbook 3.2.2.

Shaw, M., 1994. Patterns for software architecture. In: Coplien, Schmidt (Eds.), First Annual Conference on the Pattern Languages of Programming, vol. 1. Addison-Wesley, Reading, MA, pp. 453−462.

Systems Engineering and Cybernetics Centre, 1999. Multi-modeling Approach to Enterprise Analysis and Modeling. Quality Management System Guidelines.

Womack, J.P., Jones, D.T., 1996. Lean Thinking. Simon & Schuster, New York.

Zachman, J.A., 1987. A framework for information systems architecture. IBM Syst. J. 26 (3), IBM Publication G321-5298.

Linking Architecture Inception and Evolution to Economics: Experiences and Approaches

IV

Software Evolution in the Presence of Externalities: A Game-Theoretic Approach

11

Marios Fokaefs, Eleni Stroulia, and Paul R. Messinger

University of Alberta, Edmonton, AB, Canada

11.1 Introduction

Software evolves over time to include various enhancements, and these changes may increase its value. From a technical standpoint, evolution occurs to fix issues with the software behavior, to extend its functionality with improved and new features, and to improve its design qualities such as maintainability, performance, and security. Clearly, these changes have financial implications for both revenues and costs. On the one hand, maintenance and evolution imply development costs, related to modifying and retesting the software, and a learning curve for the users who need to become aware of the changes and how they may benefit from them. On the other hand, evolution should add value for the software users, which may be associated with an increased usage fee.

Our understanding of how software is developed and consumed has been changing, as have the underlying technologies, architecture styles and life-cycle processes, and so has the process of software evolution and the economic concerns around it. In order to calculate revenues and costs when considering the evolution of software, one should be aware of the architecture of the software and the nature of the relationship between production and consumption.

From an architectural perspective, software was originally thought of as a "product" of a development team. In this scenario, the decision on when and how exactly to evolve the software has to consider the estimated cost of the change, in relation to the anticipated increase of revenue that the change may bring. Eventually, technologies such as software frameworks and off-the-shelf components enabled the modularization of the software architecture and its development as an agglomeration of parts, developed and evolved by independent teams. In this scenario, the community recognized that, in addition to the trade-offs in the cost and value of the change of a component, the evolution of that component has to take into account the impact of the change on its clients, who have to decide whether to continue using the deprecated component version or to "catch-up with the evolution" by adapting their own software. More recently, software has increasingly been viewed as the composition and orchestration of "services." In this scenario, when service providers consider evolving their offerings, they also have to consider the impact of the service evolution on the consumers of their services. The decision-making process is similar to the second scenario of component evolution, yet different in an important respect: Old service versions typically cease to be available (it is too costly to support the operations of multiple versions at the same time), which makes the impact of the change to the client immediate and potentially severe.

Clearly, software evolution presents complex challenges for participants in the software market, governed by several factors. First, software production and consumption relations, enabled by software-reuse technologies, imply complex dependencies among various development teams. Second, the various parties may have different, even competing, goals during the software-evolution process; for example, while providers envision extensions to potentially attract new clients, existing clients may prefer stability. Third, the various parties may have different levels of technical adeptness and knowledge; while component providers have deep knowledge of their implementation and can easily plan its evolution, the component consumers may find it difficult to understand the change and to trace its impact throughout their own software. And fourth, economic considerations, particularly pricing, can influence the extent to which the parties involved want to develop, acquire, maintain, and utilize the software.

In the presence of such complex relationships between the various parties, the reactions of one party to the decisions of another may affect the outcome of the evolution process. When one party makes a decision and some of the associated costs or benefits are borne by another party, such costs or benefits are known in the economic literature as *externalities* (Laffont, 2008). Applied in the context of software evolution, providers' decisions (e.g., evolution) often give rise to external effects (i.e., externalities) borne by clients (e.g., adaptation costs). By their very definition, externalities on downstream users are typically not fully factored into the decisions taken by the providers in the process of software creation and enhancement. Yet the welfare of the ecosystem as a whole—including providers and consumers—depends on the actions of all the parties, and typically the presence of externalities leads to suboptimal outcomes for a system as a whole. We are interested in studying the extent to which such issues arise in the context of software evolution and identify possible remedies for this problem, including concerted action by providers and users.

In this chapter, we study the software-evolution process from the perspectives of two parties simultaneously: the perspective of the provider, which is the party that develops and enhances the software, and the perspective of the client, which is the party that consumes the software and adapts to its changes. We study the relationships of these two parties in the process of software evolution, in the context of three different software-architecture settings. We view each setting as a game in which the two parties take actions that affect the outcomes for both parties, and, for each game, we define the players' actions and calculate their payoff. Eventually, we focus on service-oriented architecture, as the most prevalent one today, and we develop a theoretical framework to study the relationship between providers and clients and the constraints that it imposes in the ecosystem. We then examine whether there can exist a viable solution for all involved parties in a service system whereby software evolves in a beneficial way for all concerned. We describe the other architectural styles in order to stress the special conditions and challenges that web services may impose and in order to show that each newer architecture introduces new parameters and constraints in the software-evolution problem. We conclude our work with propositions that summarize the results of our study and provide guidelines to providers and clients on how to make the best possible decision.

The rest of the document is outlined as follows. In section 2, we provide the background of this work, and we discuss the related literature. In section 3, we describe in detail the various evolution scenarios and examine in detail the relationship between the provider and the client in each one of them. Finally, section 4 concludes this work.

11.2 **Background**

This work touches on the areas of software-engineering economics, software evolution, and theories of software cost and value.

11.2.1 **Software engineering economics**

Software economics is a mature research area that deals with the ever challenging issue of valuing software and estimating the costs involved in its production. These issues may be exacerbated in the case of service systems because of the peculiarities of such systems, some of which we have highlighted in this work. In their work, Boehm and Sullivan (1999, 2000); Boehm (1981) outline these challenges and also show how software-economics principles can be applied to improve software design, development, and evolution. They define software engineering fundamentally as a decision-making activity over time with limited resources and usually in the face of significant uncertainties. *Uncertainties* pose a crucial challenge in software development that can lead to system failure. Uncertainties can arise from inaccurate estimation. For example, cost-estimation models developed for traditional development processes no longer apply to modern architectural styles and development processes, such as the ones around service-oriented software systems. Furthermore, due to the lack or inadequacy of economic and business information software projects may be at risk. Boehm and Sullivan also recognize the need to include the *value added* from any design or evolution decision. However, as they point out, usually there are no explicit links between technical issues and value creation. It is critical to understand that the value added by evolving a system depends not only on technical success but also on market conditions. It is stressed that the cost should not be judged in isolation. For a system to create value, the cost of an increment should be proportional to the benefits delivered (Boehm and Sullivan, 2000, p. 329). Finally, Boehm and Sullivan claim that there is a need for not only better cost estimation models but also stronger techniques for analyzing benefits.

11.2.2 **The provider–client relationship**

The provider–client game as presented in this chapter is a clear example of an ecosystem where externalities exist. An externality is an indirect cost or benefit of consumption or production activity, that is, effects on agents, other than the originator of such activity, which do not work through the price system (Laffont, 2008). External effects such as these can lead to suboptimal or inefficient outcomes for the system as a whole, whereby both parties by acting independently end up less well off than they could do if they coordinated their actions or if the decision maker (in this case the provider) took into account the external effects of any action.

The Coase theorem (Coase, 1960) argues that an efficient outcome can be achieved through negotiations and further payments between the involved parties under certain conditions (the parties act rationally, transactions costs are minimal, and property rights are well defined). The last scenario, where the provider supports the client in the adaptation process, is an example of the Coase theorem.

The relationship between a producing party (provider) and a consuming party (client) is a prevalent concept in many economic and business fields. More specifically, in the field of operations management, the relationship between the provider and the client is a special case of a supply-chain relationship, where we have the provider of an input interacting with a firm using that input in the production process (Gokhan and Needy, 2010; McGuire and Staelin, 2008; Nagurney, 2006). In the field of marketing, the relationship is referred to the channel of distribution (Choi, 1991; McGuire and Staelin, 2008). In both of these fields, there is an external relationship between the upstream supplier/provider and the downstream producer/client.

Hoffmann (2007) has studied the interbusiness relationships as a portfolio of strategic alliances and how an evolving environment can affect these alliances. According to the author, there can exist three strategies in managing the portfolio and coping with a changing environment: (1) actively *shaping* the environmental development according to firm strategy, (2) *stabilizing* the environment in order to avoid organizational change, and (3) reactively *adapting* to the changing environment. In the context of our work, we can perceive the different strategies as being part of different business partners. For instance, the provider is the one that shapes the environment by evolving the software; the client is trying to catch up with the evolved software in order to stabilize the environment and reach a previous point of balance; and other providers are trying to adapt to the changed environment in order to stay in the competition.

11.2.3 The value and cost of software evolution

Software evolution has been studied extensively, as both a technical problem and a decision-making process. In this section, we review several works that touch on various aspects of the software-evolution problem as described in our work.

In order to calculate the value that the provider expects to receive from the change, first the type of change has to be determined. According to Swanson (1976), changes in software systems can be *perfective* (e.g., to add new features), *corrective* (e.g., to fix a bug), *adaptive* (e.g., to migrate to a new language), or *preventive* (e.g., refactorings). For each of these types of changes, the value for the provider depends on different factors. For example, the value from fixing a bug can depend on the popularity of the bug (i.e., how many developers follow its updates), the importance of the code where the bug was found, its severity, and so on. To calculate the value from adding new features, Tansey (2008) used financing and accounting measures, namely, the Net Present Value (NPV) index along with software metrics to calculate cost and effort and projected the evolution of the system in the future in order to select the most profitable scenario. Finally, to calculate the value of preventive changes a lot of works in the field of software maintenance have used traditional software metrics to calculate the improvement in design quality, maintainability, and understandability of the code.

Ozkaya et al. (2007) propose a quality-guided model to evaluate architectural patterns and design decisions to support the decision process of software designers and architects. They employ real-options analysis to identify the best available design decision. In their analysis, they take into account and study the effect of the decision on a set of quality properties (rather than just one).

Many methods have been proposed to estimate the implementation cost of changing software. One of the most popular methods is Constructive Cost Model (COCOMO II) (Boehm et al., 2000). This model calculates cost as the programmatic effort required to change the software in terms of source lines of code or function points. An issue with this model is that it requires knowledge about the system's source code. When the source code is not available, for example, in the third scenario we describe, the provider cannot predict the adaptation cost for the client and therefore cannot make an informed decision. This issue is mitigated by an extension of COCOMO II, called Constructive Commercial Off-the-Shelf Cost Model (COCOTS), which calculates costs when the system is using Commercial Off-the-Shelf components (COTS). In particular, a submodel of COCOTS, the *volatility* model, calculates the costs to adapt to changed COTS, when the source code is unavailable. However, this approach requires knowledge about the source code of the client applications, which does not facilitate the provider's decision-making process.

Srivastava and Sorenson (2010) propose a method to select between functionally equivalent services based on Quality of Service (QoS) properties. They study how clients value the quality of the service and how they would react in case of a change in the QoS properties. These QoS properties are usually contained in the service-level agreement (SLA), which is an artifact that the provider can use to calculate variables concerning the value of service such as availability, security, uptime, response time and so on. Finally, the authors also argue (but do not further investigate) that the client's reaction to a change in QoS properties also depends on the price fluctuation for the service.

Having reviewed the aforementioned works (concerning both value and cost of evolution), we recognize the need for a model of the software-evolution process, in the context of an ecosystem rather than just as a process carried out by the service provider as an independent entity. This model should include all the relevant costs and benefits for providers and clients alike. As we have seen in this work, certain decisions, which might look optimal for one party, might not be optimal for ecosystem as a whole, and thus could lead to inferior outcomes for the individual parties.

11.3 **The software-evolution game**

Adopting a game-theory perspective to analyze the provider−consumer relationship in the context of software evolution, we distinguish three different scenarios in the software-evolution game. The distinction is based on the architecture and underlying technologies of the evolving software system, which, to an important extent, dictates how the software is delivered and shapes the relationship between the developing party (provider) and the consuming party (client).

- *Software is a monolithic product, produced by a single independent entity (individual or organization).*The decision on whether or not to change it is made by the producing organization with full knowledge of the complete software; thus, the decision makers can assess the full scope of the change and estimate its cost. At the same time, the software organization can also estimate the additional value that the change will embed in the software and develop a plan for its eventual monetization.
- *Software is built and delivered as a module, either an off-the-shelf component (COTS) or an extensible framework; the client application is built using these modules.* The various constituent parts are owned and are being developed by different and independent organizations. Therefore, the evolution of the reusable modules may impact their clients if they decide to migrate to the newer version. However, the clients may choose to keep using the older module versions, which remain typically available but may no longer be supported or maintained by the provider.
- *Software is built as a service; the client application is built by composing a number of services.* Software is still modular, but the fundamental distinction between this scenario and the one

above is that, in this case, the reusable components are available online and are accessible at runtime; the client does not own "copies" of earlier service versions but rather has the right to use/invoke the services, which are deployed by the provider. Given this type of tight runtime relationship between the provider and the client of reusable software components, the decision-making process around service evolution occurs in the presence of externalities. Although externalities exist in both this and the previous scenario, in the latter case they are more pronounced. Older versions of services cannot be available to the client, if they are not supported by the provider.

In fact, Kaminski et al. (2006) argue that backwards compatibility should be offered when evolving a web service, but at least until support for the older version is formally withdrawn. Practically, this means that there should be a grace period during which the clients should make efforts to migrate to the newer version. Consider, for example, Twitter[1] which released API v1.1 in September 2012 as a replacement for the old v1, which was slated for complete retirement in March 2013. At this point, the provider will cease to offer the older version since there are costs associated with maintaining multiple versions simultaneously; the clients will have to decide whether they will migrate to the new version or they will have to find a more suitable alternative.

Another important aspect of service-oriented architectures that is different from other architectures is the relationship between providers and clients. Services are conceived to implement (or support) high-level business offerings, and influence business interactions at a higher level than interdependencies between typical software components and libraries. After all, some of the most popular examples that are used to explain service systems (e.g., loan approval, product orders) describe eponymous business transactions where some data needs to persist in the system, unlike the usually anonymous interactions in modular systems. Therefore, the nature of these transactions imposes a stronger type of relationship between the provider and the client: that of business partners. In this scenario, the provider and the client may act completely independently, but, because of this business partnership, the provider may choose to support the client in the adaptation process, thus internalizing some of the client's cost for migrating to the new service version. This tighter relationship between the provider and the client and the motivation of the provider to support the client can also be explained by Williamson's transaction cost approach (Williamson, 2013). In cases of tight relationship between two parties, where the cost of transactions between the parties is high, one party may opt to include the other in what is called the "efficient boundary" of the organization, thus internalizing the transaction costs.

Although these settings differ from each other with respect to their complexity and the details of the relationship between the provider and the client, they share certain common aspects which, in this chapter, we aim to capture in a coherent provider–client game-theoretic framework. In particular, we consider a situation in which a software provider is contemplating changing old software and making the new version available to the client. We write V_o^C as the value to the client of the old software (before the change), and we write p_o as the price the client pays for the old software.

---

[1]https://dev.twitter.com/blog/planning-for-api-v1-retirement (last accessed 15 February 2013).

In order to evolve the old software, the provider is assumed to incur a cost C_e (for such things as conceptual development and implementation). The software also requires investment of effort on the part of the client to adapt, assimilate, and use in the client's own systems—and to teach the client team how to make use of the new system elements. We refer to these costs on the part of the client as adaptation costs, which we write as C_a.

In some cases, there is inherent value to the provider in improving the software, and this value, as perceived by the provider, we denote by V_e^P. For example, improvements may allow the software to more efficiently utilize the provider's resources. In all cases in our model, we assume that there is an increased value of the new version of the software to the client; this value, as perceived by the client, we denote by V_e^C. Naturally, V_e^P depends on the costs incurred to change the software, which we refer to as the evolution costs; the more effort the provider puts in the evolution, the greater the improvement that can be achieved. However, V_e^C does not depend on the adaptation costs. This is because the improvement is specific to the software and the provider's efforts; no matter how much effort the client puts in the adaptation, the improvement will be the same. The increase in the value for the client depends on the degree to which the client can benefit from the improvements that the provider built in the evolution.

Table 11.1 summarizes all the variables in our model. We observe that the notation distinguishes between two states for the software: *before* the evolution of the software and *after* the

Table 11.1 The variables and their definitions as used in the Evolution Model

Variables	Definition
Before the evolution	
V_o^C	the value of the software before evolution (based on its features and qualities)
P_o	the price the client pays for the software (assumed to be either an one-time fixed price or based on a pay-per-use contract of some duration)
After the evolution	
C_e	the cost of the evolution process
C_{ai}	the cost of adaptation to the new version of the current provider's software for the client application
C_{aj}	the cost of migration to provider j's software for the client application
p_e^E	the price differential for the updated software when the provider just evolves
p_n^E	the new price for the updated software when the provider just evolves $(p_n^E = p_o + p_e^E)$
p_e^S	the price change for the updated software when the provider supports the client
p_n^S	the new price for the updated software when the provider supports the client $(p_n^S = p_o + p_e^S)$
p_j	the price the client pays for provider j's software
V_e^P	the change in the value of the updated software, as perceived by the provider
V_e^C	the change in the value of the updated software, as perceived by the client
V_n^C	the value of the new version of the software, as perceived by the client $(V_n^C = V_o^C + V_e^C)$
V_j^C	the value of provider j's software, as perceived by the client
a	the subsidy rate, which determines what portion of the adaptation costs the provider will cover
b	the final portion of the adaptation costs that remains for the client after the provider's support

evolution. All the variables referring to the former state have the subscript o to denote that they are specific to the old version of the software, the variables referring to differentials (increase or decrease) have the subscript e, and the variables referring to the new state have the subscript n. We distinguish between three types of variables: costs (denoted with the letter C), software prices (denoted with the letter p for price), and nonmonetary benefits (denoted with the letter V for value). Finally, the variables that are specific to the "other" provider (to whom the client may choose to switch) have the subscript j.

11.3.1 Software as a monolithic product

In the case of a monolithic system, there is a single organization that designs, develops, and maintains a single piece of software. As far as the delivery and usage of the system is concerned, we can distinguish between two scenarios: Either the firm develops the software for internal purposes or the firm sells the software as a shrink wrap to anonymous end-users. In both cases, the development and maintenance of the software, as well as all decisions concerning these activities, are internal to the firm, which can make fully informed decisions on these matters. The firm (i.e., the provider) then controls who is using the software (i.e., who the clients are) and can adapt the other processes or educate the personnel to use the new version of the software. All the costs incurred from the evolution process are internal for the provider of the software. In other words, the only cost present in this scenario is C_e. Furthermore, the benefit to be obtained through the evolution process is the system improvements with respect to its features and qualities, that is, performance, design, efficiency, and so on, V_e^P. As a result, the problem of software evolution becomes a linear optimization problem in which the provider has to choose the evolution scenario that maximizes the "profit":

$$
\begin{aligned}
\text{maximize } \Pi \quad &= V_e^P - C_e \\
\text{s.t.} \quad\quad & V_e^P \geq 0 \\
& C_e \geq 0
\end{aligned}
$$

In this scenario, there are no interactions external to the system. Both decision variables in this setting (V_e^P and C_e) are determined solely by the opportunities present in the environment, since there is no strategic interaction between players with divergent interests. As a result, the decision maker will have to, first, confirm that there exists an evolution scenario that will create a profit (i.e. $V_e^P - C_e > 0$) and, second, select the most profitable scenario.

Even if the software is a shrink-wrap product sold to anonymous clients, these clients are not strategic players; instead they are an environmental variable that feeds into the estimation of V_e^P (as a function of the proposed price per piece multiplied by the estimated number of customers).

The system might reach technological stagnation if no such evolution scenario exists. This may occur if the evolution cost becomes prohibitively high, due to the low technological adeptness of the provider. In such a situation, opportunities for evolution will not be pursued, and the ecosystem will stagnate until the environment changes.

11.3.2 Software as a module

In this scenario, the decision maker has only partial control of the outcome because the provider and the client are two independent entities that jointly influence the outcome. In this case, the client develops a software application that would consume the service. As a result, the design, development, and maintenance of the system are divided between an upstream (the provider) and a downstream developer (the client). Therefore, the costs and benefits are no longer internal to a single party, and the information flow between them is somewhat reduced. Furthermore, the behavior of each party and their reaction to the evolution event may affect the other, in the presence of externalities.

In the special case where the provider evolves the software but offers some backward compatibility so that old versions of the software are still available, the client applications continue to function as intended. We call this scenario "asynchronous evolution" in order to stress the fact that the client is not disrupted immediately after the evolution takes place. An example of such a scenario is programming libraries. This kind of software is usually offered as a compressed file, which the client can download locally and use. When the library changes, a new version is created and becomes available to the clients. However, the client may opt to keep using the old (now local) copy of the software, which, however, is no longer supported by the provider.

An implication of the fact that the software is now delivered as a module to an external client is that the module is offered for a price. This price can follow any pricing model, including a fixed one-time price, a pay-per-use pricing model, or a subscription model. In any case, the price can be a function of time or instances (i.e., number of users, number of requests). We do not make any particular assumptions about how the price is calculated, but we consider it as an input to our model.

Let us formulate this scenario as a game. On one hand, the provider has two choices: either to retain the status quo of the software and make no changes (SQ), or to evolve the software (E). On the other hand, the client can continue to use the old version (O) or migrate to the new one (N). Figure 11.1 presents the offline evolution game in its extensive form.

If the client stays with the old version, then the provider still may perceive benefits from the new software, V_e^P (due, for example, to greater ease of maintaining the software), and the provider, of course, still incurs the cost of software change, C_e. But the provider does not receive revenue p_e^E for the new software, and the client does not pay for the new software. In contrast, if the client migrates to the new software, the provider does receive this revenue and the client has to pay for it. Furthermore, the client receives the net benefit of the new software, $V_e^C - C_{ai}$ (the value of the new software net of the adaptation costs).

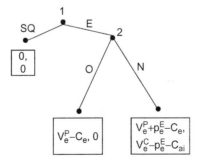

FIGURE 11.1

The provider–client game in the evolution of software as a module.

Table 11.2 Best-response Analysis for the Evolution of Software as a Module Game

		When the client prefers…	
		$O \succ N$	$N \succ O$
Provider	$E \succ SQ$	1. $V_e^P > C_e$	2. $V_e^P + p_e^E > C_e$
Client	$N \succ O$	3. $V_e^C > p_e^E + C_{ai}$	

Using the best-response analysis as shown in Table 11.2, we find under what conditions each leaf of the tree is an optimal solution. The client will always prefer to migrate to the new version ($N \succ O$), when the value of the new software for the client (V_e^C) exceeds the cost of its adaptation to the new version (C_{ai}) plus the associated price differential (p_e^E). On the other hand, if the client prefers to continue using the old version, the provider may still choose to evolve if the value of the new software for the provider exceeds the evolution costs (C_e). If the client prefers to migrate to the new version, the provider will evolve the software if the value of the new software for the provider (V_e^P) plus the additional income (p_e^E) exceed the evolution costs.

Unlike the previous scenario, where the decision-making process involved environmental variables only, in this scenario the provider has a decision to make regarding the value of the price differential (p_e^E); by controlling this value, the provider has the power to avoid stagnant situations (where the software is not evolved).

In this scenario, the client will still work with the provider after the evolution, whether by retaining the old software version or by migrating to the new one, thus guaranteeing an income for the provider. The problem that now faces the provider is to decide on a price that will motivate the client to migrate to the new version, in order to obtain the additional income associated with the price increase of the new software version. In principle, the client prefers a lower price increase for a higher additional value. In fact, from inequalities 2 and 3 we have that $C_e - V_e^P < p_e^E < V_e^C - C_{ai}$, which defines the range for the price increase within which the client will select the new version and the provider will still make profit. Naturally, the provider will try to push toward the higher end of the price range, to increase the profit. Therefore, we have $p_e^{*E} = V_e^C - C_{ai}$, provided that $V_e^C - C_{ai} > C_e - V_e^P$. This means that the final decision is driven by client-oriented factors, even if there is no immediate positive outcome for the provider. Furthermore, the provider's net software development costs ($C_e - V_e^P$) must be covered by the price increase, which will equal the net value of the evolution for the client. This amount for the price differential (p_e^{*E}) is the solution for this scenario.

11.3.3 Software as a service

In this scenario, the nature of the provider–client dependency is different from the one above. In the service-oriented paradigm, client applications are developed by consuming and composing services. Therefore, the provider and the client are highly coupled, and if a change happens to the service the consuming party is affected. Unlike the previous scenario, in the evolution of software as a service, if the sum of adaptation costs and price increase is too high, then it may be easier for the client to opt to abandon the provider. In this case, the provider not only tries to increase revenues by evolving the software, but at the same time must consider the possibility that current clients will abandon the new software.

The game corresponding to this scenario is shown in Figure 11.2. The provider has the same options as previously (SQ and E), but the client can now stay with the current provider and adapt to the new version (A) or leave the provider (L). We consider this setting to be a closed environment, and as a result we do not examine how the client will choose the new provider, but we include in the model the parameters that are relevant to the other provider. These parameters, which will be noted with the subscript j (as opposed to the subscript i for the current provider), include the value the client will get from using the other provider's service (V_j^C), the price for provider j's service (p_j) and the costs for the client to adapt to provider j's service (C_{aj}).

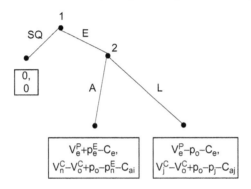

FIGURE 11.2

The provider–client game in the evolution of software as a service.

The best-response analysis for this game is shown in Table 11.3. The client will always prefer to adapt to the new version ($A \succ L$) when the total value of the service (including the original value of the service (V_o^C) and the value of the new software for the client (V_e^C)) exceed the adaptation costs plus the price differential p_e^E and the original price p_o. In this case, the provider will prefer to evolve the service if the value of the new software for the provider plus the extra income p_e^E exceeds the evolution costs of the provider.

On the other hand, if the client opts to leave the current provider, the latter will always prefer to evolve, if the value of the new software for the provider is greater than the evolution costs plus the current revenue from the client (p_o) that the provider will lose in this case.

Table 11.3 Best-response Analysis for the Evolution of Software as a Service Game

		When the client prefers...	
		$A \succ L$	$L \succ A$
Provider	$E \succ SQ$	1. $V_e^P + p_e^E > C_e$	2. $V_e^P > p_o + C_e$
Client	$A \succ L$	3. $V_n^C - V_j^C > p_n^E - p_j + C_{ai} - C_{aj}$	

Unlike the previous scenario, this is not a simple pricing problem because now the provider has to consider the competition. In order for the evolution to be a profitable option, the provider will have to either increase its own benefits or make an effort to retain the client. Benefits can be increased by

1. increasing the value of the service (V_e^P),
2. increasing the price for the new version of the service (p_n^E), and/or
3. decreasing the evolution costs.

The other option, that of retaining the client, can be achieved by

a. increasing the value of the service for the client (V_n^C) by offering additional features or better quality,
b. offering the service at a more competitive price (p_n^E) than the other provider, and/or
c. decreasing the adaptation costs of the client.

Since improving the value of the service will require more effort from the provider, it becomes obvious that condition (3) is in conflict with conditions (1) and (a). Furthermore, conditions (2) and (b) naturally contradict each other. Therefore, the only option that remains for the provider is to somehow help the client reduce the adaptation costs.

This can only be shown by condition 3 from Table 11.3. If we solve this condition for p_n^E, it will give us an upper bound for the price of the new version of the service $p_n^E < p_j + V_n^C - V_j^C + C_{aj} - C_{ai}$. Therefore, by increasing the value of the service or by decreasing the adaptation costs, the provider can increase the price of the service without losing any competitive advantage. In the next scenario, we are going to discuss how the provider can efficiently facilitate the client with the adaptation costs in order to increase the price of the new service.

11.3.4 Evolution with support

The two previous scenarios may lead to suboptimal solutions (and probably stagnation) if the adaptation costs are so high that the net benefit of the client cannot cover the provider's potential loss (i.e., $C_e - V_e^P > 0$ and $V_e^C - C_{ai} < C_e - V_e^P$). This can happen due to the client's technological inadequacy or lack of communication and reduced information flow between the two parties. For this reason, in this scenario, we consider a particular type of information flow from the provider to the client, where the provider covers part of the adaptation costs by lending additional technical support to the client, to simplify its adaptation to the new version. The concept of technical assistance in the adaptation process has been a subject of extensive research, and various methods have been proposed. Chow and Notkin (1996) have proposed that the provider give additional information about the evolution process so as to help the client in the adaptation process. On the other hand, Benatallah et al. (2005) propose a methodology to provide web service adapters on the provider side to make changes transparent to the client. Finally, Fokaefs and Stroulia (2012) propose an algorithm to support the automatic adaptation of applications on the client side.

By providing support to the client, the provider effectively "subsidizes" part of the adaptation cost. Assuming that the provider is more knowledgeable and technologically equipped with respect to the evolving service, then the provider can provide adapters with less effort than the client would need to create them. Therefore, if the provider produces adapters as a portion of the adaptation costs, say aC_{ai}, where $0 < a \leq 1$, then instead of the remaining cost $((1 - a)C_{ai})$, the client will bear a portion of the

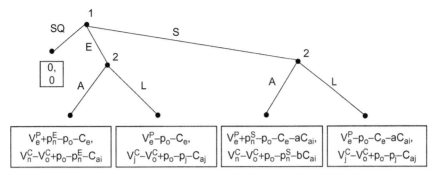

FIGURE 11.3

The provider–client game with support from the provider.

Table 11.4 Best-response Analysis for the Evolution with Support Game

		When the Client prefers...	
		$A \succ L$	$L \succ A$
Provider	$E \succ SQ$	1. $V_e^P + p_n^E > C_e + p_o$	2. $V_e^P > C_e + p_o$
	$S \succ SQ$	3. $V_e^P + p_n^S > C_e + aC_{ai} + p_o$	4. $V_e^P > C_e + aC_{ai} + p_o$
	$S \succ E$	5. $aC_{ai} < p_n^S - p_n^E$	6. $-aC_{ai} > 0$(ALWAYS FALSE)
		When the provider prefers...	
		$E \succ S$	$S \succ E$
Client	$A \succ L$	7. $V_n^C - V_j^C > p_n^E - p_j + C_{ai} - C_{aj}$	8. $V_n^C - V_j^C > p_n^S - p_j + bC_{ai} - C_{aj}$

adaptation cost, say bC_{ai}, such that $b < 1 - a$. Therefore, the provider can take advantage of this difference and charge a different price when supporting the client (p_n^S) than when just evolving the service (p_n^E). The corresponding game is similar to the previous scenario, with the difference that the provider now has the additional option of supporting the client (S), as shown in Figure 11.3.

If we solve inequalities 7 and 8 in Table 11.4, we obtain an upper bound for the new price when the provider evolves with and without supporting the client adaptation. Naturally, the provider will push toward these upper bounds to maximize revenue, and we can say that the two prices can marginally equal their upper bounds. Therefore, we have that $p_n^S = V_n^C - V_j^C + C_{aj} - bC_{ai} + p_j$ and $p_n^E = V_n^C - V_j^C + C_{aj} - C_{ai} + p_j$. If we subtract the second equation from the first, we have that $p_n^S - p_n^E = (1 - b)C_{ai}$, which means that the provider can charge a higher price for the new version, while supporting the client. However, the difference between this higher price and the normal price of the new version should not be higher than the adaptation costs the client will save from the provider's support. Eventually, we have that $aC_{ai} < p_n^S - p_n^E < (1 - b)C_{ai}$. Within this range the provider will make a profit even after supporting the client, and the client will be motivated to adapt to the new version rather than to switch to a different provider. If the client decides to abandon the current provider, the provider will not provide any support since this would be a frivolous and pointless action. This is reflected by condition 6, which is always false.

11.3.5 Propositions

Proposition 1: *The Nash Equilibrium for the provider-client game is (S, A).*

Let us assume that the provider sets $p_n^S = (1 - b)C_{ai} + p_n^E$. If the client already prefers to adapt when the provider evolves (i.e., condition 7 in Table 11.4 holds), then condition 8 (from the same table) also holds (it becomes the same as condition 7, in fact). Therefore, the client will always prefer to adapt. If condition 7 does not hold (i.e., $V_n^C - V_j^C < p_n^E - p_j + C_{ai} - C_{aj}$), condition 8 becomes $V_n^C - V_j^C > p_n^E - p_j + C_{ai} - C_{aj}$; this means that $V_n^C - V_j^C = p_n^E - p_j + C_{ai} - C_{aj}$, which will make the client indifferent between adapting or leaving the provider. Similarly, if the client prefers to adapt over leaving the provider and condition 1 from Table 11.4 holds, so does condition 3, which, in fact, becomes the same as condition 1. Therefore, the provider will never prefer to retain the status quo. If condition 1 does not hold (i.e., $V_e^P + p_n^E < C_e + p_o$), condition 3 becomes $V_e^P + p_n^E > C_e + p_o$; this implies that $V_e^P + p_n^E = C_e + p_o$, which makes the provider indifferent between retaining the status quo and evolve or support. Finally, we know that $aC_{ai} < p_n^S - p_n^E < (1 - b)C_{ai}$, which means that condition 5 holds and the provider will always prefer to support than just evolve. Therefore, if the provider selects a slightly lower value for p_n^S, then both players will strictly prefer the outcome (S, A) over any other outcome of the game.

Proposition 2: *Collaboration between the client and the provider can guarantee greater payoff for the ecosystem overall.*

In the presence of competition, the only feasible option for the provider in order to retain the current client is to provide technical support when evolving the software. Using knowledge about the software and its changes, the provider can be more efficient in covering part of the adaptation costs than the client; the savings that this efficiency makes possible can be translated into an increase in the price that the client may be able to pay for the new software version, which eventually implies increased income for the provider. If the provider simply evolves and the client adapts, the accumulative payoff of the ecosystem will be $V_e^P + V_e^C - C_e - C_{ai}$. If the provider supports and the client adapts, the total payoff will be $V_e^P + V_e^C - C_e - aC_{ai} - bC_{ai}$ which is greater than the previous payoff because $C_{ai} > (a + b)C_{ai}$.

The provider's support toward alleviating the client's adaptation costs will result in the client's increased trust of the provider. Client support is a widespread concept in modern business. For example, the automotive industry has implemented the concept of "after-sales service" with great success. Eventually, client care may guarantee greater revenue for the provider through brand loyalty.

Trust and commitment have been a central theme in marketing research. Morgan and Hunt (1994) propose a model of relationship marketing in which trust and commitment have a central role. In such a model, certain activities by the business partners, such as sharing values and better communication, may result in increasing trust, which in turn will strengthen the relationship commitment. Eventually, the propensity of the business partners to abandon the relationship and the uncertainty of the environment is reduced. In a service-oriented system, where the provider assists the client during the evolution process, trust and commitment have a similar role. Information sharing is also discussed by Li et al. (2006)) as a process that enables global optimization and strengthens the relationship between the producing party and the consuming party.

11.4 Conclusion

In this chapter, we studied the evolution of software in the context of a provider−client ecosystem. We identified a number of distinct software architecture styles, and their implications for how the software is delivered by the provider and used by the client for the downstream development of new software. We then examined a number of corresponding evolution scenarios and developed game-theoretic models of the decision-making processes of the involved parties, that is, provider and client, in each of these scenarios. Our game-theoretic approach enables us to better model the concerns around software evolution in the presence of externalities. In this work, we argue that the evolution of modern software cannot be studied from a single entity's point of view. Externalities play a very important role and should be taken into account by the decision makers. We further argue that decisions should be made with the aim of optimizinz the welfare of the ecosystem as a whole, and not driven simply by the interests of a single organization. Because of the relationship between the provider and the client, self-interested decisions will lead to suboptimal, even undesirable, outcomes in the longer run. Eventually, we put forward two propositions when evolving a service-oriented software system.

1. The Nash Equilibrium for the software evolution game is reached when the provider supports the client in the adaptation process and the client stays with the current provider and adapts to the new version (S, A). This equilibrium promotes technological progress (since the software evolves and the new version is adopted) and collaboration between the parties that can control this technological progress.
2. This collaboration between the provider and the client can lead to larger payoff for the ecosystem as a whole, since the provider's support induces the client to adapt to the new version and enables the provider to receive a higher price for its software.

References

Benatallah, B., Casati, F., Grigori, D., Nezhad, H.R.M., Toumani, F., 2005. Developing adapters for web services integration. CAiSE 415−429.

Boehm, B.W., 1981. Software Engineering Economics. Prentice Hall, Englewood Cliffs, NJ.

Boehm, B.W., Clark, Horowitz, Brown, Reifer, Chulani, et al., Software Cost Estimation with Cocomo II with Cdrom. first ed. Prentice Hall, Upper Saddle River, NJ.

Boehm, B., Sullivan, K., 1999. Software economics: status and prospects. Inf. Softw. Technol. 41 (14), 937−946.

Boehm, B.W., Sullivan, K.J., 2000. Software economics: a roadmap.. Proceedings of the Conference on the Future of Software Engineering. ACM Press, New York, pp. 319−343.

Choi, S.C., 1991. Price competition in a channel structure with a common retailer. Mark. Sci. 10 (4), 271—296.

Chow, K., Notkin, D., 1996. Semi-automatic update of applications in response to library changes. International Conference on Software Maintenance 1996, Proceedings, pp. 359—368.

Coase, R.H., 1960. The problem of social cost. J. Law Econ. 3, 1—44.

Fokaefs, M., Stroulia, E., 2012. WSDarwin: Automatic Web Service Client Adaptation, CASCON '12.

Gokhan, N.M., Needy, N., 2010. Development of a Simultaneous Design for Supply Chain Process for the Optimization of the Product Design and Supply Chain Configuration Problem 22 (4), 20—30.

Hoffmann, W.H., 2007. Strategies for managing a portfolio of alliances. Strateg. Manage. J. 28 (8), 827—856.

Kaminski, P., Litoiu, M., Müller, H., 2006. A design technique for evolving web services, Proceedings of the 2006 Conference of the Center for Advanced Studies on Collaborative research.

Laffont, J.J., 2008. Externalities. In: Durlauf, S.N., Blume, L.E. (Eds.), The New Palgrave Dictionary of Economics. Palgrave Macmillan, Basingstoke.

Li, J., Sikora, R., Shaw, M.J., Woo Tan, G., 2006. A strategic analysis of interorganizational information sharing. Decis. Support Syst. 42 (1), 251—266.

McGuire, T.W., Staelin, R., 2008. An industry equilibrium analysis of downstream vertical integration. Mark. Sci. 27 (1), 115—130.

Morgan, R.M., Hunt, S.D., 1994. The commitment-trust theory of relationship marketing. J. Mark. 58 (3), 20.

Nagurney, A., 2006. Supply Chain Network Economics: Dynamics of Prices, Flows, and Profits. Edward Elgar Publishing.

Ozkaya, I., Kazman, R., Klein, M., 2007. Quality-Attribute Based Economic Valuation of Architectural Patterns. 2007 First International Workshop on the Economics of Software and Computation, IEEE, p. 5.

Srivastava, A., Sorenson, P.G., 2010. Service Selection Based on Customer Rating of Quality of Service Attributes, IEEE International Conference on Web Services, 1—8.

Swanson, E.B., 1976. The dimensions of maintenance. Proceedings of the 2nd International Conference on Software Engineering. IEEE Computer Society Press, Los Alamitos, CA, pp. 492—497.

Tansey, B.M., 2008. Valuing Software Services: The Real Options-Based Modularity Analysis Framework. University of Alberta, Canada.

Williamson, O.E., 1981. The economics of organization: the transaction cost approach. Am. J. Sociol. 548—577.

Successful CyberInfrastructures for E-Health

12

Emilia Farcas, Claudiu Farcas, and Ingolf Krüger

University of California, San Diego, CA, USA

12.1 Introduction

The pace of medical scientific discovery and related health-care advancements have been tremendously accelerated by new technologies, multidisciplinary work, and rapid communication of results, with a significant transition from single-purpose systems to large-scale, complex systems-of-systems. However, organizational, national, and business boundaries led to intricate silos of information, ranging from human resources (HR) systems, electronic health records (EHR) providers, specialized health-care software for various medical groups, vendor-specific data repositories for wearable devices (e.g., pacemakers, insulin pumps, and glucose meters), and myriad research environments from both academia and commercial entities. Such silos lead to waste and missed opportunities for care as they lock vital information for each potential patient behind technological, social, legal, and ethical doors.

Consequently, there is a growing trend to investigate means to *integrate* these systems into *patient-centric*, community-serving information systems to address global health priorities (see Figure 12.1). We call such systems E-Health CyberInfrastructures (CIs) as they often span across organizational, geographical, and technological boundaries. Thus, CIs comprise the infrastructure—the computational, networking, and data fabric that enables access to, observation, processing and distribution of, and control over data across the integrated system—as well as the community that uses the infrastructure, a complex socio-tech-economic mix that is inherently difficult to fully describe, design, analyze, or evaluate. As a primary characteristic, these CIs would address the growing "digital divide" between the "have" and "have not" researchers and health-care practitioners who can participate in this new mode of discovery and care due to limited access to advanced computational infrastructures and high-bandwidth networks required for the integration, analysis, and sharing of valuable biomedical data collections.

E-Health CIs evolve toward very large-scale systems serving *predictive, personalized, preventive, and participatory health care*—the P4 medicine (Hood, 2009), as well as scientific discovery. They have high requirements for flexibility, scalability, governance, security, management of a vast set of resources, and serving different organizations, each with its own boundaries, economics, policies, rules, and regulations. For instance, in E-Health there are several regulations for information security: The Health Insurance Portability and Accountability Act (HIPAA) (1996) provides standards for ensuring the security and privacy of Protected Health Information (PHI). The PHI is an individual's health information that is created or received by a health-care provider related to the

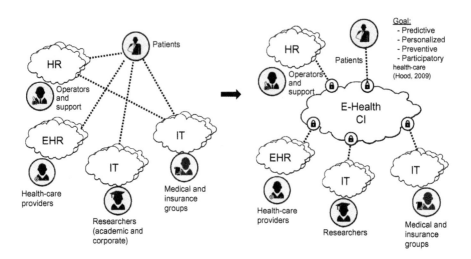

FIGURE 12.1

From information silos to patient-centric care.

provision of health care and that can identify the individual. The Federal Information Security Management Act (FISMA) (2002) requires each federal agency to implement a costly agency-wide program to provide information security for the information and systems that support its operations and assets. Therefore, CIs need to integrate a variety of distributed components to serve the heterogeneous and evolving requirements of a diverse stakeholder community, while meeting the quality constraints of the problem domain. The complexity of these systems requires proper economics-driven methodologies for requirements elicitation, value and cost prioritization, architecture specification, evaluation and refinement, system analysis, development, deployment, and evolution. Moreover, distributed development and outsourcing, release schedules, maintainability, and cost considerations add to the complexity and limit the methodologies that can be used in practice.

Most recently, outsourced and virtualized computation, storage and networking, collectively known as the cloud, has become an economically attractive alternative to owning IT infrastructure. Lowered costs ("pay-as-you-go"), higher flexibility to respond to up- and down-scale scenarios, better options for fault tolerance, and increased application of best practices for information assurance are among the frequently cited benefits of the cloud. However, this option comes with its own set of challenges. Because cloud-assets are under the domain of authority of a mix of cloud providers, "ownership" of resources is a much fuzzier concept than in a classical data-warehouse scenario. Most institutions have generic policies such as "Personally Identifiable Information (PII), which is any data that can identify an individual, does not leave this data center unless it is previously de-identified"; such policies are subject to reconsideration because the concept of "this data center" is dependent on the dynamic reorganization policies of the respective cloud providers. Information assurance policies across cloud providers differ, placing a burden on the software infrastructure and application level to ensure that policies such as HIPAA and FISMA are enforced. This, in turn, requires a much more careful and uniform design of policy capabilities into the overall software architecture of the E-Health software fabric than what is available off the shelf today. Reaping the cost, scale, fault tolerance, and information assurance benefits promised is a tremendous opportunity but does come at a price: Architecting E-Health software for the cloud requires significant expertise in distributed systems software architecture. In the following sections, we present some aspects of that expertise we have gained across a variety of E-Health and other software systems integration projects.

Much has been written on the context, trends, opportunities, and strategic directions related to CIs (Atkins et al., 2003; National Science Foundation, 2007) and ultra-large-scale systems (Northrop et al., 2006). However little has been published on the design and implementation of a CI, the process involved, trade-offs and rationale, economics, and hard-earned lessons from the field. In this chapter, we first discuss requirements of E-Health CIs and some of the challenges of designing a system that meets these needs. We then present our value-based methodology for incrementally understanding and defining these systems, creating appropriate architectures, including an economic decomposition blueprint, and evaluating outcome to make such CI endeavors a manageable technological investment. We continue by revealing several lessons from this field, and we place aspects of data ingestion, storage, and sharing between stakeholders, scaling, and federation to accommodate increasing resource needs, security, deployment, and operations in the proper context. We wrap up with a discussion of strategic success factors that are sometimes overlooked, yet critically impact the value proposition and success of a CI.

12.2 Needs and challenges for building E-Health CyberInfrastructures

By their very nature, E-Health CIs service multidisciplinary stakeholder communities, and therefore, designing and building them requires an interdisciplinary effort. For example, consider the scenario of a cancer patient who is undergoing radiation sessions and whose symptoms rapidly worsen. While she is at home, her vital signs such as blood pressure and heart rate need to be monitored and shared with her physician. For this reason, she carries sensors on her body most of the time, and she also has at home a sensor hub that collects data from the sensors and sends it off to the CI (see Figure 12.2). The patient's physician then monitors these diverse data that same day and is able to determine if changes in her treatment should be made. After securing an Internal Review Board (IRB)-approved protocol, researchers can use the CI to enroll such patients in clinical trials and to collect, store, process, and visualize their participants' data.

While all of these different stakeholders are using the CI, they have various entry points to access system capabilities, and they have diverse concerns such as privacy and dependability. For example, the patient wants to make sure her privacy is respected, and she doesn't want to send any data unencrypted. The physician and researcher do not want any of the data collected from patients to be lost, so the data should be buffered on devices when connectivity cannot be established. Moreover, the physician wants timely delivery of data, at least on a daily basis, whereas the researcher typically analyzes data at the end of a study. Hence, the CI contains a complex mix of needs for data ingestion from sensors, patient correlation, data transformation and distribution, policy management, and analytics. Ultimately, a proper CI for E-Health has to meet the requirements of such a diverse stakeholder set, while being scalable, maintainable, flexible, and so on.

Building systems that meet the needs of large and diverse stakeholder populations often involves both integrating and reusing existing systems, and adding new functionality. Key

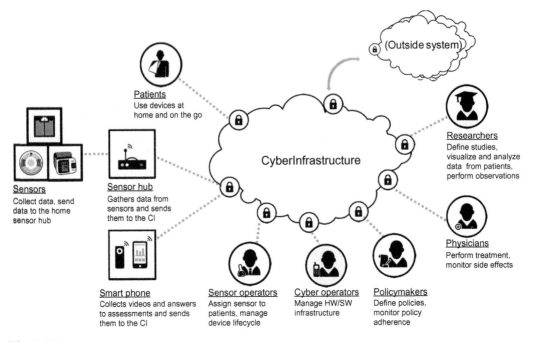

FIGURE 12.2

Generic E-Health CI incorporating patients, devices, operators, health-care providers, researchers, policymakers, and operators.

challenges involve understanding and modeling both the existing systems and the new stakeholder requirements; designing an extensible architecture for such system-of-systems integration that meets the stakeholder's needs; creating systems that are robust, performant, and maintainable; and evolving the system as requirements themselves evolve. Traditional development and integration approaches involve time-consuming rework bearing major financial and technical risk that only increases with the size of the stakeholder community and the diversity of its requirements.

12.2.1 E-Health services

Service-oriented architectures (SOAs) and service-oriented development (SOD) technologies have greatly facilitated rapid data and application integration by leveraging open standards for information exchange, service discovery and binding, and orchestration and choreography. SOAs are dynamic functional programs. That is, all capabilities of a system under consideration present themselves as functions (typically accessible via the Internet); service composition is function composition (in the mathematical sense); and the system is dynamic in that (a) services are discoverable via a registry, and (b) the behavior of any one service can change over time. Thus, SOA and SOD require identification of the adequate set of functions and compositions of these functions, as well as establishment of software fabrics that display the desired degree of dynamics. Part of the value proposition of SOA and SOD is a more finely granular level at which functionality is offered, composed, and changed over time. This helps eliminate or transition away from monolithic toward flexible and agile software architectures.

Even as successes with such technologies have effectively created systems of systems, they have exposed deeper and more complex challenges arising from the composition of business processes and associated applications from multiple enterprises having requirements such as security, policy, and governance. Reintegrating services with these and other crosscutting business concerns (e.g., manageability, scalability, and dependability), while maintaining the lightweight flavor of SOAs, is one of the key remaining challenges in design, deployment, and quality assurance, particularly as applied to modern CIs.

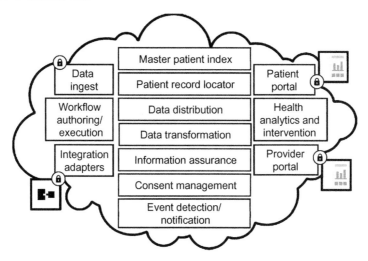

FIGURE 12.3

E-Health CIs—the big picture.

Consider a basic set of capabilities that most E-Health CIs have to provide: (a) multiple ways to collect data from internal and external sources, that is, data ingestion; (b) integration points and adapters to interface with external systems across organizational or geographical boundaries; (c) data transformation tools to support the multitude types of data used by its stakeholders; (d) data distribution mechanisms to deliver data artifacts at the necessary service endpoints; (e) analytics tools to make sense of the data and derive intervention solutions; (f) record locators to retrieve data of interest for these interventions; (g) indexes of patients; (h) portals for data access, both for providers and patients; (i) streamlined tools for privacy, consent management, and information assurance; (j) complex computational workflows and related authoring tools.

Building a successful system-of-systems requires an architecture that achieves coherent system integration out of these capabilities and that manages the life cycle of all resources (such as sensors, data, studies, policies, and algorithms) scalably and adaptively throughout the life span of the system, while addressing crosscutting concerns such as security, policy management, governance, high availability, and resilience.

SOAs enable functionality expansion through new services or by modifying communications among existing services. Services are the mechanism by which specific needs (e.g., a researcher's need to visualize data in a web browser) and capabilities (e.g., obtaining data from sensors) are brought together within a single software system (MacKenzie et al., 2006). However, most advances in the area of SOD so far have been made at the deployment and implementation technology level.

The introduction of web services led to a much needed separation of concerns: First, the core interoperability issue was addressed by using standard communication protocols (HTTP/SOAP), data marshaling (XML), and interface description (WSDL) technologies. REST further enables cleaner separation between system boundaries and leverages standards, such as XML/SOAP and JSON, to loosely couple distributed functionality. Second, some of the crosscutting technological and business issues were addressed in a separate step (e.g., the need to discover and connect to services at runtime led to the creation of UDDI, and security concerns led to the enhancement of SOAP via WS-Security (Nadalin et al., 2006)). Two interesting directions for web service composition are the semantic web and business workflows. Extensions to include semantic/ontology information (e.g., OWL-S (Martin et al., 2004; Berners-Lee et al., 2001)) aim to enrich the WS core technologies through meaningful and flexible runtime discovery, binding, and automatic composition of newly published services. Extensions toward service orchestration (e.g., WS-BPEL (Alves et al., 2007)) and choreography (e.g., WSCL (Banerji et al., 2002), WS-CDL (Kavantzas et al., 2005)) focus on the coordination of web services to support a business process.

The move toward tailored web service standards and technologies layered over a lean technological core resulted in a *fragmentation* of concerns. This fragmentation created the challenge *of how to integrate the pieces of the puzzle back into a coherent picture suitable for enterprise-scale SOAs.* A combination of SOD and Model-Driven Architecture® (MDA®) (Object Management Group® [OMG®], 2003) and Design (MDD) techniques is, thus, essential to address the integration and quality assurance challenges of E-Health CIs. Therefore, we have created the Rich Services architecture (Arrott et al., 2007) and related development process (Demchak et al., 2007) for organizing complex systems and managing distributed capabilities that may be under the control of different ownership domains.

12.3 Value-based Rich Services methodology

Surveys such as the Standish Group's CHAOS reports (The Standish Group, 1995, 2001) show that most software-project failures are caused not by technical aspects, but by business value and management aspects. Thus, value-based software engineering (Boehm, 2006; Boehm and Jain, 2006) integrates value considerations within the full range of software engineering activities from requirements engineering to architecture, development, verification and validation, and management.

In this section, we introduce our value-based methodology for architecting E-Health CIs. The underlying architectural pattern—Rich Services (RS) (Arrott et al., 2007)—allows for organizing complex systems in a hierarchical fashion, while addressing crosscutting concerns such as privacy and security, which are paramount in CIs involving patient data. In a nutshell, the Rich Services architecture integrates application services (which provide core application functionality) with infrastructure services (which transform messages defined by the application services, providing the underlying mechanisms to inject crosscutting concerns).

An architecture and its implementation have to meet all stakeholder needs, and not just user needs. Stakeholders include program managers, architects, developers, and operators. Needs are often conflicting, being related to features, timeline, cost, and personal satisfaction. Therefore, it is necessary to disentangle key requirements from nice-to-have ones. Program managers need to coordinate a successful project within budget constraints. Architects need to develop an architecture that reflects the requirements and can be implemented with the available resources within the timeline constraints. Developers need to use their skills to bring them satisfaction and contribute to a successful system, and they also need time to program in a way that will be less painful in the future when requirements inevitably change. Operators and maintainers have their own requirements of the system, and they need to be able to diagnose and fix things when issues arise. And researchers and clinical users might have lots of requirements because they need a system that can bridge the gap in their current practice and there are so many opportunities for a CI to contribute to E-Health. However, as it becomes clear, not all requirements can be implemented to satisfy the diverse needs of all stakeholders.

12.3.1 Development process overview

Given their size and complexity, E-Health CIs do not follow a single regular design/deploy/operate pattern as a whole; instead, they evolve continuously through successive iterations. Consequently, classic waterfall development processes are hardly applicable; instead, agile development processes (Boehm and Turner, 2003) with several iterations and corresponding system releases are required for dealing with emergent, evolving, and ever-changing requirements that affect CIs. The RS development process (Demchak et al., 2007) is iterative and leverages the spiral (Boehm, 1998) model of agile development methodologies (Boehm and Turner, 2003), where requirements often resolve to partial specifications, and refinements or additions of requirements at one stage can trigger iterations beginning at an earlier stage. For example, at later stages of architecture definition, it is common to discover additional opportunities for crosscutting concerns, such as Quality of Service (QoS) monitoring. These concerns reflect functional and nonfunctional facets of requirements, which may generate additional use cases resulting in spiraling back to the initial requirements elicitation stages.

We employ an iterative, end-to-end software engineering process that involves multiple stages from requirements elicitation to physical network deployment. This process provides a good fit of modern agile software development techniques, with traditional waterfall or more rigorous, plan-driven methodologies employed by many projects in the E-Health domain. Furthermore, our process has *three phases* (each of which is further divided into stages that can also be iterated for incremental refinement): service elicitation, RS architecture, and system architecture definition (see Figure 12.4), which are discussed in detail are in the rest of this section. Typical iterations span two to six weeks, depending on the size of the project and its stakeholder community.

In our experience, the diversity and complexity of various personal, institutional, business, operational, and quality concerns that arise in E-Health systems further create a strong demand for a richer service-oriented framework that is scalable and dynamic, and that provides decoupling between various concerns. Hence, the resulting RS architecture targets key integration and extensibility requirements, while providing a systematic way to model various stakeholders' crosscutting concerns. Perry and Wolf (1992) define software architectures as the configuration of architectural

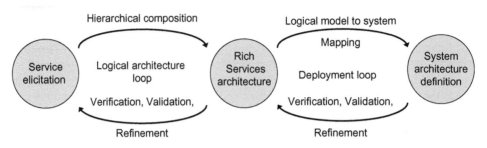

FIGURE 12.4

Rich Services development process overview.

elements, their interactions, and constraints. Song et al. (2008) argue that to provide adaptability for large-scale systems, we need to pay particular attention to coupling software artifacts and processes with the stakeholders and environments that influence the decisions to which systems must adapt. Similarly, for E-Health CIs we consider that it is critical to identify stakeholder concerns early and to address them uniformly in the infrastructure. Hence, our service-oriented development process encompasses activities from requirements and use case elicitation, service definition, mapping to RS architecture, through physical network deployment, while keeping the traceability of crosscutting concerns at each stage of development.

Using agile methodologies, our process directly addresses some of the core aspects identified in the CHAOS reports, such as user involvement, clear business objectives, changing requirements, and minimized scope. However, a question that remains is how to establish realistic expectations and plan software releases in large-scale systems. Thus, we extended our service-oriented development process from (Demchak et al., 2007) with value-based considerations, which we introduce in the following.

12.3.2 Service elicitation

Service elicitation is primarily a requirements elicitation phase, although requirements can be identified in later phases leading to new iterations of the process. In this phase depicted in Figure 12.5, we identify requirements, elicit their values and prioritize them, express them as use cases, identify crosscutting concerns, construct a domain model of the system, identify service roles, and, lastly, define interaction patterns for specifying services and workflows. Often, requirements engineering involves negotiations and trade-off analysis. In the following, we elaborate on each of the stages from this elicitation phase.

We start by identifying the *stakeholder group*, the CI *user roles*, and pertinent *business and process constraints* per stakeholder group. Stakeholders include users, managers, architects, developers, and administrative personnel. Users are the stakeholders that actually use the running systems, and users can play several roles when interacting with the system (a user can play more than one role). Therefore, it is important to identify the abstract user roles and their goals, or what is referred in the Department of Defense Architecture Framework (DoDAF) as the concept of operations. Some typical user roles in E-Health are depicted in Figure 12.2: Participants (patients or the general

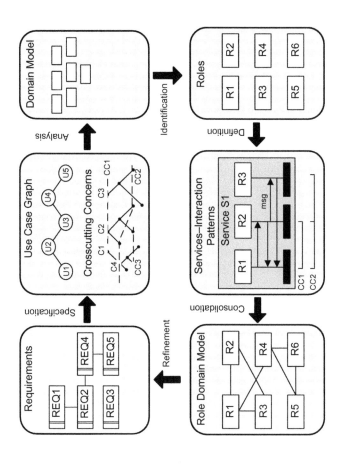

FIGURE12.5

Service elicitation phase from the Rich Services development process.

public) are enrolled in a study, researchers analyze data obtained in studies, physicians treat patients, sensor operators manage study devices, study assistants help in study management, policy-makers perform system audit, and cyber-operators manage user accounts and maintain the CI.

Business and process constraints include the cost model, laws, and regulations, which all can affect timelines and create functional and nonfunctional requirements. It is important to identify up front which aspects of the system are subject to regulations, such as HIPAA. For example, transmitting de-identified information simplifies the system requirements. If the system has to be HIPAA compliant, then strategies should be defined up front on how to manage topics, such as encryption in storage and in flight, access control on servers and websites, minimizing data sent over networks, backups and disaster recovery, audit, employees access privileges, and so on. We also identify operational infrastructure constraints, including mandated deployment contexts, acceptable standards, and technologies options.

12.3.2.1 Value-based model for Rich Services

We propose the model from Figure 12.6—specified as a Unified Modeling Language™ (UML®) class diagram (OMG, 2010)—for incorporating value-based considerations in the Rich Services process, focusing on the mapping from Requirement to the Rich Services architecture. A Requirement is specified as Use Cases and is constrained by Crosscutting Concerns; a Requirement can also be related to/depend on other Requirements. Use Cases are specified by one or more Interaction Patterns (together with the specification of how these are composed). Crosscutting Concerns are applied to the Interaction Patterns and composed as needed; more Interaction Patterns can be created specifically for the Crosscutting Concerns. Rich Services implement all Interaction Patterns, realizing both the Use Cases (via Rich Application Services) and the Crosscutting Concerns (via Rich Infrastructure Services, explained later in Figure 12.7).

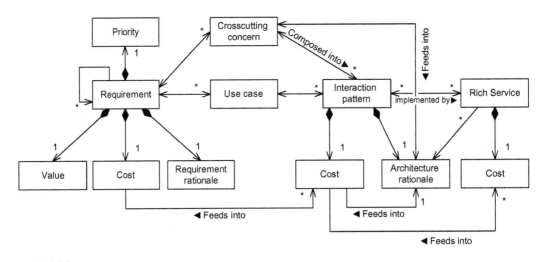

FIGURE 12.6

Domain model for value-based considerations in the Rich Services development process.

Traceability should be done in both directions: from Requirements to Rich Services and the other way around. In the UML model, we have used navigability at both ends of the associations to highlight this aspect. Traceability helps in assessing the impact of requirements changes (Nuseibeh and Easterbrook, 2000) and also in computing the cost of a requirement, as we discuss in more detail in this section.

In the literature, requirements are often categorized as functional requirements or nonfunctional requirements. All nonfunctional requirements tend to crosscut system functionality and influence the architecture and the development process used; some of them (such as maintainability, scalability, testability, flexibility, affordability, and reusability) are often more general, whereas others (such as governance, security, usability, performance, and fault tolerance) directly apply to particular functionality. We recognize that sometimes it is difficult to make the distinction between requirements because a requirement as identified from stakeholders can have both functional and nonfunctional concerns.

In our model, we associate each Requirement with a set of Use Cases and a set of Crosscutting Concerns (one of the sets can be empty). In other words, the Use Cases describe the functional part, and the Crosscutting Concerns describe nonfunctional properties. Other approaches often focus on the requirements engineering process for functional requirements, and then nonfunctional properties are specified separately, which makes their traceability difficult. In our approach, crosscutting concerns are first-class citizens, are linked to the use cases, and are traced in the same way as any functional requirement. Moreover, such concerns are specified in as detailed a manner as possible. For example, when discussing extensibility, a number of requirements are identified related to adding new types of devices easily, ingesting new sources of data from a common ingestion interface, exporting data in various formats, and so on.

Requirements engineering is not the only topic that we cover in our frequent stakeholder meetings, but we also discuss the decisions (those already taken or those that need to be taken soon) and the reasons behind them. E-Health CIs involve multidisciplinary teams for both users and developers. Thus, communicating rationale is important for collaboration and management, such that every team member is aware of how the decisions of others affect their work. Rationale-based software engineering (Burge et al., 2008) provides methods for documenting and using rationale for decision making throughout the system life cycle. Although more sophisticated methods for managing rationale have been proposed, we try to keep a lightweight process in the spirit of agile methodologies: We focus on eliciting rationale from stakeholders, documenting it in simple textual form, and communicating rationale within the teams so that conflicts can be identified and eliminated.

In the Requirement Rationale for Rich Services we propose to capture: (1) the *benefits* of incorporating the requirement in the system and the *consequences* of not incorporating it (Carroll et al., 1998), (2) the source *stakeholder* that identified the requirement, as well as the key stakeholders or stakeholder roles that need this requirement (if the details are not available, the requirement can be annotated with the date of the discussion/workshop when it was identified) and (3) the high-level *goal* that this requirement supports (for E-Health projects involving various trials/studies, the specific study name can be used instead of the high-level goal). Thus, the rationale helps in trade-off analysis, negotiation, and prioritization of requirements to achieve consensus between stakeholders (Burge et al., 2008, Chapter 11).

The Architecture Rationale pertains to each Interaction Pattern and explains why the specific Rich Services were chosen to implement it at their level in the Rich Services hierarchy.

The Architecture Rationale also helps in evaluating the cost of an Interaction Pattern. The Crosscutting Concerns have a major influence on architecture decisions.

Cost can be associated with each element from the model; for requirements prioritization, we are interested in the cost of a Requirement, which means adding the costs of the identified Interaction Patterns. The cost evaluation comes from the choice implementation of Rich Services. Note that the cost of an Interaction Pattern is not the sum of the cost of Rich Services because a service implements a number of interactions. The cost of an Interaction Pattern is the cost of *adding* an interaction to a set of services (which can include the cost of creating the services and their elements if they do not exist yet).

12.3.2.2 Stakeholder value elicitation

We identify the set of requirements by discussing the *functions* and workflows expected of the system by the stakeholders. It is useful to start with high-level activities performed by stakeholders and then to detail them and start the construction of use cases (Holbrook, 1990; Cockburn, 2000). Because various stakeholders have different views and goals for the system, their value propositions for requirements also might differ. Hence, part of our requirements negotiation is to arrive at mutually satisfactory agreements regarding what the exact requirements are and which are their values. Another part of requirements negotiation is to establish priorities based on value and cost.

Detailed approaches for requirements negotiation, such as WinWin (Boehm and Bose, 1994; Boehm et al., 1994; Lee, 1996; Boehm and Kitapci, 2006) and EasyWinWin (Boehm et al., 2001; Grünbacher et al., 2006) can be integrated into the Rich Services process. They are based on *Theory W* (Boehm and Ross, 1989), whose main concept is that an enterprise is successful if all its success-critical stakeholders are "winners." The WinWin approach uses Win conditions, agreements, issues, and options to guide stakeholders to converge on mutually satisfactory agreements. Stakeholders express their goals as *Win conditions*. If everyone concurs, the Win conditions become *agreements*. If they do not concur, stakeholders register their conflicts as *issues* and explore *options* for mutual gain. When everyone concurs, options are turned into agreements.

The WinWin Spiral Model (Boehm and Bose, 1994; Boehm et al., 1998) extends the spiral model of development (Boehm, 1988) with negotiation activities that are performed at the beginning of each spiral cycle. The first activities in the spiral model are to elaborate the system's objectives, constraints, and alternatives; the WinWin spiral model includes front-end activities to identify Win conditions and negotiate win—win reconciliations, which guides the identification of objectives, constraints, and alternatives.

The EasyWinWin approach builds on the WinWin negotiation model and further leverages a Group Support System, which is a suite of collaborative software tools. Various generations of groupware tools for WinWin negotiation, which led to EasyWinWin, are discussed in Boehm et al. (2001). Possible extensions to the EasyWinWin approach are suggested in Grünbacher et al. (2006) to account for conflicting stakeholder interests, individual preference elicitation, integrative negotiations, complexity, traceability of negotiation results, and distributed negotiations.

In the EasyWinWin approach, one output of the negotiation process is the decision rationale showing the negotiated history (i.e., comments, Win conditions, issues, and options). Captured rationale can improve later decisions and enable better context for change impact analysis when requirements changes arrive (Boehm and Kitapci, 2006). EasyWinWin simplifies capturing rationale by providing a well-defined process and structure for the artifacts in negotiations.

If EasyWinWin is used for the Rich Services process, then the negotiation results can be linked to the Requirement Rationale (see Figure 12.6) to provide traceability from negotiations to requirements and architecture.

In practice, however, we have used a more flexible, informal process for requirements negotiation and consistency checking based on discussing rationale, defining a glossary of terms, and constructing domain models in requirements workshops, where the lead requirements engineer facilitated discussions. Such a process has worked for our E-Health CI projects because specific conflicting value propositions between stakeholders have been less of an issue than the general conflict between a long "wish list" for requirements and a reduced set of resources available for implementation. Therefore, cost is a major player in requirements negotiation to establish priorities.

Similar to the WinWin Spiral Model, we also start each iteration with a stakeholder win–win stage to determine the set of requirements; the difference is that we have not used the WinWin formal process to achieve consensus. In the spirit of a lean agile process and to address system complexity, we adopt a few simplifications and do not collect all information on all requirements. Comprehensive approaches for value proposition reconciliation are difficult to scale to large-scale systems because of the vast number of stakeholders, distributed teams leading to distributed negotiations, the large set of heterogeneous requirements, and the complexity of the interdependencies between them. Therefore, we focus on efficiency rather than completeness.

When a requirement is identified, we elicit its value, which could have various interpretations for different stakeholder groups, such as time savings, new capabilities, potential for grants, and prestige. If consensus is not reached reasonably easy, then we continue negotiations for value reconciliations only for the requirements that have high value for at least one stakeholder or group. This process bears similarities to the speculate cycle of the Adaptive Software Development (ASD) (Highsmith, 2000), where stakeholders have partial views of the system and thus different values and expectations. Therefore, at the beginning of any iteration, we discuss again the value (in case it has changed since the last iteration), and we evaluate the cost only for the top-valued requirements. Thus, at any given point in time, the requirements information is likely incomplete, as, for example, there are requirements that have no cost evaluation and there might even be requirements that have no consensus for the value proposition.

12.3.2.3 Requirements prioritization

According to a survey from Wohlin and Aurum (2006), the most crucial criteria for prioritizing requirements are related to customers, markets, development time, cost and benefit, and resources. We base the prioritization of requirements on the (1) *Value* defined by stakeholders, (2) *Cost* of a requirement as evaluated based on the Rich Services architecture implementing the interaction patterns needed for this requirement, (3) *Requirement Rationale*, and (4) *Architecture Rationale* (see Figure 12.6).

The Pareto principle can help us with a simple rule of thumb, as it applies to system design (80% of a system's value comes from 20% of its features), development, and later on operation (Rooney, 2002). The Pareto analysis can be used to identify the top features to implement first as ranked by customers, identify the best placement of user-interface elements according to their common usage scenario, focus the bug-fixing efforts on the components that contribute heavily to faults, and so on.

It is important to recognize that the Pareto principle applies differently to each project, and within each project it applies differently to its constituents. For instance, the 20% most used features of a project might be the most overlooked ones in another project; 20% of the customers using 80% of the bandwidth might not be the same 20% producing actual useful content. Similarly, software quality metrics could also be applied, with statistical methods such as factor analysis (Ebert, 1992) and principal component analysis (Munson and Khoshgoftaar, 1990), and classification methods (Selby and Porter, 1988; Porter and Selby, 1990) to predict and manage the expected quality and productivity during the project life cycle.

A major challenge in software development is the volatility of user requirements (Rajlich, 2006). This is especially true for E-Health CIs because software brings significant added value to existing workflows involving different stakeholders; thus, the new E-Health requirements and contributions are not clearly understood yet. Furthermore, the environment and technologies change so rapidly that new needs or new opportunities arise from one release to the next. Thus, our approach focuses on short iterations, and in each iteration the requirements set and their priorities are reevaluated.

At the beginning of each iteration, we execute the following steps: We pick the top 10–20% of requirements (at least five requirements, but still a small, manageable number) sorted by stakeholder value (similar to agile backlogs as seen by the stakeholders), sketch the architecture changes needed, evaluate the architecture rationale and the cost of implementing the new features, and establish the priorities together with the stakeholders. The steps described above have to be performed in each iteration because new requirements can be identified from one iteration to another, the cost changes in time as more features are implemented, and also the user value can change based on stakeholders using the previous release of the system and gaining more insight into how it modifies existing workflows.

We evaluate costs in both persons per month and calendar weeks, which account for developer availability and conflicts in resource allocations. Costs are sometimes hard to estimate correctly or translate into actual monetary value. Even in those cases, however, discussions about costs are very valuable. One of the outcomes is a shared understanding of project budget, staffing, schedules, and other constraints. In the EasyWinWin approach, stakeholders rate each Win condition along two criteria: value and feasibility. In our case, users rate the value, whereas architects provide the cost estimate. Then, all stakeholders (e.g., users, architects, and decision makers) decide on the priorities together.

Requirements can be plotted on a graph, with *value* and *cost* on the X and Y axis, respectively (after normalizing the numbers). Similarly, the EasyWinWin approach organizes the portfolio of Win conditions in four categories depending on combinations of high and low for *value* and *feasibility*. Obviously, requirements of high value and low cost are immediately appealing to implement, whereas requirements of low value and high cost will be deferred and might never be implemented (recall the 80%/20% Pareto rule). However, it is hard to define a function of value and cost to produce the requirements priorities because the prioritization process is heuristic and depends on the stakeholders' preferences. Moreover, the estimates for values and costs are never perfect and might not reflect the right relationships between requirements. It is possible to have the scenario when requirements of similar declared value have significant differences in cost, and after discussions, the stakeholders reestablish the values and pick the top priority for the requirement with the highest cost of implementation. Such scenarios are possible because requirements engineering is a process of cooperative learning in which stakeholders learn from one another and continuously refine their understanding of the current system, of what they want, of what others want, and of what is technically possible to implement within each iteration. This is a key reason why we adopt an iterative development process.

Requirements negotiation and architecture definition are not sequential activities. Prioritization of requirements is done concurrently with exploration of the solution architecture because the cost of the proposed architecture and implementation dictates the cost of the requirements. However, it is not practical to design the solution in detail for each requirement just for defining the priorities of requirements, from which only a subset will be actually architected and implemented. Thus, we follow the process from requirements to architecture as far as needed to provide a cost estimate. Then, after requirements are prioritized, we revisit the sketches and follow the process in detail for the requirements selected to be implemented in this iteration.

12.3.2.4 From requirements to services

Traditional approaches to system engineering define clear boundaries between a system and its environment and describe a development process that assigns clear requirements to specific components in the architecture. In systems-of-systems (SoS), individual systems are no longer seen as bounded entities, but rather as interacting with other participants to form a larger system based on end-to-end business processes and requirements (Lane and Dahmann, 2008). This is also true in E-Health CIs as we move from silos to patient-centric care. Thus, we emphasize that system requirements are generally not defined in terms of architectural components; instead, they typically span across the various components of the system, establishing complex interaction dependencies. Consequently, we focus on eliciting the interaction patterns among the system entities involved in establishing a particular piece of functionality, as well as the policies and other crosscutting concerns that govern the interaction.

From the selected requirements, we identify the internal and external *actors* and *data entities* involved in these functions, and then present the *interactions* (event-, message-, control-, and dataflows) among the identified actors. We iterate over the identified functions to identify the actors and data entities needed to address the crosscutting concerns that apply to the respective use cases; we associate the artifacts for the crosscutting concerns with the artifacts of the use case. Thus, we construct a use case graph and, at the same time, we construct a *domain model* (Evans, 2004), which integrates the functional requirements with the main business concerns and crosscutting system concerns, such as security, fault tolerance, and logging.

In E-Health, we find it particularly useful to hold focused stakeholder workshops, within and across stakeholder groups, to bring out functional and crosscutting requirements. In these workshops, we typically execute the steps previously described (identifying functions, actors, data entities, interactions, and crosscutting concerns) with the workshop participants to create initial domain model candidates on the spot. These models provide the basis for stakeholder value negotiation and estimates for implementation costs. The domain modeling activities with the participating stakeholders lead to developing an ontology (Gruber, 1993) and behavioral model of the core concepts that make up the domain model of the system as commonly understood at a particular point in time. Ultimately, this model captures the entities and relationships relevant to the problem domain and its associated stakeholder groups. For the structural aspects of this domain model we use the Unified Modeling Language™ (UML®) Class Diagrams (OMG, 2010) to capture the actor and data classes and their structural relationships. For the associated interaction model, we use Message Sequence Charts (MSCs) (Krüger, 2000) or UML Sequence Diagrams (OMG, 2010) to capture the interaction and various role states.

From the structural diagrams, we then extract the *role domain model* capturing actors (i.e., unique, abstract entities) that participate in interaction scenarios. Examples of roles include user roles (e.g., researcher), devices (e.g., sensor), subsystems (e.g., data management subsystem), and processes (e.g., data acquisition handler). Depending on the mapping to the deployment architecture (as in the System Architecture Definition phase), the logical roles from the role domain model can be played by several distinct functional implementations. We maintain a traceability mapping between roles and use cases, and the role domain model provides a roadmap of role interaction issues to consider when a use case is changed. Furthermore, the set of roles needs not be fixed over time. This supports flexibility and dynamic adaptation, which are relevant for the system evolution. Because roles are tagged with the use cases that contributed them, when use cases evolve, roles can be added, changed, and retired as appropriate.

Furthermore, we define individual *services* through *interaction patterns* between roles (Krüger & Mathew, 2005) for the realization of each use case. Each service "orchestrates" interactions among system entities to achieve a specific goal (Evans, 2004). Within a service, roles exchange messages, thereby switching from one state to another. We use services as first-class modeling entities. Our service notion includes structural information (types of messages and data that can be exchanged) and the service behavior (interaction pattern among roles). Thus, services are specified by MSCs or UML sequence diagrams, which can be augmented with constraints that reflect the crosscutting concerns (e.g., precondition checking, postcondition checking, deadlines, or complex crosscutting concerns modeled as a separate MSC that can be composed with the service MSC). In this way, the crosscutting concerns are available for explicit validation and verification, rather than being an implicit, inaccessible aspect of the requirements model. Finally, all services are collected in a service repository.

12.3.3 Logical Rich Service architecture

The Rich Service Architecture is a type of SOA. It complements the OASIS SOA Reference Model (MacKenzie et al., 2006) and W3C Web Services Architecture (Booth et al., 2004) by providing an architectural style that is particularly suitable to integrating complex distributed applications. Architectural styles and patterns (Monroe et al., 1997) define families of architectures whose elements are configured according to given constraints. For example, with multiple-user communities in E-Health, each institution may have its own policy for the use of resources and data. RS allow for infrastructure services, such as encryption, policy management (e.g., authorization, privacy, and auditing), and identity management to be plugged into the architecture without modifying core system functionality (Farcas et al., 2010). This feature ensures the scalability of the system, so it can grow as new needs are identified, and new users engage with the system without changes to the underlying CI.

We distinguish the terms *logical architecture* and *deployment architecture* as follows. Logical architecture is the decomposition of the system into functional components/services independent of the platform that will execute them, whereas deployment architecture specifies the representation of the logical components in terms of platform-specific entities. In this section, we focus on the logical RS hierarchy, the infrastructure and application services, and the mapping to the individual services identified during requirements elicitation.

The RS architectural blueprint (Figure 12.7) can be used to recursively decompose the CI functionality into business and infrastructure services (i.e., structural decomposition), leading to a hierarchy of policies and concerns (i.e., cross-functional behavioral decomposition). We use the term

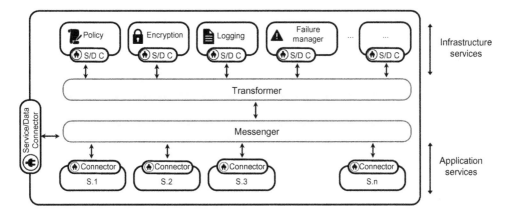

FIGURE 12.7

Rich Services blueprint.

service composition to refer to the order in which services are invoked and the conditions under which the service may be invoked. Additionally, a service composition is viewed as the binding of participating services with respect not only to the behavior of the services but also to their requirements and policies.

Of the many possible hierarchical decompositions, the ones we choose for the RS hierarchy are driven by client values, such as architecture comprehensibility, business manageability, performance, and organization domains. In the process of defining infrastructure and application services, it is common to discover additional opportunities for crosscutting processing, such as QoS property monitoring, failure detection and mitigation, and role interaction monitoring. The newly identified crosscutting concerns typically lead to spiraling back to the service elicitation phase.

The architecture is organized around a message-based communication infrastructure that supports the interaction between all services within one RS and across RSs. A Service/Data Connector encapsulates the internal structure of the service and exposes a uniform interface for each service instance; the connector serves as the sole mechanism for interaction between a service and its environment. To manage service orchestration, the communication infrastructure has two main layers: (1) the *Messenger layer*, which is responsible for transmitting messages between services, and (2) the *Transformer layer* (also called Router/Interceptor), which is responsible for intercepting messages placed on the Messenger and then routing them among all services involved in providing a particular capability. This separation enables an efficient monitoring and enforcing of the QoS properties required by the system at all levels of the hierarchy.

An RS could be a simple functionality block, or it could be hierarchically decomposed into further services. Thus, services S.1 to S.n from the bottom part of Figure 12.7, as well as the infrastructure services, can be further decomposed following the same RS pattern. The high-level domain model for Rich Services is depicted as a UML class diagram in Figure 12.8. Application services provide core application functionality, mandating the business flow. Infrastructure services reroute or filter messages defined by the application services. Failure management, security,

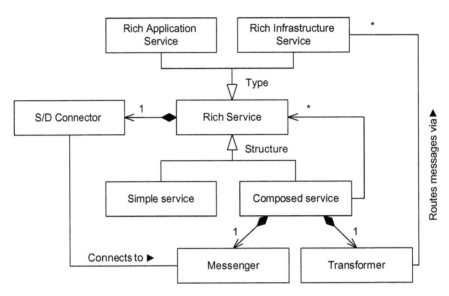

FIGURE 12.8

Domain model for Rich Services.

authorization, and policies are typical examples of infrastructure services that are typically encountered in CIs. The communication infrastructure enables loose coupling and seamless communication between services. Such capability drives the evolution of the system by providing the underlying mechanisms to handle changes, dynamic reconfiguration, and policy enforcement. It also provides a great economic advantage for implementing a CI; for example, the encryption concern can be addressed in a separate infrastructure service rather than hard-coding it into every other service in the system.

The separation of concerns also simplifies the cost evaluation for a RS. Every entity from Figure 12.8 has a cost that can be evaluated separately, making it easy to compute the cost of a Composed Service by summing the costs of the constituent Rich Services, S/D Connectors, Messenger, and Transformer. If a new requirement arises to address a crosscutting concern, then the cost of the existing services remains unchanged: One needs to create a new infrastructure service, decompose it internally if needed, and add the new routing rules to the Transformer.

RS organizes systems-of-systems into a hierarchically decomposed structure that supports *horizontal* and *vertical* service integration. The horizontal integration involves managing the interaction of application services and crosscutting concerns on the same level. On the other hand, vertical integration involves the hierarchical decomposition of an application service into a set of subservices. The environment of the subservices, their composition and interaction, and their structural/behavioral complexity are covered inside the application service and hidden from the other application services on the same level.

The role domain model (see Figure 12.5) presents a high-level view of the interaction of roles across all services, and provides a framework that advises the organization of roles and services into the RS hierarchy. From the role domain model, we can identify the decomposition boundaries and determine the interactions that occur across these boundaries. Each RS in the hierarchy presents itself to its environment via a dedicated Service/Data Connector that encapsulates its internals and adapts the inputs and outputs of a the RS to any of the services that use it. In the process of mapping roles and services to RSs, we set up the communication channels, decide the location of each crosscutting concern, and decide what service interface to publish through the Service/Data Connector. In particular, for each RS interface, we associate the MSCs that define the communication patterns and protocols between roles outside the RS (i.e, imported roles) and roles inside it (i.e., exported roles).

The RS architectural blueprint described above leverages well-known enterprise integration patterns and the asynchronous messaging pattern. The communication is carried out by Messages exchanged over Messages Channels (Hohpe and Woolf, 2004). To remove service interdependencies, the Transformer is an instance of the Mediator pattern (Gamma et al., 1995) and leverages the Interceptor pattern (Schmidt et al., 2000) to facilitate dynamic behavior injection of policies governing the integration of a set of horizontally decomposed services. Services are also decoupled via the Plugin pattern (Fowler, 2003). Furthermore, the Façade, Proxy, and Adapter patterns (Gamma et al., 1995), as well as the Messaging Gateway pattern (Hohpe and Woolf, 2004) inspired our Service/Data Connector. Finally, the Composite pattern (Gamma et al., 1995) enables the hierarchical nesting of Rich Services.

12.3.4 System architecture definition

System Architecture Definition is the phase for creating the deployment architecture. A logical architecture can be mapped to multiple deployment architectures, each capturing all aspects of a particular deployment. The RS pattern is a logical model, and it can be used at both the logical and deployment level. Various other terms are used in the literature to distinguish between logical and deployment system aspects: MDA distinguishes between a Platform Independent Model and a Platform Specific Model, whereas the DoDAF (Department of Defense, 2010) distinguishes between operational views and systems views. We maintain the use of logical and deployment architecture to encompass both of these standards.

We first inventory the components and subsystems already available, and analyze the topology of the existing systems in terms of computational, input/output, control, and storage nodes, and available networks. Then, we choose the deployment technologies, create the implementation of services, and map them onto the available set of physical networks and compute engines.

When a physical infrastructure is not yet defined or available, we start prototyping the high-risk, critical services of the project to gain insights into the minimum system performance requirements and establish a baseline platform with an associated cost. The baseline cost is typically actored into the early decision-making process associated with the target performance and expected cost. In successive iterations of the development process, we continuously refine this baseline by profiling the computation, storage (i.e., both memory and disk space), and communication needs of each developed RS from the logical architecture, and we inform the project stakeholders about any perceived cost or performance overrun risks. Therefore, we refine the chosen platform according to the available budget and QoS requirements of the project.

We also need to implement the RS communication infrastructure for messaging, intercepting, and routing among services, unless such an infrastructure is leveraged from an available technology. Furthermore, the specific interception and routing rules have to be defined for the application. Because the logic needed to orchestrate the message flow is captured by MSCs (Krüger, 2000), we can leverage our work on state machine generation to synthesize the routing required (Krüger & Mathew, 2005). This greatly reduces the cost of the implementation. An alternative option is to describe the orchestration logic through existing technologies, such as WS-BPEL (Alves et al., 2007).

Operational and maintenance use cases are refined at this phase to address the system evolution concerns. Moreover, analysis of the message flow, volume and frequency of the data exchange, and the relationships between the hosts implementing the business logic is important to identify possible bottlenecks and best places to address the crosscutting concerns in the RS deployment to meet QoS properties. When mapping the RS logical architecture to the deployment architecture, levels in the hierarchy can be flattened during deployment, or some services can be duplicated, whereas other duplicated services can be replaced with proxies for unique services. This is particularly important in cases where services operate across networks owned by different entities, which may significantly impact the costs of invoking them during system operation (e.g., per transaction costs in cloud deployments).

We use the RS architectural blueprint both as a logical model and as a guide to a deployment architecture. In particular, the logical architecture maps well to existing web services deployment technologies for dynamic discovery, binding, choreography, and orchestration. In addition, Enterprise Service Bus (ESB) technologies such as the Mule ESB framework (MuleSoft, 2012) can provide message routing among well-defined, loosely coupled services and increase code reuse due to built-in services and intercepting mechanisms. RSs conceptualize and extend the benefits offered by ESBs at the deployment level. Thus, RSs are a consistent architectural blueprint that has a direct mapping to ESBs but also to other deployment technologies. We have used the logical architecture blueprint in a number of projects, and we implemented it in various ways, depending on the specific project needs and available development talent: flattened versus hierarchical deployments, ESBs versus Java Virtual Machine (JVM), message passing versus Clojure (Hickey, 2012) —a functional language executed on top of the JVM.

Our process can also be integrated with SoS development processes such as the Systems-of-Systems Engineering model (SoSE) (Dahmann et al., 2008) and the Incremental Commitment Model (ICM) (Boehm and Lane, 2007), which address the issue of responsibilities and coordination between the integrated SoS and the constituent subsystems. Furthermore, cost estimation models and tools (Lane and Boehm, 2008) can be used to support estimating the effort for the development and evolution of the system.

In particular, all e-Health projects we encountered rely heavily on resource virtualization to maximize the utilization potential of the available hardware infrastructure and accommodate a changing variety of needs, including scale scenarios from the region to the state to the nation to the world. Given the uncertainty of privacy, security, and data retention policies in public clouds, most large-scale projects employ a mix of modern cloud technologies to power their own private clouds, along with a comprehensive set of services to drive them.

Key drivers for the adoption of cloud technologies in these projects are the flexibility and scalability given by the expression of resources as services, followed by the lower upfront cost that would otherwise hinder development and slow down scientific advancement. At the deployment level, RS allows us to use technologies of a commercial nature, such as VMware's vCloud, or community-supported open-source solutions, such as OpenStack (OpenStack, 2012) and OpenNebula (Sotomayor et al., 2009; OpenNebula, 2012). Often, each subproject or subsystem has specific allocations of storage and computing resources based on initial needs and planned growth patterns. In contrast with public, massive clouds, where such allocations can be simply provided on the spot through dedicated user-facing services, such as Amazon's Web Services [AWS] most projects we encountered have a tighter allocation of resources that can involve management or security approval prior to enactment. Such processes can be fully automated based on policies implemented as infrastructure services, or require human intervention that may introduce additional overhead to those involved. Nevertheless, they are necessary safeguards to ensure the privacy and security of the data entrusted by the data providers and (ultimately) patients contributing to medical research (e.g., when dealing with sensitive data); and also to preserve the integrity and quality of service of the CI (e.g., for large allocations that require prior reservation).

12.3.5 Architectural evaluation and refinement

Once the architecting process has started, the architecture can be incrementally evaluated and refocused to ensure that it meets the expectations of its stakeholders during each iteration of the development process. Architecture evaluation methods have been proposed, formalized, and compared (Bass et al., 2003) for more than a decade. The Dobrica and Niemela (2002) survey focuses on the end-goals, whereas Bass and Nord (2012) focuses on the contextual factors. Bosch (2000) specifies other classes of evaluation techniques, such as scenario-based that evaluate software qualities in the context of usage scenarios; simulation-based where models and simulation environments help refine the architecture to meet its requirements; mathematical modeling that relies on statistics, probabilities, and similar techniques to predict hard-to-evaluate qualities such as reliability and efficiency; and experience-based reasoning that intends to leverage the practical experience in the context of an organization to reveal reasonable expectations about the intended product or system —a difficult proposition when the evaluation is performed by external assessment teams that have limited insight into the organization and its practices.

Relevant scenario-based architecture evaluation approaches are the Software Engineering Institute's Architecture Tradeoff Analysis Method (ATAM) (Clements et al., 2002) and the Cost Benefit Analysis Method (CBAM) (Kazman et al., 2001, 2002), the Tiny Architectural Review Approach (TARA) (Woods, 2011), the Lightweight Architecture Alternative Assessment Method (LAAAM) (Carriere, 2009), and Scenario-based Peer Reviews (Bachmann, 2011).

ATAM is a more complete evolution of the earlier Software Architecture Analysis Model (SAAM) from the same authors, starting from the business perspective behind the system, which precedes the requirements. This strategy allows for a methodological guidance of the requirements prioritization process with business goals in mind and a more rigorous evaluation of the presented architecture along with the architectural options available based on the identified risks, sensitivity points, and trade-offs.

We apply similar techniques to focus the stakeholders' discussions on high-payoff areas. ATAM could be integrated with the Rich Services approach to provide a more formal process for evaluating architectural alternatives within iterations. Our model from Figure 12.7 considers the architectural solution that has already been chosen to realize a large number of requirements frequently encountered in this field. Often, however, there are several architectural choices, each one with its own cost and trade-offs. ATAM results in a hierarchical model of the driving architectural requirements (i.e., the utility tree), with a documented basis for architectural decisions and involved risks. Yet, it concludes at the architecture definition level, without any guidance for architecture evolution or iterative requirements reprioritization, or any consideration for the economic impact of the identified trade-offs.

Our approach also maps well over the decomposition into dimensional views from Bosch (2000) by distinguishing between individual business services (our Rich Application Services) (i.e., component views) and hierarchical aggregation of capabilities to form the system views, which is also similar to the Attribute-Driven Design Method (ADD) (Bachmann and Bass, 2001; Wojcik et al., 2006); interaction patterns for the business, organization, process views; a dedicated phase for technical views; and development and evolution views through continuous refinement of the requirements and logical architecture. Applying such product-line concepts to our design and development process promotes reusability and helps us evolve the architecture during our frequent development iterations. However, the approach from Bosch (2000) cannot help us strategize on the architectural choices to take from an economic point of view.

CBAM emerged from a quantitative economic approach to make design decisions based on architectural strategies (i.e., options) affecting quality attributes (i.e., crosscutting concerns) that return benefits (i.e., value) to the system's stakeholder. By aiding in the decision-making process to reduce the uncertainty of architectural investments, CBAM is an excellent foundation for building value-based methods and tools.

As asserted by the CBAM authors (Moore et al., 2003), we found that such rigorous methods are difficult to implement comprehensively in practice in large-scale systems, but the real benefits remain in the increased communication between stakeholders and the ability to quickly prototype new functionality that helps them refine the requirements. We also found that the efforts and associated costs spent on heavy documentation were less effective as the documentation was painfully written but hardly ever read. Instead, most end-user stakeholders reacted positively when presented with simple, intuitive interfaces; and well-structured code proved to be a more cost-effective and sustainable solution for system evolution.

More lightweight approaches such as LAAAM refocus the discussion around the quality attributes and the related quality tree to help stakeholders reach agreement faster. It brings structure to the ATAM scenarios: the context of the scenario, the stimulus that triggers the scenario, and expected system response.

In our experience, any nontrivial project presents multiple scenarios (i.e., Use Cases in our model from Figure 12.6) that represent requirements and significant interdependencies between them. Our approach places emphasis on a clear separation between business requirements and the crosscutting requirements (i.e., the quality attributes) and their interplay that gets expressed as interaction patterns. By blending in domain modeling and MDA, we were able to further enrich the stakeholders' understanding of the planned or existing system capabilities and its realistic potential for expansion. Hence, we can reuse the same "rank-order centroids" (ROC) (Hutton Barron and Barrett, 1996) ranking and weighting scheme of LAAAM for the quality attributes but with an improved accuracy. The LAAAM-rebranded Quality-Oriented Decision Assessment (QODA) Tool can be used here as a web-based mechanism to calculate the necessary scenario to alternative weight mappings in a simplified way.

TARA is another lightweight approach for architecture evaluation that works best for small-to-medium scale assessments of already existing systems, where the number of stakeholders and their commitment time and levels is relatively small. It trades simplicity for accuracy and requires prior domain knowledge to be effective. However, it can be used to quickly gain an understanding of whether the project and its architecture are on the appropriate track. We use a similar process to gain this insight and make best use of the precious stakeholder time we have allocated in our meetings.

12.3.5.1 Cost-based dynamic system reconfiguration

As an alternative to upfront system architecture definition and refinement, the Rich Services framework allows for post design and implementation system reconfiguration by using up-to-date information available only during the actual system operation. The transformer (i.e., router-interceptor) mechanism enables a powerful, dynamic system adaptation to economic or environmental factors. Often, invoking a specific service is found to cost significantly more than another service in terms of latency, performance, or actual monetary cost, which can be difficult to predict during design time. Requirements for reliability may drive the system architecture toward an N-version modular approach where at runtime the system would choose between multiple-service implementations with emphasis on those that cost less to invoke (e.g., faster) or deliver better (e.g., more accurate) results. Lastly, actual monetary factors can come into play for service invocations, for instance, when leveraging cloud-computing platforms that have per transaction costs (e.g., Amazon S3), where choosing bulk transfers instead of frequent request would yield significant savings.

12.4 Lessons from practice

We have applied the Rich Services methodology with success in multiple E-Health interdisciplinary projects at the University of California, San Diego. Among these projects are CYberinfrastructure for COmparative effectiveness REsearch (CYCORE) (Patrick et al., 2011) for cancer clinical trials; Personal Activity Location Measurement System (PALMS) (Demchak et al., 2012; Demchak and Krüger, 2012) for studying human activity patterns; CitiSense (Nikzad et al., 2011, 2012) for sensing city pollution; and Integrating Data for Analysis, Anonymization, and Sharing (iDASH) (Ohno-Machado et al., 2012), which is a National Center for Biomedical Computing.

CYCORE provides a CI for the collection and analysis of home-based physiological, behavioral, social, and environmental data from patients undergoing cancer treatment (see Figure 12.2). The monitoring capabilities of the platform via wireless devices include weight scale, blood pressure monitor, heart rate monitor, accelerometer (which measures the number of walking and running steps), carbon monoxide monitor, global positioning system (GPS), video, and self-report data via a questionnaire/response application delivered via smart phone. The CYCORE CI has been successfully used in feasibility trials at the M.D. Anderson Cancer Center in three populations: advanced colorectal cancer patients, head and neck cancer patients, and cancer survivors who were smokers. The CI provides data about symptoms, quality of life, performance status, and physiological parameters that signal how well participants are doing with their treatment, and they also provide key information for cancer prevention and control research.

PALMS supports merging and processing data from physical activity sensors (e.g., accelerometers and heart rate monitors) with GPS data, and it constructs a detailed picture of a participant's day: travel patterns, locations, durations, and levels of physical activity and sedentary periods. PALMS supports the research of a worldwide community of exposure biologists, which study human health as a function of geographical location and ambient conditions. Thus, PALMS employs a number of principal investigators, each defining distinct studies involving study participants, data collection, and analysis. Each study is unique as to content, funding agency requirements, and personnel organization.

CitiSense uses sensors placed in the environment and carried by users to collect data about city pollution (such as ozone and carbon monoxide) and mobile phones to send the collected data to the backend infrastructure, which stores the data and serves it to the outside world. The data is used to provide real-time feedback to users, and it allows them to make healthier choices about where they live, work, and play. The data can also be shared within the CI for further processing and modeling, helping other stakeholders better understand how diseases such as asthma develop and coordinate efforts within a user's community to improve conditions.

iDASH provides a biomedical CI as a computational collaborative environment to enable wide access to quality biomedical data and software, and to provide a sophisticated computational infrastructure that allows researchers to share data and accelerate discoveries. iDASH focuses on algorithms and tools for sharing data in a privacy-preserving manner, and creates a private Health Insurance Portability and Accountability Act (HIPAA)-compliant cloud. Furthermore, training and dissemination efforts connect iDASH with its stakeholders and educate data owners and data consumers on how to share and use clinical and biological data. Its rich repository of medical data is not restricted by data type, and it includes structured biomedical data, images (e.g., CT and MRI), and text (e.g., clinical reports and notes) accompanied by meta-data (e.g., annotations).

Moreover, we have also designed CIs for ultra-large-scale systems in other domains, such as oceanography—the Ocean Observatories Initiative, which combines oceanographic instrument and sensor and actuator networks, data and computation grids, and a broad set of end-user applications in a CI (Chave et al., 2009; Arrott et al., 2009; Meisinger et al., 2009; Farcas et al., 2011) with novel capabilities for data distribution, modeling, planning, and control of oceanographic experiments.

All of these projects have requirements for integrating heterogeneous trust, security, and privacy zones. Each stakeholder brings its own business processes, capabilities, and requirements. We learned that these concerns should be treated up front in any project and refined through all phases of the development process. Following a blueprint, such as Rich Services, enables hierarchical structuring of the stakeholders' logical roles and encapsulation of crosscutting concerns according to their individual policies. Furthermore, these projects integrate systems-of-systems that require loose coupling between existing and emergent services.

12.4.1 Typical architecture

CIs comprise a variety of subsystems and are inherently subject to the effects of requirements changing over time. Not only do the requirements for the integrated system change over time in both short-lived and long-lived CIs, but the requirements for their constituent subsystems also evolve independently from the composite. This entails continually adapting the integrated system to avoid negative feature interactions in the integration solution. In essence, this concern affects not only the requirements gathering and design process, but also the architecture for the integrated system. On the one hand, the pertinent requirements for all the subsystems and the integration solution

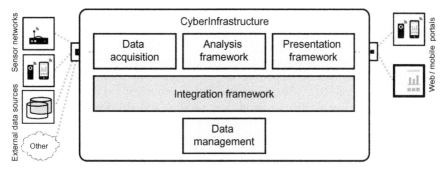

FIGURE 12.9

Typical E-Health CI logical architecture.

must be understood, updated, and transitioned into the architecture. On the other hand, the more flexible the architecture is with respect to updating or substituting existing subsystems, the more reactive the CI will be to changes in the environment in which it operates. This is particularly important in the context of dynamic system reconfiguration, as such flexibility is needed for self-healing systems that recover gracefully from failures or attacks. Our experience with the aforementioned E-Health projects revealed a number of shared requirements and reusable strategies for addressing them that can be leveraged to both reduce implementation times and further provide more accurate cost estimates. Having baselines of capabilities also enabled us to point the stakeholders of each project at examples of existing systems to help them better define their needs and ground the discussions on feasible solutions within their specified time frames. In the following, we detail key requirements for E-Health CIs and describe how our architectural choice helps us solve the challenges posed by these requirements.

Most E-Health CIs have at least five subsystems (see Figure 12.9), such as Data Acquisition (DA), Analysis Framework (AF), Data Management (DM), Presentation Framework (PF), and the Integration Framework (IF). These subsystems group together logically related functionalities that may be provided by different systems or stakeholders. Such structural decomposition is generally accepted and aligned with the needs of the involved stakeholder communities. It helps us bring together in meetings only the necessary parties and focus the discussions on shared values and perceived needs and capabilities. Often the development of each subsystem follows an iterative, spiral development process to release core functionality according to a manageable timeline. Third-party software is integrated through wrappers, virtualization/ encapsulation, or decomposition as applicable. System releases crosscut subsystems, as user requirements often translate into multiple services provided by different subsystems. For example, the requirement to integrate a specific sensor involves at least the Data Acquisition and Data Management subsystems, and then it will generate requirements for how to further process and visualize the data coming from that sensor.

12.4.1.1 Data acquisition

The Data Acquisition (DA) subsystem is the entry point into the CI for sensor, genome, and clinical data that encompasses capabilities for retrieval of complex datasets (Figure 12.9) from multiple sources over various protocols and access patterns. Besides data access, research reproducibility is a classical issue of the "secret sauce" availability that is directly related to data sharing. The acquisition and then broad access to data are understandably subject to societal norms, including patient's consent, data owner's privacy preferences, IRB approval, and federal, state, or local regulations.

To alleviate these challenges, in large-scale projects, such as iDASH, we rely on a legal framework of data-use agreements (DUA) between both (a) data providers and the data repository as custodian (i.e., an honest broker similar to an escrow service) and (b) data recipients and the data repository. These DUAs allow the provider to specify precisely what is shared and when (e.g., embargo prior to article publication), the sensitivity of the data (e.g., PHI/PII vs. anonymized), and restrictions on who can access the data with a fine granular control. Such specifications are then implemented as policies through infrastructure services that enforce them upon all data transfer requests.

Additionally, there are technical constraints, such as data formats (e.g., proprietary, ad-hoc, standard, or raw), meta-data availability (e.g., protocol description, contextual or environmental factors,), and storage and network bandwidth requirements. Having focused stakeholder meetings helps to identify the proper strategies to alleviate these constraints and reach value/cost consensus sooner. The solutions are generally different in each project and may involve services from the Data Management or Analysis Framework.

12.4.1.2 Data management

E-Health CIs have to integrate complex and diverse datasets into aggregates that support science and health-care services. Data Management (DM) provides the persistence/storage, cataloging, curation, backup, and retrieval services. At the logical level, the DM subsystem is not bound to use any particular technology, such as relational databases. It is also an enforcing point for policies, security, and other critical services. However, at the implementation level, they employ a mix of technologies to identify the data types, underlying structural representation, built-in or associated meta-data, and then store such rich datasets into data repositories. These repositories typically implement policy or role-based access controls to limit access for reading, writing, or updating data to the appropriately credentialed stakeholders or services acting on their behalf.

Our data repositories rely on proven open-source or commercial technologies, including relational, object, and partially consistent databases. Often, structured data (such as data from CYCORE clinical trials) is deposited in SQL-based databases, either completely normalized or just through references to various storage means, such as files on local and networked file systems (e.g., video files), objects or blocks in raw storage, and so on.

Recently, we used a variety of NoSQL databases for unstructured data to achieve greater flexibility and scalability without requiring upfront schema definitions. Specialized services then interface with these underlying storage technologies to deliver indexing, cataloging, search, and listing capabilities.

For instance, in iDASH we used popular open-source platforms, such as XNAT (NRG, 2012) and MIDAS (Kitware, 2012), to accommodate a variety of datasets and support capability extensions through plug-ins. The plug-ins streamline the end-user interaction and can perform in-situ data analysis and visualization, or even handle complex workflow execution. Furthermore, certain types of data, such as medical imaging, sensory data, and genomics, require dedicated storage solutions, such as PACS (Picture Archiving and Communication System) or proprietary software, to be able to interface with higher-level services for analysis.

12.4.1.3 Analysis framework

Interoperability among E-Health systems is currently challenged by a variety of choices and circumstances in the existing E-Health landscape. This includes legacy databases and formats, such as MUMPS (ANSI, 1977) with proprietary interchange scenarios, as well as interoperability middleware that is hard to scale and make fault-tolerant beyond a citywide usage scenario. This makes it challenging to even conceive of the planetary-scale Health Information Exchanges (HIEs) and Medical Record Systems (MREs) that hold tremendous potential for integrated P4 care (see Figure 12.1).

The Analysis Framework (AF) consists of a collection of data analysis tools including annotation, anonymization, and machine learning, which may be invoked on demand or as part of various biomedical workflows. In addition, the integration and compression tools may be invoked automatically with the resulting new data streams delivered to the DM.

12.4.1.4 Presentation framework

A system can have a great architecture and implementation, but will have difficulty being adopted if the user interface does not meet usability needs. Users ultimately interact with the user interface and do not see the internal details. This does not mean the user interface is the most important, because a nice cover on a system that is not working properly or cannot be maintained is not going to work in the long run. However, ignoring the user interface and focusing only on internal details will lead to user dissatisfaction. Because building a CI is such a complex endeavor, we have witnessed the trend whereby user interfaces are often simplified and deferred with unfavorable results.

The Presentation Framework (PF) represents a collection of all services that enable CI's stakeholders to interact with the provided functionality, including domain-specific interfaces from privacy-preserving data querying to dashboards and administrative portals. We have found that especially in E-Health systems where clinical doctors will be part of the users, it is essential to produce a streamlined interface, because the system will be used on a daily basis in an environment where the information has to be available quickly and as expected. This requires architects and developers to have many iterations with stakeholders to review the interface, the envisioned workflow, and overall experience, then refine exactly what information they want displayed, how, and where. In fact, user experience requirements have often been ranked as high priority in stakeholder workshops after the core services were in place.

12.4.1.5 Integration framework

The Integration Framework (IF) is provided by the RS architecture. It is the bridge to the underlying infrastructure (represented as services), and it supports the operation of the other subsystems and their interactions, including distributed messaging, federation, governance, and policies (e.g., authentication, authorization, privacy, security, encryption, logging, and notifications). Often the security processes required by E-Health CIs bring forward issues that typically are second thoughts for most researchers in the community (e.g., the safety of PHI data on mobile devices, including laptops, used for research on human subjects).

Regardless of the support reference of all involved technologies, CIs require highly skilled personnel to build, operate, and maintain the virtualized infrastructure in compliance with project requirements, and local, state, or federal regulations (e.g., firewalls, intrusion detection systems, and multiple-site encrypted storage of critical data). They also require professional development teams to deliver quality services on an ongoing basis.

Through frequent meetings, we point out weaknesses in common practices (e.g., shipping PHI data across the country on unencrypted hard drives) and educate the stakeholders about improved solutions, which are often readily achievable with existing, cost-effective technologies. This leads to both dissemination activities that educate the community into adopting better practices into their own environments, and also service offerings for those lacking adequate technical capabilities and resources at their home institutions.

12.4.1.6 Deployment, operations, maintenance

A flexible architectural blueprint such as RS allows the cyber-operators to partition the underlying physical infrastructure into classical production, quality-assurance, and development environments that allow for strategic containment of data, processes, and related software artifacts. Such practice supports proper development processes and helps achieve timely releases of new or improved functionality. Furthermore, it is perfectly suited to accommodate automated mechanisms that support its software stack.

Each service can have its own implementation instantiated as many times as needed, which allows for simple containment of upgrades and new functionality rollouts. Complex software can be decomposed into parts and deployed in different capability containers (i.e., virtual machines) for performance, security, or fault-tolerance reasons.

In general, multiple deployment options are available for any service, with proper allocations representing the trade-off of performance, scalability, and reliability. In our experience, the setup, configuration, and packaging of such specialized software for operation in the CI are best performed with well-supported open-source software, such as Chef (Opscode, 2012), Puppet (Puppet Labs, 2012), or Zookeeper (Apache Zookeper, 2012) for configuration management; Fabric (Fabfile, 2012) or Capistrano (Buck, 2012) for deployment; Func (Redhat, 2012) or Tentakel (Stark and Berlin, n.d.) for distributed task execution; Galaxy (Nekrutenko, 2012) or Taverna (Wolstencroft et al., 2013) for scientific workflow management; Oracle Grid Engine (OGE) (Oracle, 2010) or HTCondor (CHTC, 2012) for batch job execution, and so forth. These tools bring tremendous savings in keeping the CI operating according to its QoS requirements.

12.4.2 Additional success factors

While each CI project has specific scope, budget, duration, and organizational fabric, our experience revealed a number of key success factors that must be addressed to ensure a positive outcome for the project. As discussed in the previous sections, the RS architecture and development process involve various steps where these factors are addressed explicitly, early and throughout the duration of each project.

Involving stakeholders. A lot has been written about the importance of requirements gathering and involving stakeholders during requirements engineering, as well as validating architecture and prototypes. Nevertheless, we continue to witness projects that fail due to not meeting stakeholders' needs. The reasons cover a wide spectrum, such as overengineering, poor management, lack of involved stakeholders, lack of early prototyping, and focus on features that do not bring immediate value. We highlight the importance of identifying stakeholder groups and of holding requirements workshops within and across these groups for identifying features and crosscutting concerns as early as possible. We also take the approach from agile development and continuously involve the customers and main stakeholder groups in all iterations of the system for validating the current implementation and prioritizing the features for the next iteration. Moreover, an early, continuous, and far-reaching organizational engagement ensures fruitful cross-disciplinary collaborations and fosters larger communities of interest that keep projects in contact with the realities of their field and help keep up to date with inherent requirements' changes.

Furthermore, users rarely think of life-cycle management requirements because they tend to imagine a snapshot of the system when all required entities exist in an appropriate state. In reality, every entity has a life cycle in the system, whether a sensor, study, patient, data stream, and the like. Entities come and leave, and may change various states during their existence in the system. It is very important to uncover these requirements for life-cycle management up front to ensure proper interoperability across subsystems.

Common vocabulary. In a domain such as E-Health, there are so many terms that computer scientists are not familiar with, and vice versa, clinical stakeholders might not be familiar with computer science terms. Therefore, establishing a common vocabulary and clarifying all terms is key to having a shared understanding of the problem domain and the solution. We employ mind maps extensively at the beginning of a project, and then we continue to use them whenever new terms come up. A more formal alternative, domain models define "the language" of the system by capturing domain entities in a structural way. This involves extracting the main entities and their relationships from use cases, user stories, or business-process documents, and then expressing them, typically, in a set of UML class diagrams.

Moreover, requirements are often expressed in the user language, which inevitably leads to inconsistencies because each stakeholder has his or her own description and understanding. This risk can be mitigated by frequent requirements reviews involving all stakeholders and using ontologies to communicate requirements. Complex requirements also benefit from domain models that clearly depict relationships between critical entities and help ground a common understanding shared by all involved stakeholders. Constructing domain models is a very important process that supports aligning the architecture effort with the stakeholder needs and often involves several iterations with domain experts. Moreover, in large systems-of-systems integration projects, domain models help in understanding the different languages of each system and in defining the interfaces between subsystems.

We have used both mind maps and formal domain models during requirements workshops with stakeholders: Mind maps are always easier to grasp by all participants, and they facilitate interactions between the architecture team and the domain experts, resulting in efficient and effective knowledge transfer. Mind maps often lead to immediate augmentation and refinement of vocabulary, requirements, and entity relationships; thus, they are a valuable asset in identifying inconsistencies and facilitating the transition from use cases to domain models. Then, we share the formal domain models with key stakeholders for checking correctness and internal consistency.

Iterative development. In practice, use case sets are often incomplete in important ways: omitting key requirements and relationships; implying the existence of important stakeholders and resources without specifically identifying them; omitting entire use cases; and omitting preconditions, postconditions, exceptions, and guarantees. As such, use case sets are often open to interpretation and speculation, leading to volatile requirements. Choosing an appropriate iterative development process, such as RS, is essential to accommodate the re-specification and refinement of use cases over time through multiple design iterations. We need not fully resolve an imperfect and incomplete use case set before proceeding from one stage to the next, though the more complete and coherent a use case set is, the fewer iterations we will need.

Scalability and federation. Serving large and diverse communities of stakeholders, CIs have by their nature a stringent need for horizontal scalability and federation with other similar systems and services. The classical technique of throwing a faster or larger hardware at the scalability issue simply does not work for CIs, as they are inherently complex and distributed. Hence, strategic separation of concerns at the architectural level and then careful implementation through loosely coupled services are essential to be able to scale horizontally at the deployment level. Often, scalability is not just a question of processing or storage requirements, but also a matter of communication bandwidths and latencies involved. Hence, service and algorithm implementations must account for large networks, intermittent connectivity, and unscheduled downtime, in-transit data loss, and other such factors that can affect the correctness and quality of service delivered. Certain applications further shift the focus from local to global optimizations to be able to scale properly.

Architectural spiking. We have found that focusing on use cases end to end, from requirements to architecture to a working prototype, is key in mitigating project risks related to both unclear requirements and technology concerns. Therefore, the RS process has iterations within each phase and across all three phases of service elicitation, RS architecture, and system architecture definition. Stakeholders have the opportunity to see a live product with limited functionality, and they can provide valuable feedback regarding what they really want. More and more use cases are added over subsequent rounds. Architectural spiking allows domain and application knowledge to be developed incrementally instead of in grand exercises, thereby managing complexity and mitigating development risks.

Nonfunctional/crosscutting concerns. In E-Health, systems are constrained by privacy and security regulations, which are pervasive and crosscut all functional services provided by the system. The security solution should be designed upfront and decoupled as much as possible from the implementation of other services to ensure the system's extensibility and maintainability. This is where a decoupling architecture such as RS shines, as all security use cases can be implemented transparently. Other crosscutting concerns include policy management, monitoring, and reliability. The choice of the high-level architecture is key in managing the trade-offs between requirements. A major feature of the RS process is the identification and abstraction of crosscutting concerns early in the development process. Historically speaking, addressing such concerns as afterthoughts notoriously increases the integration costs and leads to incomplete or incorrect system implementations.

Traceability. Traceability between requirements and architecture and implementation is a daunting task, and yet it is necessary in order to navigate between one space to another in forward engineering to realize a system that meets the requirements, as well as in reverse engineering to maintain, analyze, and diagnose the operational system. We have found that when implementing traceability, it is more important to focus on validation and correctness than on full coverage. By this we mean that in incremental development, inevitably some requirements will be deferred for future iterations and cannot be traced to the architecture at a given point in time. The same is true for architecture elements that are designed from the beginning to see how they fit in the big picture but they will not be implemented in the initial iterations. However, it is important to ensure that every element in the architecture is justified by some requirements, in order to avoid overengineering or designing the wrong system.

Furthermore, traceability is important in respect to crosscutting concerns. These concerns should be linked to the use cases, and later to the services to which they apply. Thus, the crosscutting concerns can be included in explicit validation and verification.

Architecture stability. Traceability is also key in maintaining systems when requirements change and new requirements appear. The system's architecture should be created to accommodate requirement changes by extension of the design elements, instead of radical changes to the existing ones, to ensure architecture stability over time. However, the stability of the architecture is also influenced by the flexibility of the middleware in implementing nonfunctional requirements. This was argued in Bahsoon et al. (2005) based on an option−based model for trade-off analysis and a case study of a system instantiated in two versions, using CORBA and J2EE, respectively.

We separate between logical and deployment architectures, and it is possible to implement a logical RS architecture in a variety of languages and middleware. It is often more obvious how the logical architecture constrains the decisions for the deployment architecture, than the other way around. However, nonfunctional properties such as scalability and performance depend significantly on the deployment architecture and the mapping between RS hierarchy to the deployment nodes. If the implementation does not meet nonfunctional requirements, it might require changes to the mapping or even to the logical architecture to accommodate the constraints of the platform; switching the entire implementation to a different platform is often too costly. Thus, an advantage of the RS architecture is the 1:1 mapping to an ESB deployment. In this way, there is a direct correspondence between the quality properties of the logical architecture and the middleware used for implementation.

12.5 Future research directions

E-Health CIs are key to turning waste into value across our health system. They are the enablers necessary to let Hood's P4-style health approach come to life. While we have taken significant steps toward producing a value-driven, end-to-end process for constructing and deploying E-Health solutions on corresponding CI fabrics, there is much room left for further consolidation and improvement. Specifically, the interface between health domain experts and software engineers has yet to be fully explored, modeled, and more flexibly taken into account throughout the process. This will enable domain experts rather than software engineers to drive application development and maintenance. One key to this is further improvement of our understanding of highly configurable, and automatically reconfigurable, standard architectures and implementations of E-Health CIs. This will include development of a mix of modeling and analysis techniques for E-Health architectures through appropriate and yet-to-be-designed domain-specific languages. These languages need to take stakeholder values into account to enable cost-effective, responsible systems engineering in this complex yet highly impactful application domain.

12.6 Conclusion

Fueled by advancements in CIs, the E-Health landscape is continuously evolving at a higher pace than before. Our experiences in multiple projects from this domain reveal that success is an interesting mix of business lessons, technology choices, architectures, processes, and people that intersect and interact in novel ways to make way for a new era of discovery and health care. In this chapter, we presented a strategic end-to-end recipe for building CIs, along with lessons learned along the way. Far from being a solution for everybody and every problem, it illustrates a proper way to economically address the needs and challenges presented by this field.

Acknowledgments

This work was supported in part by the National Institutes of Health (NIH) Roadmap for Medical Research iDASH program grant U54HL108460; the American Recovery and Reinvestment Act (ARRA) Grand Opportunity CyCORE grants 1 RC2 CA148263-01 and 5 UC2 CA148263-02; the NSF Cyber-Physical Systems CitiSense project grant CNS-0932403; and the NIH National Center for Research Resources P41 Computational Center for Mass-Spectrometry grant 1-P41-RR024851. In part, this research was performed while the third author was on sabbatical leave from UCSD at TU Munich, TU Aachen, Saarbrücken University, and Paderborn University.

References

Alves, A., Arkin, A., Askary, S., Barreto, C., Bloch, B., Curbera, F., et al., 2007. OASIS Web Services Business Process Execution Language (WS-BPEL) Version 2.0. OASIS Standard. Retrieved from: <http://docs.oasis-open.org/wsbpel/2.0/wsbpel-v2.0.html>.

American National Standards Institute (ANSI), 1977. MUMPS (Massachusetts General Hospital Utility Multi-Programming System). Standard X11.1-1977.

Apache Software Foundation, 2012. ZooKeeper. Version 3.4.5. <http://zookeeper.apache.org/>.

Arrott, M., Demchak, B., Ermagan, V., Farcas, C., Farcas, E., Krüger, I.H., et al., Rich services: the integration piece of the SOA puzzle. Proceedings of the IEEE International Conference on Web Services (ICWS). IEEE Computer Society, Salt Lake City, Utah, pp. 176–183.

Arrott, M., Chave, A.D., Farcas, C., Farcas, E., Kleinert, J.E., Krüger, I., et al., Integrating marine observatories into a system-of- systems: messaging in the U.S. Ocean observatories initiative. OCEANS 2009 MTS/IEEE Biloxi. IEEE Ocean Engineering Society, Biloxi, MISS, p. 9.

Atkins, D., Droegemier, K., Feldman, S., Garcia-Molina, H., Klein, M.L., Messerschmitt, D.G., et al., Revolutionizing Science and Engineering Through Cyberinfrastructure: Report of Blue-Ribbon Advisory Panel on Cyberinfrastructure. National Science Foundation, Washington, DC.

Bachmann, F., 2011. Give the stakeholders what they want: design peer reviews the ATAM style. CrossTalk .

Bachmann, F., Bass, L., 2001. Introduction to the attribute driven design method. Proceedings of the 23rd International Conference on Software Engineering (ICSE '01). IEEE Computer Society, Washington, DC, pp. 745–746.

Bahsoon, R., Emmerich, W., Macke, J., 2005. Using real options to select stable middleware-induced software architectures. IEE Proc. Softw. 152 (4), 167–186.

Banerji, A., Bartolini, C., Beringer, D., Chopella, V., Govindarajan, L., Karp, A., et al., 2002. Web Services Conversation Language (WSCL) 1.0. W3C. Retrieved from: <http://www.w3.org/TR/wscl10/>.

Bass, L., Nord, R.L., 2012. Understanding the Context of Architecture Evaluation Methods. 2012 Joint Working IEEE/IFIP Conference on Software Architecture (WICSA) and European Conference on Software Architecture (ECSA), pp. 277–281.

Bass, L., Clements, P., Kazman, R., 2003. Software Architecture in Practice. second ed. Addison-Wesley, Boston.

Berners-Lee, T., Hendler, J., Lassila, O., 2001. The semantic web. Sci. Am. 284 (5), 34–43.

Boehm, B., 2006. Value-based software engineering: overview and agenda. In: Biffl, S., Aurum, A., Boehm, B., Erdogmus, H., Grünbacher, P. (Eds.), Value-Based Software Engineering. Springer, Berlin, pp. 3–14. , Chapter 1.

Boehm, B., Bose, P., 1994. A collaborative spiral software process model based on theory W. Proceedings of the 3rd International Conference on the Software Process, Reston, VA, pp. 59–68.

Boehm, B., Jain, A., 2006. An initial theory of value-based software engineerin. In: Biffl, S., Aurum, A., Boehm, B., Erdogmus, H., Grünbacher, P. (Eds.), Value-Based Software Engineering. Springer, Berlin, pp. 15–37. , Chapter 2.

Boehm, B., Kitapci, H., 2006. The WinWin approach: using a requirements negotiation tool for rationale capture and use. In: Dutoit, A., McCall, R., Mistrík, I., Paech, B. (Eds.), Rationale Management in Software Engineering. Springer, Berlin, pp. 173–190.

Boehm, B., Lane, J., 2007. Using the incremental commitment model to integrate system acquisition, systems engineering, and software engineering. CrossTalk 19 (10), 4–9.

Boehm, B., Turner, R., 2003. Balancing Agility and Discipline: Guide for the Perplexed. Longman Publishing Co, Boston.

Boehm, B., Bose, P., Horowitz, E., Lee, M.J., 1994. Software requirements as negotiated win conditions. Proceedings of the First International Conference on Requirements Engineering. IEEE Computer Society Press, Colorado Springs, CO, pp. 74–83.

Boehm, B., Egyed, A., Kwan, J., Port, D., Shah, A., Madachy, R., 1998. Using the WinWin spiral model: a case study. IEEE Comput. 7, 33–44.

Boehm, B.W., 1988. A spiral model of software development and enhancement. Computer 21 (5), 61–72, IEEE Computer Society.

Boehm, B.W., Ross, R., 1989. Theory-W software project management: principles and examples. IEEE Trans. Softw. Eng. 15 (7), 902–916.

Boehm, B.W., Grünbacher, P., Briggs, R.O., 2001. Developing groupware for requirements negotiation: lessons learned. IEEE Softw. 18 (3), 46–55.

Booth, D., Haas, H., McCabe, F., Newcomer, E., Champion, M., Ferris, C., et al., 2004. Web Services Architecture. W3C Working Group Note. Retrieved from: <http://www.w3.org/TR/2004/NOTE-ws-arch-20040211/>.

Bosch, J., 2000. Design and Use of Software Architectures: Adopting and Evolving a Product-Line Approach. ACM Press/Addison-Wesley Publishing, New York, ISBN 0-201-67494-7.

Buck, J., 2012. Capistrano. Version 2.13.0. <http://capistranorb.com/>.

Burge, J.E., Carroll, J.M., McCall, R., Mistrik, I., 2008. Rationale-Based Software Engineering. Springer, Berlin, p. 316.

Carriere, S.J., 2009. Lightweight Architecture Alternative Assessment Method. <http://technogility.sjcarriere.com/2009/05/11/its-pronounced-like-lamb-not-like-lame/>.

Carroll, J.M., Rosson, M.B., Chin Jr., G., Koenemann, J., 1998. Requirements development in scenario-based design. IEEE Trans. Soft. Eng. 24 (12), 1156–1170.

Center for High Throughput Computing (CHTC), 2012. HTCondor workload management system. Department of Computer Sciences. University of Wisconsin-Madison (UW-Madison), <http://research.cs.wisc.edu/htcondor/>.

Chave, A., Arrott, M., Farcas, C., Farcas, E., Krüger, I., Meisinger, M., et al., Cyberinfrastructure for the U.S. Ocean observatories initiative: enabling interactive observation in the Ocean. IEEE OCEANS'09. IEEE Ocean Engineering Society, Bremen, Germany, p. 10.

Clements, P., Kazman, R., Klein, M., 2002. Evaluating Software Architecture: Methods and Case Studies. Addison-Wesley, Boston.

Cockburn, A., 2000. Writing Effective Use Cases. Addison-Wesley, Boston.

Dahmann, J., Lane, J., Rebovich, G., Baldwin, K., 2008. A model of systems engineering in a system of systems context, Proceedings of the Conference on Systems Engineering Research, Los Angeles, CA.

Demchak, B., Krüger, I., 2012. Policy driven development: flexible policy insertion for large scale systems. 2012 IEEE International Symposium on Policies for Distributed Systems and Networks. IEEE Computer Society, Chapel Hill, NC, pp. 17–24.

Demchak, B., Farcas, C., Farcas, E., Krüger, I., 2007. The treasure map for rich services. Proceedings of the 2007 IEEE International Conference on Information Reuse and Integration (IRI). IEEE, Las Vegas, pp. 400–405.

Demchak, B., Kerr, J., Raab, F., Patrick, K., Krüger, I., 2012. PALMS: a modern coevolution of community and computing using policy driven development. 45th Hawaii International Conference on System Sciences (HICSS). Maui, Hawaii.

Department of Defense, 2010. The Department of Defense Architecture Framework (DoDAF) Version 2.02. DoD.

Dobrica, L., Niemela, E., 2002. A survey on software architecture analysis methods. IEEE Trans. Softw. Eng. 28 (7), 638–653. Available from: http://dx.doi.org/10.1109/TSE.2002.1019479.

Ebert, C., 1992. Visualization techniques for analyzing and evaluating software measures. IEEE Trans. Softw. Eng. 18, 1029–1034.

Evans, E., 2004. Domain-Driven Design: Tackling Complexity in the Heart of Software. Addison-Wesley, Boston, p. 560.

Fabfile, 2012. Fabric library. Version 1.5. <http://docs.fabfile.org/en/1.5/>.

Farcas, C., Farcas, E., Krüger, I., 2010. Requirements for service composition in ultra-large scale software-intensive systems. In: Choppy, C., Sokolsky, O. (Eds.), Foundations of Computer Software: Future Trends and Techniques for Development. 15th Monterey Workshop, Budapest, Hungary, September 24–26, 2008, Revised Selected Papers, Lecture Notes in Computer Science, 6028, Chapter 6:93–115, Berlin: Springer.

Farcas, C., Meisinger, M., Stuebe, D., Mueller, C., Ampe, T., Arrott, M., et al., Ocean observatories initiative scientific data model. Proceedings of OCEANS'11—MTS/IEEE Kona. IEEE Ocean Engineering Society, p. 10 (paper 110422-240).

Federal Information Security Management Act of 2002, Title III, E-Government Act of 2002, P.L. 107–347.

Fowler, M., 2003. Patterns of Enterprise Application Architecture. Addison-Wesley Professional, Boston.

Gamma, E., Helm, R., Johnson, R., Vlissides, J., 1995. Design Patterns: Elements of Reusable Object-Oriented Software. Addison-Wesley Professional, Boston.

Goble, C., et al., n.d.. Taverna Project. School of Computer Science at the University of Manchester, UK. <http://www.taverna.org.uk/>.

Gruber, T., 1993. A translation approach to portable ontology specications. Knowl. Acquis. 5, 199.

Grünbacher, P., Köszegi, S., Biffl, S., 2006. Stakeholder value proposition elicitation and reconciliation. In: Biffl, S., Aurum, A., Boehm, B., Erdogmus, H., Grünbacher, P. (Eds.), Value-Based Software Engineering. Springer, Berlin, pp. 133–154. , Chapter 7.

Health Insurance Portability and Accountability Act of 1996. P.L. 104–191.

Hickey, R., 2012. Clojure Dynamic Programming Language. Version 1.4. <http://clojure.org/>.

Highsmith, J.A., 2000. Adaptive software development. A Collaborative Approach to Managing Complex Systems. Dorset House, New York, pp. 392, ISBN 0-932633-40-4

Hohpe, G., Woolf, B., 2004. Enterprise integration patterns: designing. Building, and Deploying Messaging Solutions. Addison-Wesley Professional, Boston.

Holbrook, I.H., 1990. A scenario-based methodology for conducting requirements elicitation. SIGSOFT Softw. Eng. Notes 15 (1), 95−104.

Hood, L., 2009. A doctor's vision of the future of medicine. Newsweek Mag. Retrieved from: <http://www.thedailybeast.com/newsweek/2009/06/26/a-doctor-s-vision-of-the-future-of-medicine.html>.

Hutton Barron, F., Barrett, B.E., 1996. Decision quality using ranked attribute weights. INFORMS Institute for Operations Research and the Management Sciences (INFORMS), Linthicum, MD. Management Science, 42 (11), 1515−1523.

Kavantzas, N., Burdett, D., Ritzinger, G., Fletcher, T., Lafon, Y., Barreto, C., 2005. Web Services Choreography Description Language Version 1.0. W3C Candidate Recommendation. Retrieved from: <http://www.w3.org/TR/2005/CR-ws-cdl-10-20051109/>.

Kazman, R., Asundi, J., Klein, M., 2001. Quantifying the costs and benefits of architectural decisions. Proceedings of the 23rd International Conference on Software Engineering (ICSE '01). IEEE Computer Society, Toronto, Ontario, Canada, pp. 297−306.

Kazman, R., Asundi, J., Klein, M., 2002. Making Architecture Design decisions: An Economic Approach (CMU/SEI-2002-TR-035, ESCTR-2002-035). Software Engineering Institute, Carnegie Mellon University, Pittsburgh, PA.

Kitware, Inc., 2012. MIDAS Platform—The Multimedia Digital Archiving System. MIDAS Server version 3.2.8. <http://www.midasplatform.org/>.

Krüger, I.H. (2000). Distributed System Design with Message Sequence Charts. Doctoral dissertation, Fakultät für Informatik, Technischen Universität München.

Krüger, I.H., Mathew, R., 2005. Component synthesis from service specifications. scenarios: models, transformations and tools, international workshop, dagstuhl castle, germany, September 7−12, 2003, Revised Selected Papers. In: Leue, S., Systä, T.J. (Eds.), Lecture Notes in Computer Science, 3466. Springer, Berlin, pp. 255−277.

Lane, J., Boehm, B., 2008. Modern tools to support DoD software intensive system of systems cost estimation. Data and Analysis Center for Software, Rome, NY.

Lane, J.A., Dahmann, J.S., 2008. Process evolution to support system of systems engineering. ULSSIS '08 Proceedings of the 2nd international Workshop on Ultra-Large-Scale Software-intensive Systems. ACM Press, New York, Leipzig, Germany, May 10−11, 2008, pp. 11−14.

Lee, M.J., 1996. Foundations of the WinWin Requirements Negotiation System. PhD dissertation, University of Southern California.

MacKenzie, C., Laskey, K., McCabe, F., Brown, P., Metz, R., 2006. Reference Model for Service Oriented Architecture 1.0. OASIS Standard. Retrieved from: <http://docs.oasis-open.org/soa-rm/v1.0/soa-rm.pdf>.

Martin, D., Burstein, M., Hobbs, J., Lassila, O., McDermott, D., McIlraith, S., et al., 2004. OWL-S: Semantic Markup for Web Services. W3C Member Submission. Retrieved from: http://www.w3.org/Submission/2004/SUBM-OWL-S-20041122/.

Meisinger, M., Farcas, C., Farcas, E., Alexander, C., Arrott, M., Beaujardière, J.D.L., et al., Serving ocean model data on the cloud. OCEANS 2009 MTS/IEEE Biloxi, Biloxi, MISS. IEEE Ocean Engineering Society, p. 10.

Monroe, R., Kompanek, A., Melton, R., Garlan, D., 1997. Architectural styles, design patterns, and objects, IEEE Software, vol 14. IEEE Computer Society Press, 1 (Jan), pp. 43−52.

Moore, M., Kaman, R., Klein, M., Asundi, J., 2003. Quantifying the value of architecture design decisions: lessons from the field. Proceedings of the 25th International Conference on Software Engineering, pp. 557−562.

MuleSoft Inc, 2012. Mule Open Source ESB and Integration Platform. Community Edition Version 3.3. <http://www.mulesoft.org/download-mule-esb-community-edition>.

Munson, J.C., Khoshgoftaar, T.M., 1990. Regression modelling of software quality: empirical investigation. Inform. Soft. Technol. 32, 106−114.

Nadalin, A., Kaler, C., Monzillo, R., Hallam-Baker, P., 2006. Web Services Security: SOAP Message Security 1.1 (WS-Security 2004) OASIS Standard Specification. Retrieved from: <https://www.oasis-open.org/committees/download.php/16790/wss-v1.1-spec-os-SOAPMessageSecurity.pdf>.

National Science Foundation, 2007. NSF's Cyberinfrastructure Vision for 21st Century Discovery. NSF Cyberinfrastructure Council. Retrieved from: <http://www.nsf.gov/pubs/2007/nsf0728/nsf0728.pdf>.

Nekrutenko lab in the Center for Comparative Genomics and Bioinformatics at Penn State, 2012. Galaxy project. <http://galaxyproject.org/>.

Neuroinformatics Research Group (NRG) at the Washington University School of Medicine, 2012. XNAT imaging informatics platform—version 1.6. <http://xnat.org/>.

Nikzad, N., Ziftci, C., Zappi, P., Quick, N., Aghera, P., Verma, N., et al., CitiSense—Adaptive Services for Community-Driven Behavioral and Environmental Monitoring to Induce Change, Tech. Rep. CS2011-0961. University of California, San Diego.

Nikzad, N., Verma, N., Ziftci, C., Bales, E., Quick, N., Zappi, P., et al., 2012. CitiSense: improving geospatial environmental assessment of air quality using a wireless personal exposure monitoring system. Wireless Health (Best Paper).

Northrop, L., Feiler, P., Gabriel, R.P., Goodenough, J., Linger, R., Longstaff, T., et al., Ultra-Large-Scale Systems: The Software Challenge of the Future. Software Engineering Institute, Carnegie Mellon University, Pittsburgh, PA.

Nuseibeh, B., Easterbrook, S., 2000. Requirements engineering: a roadmap. Proceedings of the Conference on the Future of Software Engineering. Limerick, Ireland, pp. 35−46.

Object Management Group, 2003. Model Driven Architecture (MDA) v1.0.1. omg/03-06-01, OMG.

Object Management Group, 2010. Unified Modeling Language (OMG UML), Superstructure, Version 2.3. formal/2010-05-05, OMG.

Ohno-Machado, L., Bafna, V., Boxwala, A.A., Chapman, B.E., Chapman, W.W., Chaudhuri, K., et al., 2012. iDASH: integrating data for analysis, anonymization, and sharing. J. Am. Med. Inf. Assoc. JAMA 19 (2), 196−201. Available from: http://dx.doi.org/10.1136/amiajnl-2011-000538.

OpenNebula, 2012. OpenNebula −Open Source Data Center Virtualization. Version 3.8. <http://www.opennebula.org/>.

OpenStack Foundation, 2012. OpenStack—Open Source Cloud Computing Software. <http://www.openstack.org/>.

Opscode, Inc., 2012. Chef Integration Framework. Apache Foundation supported community edition. Version 10.16.2. <http://wiki.opscode.com/display/chef/>.

Oracle Corporation, 2010. Oracle Grid Engine. Previously known as Sun Grid Engine (SGE), version 6.2. <http://www.oracle.com/technetwork/oem/grid-engine-166852.html>.

Patrick, K., Wolszon, L., Basen-Engquist, K., Demark-Wahnefried, W., Prokhorov, A., Barrera, S., et al., 2011. CYberinfrastructure for comparative effectiveness research (CYCORE): improving data from cancer clinical trials. J. Transl. Behav. Med. Pract. Policy Res. 1 (1), 83−88. Available from: http://dx.doi.org/10.1007/s13142-010-0005-z.

Perry, D., Wolf, A., 1992. Foundations for the study of software architecture. SIGSOFT Softw. Eng. Notes 17-4, 40−52.

Porter, A.A., Selby, R.W., 1990. Empirically guided software development using metric-based classification trees. IEEE Softw. 7, 46−54.

Puppet Labs, 2012. Puppet Open Source. IT Automation Software for System Administrators. <http://puppet-labs.com/puppet/puppet-open-source/>.

Rajlich, V., 2006. Changing the software paradigm. Commun. ACM 49 (8), 67−70.

Redhat, Inc., 2012. Func: Fedora Unified Network Controller. <https://fedorahosted.org/func/>.

Rooney, P., 2002. Microsoft's CEO: 80-20 Rule Applies to Bugs, Not Just Features. Available at: <http://www.crn.com/news/security/18821726/microsofts-ceo-80-20-rule-applies-to-bugs-not-just-features.htm>.

Schmidt, D.C., Stal, M., Rohnert, H., Buschmann, F., 2000. Pattern-Oriented Software Architecture: Patterns for Concurrent and Networked Objects, vol. 2. Wiley, New York.

Selby, R.W., Porter, A.A., 1988. Learning from examples: generation and evaluation of decision trees for software resource analysis. IEEE Trans. Softw. Eng. 14, 1743−1757.

Song, Y., Rai, D., Sullivan, K., 2008. Adaptation architectures cross levels. ULSSIS '08 Proceedings of the 2nd International Workshop on Ultra-Large-Scale Software-intensive Systems, Leipzig, Germany. New York, pp. 27−28.

Sotomayor, B., Montero, R.S., Llorente, I.M., Foster, I., 2009. Virtual infrastructure management in private and hybrid clouds. IEEE Internet Comput. 13 (5), 14−22.

Stark, S., Berlin, M., n.d.. Tentakel Distributed Command Execution. <http://tentakel.biskalar.de/>.

The Standish Group, 1995. CHAOS report. The Standish Group. <www.standishgroup.com>.

The Standish Group, 2001. Extreme CHAOS Report. The Standish Group. <www.standishgroup.com>.

Wohlin, C., Aurum, A., 2006. Criteria for selecting software requirements to create product value: an industrial empirical study. In: Biffl, S., Aurum, A., Boehm, B., Erdogmus, H., Grünbacher, P. (Eds.), Value-Based Software Engineering. Springer, Berlin, pp. 179−200. Chapter 9.

Wojcik, R., Bachmann, F., Bass, L., Clements, P., Merson, P., Nord, R., et al., 2006. Attribute-Driven Design (ADD), Version 2.0 (CMU/SEI-2006-TR-023). Retrieved April 11, 2013, from the Software Engineering Institute, Carnegie Mellon University website: <http://www.sei.cmu.edu/library/abstracts/reports/06tr023.cfm>.

Woods, E., 2011. Industrial architectural assessment using TARA, Ninth Working IEEE/IFIP Conference on Software Architecture (WICSA).

Wolstencroft, K., Haines, R., Fellows, D., Williams, A., Withers, D., Owen, S., et al. The Taverna workflow suite: designing and executing workflows of Web Services on the desktop, web or in the cloud. Nucleic Acids Research, First published online May 2, 2013. Available from: http://dx.doi.org/10.1093/nar/gkt328.

The Design Implications of Users' Values for Software and System Architecture

13

Alistair Sutcliffe[1] and Sarah Thew[2]

[1]University of Lancaster, Lancaster, UK
[2]University of Manchester, Manchester, UK

13.1 Introduction

At first sight, sociopolitical "soft issues" in software engineering may seem to have few, if any, direct implications for software architecture. In this chapter we argue that users' values as examples of soft issues, such as moral views, creativity, and aesthetic sensitivities, do indeed have considerable architectural implications. Appropriate consideration of social and political issues has for some time been recognized as a key aspect of developing successful systems (Gougen, 1994). Stakeholder conflicts and their sociopolitical causes have been analyzed as critical issues in requirements analysis (Bergman et al., 2002; Finkelstein and Dowell, 2006). Stakeholder conflicts often arise from users' values where adverse emotional responses can lead to system rejection (Ramos & Berry, 2005a; Ramos et al., 2002). For example, stakeholder values of ownership and control can lead to frustration and rejection of (enterprise resource plan (ERP)) systems. User values have been analyzed at a high level of cultural attributes such as power distance and individualism (Viega et al., 2001), while Sutcliffe et al. (2006) argued that cultural values should have an important influence on requirements definition. However, apart from some examples in specific applications (Krumbholz et al., 2000), few reports of applications of value-based requirements analysis have emerged. Analysis of user values can facilitate design decisions/rationale, requirements-design trade-off negotiations in the development process, and the transition from requirements to the design of system architecture.

Investigation of user values focuses attention on the connection between users' beliefs and their implications for architectural design, as the inevitable intertwining of requirements and architecture (Sutcliffe, 2008), following the twin peaks model (Nuseibeh, 2001) that argued for the close association between requirements and design (i.e., architectural) decisions. User values are closely related to nonfunctional requirements (NFRs) or architectural qualities (Bass et al., 2003). Some NFRs have clear architectural implications, with security being the best example. Security requirements and generalized architectures have been specified using problem frames as a starting point to understand the connection between requirements, assumptions, constraints, and solution designs (Haley et al., 2004; Rapanotti et al., 2004). More general interest in self-aware adaptive systems (Sawyer et al., 2010; Souza et al., 2011) has led to development of general conceptual models of sense-making systems, where user values/NFRs for privacy, flexibility, and control may have considerable architectural implications in terms of autonomy and control coupling between components.

In this chapter we argue for the merit of analyzing requirements using informal ontologies of values to extend the concept of NFRs by linking them to generic models of system architecture. We do not deal with NFRs directly since the architectural implications of NFRs have been extensively researched by others (e.g., Bass et al., 2003). However, we do explain where user values and NFRs intersect, for instance, in issues such as privacy and security. In the following sections, first user values are defined and related to other "soft" socioeconomic concerns in software engineering (SE). Then a preliminary taxonomy of values is elaborated, with implications for product design as well as for project management. This leads to the main proposition: that the implications of user values can be understood as extensions of NFRs, with implications for the design of system architecture. Then a case study applying value-based requirements analysis to design of systems architecture in a medical research decision support system is described. The chapter concludes with a discussion of the future implications for value analysis for software architecture.

13.2 Values and related social issues

Requirements engineering (RE) methods have been proposed for analyzing values in the sense of economic worth for services (Gordijn and Akkermans, 2002); and for anticipating overall customer value in product lines by applying a road-mapping process in strategic product-release planning (Komssi et al., 2011). However, only general advice about considering political and social issues is given in most RE methods (Sommerville and Sawyer, 1997; Robertson and Robertson, 1999; Van Lamsweerde, 2009). In an application of activity theory to RE, Fuentes-Fernandez et al. (2010) elaborated UML (Unified Modelling Language) schema for social issues and proposed patterns for recognizing stakeholder conflicts; however, they did not give specific advice about eliciting or analyzing users' values. While some soft issues and social relationships, such as responsibility and authority, are modeled in i* (Yu, 2009) and extensions thereof (Sutcliffe, 2010), user values have not been explicitly included in requirements processes to date. In a recent review of power and political issues in RE, Milne and Maiden (2011) pointed out that requirements are socially constructed in a political context, and they advocated development of techniques for social power modeling. A more detailed taxonomy of social and political issues with guidelines for recognizing affective reactions among stakeholders, was proposed by Ramos et al. (2002) who applied their approach in analyzing requirements for ERP applications. In conclusion, while the importance of values and social issues has long been recognized in software development, advice on how to elicit and deal with such issues is scarce.

In human—computer interaction (HCI), the value-based design method (Friedman, 2008) provides a process for eliciting user feelings and attitudes to potential systems by presenting cue cards associated with possible emotional responses and user values. Scenarios and storyboarding techniques are used to elicit stakeholder responses, but value-based design does not focus directly on requirements definition. Instead, it aims to elicit users' attitudes and feelings about products and prototypes as an aid toward refining requirements with human-centered values. Values and affective responses have been investigated by Cockton et al. (2009) in worth maps, which attempt to document stakeholders' views about products or prototypes. Worth maps may include values and emotional responses, but their main focus, similar to value-based design, is to elicit informal descriptions of potential products expressed in stakeholders' language as feelings, values, and attitudes.

13.2.1 Definition of user values

Several authors have noted the importance of values. For example, Shiell et al. (1997) considered values as fundamental aspects of life, including health, happiness, and prestige; while Keeney (1992, 1996), who proposed value-focused thinking, considered values to be fundamental and a driving force in decision making. Definitions of value vary from worth and desirability to judgment of what is valuable or important in life (Oxford English Dictionary (OED)). In psychology, values are the beliefs and attitudes held by people about other people, organizations, or artifacts; for instance, in small group theory (Arrow et al., 2000), values, beliefs, and attitudes are held by group members and influence group operation, collaboration, and performance.

Rescher's value theory (1969) provides a useful classification of the objects to which values may be applied: things, the environment, people, groups, and whole societies, while another facet of the theory classifies the potential benefit of applying values such as economic, moral, social, political, aesthetic, and religious. Rescher proposed five principles as criteria to explain the concept of values. One criterion, for example, classifies the type of benefits arising from values into material and physical, economic, moral, social, political, aesthetic, religious (spiritual), intellectual, professional, and sentimental. Kluckhohn (1951) gave an alternative faceted classification, including modality (positive or negative), intensity (of belief), content (with a very limited subtaxonomy of aesthetic, cognitive, or moral), generality (of application), extent (of belief in a population) and explicitness (in articulation). In a more detailed value survey, Rokeach (1973) classified 18 terminal values (e.g., happiness, equality, freedom, social recognition) and 18 instrumental values (e.g., ambition, love, courage, honesty, independence). Schwartz and Bilsky (1990) produced an even richer taxonomy, specifying 56 basic human values grouped into 10 value types (achievement, benevolence, conformity, hedonism, power, security, self-direction, stimulation, tradition, and universalism). Closely related to values are theories of motivation (Maslow et al., 1987) which describe driving influences on human behavior such as achievement, power, self-esteem, self-actualization (realizing one's potential), and more socially oriented concepts of social inclusion and altruism. Sheldon's taxonomy of needs (Sheldon et al., 2001) provides a slightly different perspective with 10 categories: autonomy, competence, belonging, popularity, security, physical health, money-wealth, pleasure, self-esteem, and self-actualization. Many values in these taxonomies describe individual users' characteristics and personal predispositions, so while they are relevant to the design of personalized systems, they are less relevant as general NFR-style values.

Psychological definitions of values are usually informal. For example, Kluckhohn (1951) defines a value as "a conception explicit or implicit, distinctive or an individual or characteristic of a group, of the desirable which influences the selection from available modes, means and of action." Management science researchers have used questionnaires to investigate people's values (Bjorn-Andersen et al., 1979), covering specific topics such as commitment to employment, the Protestant work ethic, personal development, professionalism, and social status. However, the questions are usually framed at a specific level, which hinders their application to general requirements

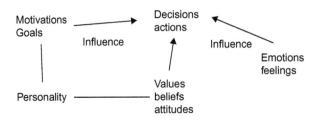

FIGURE 13.1

Conceptual structure of values and related cognitive constructs.

analysis. The more general Models of Man questionnaire (Cook, 1982) assesses the impact of systems change within organizations, covering the personal background of respondents, their perceptions of different groups, their objectives, their criteria for job satisfaction, and their personal values.

In conclusion, "values" have referred to a wide variety of concepts, interests, pleasures, likes, preferences, duties, moral obligations, desires, wants, goals, needs, aversions, and attractions, and many other kinds of selective orientations (Williams, 1979).

One reason for the absence of concise definitions is that values are closely related to other mental constructs such as intent, motivation, and belief. People have value systems consisting of a complicated web of concepts, and as Schwartz (1996) pointed out that attitudes and behaviour are guided by trade offs between competing values rather than prioritisation of unitary values. Hence values are better understood as conceptual structures, relating them to other aspects of our psychology, as illustrated in Figure 13.1.

Values are almost synonymous with beliefs and attitudes which are knowledge schema in our memory, shaped by our personality and motivations. Values influence our decisions; for example, one may believe in the "green" values associated with conservation, sustainability, and ecological awareness. This belief might lead me to take a stance on climate change and make decisions about recycling, energy use, and transport. We interpret our perceptions of the world by reference to complex memories that preserve the effects of past judgments (values, beliefs, and attitudes), and motivations that can be considered as long-term personal goals. Our responses and actions are shaped by events and our perceptions of the world which are influenced by value, feelings, and emotions.

A reasonably concise working definition is as follows:

> Values are conceptual structures or knowledge schema, related to our beliefs and attitudes, which shape our decisions and actions.

In the next section, the implications of values for requirements and software development are reviewed.

13.3 Taxonomy of values and system implications

Because many taxonomies of values in the literature describe similar concepts, a synthesis of several taxonomies was carried out. Some taxonomies are very detailed—for instance, Schwartz and Bilsky's (1990) 56 categories. Although, richer and more extensive taxonomies might prove more

Table 13.1 Values: Elicitation Hints and System Implications

Value	Related Terms	Potential Sources	System Implications
Trust	openness, integrity, loyalty, responsibility, reliability	Relationships with other individuals/departments Privacy policies	Less control, milestone checks, improved team, confidence
Sociability	cooperation, friendship, sympathy, altruism	Relationships with others; awareness of others; office politics	Improved team, cooperation, shared awareness
Morals/Ethics	justice, fairness, equality, tolerance	Behaviour towards others Opinions of others' behaviours	Openness and honesty in teams
Creativity/ Innovation	originality, adventure, novelty	Work processes, problem solving	Creativity, workshops, facilitators
Aesthetics	beauty, nature, art	Self-appearance, reaction to images, shapes, art and design	Team members, designers, storyboards
Security	safety, privacy, risk	Data management policies, hazards, threats, change	Hazard/threat, analysis, safety cases
Personal characteristic	openness, conscientiousness, extroversion, agreeableness, neuroticism	Self-image, personae scenarios, psychological questionnaires Role playing	Customisation analysis, personalisation, team conflict management
Motivation	ambition, power, achievement, self-image, peer esteem	Ambitions, goals, career plans	Stakeholder analysis, rewards, incentives for members
Beliefs & attitudes	cultural, political, religious topics	Leisure interests, user background, reaction to news events	Stakeholder analysis, team composition, incentives

useful for research purposes, more concise taxonomies are desirable for practical application. Hence, a parsimonious taxonomy of values and their consequences for process guidance was created, as illustrated in Table 13.1. Nine upper-level value categories are proposed based primarily on Rescher's theory (1969), supplemented by categories produced from card-sorting experiments and experts interviews (Thew and Sutcliffe, 2008). Six categories are commonly recognized concepts across most taxonomies: trust, morals, aesthetics, privacy/security, sociability, and creativity/innovation. Synonyms that express variations on the core value are given in the related terms in column two of the table, while potential sources and hints for eliciting user values are given in column three. Column four contains implications at the system level, that is, issues for organizations, management, and system design for people. These system implications can be applied to the project management of the development process or to the design of the human part of a sociotechnical system.

Trust, sociability, and ethics/morality values are all properties of relationships with others or within groups, whereas creativity is closely linked to curiosity, experimentation, and the personality attributes agreeableness and extroversion. Personal characteristics values are taken directly from the "big five" framework, which is the accepted standard of personality theory (McCrae and John, 1992): openness (inventive/curious vs. consistent/cautious), conscientiousness (efficient/organised vs. easygoing/careless), extroversion (outgoing/energetic vs. solitary/reserved), agreeableness (friendly/compassionate vs. cold/unkind), and neuroticism (sensitive/nervous vs. secure/confident). Unlike other values, personal characteristics are attributes that describe people. Personality characteristics are closely related to motivations, and both have implications for team management in the development process and customization for personalized application.

Motivations are a placeholder for a more detailed taxonomy beyond the scope of this chapter, although more detail can be found in Thew and Sutcliffe (2008). Beliefs and attitudes are a diverse category including sociopolitical, cultural, and religious beliefs. These values change more rapidly, driven by social, cultural, and political issues as well as events, so this category is an open-ended set that varies across time and cultures, whereas the other values are general time-invariant conceptual structures or belief systems, independent of culture.

The potential sources in column three suggest questions and interview topics for eliciting particular values. The system implications in column four vary from organizing the team composition in response to aesthetic needs (i.e., including aesthetically aware designers), specialization of the development process to include safety and risk analysis (Sutcliffe, 1998), to more general heuristics for project team management such as the need for fewer controls when trust is high, or the converse when mistrust is discovered. Sensitivity to moral values indicates the need for honesty, openness, and fairness in all parts of the development process. In many cases, especially with regard to motivations, beliefs, and attitudes, value analysis may alert the analyst to potential stakeholder conflicts, in which case negotiation will be necessary to arrive at a common set of values. Alternatively, system configuration/customization may need to be considered (e.g., different levels of security controls mapped to stakeholders who regard security as very or not important).

When a value is absent, the only process consequence is usually not to invest in analysis effort for understanding the needs for aesthetics, security, creativity, and so on. However, the absence of, or negative values for, trust, sociability, or morals will need corrective action to ensure a productive relationship among the project team.

13.4 Analyzing stakeholders' values

The taxonomy of values is used in the value-based requirements engineering (VBRE) method which guides eliciting user values and motivations. Interviews are combined with scenario/narrative probes, user observations, and reflections on the users' discourse to elicit values by direct questioning with scenario analysis of value-laden situations for use of the future system. Work shadowing, observation, and ethnographic techniques help gather insight into values and emotions from implicit expression of users' likes and dislikes in nonverbal as well as verbal communication. Scenarios, storyboards, and evaluation of prototypes help to elicit user feedback when their comments reveal how the system reflects (or does not reflect) their values or motivations.

The key steps of the VBRE method are summarized in Figure 13.2.

The method can be used in two modes to suit novice or expert analysts and the time resources available. In expert mode, the taxonomy and process are learned in training courses and by

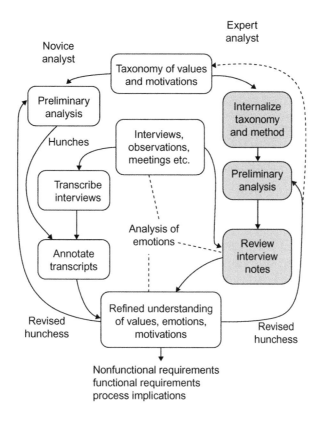

FIGURE 13.2

Process stages and expert and novice pathways in the VBRE method.

preliminary experience. The method knowledge is internalized, so it can be used to formulate appropriate questions framed by the analyst's understanding of the application domain (cf. hunches in novice mode). The method becomes part of the expert's battery of techniques in scenario analysis and questioning using storyboard and prototype probes.

In novice mode, preliminary analysis in feasibility studies leads to identification of key issues or "hunches,", that is, a subset of the users' values, motivations, or emotions from the taxonomy which seem to be relevant to the application. For example, we may suspect that our users prioritize certain aspects of their work: creativity, aesthetics, and collaboration. Making these intuitions explicit encourages gathering evidence to support or challenge initial hunches.

Interview audio-recordings are transcribed to create text records. Annotation involves reviewing transcribed interview notes for evidence of the expression of values, emotions, or motivations and marking text segments with the taxonomic category, using either the key issues or the tables directly. The transcript is marked up, summarizing each interview response or segment. If time resources are constrained, an alternative is to use the expert mode's review interview notes stage by listening to audio recordings and taking notes.

Table 13.2 Sample of a marked-up transcript. *Italics* and <u>underlining</u> are used to show the Links between the Transcript and the Annotation, with the Taxonomy Categories in **Bold**

Transcript	Annotations
<u>Interesting as in a good position to do this kind of work</u> – and *would like to develop links with Experimental Medicine given the upcoming rearrangement of schools*.	<u>Potential of work</u> – for development of science, **Motivation- achievement** also *for positioning of NIHBI*
<u>I'm still in the literature. I want a good understanding of the problem if it's tricky.</u>	<u>Very thorough</u> **Systematic**

For annotation and review stages, the checklists (see Table 13.1) are used to identify values and motivations for different interview segments, as illustrated in Table 13.2.

The tables may be used in conjunction with existing taxonomies of nonfunctional requirements which already provide lists of quality attributes, for example, accuracy or reliability (Bass et al., 2003), so the VBRE method augments analysis of nonfunctional requirements by drawing attention to issues that might be omitted from a conventional analysis. Most values and motivations held by the user (self) will be positive, but those related to colleagues, design features, and the environment may well be negative, thereby indicating problems that the design needs to solve. Emotional responses of frustration, anxiety, and fear during interviews provide corroborating evidence of such problems.

Once the annotation is complete the transcript is inspected for frequent value and motivation categories, and for differences between individuals and groups. The "hunches" list may be modified following each cycle of interviews, so it develops incrementally into a rich picture of the stakeholders' values and motivations. Finally, the implications of the analysis for both the system design and architecture are reviewed by referring to the tables in the previous and following sections (Table 13.1 and 13.3) and the annotated notes. The output consists of lists of functional and nonfunctional requirements, with recommendations for system organization, user procedures, functional allocation, and work design.

13.5 Values and architecture implications

User values have implications for NFRs and directly impact design decisions concerning software architecture. In this section, the implications focus on software design rather than organizational or human team management, although the implications at the system and software levels are often closely coupled; for instance, encouraging creativity in teams implies software tools for sharing ideas. While many user values will have domain-specific interpretations that cannot be analyzed a priori, there are general implications that can be recorded as generic functional requirements with architectural implications, as illustrated in Table 13.3.

Trust. This value concerns trust of another agent (which may be human or automated) or trust in data. Psychologists argue that trust has a reputation and a behavior component, so we assume

Table 13.3 User values with Associated Generic Functional Requirements and Architectural Implications

Value Concept	Generic Functional Requirements	Architectural Implications	Notes
Trust	Reputation mechanisms Visibility & identity	Behaviour monitors Audit trails	Reputation is associated with identity and membership
Sociability	Shared awareness Cooperation functions Communication channels/media	P2P architecture e-communities, CSCW	Social values may encourage social relationships (media)
Morals/ Ethics	Visibility & transparency Data access, shared controls	Behaviour monitors, configurable controls	Closely related to trust
Creativity Innovation	Extendable tools, customisation, configuration	End-user development tools	Creativity, workshops, facilitators
Aesthetics	User interface design, media choice	More complex UI components	User experience NFRs
Security Safety	Error prevention Warnings, mitigation: recovery, access controls	Safety kernels, firewalls, sensors, awareness	Hazard/threat analysis
Personal characteristics	Matching functions to individual users	Personalisation, customisation	Cost of adaptation trade-off
Motivation	More complex functional requirements	Functional layers Adaptable systems	Component-based architectures

that data or a person is trustworthy if they are associated with reputational markers, such as certificates, badges of membership of reputable organizations, or affidavits from friends. We also base trust on what people do, the reliable behavior of agents, and accurate content of information. This requires behavior to be visible and inspectable. Trust therefore implies generic requirements for reputation mechanisms as recommended in web services—for example, security certificates, membership of reputable organizations, and references of repute from others. Visibility and transparency requirements are for all behavior to be accessible and shared with others, with graphical shared-awareness displays of where agents are, what they are doing, statements of intent, and so on. Architectural implications are for developing monitors for user behavior, database updating, and audit trails of agents' and system activity.

Sociability. This value is oriented toward cooperating with other people and seeking social relationships rather than being more content with "going it alone." It is closely related to the personal characteristics of agreeableness and extroversion. Users who hold strong positive social values will expect collaboration tools if they are appropriate for the application. They may also require social media and e-community architectures if the domain has a community of users. Some functional requirements for cooperation are shared with trust values—for example, shared-awareness displays, progress tracking in collaborative tasks, visibility of each individual's activity, identity, and status. Social values may conflict with security since social orientation and trust favor open access to data and functionality, whereas security necessitates access controls and restricted visibility. The architectural connotations of social and collaborative systems are peer-to-peer networking with multiple clients, shared databases, and shared functions for CSCW (computer-supported collaborative work).

Morality and Ethics. These values are difficult to define with precision, although moral predisposition toward others implies fairness, equitable treatment, and behavior governed by humanist or religious moral standards. Although the connection of such values to architecture may seem to be weak, these values have implications shared with trust. Moral and ethical behavior implies conformance to some norm; hence, first the moral code needs to be communicated, and then any transgressions of the code should be made visible. This implies functional requirements for behavior tracking, audit trails, penalty/reward mechanisms, and displays to encourage transparency in behavior and data. Information about the behavior and reputation of individuals and organizations showing how they follow ethical codes is closely related to trust requirements. Architectural implications are shared with trust; such as monitors for behavior and data transactions, transparency displays, and inspectable audit trails.

Creativity. This value is related to the personality characteristic of openness. Creative users wish to experiment and extend the system. This suggests functional requirements for customization and adaptable systems, where the basic functionality can be tailored by users. For more ambitious users, end-user development tools may be advisable to provide the basic building blocks of the system, supported by design tools. Creativity support has led to development of architectures such as domain-oriented development environments (Fischer, 1994; Fischer et al., 2004; Repenning, 1993), made up of components for design by reuse, tools for component editing and composition, supported by patterns, templates, explanation facilities, critical experts to guide users, and libraries of components with search facilities. Creativity may also be collaborative, so the architectural implications of sociability may also be relevant, such as shared components, designs, and experiences.

Aesthetics. Users with aesthetic predispositions value beauty in design, the content and media of websites, and interaction. Aesthetic values have few direct functional requirements or architectural implications; instead, these values guide investment in user interface design. Users with aesthetic values will expect more beautiful and more engaging user interfaces that require the skills and services of interaction and multimedia designers. The implications are for project management and investment in multidisciplinary teams that can deliver aesthetically pleasing products with positive user experience; see Sutcliffe (2009).

Security. This value, which is closely related to privacy, has received considerable attention in the literature, so there are many requirements and architectural recommendations (Haley et al., 2004; Rapanotti et al., 2004). Generic requirements are for access barriers (password and other controls), protection (encryption and secure data transmission), and remediation if security is compromised (audit trails, recovery procedures). Architectures for security involve firewalls, security kernels for critical components, and monitors to detect threats and attempts to penetrate the system. With the ever-present threat of viruses, multilayer architectures to detect and prevent security penetration are a specialist area of research.

Personal characteristics. Users' personalities have a general implication for architectural strategy as a decision to customize/personalize functionality and the user interface to fit individual users or user groups who share similar characteristics. Although it is difficult to determine the personality of individual users without asking them to complete questionnaires, some roles may tend to select for certain characteristics such as extroversion in sales and marketing. Personal characteristics may confirm other values; for example, agreeableness and sociability with cooperation, or openness and mild neuroticism tend to be associated with creativity.

Motivation. Motivations are not strictly values, so in-depth treatment is beyond the remit of this chapter. They can be considered as long-terms goals, some of which are related to values such as sociability. The more important implications of motivation are to achieve goals and possess resources. Users with these motivations may expend more effort in learning to use the system and customize it for their own purposes; hence they can accept more complexity. Complexity per se has only an indirect influence on architecture and requirements. It modulates the decision about how many functional requirements to include and how complex the system should be. Better motivated users will tolerate more complexity; furthermore, motivation may be related to creativity when users wish to extend the system's functionality.

Sociocultural values. This open-ended set of values is not described in detail. However, because they can have implications for requirements and architecture in specific applications, one example is presented. Take the value for a green-environmental predisposition. This may involve all or part of a complex schema, illustrated in Figure 13.3.

Most schema components are related to information or content, so functional requirements are hidden behind the action component. Many sociocultural values concern groups who wish to spread their values to others and persuade them to join their cause and, where necessary, take action. A set of generic community requirements may therefore be appropriate for a range of these values—for example, functional requirements to donate money to the cause, join a group, share news and views, author new content, and coordinate activity. Hence, sociocultural values will share many requirements with sociable values, with similar architectural implications for peer-to-peer networking and e-community applications. A prototype generic architecture, as shown in Figure 13.4, may be proposed to support a range of sociocultural values, where the components support the goals of recruiting people to the community sharing the value, as well as coordinating community action and sharing information. This is derived from content management system architectures for web applications, with the addition of functions for coordinating action, recruiting new members, and wiki/blog facilities for sharing information. While this pattern is not directly motivated by any one socioeconomic value, it is applicable to many values when specialized with appropriate information content.

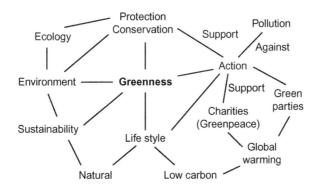

FIGURE 13.3

Knowledge schema of concepts related to a "greenness-sustainability" value.

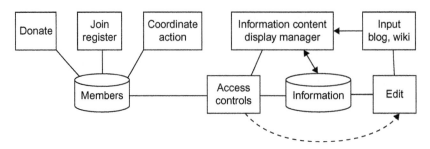

FIGURE 13.4

Architecture pattern for e-community support where the content reflects the shared socioeconomic value.

Now that it has been argued that user values deserve to be analyzed as an important influence on software development, the next section connects values with nonfunctional requirements and further implications for software and systems architecture.

13.6 Values, nonfunctional requirements, and architecture patterns

Nonfunctional requirements (NFRs) can be divided into performance and quality issues pertaining to systems. We argue that user values are related to NFRs and that both can be linked to architecture patterns, as illustrated in Figure 13.5.

Architecture patterns are more general than patterns associated with program-level components, and contain functional components associated with abstract user-oriented concerns (i.e., values) with heuristics and notes guiding design decisions. The value-oriented architecture patterns Iproposed here are intended to be conceptual models that form a bridge between requirements analysis and the design level, in contrast to most software architecture which is motivated by implementation design concerns (Bass et al., 2003).

Privacy and security, which are both values and NFRs, motivate the secure systems pattern (see Table 13.4) that has components for secure communication channels, encrypting messages and data, as well as access controls such as password and biometric checks on user identity. The secure pattern applies to a wide variety of applications with sensitive data and processing. Models of data may have depersonalized records for privacy protection, and models of potential threats and hazards are necessary to improve access controls. The secure pattern shares components with monitor and control for logging and control access, and for providing audit trails.

Three values—trust, privacy, and ethics/morality—share the monitor and control architecture pattern for monitoring agent (user or system) behavior. This pattern is composed of three types of component: for capturing events and environmental information (monitors-sensors), for making sense of such information (interpreters-analyzers), and then for planning appropriate responses (see Figure 13.5). Components from this pattern may be applied to a wide variety of applications ranging from security systems to detect and manage threats to intelligent user interfaces that adapt to individual people, recommenders for personal services and information, and the increasing number of adaptive systems. The safety NFR motivates a specialization of this pattern where monitors and

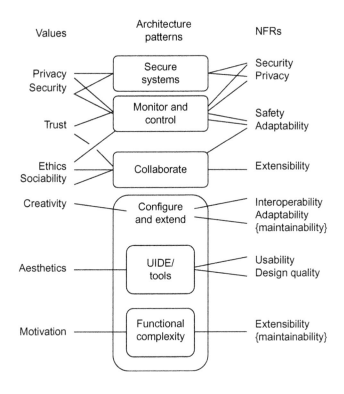

FIGURE 13.5

Connections between user values, architecture patterns, and NFRs.

interpreters focus on dangerous events and states, with adaptive mechanisms to return the systems to safe operation and mitigate any hazards. This architecture pattern frequently depends on models of the external world and the system that is being monitored. Furthermore, these models need updating, so there is a recursive embedding of monitors on the monitoring system. Monitor and control components are associated with facilities that form part of the collaboration architecture pattern: Visibility and transparency display functions for trust and ethical considerations.

The purpose of collaboration architectures is to support all forms of shared multiuser activity ranging from communication (CMC: computer-mediated vommunication), information sharing to hands-on joint activity (i.e., CSCW) which appears in applications such as joint authorship of documents, to design, workflow coordination, and collaborative telepresence in virtual reality. Collaboration involves functional components to support communication and joint actions, with shared awareness to keep all users informed of each other's activity, and access controls when applications are structured with different user roles, privileges, and responsibilities. Collaboration is suggested by sociability values that may drive the development of e-community and socio-media approaches, and by more goal-oriented function needs for collaboration in e-commerce, e-science, and many systems that involve group-level activity.

Table 13.4 Architecture Patterns: Components, Application Areas, and Supporting Models

Pattern	Component Functions	Applications	Models
Secure systems	Access controls, encrypt-decrypt, secure channels	All applications with sensitive data and communications	De-personalised data, hazard and threats
Monitor & control	Monitors: sensors, interpreters:analysers, planning adaptation	Security, self-aware adaptive systems, intelligent user interfaces, recommender systems	Environment, context, agents, phenomena the system needs to be aware of
Collaboration	Shared awareness, collaboration tools, communication support, access controls, progress tracking, visualisation	All groupware, CSCW, CMC, social media, wiki-style applications	Agents, shared activity, share content, history updates, versions
Configuration	Functional components, search matching, editor: customisers, service/component composers, explanation facilities, critics	Applications with personalisation, customisation, localisation, ERP, product lines, creativity and design support	Design patterns, templates, component specifications
User Interface Development Environment	UI components, customisers, explanation facilities, critics	Personalisation, adaptive and adaptable UIs	UI design patterns, templates, component specifications, design exemplars, principles
Complexity	Functional components, explanation facilities	Domains with more expert and ambitious users	Templates, component specifications

The purpose of the configure pattern is motivated by creative values and the extensibility/flexibility NFRs, that is, design goals to enable the system to be extended by its users to meet an increasing range of functional requirements after its initial implementation. The configure pattern is related to adaptable systems (Fischer, 2003), end-user development, and component-based software engineering. In contrast, self-aware adaptable system architectures are associated with the monitor control pattern and automatically adapt to their environment. Configurable architectures are made up of components enabling user-designers to extend the base system capabilities, and support tools that enable users to search for and match their requirements to components in reuse libraries and then design system extensions with these components. This pattern may also include facilities to develop new components motivated by the creativity value for end-user development. Configuration tools are also useful for ethical users, allowing them to choose functions and the degree of surveillance that matches their moral viewpoint. Applications range from any system with needs for customization, personalization, or localization to more ambitious configuration and tailoring in product lines and ERP approaches to creativity-support design environments. Both the collaboration and configuration architecture patterns have an impact on extensibility (of collaboration and user communities); as well as on maintainability, for end-user configuration of systems may become a maintenance issue as design inconsistencies and poor practices are introduced.

Aesthetics may be cited as an NFR design quality, but it is also a user value with direct implications for user interface design. The User Interface Development Environment (UIDE) architecture pattern is a specialization of the configure patterns, so it contains similar components except that they are specialized for user interfaces and the models include design exemplars of good practice. Finally, complexity is a response to well-motivated and more sophisticated users who are willing to learn and adapt to more complex functionality. Complexity extends the configuration pattern and hence shares the components for supporting end-user development and configuration of extensible systems.

The three base architecture patterns share many concerns and components, and conflicts may arise when values and NFRs impose incompatible requirements. For example, security motivates higher degrees of monitoring of system functions that imply increased intermodule coupling, which in turn impose a further maintenance load. Security is a shared user value in monitoring and collaboration, with high-level functional requirements for access controls, identity tracking, encryption, and audit trails. Creativity, and to an extent ethical values, highlight end-user development tools and configurable, customizable architectures. These goals may have an impact on maintainability and require extensibility of the system, but there may also be impacts on interoperability because end-user extensions may not be backwardly compatible with existing software. Usability may also be affected since design standards may be lax and different end users produce varying look-and-feel designs, resulting in an inconsistent user interface. Users' motivations, though not strictly values, can be linked to consideration of functionally rich and more complex architectures, which then have an impact on maintainability and usability, particularly for novices and less well-motivated users. One solution to this dilemma is to provide adaptive and adaptable systems, although this produces more complexity and hence exacerbates the maintenance burden. User values, therefore, have a close relationship to soft goals and NFRs, while both demonstrate the close link between requirements and design architecture.

Value analysis and the architecture patterns were used in the design of a medical research support system, which is reported in the next section.

13.7 Case study: value-based design of e-science applications

This section illustrates the experiences that emerged during application of a value-based requirements analysis method in the ADVISES project (Thew et al., 2009). ADVISES is a decision-support system for academic researchers and National Health Service public health analysts who investigate epidemiological problems. The project had two research aims: first, to design high-level interfaces for data-driven hypothesis discovery in large-scale epidemiological datasets, essentially providing facilities for researchers to pose research questions in their natural language which the system translates into appropriate analysis routines; and second, to design usable and effective visualizations for bio-health informatics. There were two distinct user communities who had different goals. For academic researchers, understanding the generic causes of childhood obesity by statistical analysis of health records was a high-level goal. In contrast, the goal of public health analysts was local health management—for example, identifying the best target for interventions, such as promotion of local sports facilities and healthy-eating campaigns. The value-based analysis method was applied during interviews, scenario-storyboard requirements exploration sessions, and

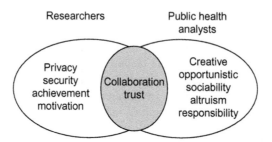

FIGURE 13.6

Value map for the ADVISES stakeholders.

requirements analysis workshops; see Thew et al. (2008) for more details. The value map resulting from the analysis is illustrated in Figure 13.6.

Much of the insight into the values and motivations of academic researchers came from reviewing interview recordings about their work practices. They talked about working in isolation, being responsible for their own success and productivity, the methodical ways they organize and check their results, and the care they take to keep their research data and practices secure. Similarly, observation of meetings between academic researchers showed them generating and reviewing ideas for new analysis or research, always considering the potential for publication or grant applications.

Similarly, interviews and meeting observations provided a rich source of values and motivations when talking to public health analysts. A strong sense of altruism was evident, both in working with and sharing resources with other analysts, and in a desire to see positive change in the health of children in their local areas.

Collaboration and trust were shared values, but the stakeholders prioritized different values and motivations, in particular customization, adaptability, and security. The researchers were more concerned with data security and privacy as well as with a systematic and reliable process that matched their motivation to achieve high-quality research. These values were addressed by functions from the secure pattern for encryption data security on servers, and set workflows. In contrast, the health analysts were more creative and social, so their values indicated configurable workflows to match systematic or more opportunistic processes, while creative values were supported by interactive visualization for data analysis. Sociability and altruism values informed decomposition of stakeholder goals. For instance, altruism and systematic values led to a subgoal to record analytic procedures, first to allow researchers to track their own work, and second to support public health analysts in sharing analysis techniques and results with colleagues. Investigation of user motivations revealed a strong desire to improve the effective use of epidemiological data in research (academic users' achievement motivation); and to share data and results with peers. Both user groups were strongly motivated by the system objectives, which indicated that more complex functionality could be deployed.

As well as producing usable and useful applications for our users, the design brief pointed toward a configurable architecture since ADVISES had to produce generic methods and research support tools for e-science. The initial systems architecture to deliver the baseline requirements is illustrated in Figure 13.7.

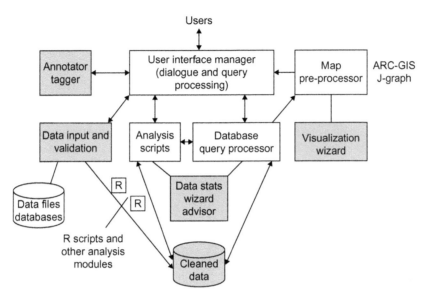

Users

FIGURE 13.7

ADVISES basic functional architecture; components influenced by value analysis are shaded.

The architecture is derived from a basic database query processing the results display pattern (Withall, 2007). The system uses epidemiological datasets (e.g., complex records of childhood obesity, with variables of age, sex, weight, height, address, socioeconomic background, medical history, etc.). These datasets come from local health authorities, but the data frequently contain inaccuracies, so functions for data cleaning and validation are required. Value analysis influenced the initial architecture design for data security and data sharing. Privacy and security values/NFRs motivated components for depersonalizing data, and checking records for completeness and consistency. The addresses of individuals have to be mapped to postcodes to create area aggregate data. User queries are interpreted into the Data Base Management Systems (DBMS) query languages, and results are displayed in a variety of media: tables, maps, graphs, and lists. A variety of statistical routines may be run on the data (correlations, analysis of variance, and regressions) before outputting the results using maps and graphs. The user interface allows the user to compose queries from menu lists, which then call for the appropriate statistical routines and graph/mapping functions.

Other modules in the system included a visualization expert who decides how to represent different variables, for example, averages, data, and continuous/discrete data, on maps by color coding, texture shading, size, and so on. A statistical advisor warned novice users when the statistical tests implied in the users' questions might be invalid with respect to the data (e.g., use of parametric tests on non-normal distributions). Inclusion of these "expert modules" arose from a clash of values between the two groups of stakeholders. The health analysts wanted to be creative, but they were not motivated to design their own displays; while the academic researchers were concerned about the accuracy of results and the need to apply systematic analysis procedures. The visualization expert saved the health analyst's work by automatically configuring map and graph displays, while the statistics expert enforced the researchers' desire for accurate results. The trust–sociability values did indicate application of the collaborate pattern. However, in discussion with the stakeholders, it was decided that cooperation would be primarily same-place, same-time, cooperation could be delivered by sharing the same user interface and, if necessary, projecting the results display for larger groups. Nonetheless, some support for asynchronous collaboration did motivate inclusion of an annotation-tagging function, so results (and the query that motivated them) could be stored as a persistent "research object." These objects could be annotated with comments, enabling them to be passed on to other research teams as well as facilitating collaborative work between the researchers and health analysts. The baseline architecture only served the needs of the immediate users in a limited range of epidemiological investigations. In the next phase, the configure pattern was applied to create a more generalized architecture that could be tailored to a wide variety of health informatics decision-support applications.

13.7.1 **Architecture extensions for configuration**

The user values of creativity, coupled with the motivation to deal with complex analysis, indicated the need for a flexible extensible architecture so that the system could be configured to support a range of epidemiological research purposes and other database-oriented analyses in health care. Furthermore, a design goal for the ADVISES tools was to create a generic architecture to serve a wider range of users in the e-science medical informatics community. The configure architecture pattern was adopted. However, further design options needed to be considered to address the trade-off between the creativity value that suggested extensive configuration and the users' effort involved in implementing new configured solutions. From earlier motivation analysis, we were aware that the health analyst users had limited resources to devote to extensive configuration. Two architecture extension strategies were considered. The first strategy was to make the tools customizable and to rely on the programming expertise of the end users. This is possible to some extent since some medical researchers are expert in statistical programming languages such as R, but this approach would still limit configurability to the statistical analysis routines. The second approach was to add configuration editors, so that health analysts who were not programming experts could configure the tools for their own datasets and analysis goals.

The value conflict between a systematic approach (achievement motivation) of the academic researchers and the more opportunistic, creative use by health analysts had additional implications for configuration, since the "expert modules" depended on configuration of analysis and display of User Interface (UI) components. One compromise was to produce two versions of the architecture, one without the "expert" components allowing more configuration freedom, targeted at health analysts, while the single version would be based on the architecture illustrated in Figure 13.7 and followed the values of both sets of users. Cost implications resolved this debate, since maintenance of two versions, as well as increased development costs, argued for a single configurable architecture, with constrained freedom for tailoring. This approach has been followed in several e-science applications by providing configurable workflow editors which then calls for web services to compose user-selected analysis processes.

The additions to the ADVISES architecture for configurability are shown in Figure 13.8. Several editors have been added to allow users to change validation checks and error messages for input data files, edit workflows to configure statistical analyses, and change annotations on results.

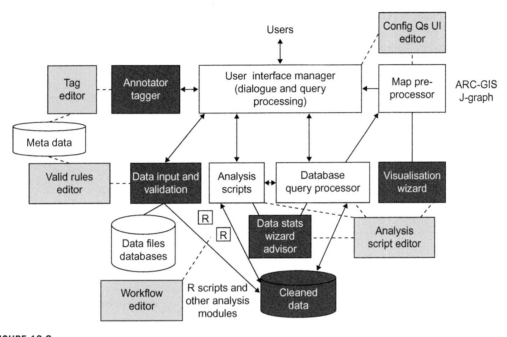

FIGURE 13.8

Extended ADVISES architecture for configurable applications. Additional configuration components are shaded dark grey.

Configuration therefore adds considerable functionality to the basic requirements, in the form of data editors that change messages and tags, new query terms and interpreters for changing UI operation and layout, diagram editors to compose statistical analysis sequences, and rule editors to change the functionality of the rule-based experts for analysis advice and visualization.

Even this level of complexity hides other requirements that are necessary to enable interpretation of the user changes. For instance, workflow modules have an embedded diagram interpreter with rules that link diagram nodes to appropriate statistical analysis functions, and validation checks to ensure that users compose legal analysis sequences. Further configuration could make the workflow fully generic, so new analysis functions can be added. This requires script editors or component reuse support to link new analysis function Application Program Interfaces (APIs) to diagram nodes and rule generation in the diagram interpreter. This option could have been implemented using generic workflow management tools such as TAVERNA (Oinn et al., 2006). However, the tight coupling of the core ADVISES modules (i.e., query processing and visual displays) meant that considerable redesign was necessary to fit these components into the TAVERNA workflow management process.

The cost of developing configuration facilities led to rationalization of the development strategy. Given that something in the order of 20−30% of the extended system components are fulfilling configuration needs alone, this represents a considerable investment in reaching more users. Layers of configuration were planned to reach, first, other epidemiologists, who require their own research questions, datasets, and analysis routines. Later, layers could extend the system for other research scientists if a wider-ranging ontology of research questions could be developed. The critical question was, will the users accept the effort of configuration, or will they just demand that a default version be prepared for them? Hence, a dilemma arose about who the target users of configuration facilities may be. Most research scientists are very busy and dislike spending time that is not directly linked to their own research work. We therefore targeted the configuration editors toward expert end-users of e-science support staff who can configure applications for end-users.

As illustrated in the preceding sections of this chapter, requirements intrudes into the design process as user values are analyzed. This leads to several decisions that shape the system architecture, such as exploring the possibilities for intelligent processing to guide users, and configuration that enables several groups of stakeholders to be served by one application, although at a cost of involving the users in discussions about how configuration may be implemented.

13.8 Conclusions

In this chapter we have argued that user values need to be added as important constructs in requirements analysis, which can augment the design of software and system architecture with a user orientation. Values can be held by individual user agents, roles, or organizational entities and have appeared in other software development approaches such as soft systems methods (Checkland, 1999) where the organization's values are recorded under the world view (*Weltanschauung*) in the CATWOE mnemonic. Ethics were the focus of Mumford's (1981) approach to systems analysis. Values are implicit in many requirements analysis methods, for example in sociopolitical issues recorded in the Volere template (Robertson and Robertson, 1999) and in requirement elicitation methods (Gause and Weinberg, 1989). Values therefore need to be systematically readopted into software development approaches. Taxonomies of values have been applied in RE (Ramos and Berry, 2005a; Thew et al., 2008), whereas this chapter has reported the application of the value-based RE method (Thew and Sutcliffe, 2008) for analyzing user values and motivations in showing the consequent decisions for the system architecture.

Values are related to goal-oriented approaches to architecture development (e.g., Chung et al., 2011; Bass and Clements, 2011); however, values have a less direct impact on architecture than functional requirements or architecture attributes/nonfunctional requirements. Instead, the implications of stakeholders have to be transformed into architectural components and heuristics to address design issues such as autonomy, coupling, and control via methods, as illustrated with VBRE described in this chapter. The closest relative of value analysis is business goals (Bass and Clements, 2011), where business goals such as "responsibility for customers or to the organisation and society" map to trust and possibly morals/ethical values in our taxonomy. Elaborating the intersections of business goals, organizational, and brand values with architectural implications is an area that deserves further research.

The value-oriented architecture patterns described in this chapter could inform design choices in many commercial system architectures such as product lines (Pohl et al., 2005) and enterprise resource plans (Keller and Teufel, 1998; Moon, 2007). ERPs have often encountered user resistance and rejection because user motivations, emotions, and cultural values have not been considered (Ramos and Berry, 2005b; Krumbholz et al., 2002). Another potential application of value analysis and related patterns is orchestration in service-oriented architectures (Endrei et al., 2004) where a user-centered approach is necessary for composition of transaction processing and information processing in business systems. The role of the value-based architecture framework is to bridge the gap from requirements and stakeholder views to design, so the value patterns could be synthesized with architectural strategies (Bass et al., 2003) and tactics (Bachman et al., 2003) to inform structural design as well as highlighting application domain concerns. The heuristics and metrics of design architecture strategies could be informed by value analysis to improve trade-off analysis in architecture design as well as shaping metrics for monitoring conformity with quality criteria and NFRs. The VBRE method should scale to larger systems since the process and taxonomy can be applied to subsystems in a divide and conquer approach. Further work is necessary, however, to specify the links between values and architecture patterns at the application level.

The value-based architecture framework described in this chapter did stand the test of application in design in the ADVISES project, contributing to several design decisions. Furthermore, it was produced by a systematic process for bridging user views in requirements analysis to architecture design. Value analysis coupled with design implications and rational knowledge contained in the patterns offers a new approach to architecture design. Value clashes between stakeholders encountered in the case study were solved by a configurable architecture. We believe that this approach will generalize, for example, configuration to add modules for visibility of users' action to match sociability and trust values. However, configuration has a cost, so it may be advisable to resolve some value conflicts where conflicts cannot be easily addressed in design (e.g., ethical requirements for transparency in the use of information and security—privacy values).

Although the VBRE approach to architecture has made a promising start, application in one case study does not provide sufficient evidence to validate the approach. Further research is necessary to apply the value-based framework in more wide-ranging domains where users' views are important (e.g., adaptation in training and educational applications). In addition, the framework needs more detail to be added in the patterns for modeling value implications as generic requirements and design issues, as well as linking these to architectural tactics and strategies.

The worth of the value-oriented conceptual-level architectures may be realized in several ways. First is by the route described in this chapter as a "tool for thought" and a source of design knowledge that can be applied to designing specific applications as well as generic systems. The value analysis method and architecture patterns could complement existing architecture design methods such as BAPO (Van der Linden et al., 2004), ADD (Bass et al., 2003), or RUP 4 + (Kruchten, 2003; Shuja and Krebs, 2007). In their review of architecture-driven design methods, Hofmeister et al. (2007) note that user views are common concerns in most methods, and they argue for "architecture-significant requirements" as an important component of the development process. Values contribute such requirements, and the patterns encapsulate reusable knowledge to inform attributes in attribute-driven design (Bass et al., 2003) or use case viewpoints/perspectives in RUP-based (Krutchen, 2003) approaches. Although user-oriented values focus on individuals or user groups, most values also apply to organizations, thereby providing content for the business and organization views in the BAPO framework. The second route for the value patterns architecture is to integrate them with reference frameworks of conceptual models for software development such as the domain theory (Sutcliffe, 2002) or analysis patterns (Fowler, 1997), either to provide reusable knowledge directly for architecture design or to index open-source components to facilitate matching application requirements to appropriate architecture components. Open-source components are currently classified by application domains (Wikipedia, 2013; SourceForge, 2012), which can hinder reuse as many components are specialized within domains. Indexing could be extended to using conceptual architectures to reengineer components for more general and wide-ranging reuse. Requirements patterns (Withall, 2007) have a similar motivation to the value-oriented architecture patterns, with related components in groupings for flexibility (configure), user function, and access control. However, requirements patterns are documented experiences that are neither motivated by a requirements analysis process nor based on a systematic taxonomy of user views or values. The third route may be to implement conceptual architectures as configurable application generators (Sutcliffe, 2008), so that the architecture drives an end-user design dialogue for acquiring sufficient detail to generate specific applications.

The connection between values and NFRs via architecture shows that many stakeholder values share common architectural concerns. However, stakeholders' values may well clash, so design is inevitably a matter of trade-off analysis and reconciliation of conflicts. For example, the need for access controls for security may well conflict with a mode/ethics value for transparency and open access. The trade-off may be to use the configuration pattern and produce different versions of an architecture to suit stakeholder groups. Unfortunately, this might then trigger a clash with cost and maintainability NFRs. The space of possible intervalue and value-NFRs clashes is extensive and requires considerable further research before trade = off guidelines can be given.

While the focus of this chapter has been on user values (Friedman, 2008) rather than on value in an economic sense (Gordijn and Akkermans, 2002), it is worth reflecting on the economic implications of user values. For example, developing multiuser CSCW features to satisfy a sociability value or end-user development for creativity both incur considerable costs beyond the basic functional system architecture. Aesthetics values will necessitate additional user interface development resources, while privacy and trust require development of additional components to protect access or to make information visible. Economic considerations involve further trade-offs, as noted above. The configuration architectural pattern can be invoked to deal with value conflicts, but only at economic penalty of producing and maintaining different versions of a software architecture.

Finally, the value-based approach to architecture design and the patterns proposed in this chapter are an initial proposal that needs to be applied in further case studies and developed to create a library of more detailed patterns, since one of the lessons apparent from their application was the extent of architecture design that was informed by domain-specific analysis. The growing interest in service patterns and architectures may provide a useful means of advancing research in such a way as to narrow the gap between user- and developer-oriented views of system architecture by bringing values and social issues to bear on design decisions.

References

Arrow, H., McGrath, J.E., Berdahl, J.L., 2000. Small Groups as Complex Systems: Formation, Coordination, Development and Adaptation. Sage Publications, Thousand Oaks, CA.

Bachman, F., Bass, L., Klein, M., 2003. Deriving Architectural Tactics: A Step Towards Methodical Architectural Design. Carnegie Mellon University Software Engineering Institute, Pittsburgh.

Bass, L., Clements, P., 2011. Business goals and architecture. In: Avgeriou, P., Grundy, J., Hall, J.G., Lago, P., Mistrík, I. (Eds.), Relating Software Requirements and Architectures. Springer, Berlin, pp. 183–195.

Bass, L., Clements, P., Kazman, R., 2003. Software Architecture in Practice. Addison-Wesley, New York.

Bergman, M., King, J.L., Lyytinen, K., 2002. Large-scale requirements analysis revisited: the need for understanding the political ecology of requirements engineering. Req. Eng. 7, 152–171.

Bjorn-Andersen, N., Hedberg, B., et al., The Impact of Systems Change in Organisations. Sijthoff & Noordoff, Alphen aan den Rijn, Netherlands.

Checkland, P.B., 1999. Systems Thinking, Systems Practice. Wiley, Chichester, UK.

Chung, L., Supakkul, S., et al., 2011. Goal-oriented software architecting. In: Avgeriou, P., Grundy, J., Hall, J.G., Lago, P., Mistrík, I. (Eds.), Relating Software Requirements and Architectures. Springer, Berlin, pp. 91–109.

Cockton, G., Kujala, S., Nurkka, P., Hölttä, T., 2009. *Supporting Worth Mapping with Sentence Completion* (LNCS, 5727). Springer, Berlin.

Cook, J., 1982. The Experience of Work: A Compendium and Review of 249 Measures and their Use. Academic Press, New York.

Endrei, M., Bolnick, J., Flood, G., et al., 2004. Patterns: Service-Oriented Architecture and Web Services. IBM/Redbooks, New York.

Finkelstein, A.C.W., Dowell, J., 2006. A comedy of errors: the london ambulance service case study. Proceedings of the 8th International Workshop on Software Specification and Design. IEEE Computer Society Press, Los Alamitos, CA, pp. 2–4.

Fischer, G., 1994. Domain-oriented design environments. Autom. Softw. Eng. 1 (2), 177–203.

Fischer, G., 2003. Beyond human computer interaction: designing useful and usable computational environments. Proceedings of the HCI 93 Conference. Cambridge University Press, Cambridge, UK, pp. 17–31.

Fischer, G., Giaccardi, E., et al., 2004. A framework for end-user development: socio-technical perspectives and meta-design. Commun. ACM 47 (9), 33–39.

Fowler, M., 1997. Analysis Patterns: Reusable Object Models. Addison-Wesley, Reading, MA.

Friedman, B., 2008. Value-sensitive design. In: Schular, D. (Ed.), Liberating Voices: A Pattern Language for Communication Revolution. MIT Press, Cambridge, MA, pp. 366–368.

Fuentes-Fernadez, R., Gomez-Sanz, J., Pavon, J., 2010. Understanding the human context in requirements elicitation. Req. Eng. 15, 267–283.

Gause, D.C., Weinberg, G.M., 1989. Exploring Requirements:Quality Before Design. Dorset House, New York.

Gougen, J., 1994. Requirements engineering as the reconciliation of social and technical issues. In: Gougen, J., Jirotka, M. (Eds.), Requirements Engineering: Social and Technical Issues. Academic Press Professional, New York, pp. 165–199.

Gordijn, J., Akkermans, H., 2002. Value-based requirements engineering: exploring innovative e-commerce ideas. Req. Eng. 8, 114–134.

Haley, C.B., Laney, R., et al., The effect of trust assumptions on the elaboration of security requirements. Proceedings 12th IEEE International Conference on Requirements Engineering. IEEE Computer Society Press, Los Alamitos, CA.

Hofmeister, C., Kruchten, P., et al., 2007. A general model of software architecture design derived from five industrial approaches. J. Syst. Softw. 80, 106–126.

Keeney, R., 1992. Value-Focused Thinking: A Path to Creative Decision Making. Harvard University Press, Cambridge, MA.

Keeney, R., 1996. Value-focused thinking: identifying decision opportunities and creating alternatives. Eur. J. Oper. Res. 92, 537–549.

Keller, G., Teufel, T., 1998. SAP/R3 Process Oriented Implementation. Addison Wesley-Longman, Reading, MA.

Kluckhohn, C., 1951. Value and value-orientations in the theory of action. In: Parsons, T., Shil, E. (Eds.), Towards a General Theory of Action. Harvard University Press, Cambridge, MA.

Komssi, M., Kauppinen, M., et al., Integrating analysis of customers' processes into roadmapping: the value-creation perspective. Proceedings of the 19th IEEE International Requirements Engineering Conference. IEEE Computer Society Press, Lòs Alamitos, CA, pp. 57–66.

Kruchten, P., 2003. The Rational Unified Process: An Introduction. third ed. Addison-Wesley, Boston.

Krumbholz, M., Maiden, N., Wangler, B., Bergman, L., 2000. How culture might impact on the implementation of enterprise resource planning packages. Advanced Information Systems Engineering (1789). Springer, Berlin, pp. 279–293.

Maslow, A.H., Frager, R., et al., Motivation and Personality. Addison Wesley-Longman, New York.

McCrae, R.R., John, O.P., 1992. An introduction to the five-factor model and its applications. J. Pers. 60 (2), 175–215.

Milne, A., Maiden, N., 2011. Power and politics in requirements engineering: a proposed research agenda. Proceedings 19th IEEE International Requirements Engineering Conference. IEEE Computer Society Press, Los Alamitos, CA, pp. 187–196.

Moon, Y.B., 2007. Enterprise Resource Planning (ERP): A review of the literature. Int. J. Manage. Enterp. Dev. 4 (3), 235–264.

Mumford, E., 1981. Values, Technology and Work. Nijhoff, Amsterdam.

Nuseibeh, B., 2001. Weaving together requirements and architecture. IEEE Comput. 34 (3), 115–117.

Oinn, T., Greenwood, M., Addis, M., Alpdemir, N., Ferris, J., Glover, K., et al., 2006. Taverna: lessons in creating a workflow environment for the life sciences. Concurrency Comput. Pract. Exp. 18 (10), 1067–1100.

Pohl, K., Böckle, G., Van der Linden, F., 2005. Software Product Line Engineering: Foundations, Principles, and Techniques. Springer, Berlin.

Ramos, I., Berry, D.M., 2005a. Is emotion relevant to requirements engineering? Req. Eng. 10 (3), 238–242.

Ramos, I., Berry, D.M., 2005b. Social construction of information technology supporting work. J. Cases Inform. Technol. L2 <http://hdl.handle.net/1822/4793>.

Ramos, I., Berry, D.M., Carvalho, J., 2002. The role of emotion, values, and beliefs in the construction of innovative work realities. *Proceedings First International Conference, SoftWare* (LNCS, 2311). Springer, Berlin, pp. 3–31.

Rapanotti, L., Hall, J., Jackson, M., Nuseibeh, B., 2004. Architecture-driven problem decomposition. Proceedings 12th IEEE International Requirements Engineering Conference. IEEE Computer Society Press, Los Alamitos, CA, pp. 80–89.

Repenning, A., 1993. Agentsheets: A Tool for Building Domain Oriented-Dynamic Visual Environments. Department of Computer Science, University of Colorado, Boulder, CO, Technical report, CU/CS/693/93.

Rescher, N., 1969. Introduction to Value Theory. Prentice-Hall, Englewood Cliffs, NJ.

Robertson, J., Robertson, S., 1999. Mastering the Requirements Process. Addison-Wesley, Harlow.

Rokeach, M., 1973. The Nature of Human Values. Free Press, New York.

Sawyer, P., Bencomo, N., et al., Requirements-aware systems: a research agenda for RE for self-adaptive systems. Proceedings RE-10. IEEE Computer Society Press, Los Alamitos, CA, pp. 95–103.

Schwartz, S., 1996. Value priorities and behavior: applying a theory of integrated value systems. The Psychology of Values: The Ontario Symposium, 8. Lawrence Erlbaum Associates, Hillsdale NJ.

Schwartz, S.H., Bilsky, W., 1990. Toward a theory of the universal content and structure of values: extensions and cross-cultural replications. J. Per. Soc. Psychol. 58, 878.

Sheldon, K.M., Elliot, A.J., Kim, Y., Kasser, T., 2001. What is satisfying about satisfying events? Testing 10 candidate psychological needs. J. Per. Soc. Psychol. 80, 325–339.

Shiell, A., Hawe, P., Seymor, J., 1997. Values and preferences are not necessarily the same. Health Econ. 6, 515.

Shuja, A.K., Krebs, J., 2007. IBM Rational Unified Process Reference and Certification Guide: Solution Designer (RUP). IBM Press/Pearson, New York.

Sommerville, I., Sawyer, P., 1997. Requirements Engineering: A Good Practice Guide. Wiley, Chichester, UK.

Sourceforge, 2012. <http://sourceforge.net/>. (Accessed 22.02.2013.).

Souza, V.E., Lapouchnian, A., Robinson, W.S., Mylopoulos, J., 2011. Awareness requirements for adaptive systems. Proceedings of SEAMS-11, 6th International Symposium on Software Engineering for Adaptive and Self-Managing Systems. ACM Press, New York, pp. 60−69.

Sutcliffe, A.G., 1998. Scenario-based requirements analysis. Req. Eng. 3, 48−65.

Sutcliffe, A.G., 2002. The Domain Theory: Patterns for Knowledge and Software Reuse. Lawrence Erlbaum Associates, Mahwah, NJ.

Sutcliffe, A.G., 2008. The socio-economics of software architecture. J. Autom. Softw. Eng. 15, 343−363.

Sutcliffe, A.G., 2009. Designing for user engagement: aesthetic and attractive user interfaces. In: Carroll, J.M. (Ed.), Synthesis Lectures on Human Centered Informatics. Morgan Claypool, San Rafael, CA.

Sutcliffe, A.G., 2010. Analysing the effectiveness of human activity systems with i*. In: Georgiini, P., Yu, E. (Eds.), i* Requirements Modelling. MIT Press, Cambridge, MA, pp. 1139−1195.

Sutcliffe, A.G., Fickas, S., Sohlberg, M.M., 2006. PC-RE: a method for personal and contextual requirements engineering with some experience. Req. Eng. 11, 157−173.

Thew, S., Sutcliffe, A.G., 2008. Investigating the role of soft issues in the RE process. Proceedings 8th IEEE International Conference on Requirements Engineering. IEEE Computer Society Press, Los Alamitos, CA, pp. 63−66.

Thew, S., Sutcliffe, A.G., et al., Experience in e-science requirements engineering. Proceedings, 16th IEEE International Requirements Engineering Conference RE 2008. IEEE Computer Society Press, Los Alamitos, CA, pp. 277−282.

Thew, S., Sutcliffe, A., et al., 2009. Requirements engineering for e-science: experiences in epidemiology. IEEE Softw. 26 (1), 80−87.

Van Lamsweerde, A., 2009. Requirements Engineering: From System Goals to UML Models to Software Specifications. Wiley, Chichester, UK.

Van der Linden, F., Bosch, J., et al., Software product family evaluation. Proceedings Software Product Lines, Third International Conference, SPLC 2004. Springer-Verlag, Berlin, pp. 110−129.

Viega, J., Kohno, T., Potter, B., 2001. Trust (and mistrust) in secure applications. Commun. ACM 44, 31−36.

Wikipedia, 2013. List of free and open-source software packages. <http://en.wikipedia.org/wiki/List_of_free_and_open-source_software_packages> (accessed 22.02.13.).

Williams, R.M.J., 1979. Understanding human values. In: Rokeach, M. (Ed.), Change and Stability in Values and Value Systems: A Sociological Perspective. Free Press, New York, pp. 15−46.

Withall, S., 2007. Software Requirement Patterns. Wiley/Microsoft, New York.

Yu, E., 2009. Social modelling and i*. In: Borgida, T., Chaudhri, V., Georgini, P., Yu, E. (Eds.), Conceptual Modeling: Foundations and Applications: Essays in Honor of John Mylopoulos (LNCS, 5600). Springer, Berlin, pp. 99−121.

Glossary

4 + 1 view A view model for describing the architecture of software systems, which contains logical view, development view, process view, physical view and a set of use cases

Adaptation goals The adaptation capabilities in the system at the requirements level

Additive weighting methods A type of methods for multicriteria decision making in which the sum of the individual attributes' contributions and the weights are used to reflect the preferences of the individual

ADDSS A tool named Architecture Design Decision Support System, which enables capturing a documenting architectural design decisions

ADkwik A wiki-based tool that is able to create architecture documentation

Agency conflicts Conflicts that occur between stakeholders whose interests are different from those of majority stakeholders

Agile process A software development process based on iterative and incremental development, in which the rules of project behavior are light-but-sufficient and also communication and people oriented, allowing fast delivery of projects

Architectural design decisions The design decisions made in the system at the architecture level with accompanying design rationale

Architectural technical debt A type of technical debt at the architecture level, which is caused mainly by architectural design decisions that compromise the maintainability and evolvability of a system

Architecturally Significant Requirements (ASR) A type of requirements that determines and constrains the architecture of the system

Architecture Business Cycle (ABC) The relationship between a system's architecture and its technical, business, and social environment influences

Architecture Description Language (ADL) A language that is used to describe software architecture

Architecture pattern Logical components of a to-be-designed system linked to appropriate design knowledge

Architecture Trade-off Analysis Method (ATAM) A method for software architecture evaluation, which considers multiple quality attribute requirements and explores how they interact with each other

Aspiration-level methods A type of methods for multicriteria decision making, in which sets of aspiration levels are assigned to different criteria in a system

Attribute-Driven Design (ADD) An approach that defines the software architectures of a system based on the quality attribute requirements

BAPO A model that defines the logical relationship between business, architecture, process, and organization concerns

Big design up front A software development method in which the design is to be completed before coding and testing take place

BPEL Business Process Execution Language, a language that enables specifying business process behavior for web services

Bunch tool A clustering tool for automatically creating subsystem decomposition by using search techniques

Business decision Basing a decision on business-relevant criteria, for example, in terms of the net present value of each alternative

CAFCR A decomposition of an architecture description into five views: Customer objectives, Application, Functional, Conceptual, and Realization

Capitalization A process of spreading a durable asset's acquisition cost over several tax years. It is how tax authorities attempt to make each year's income taxes as realistic as possible. See also Depreciation

Cash flow diagram A two-dimensional graph describing the cash flow stream for an alternative. Time is shown from left to right; each cash flow instance is drawn at a horizontal position relative to its timing. Amounts of money are shown vertically, upward arrows represent income, and downward arrows represent expense. The length of the arrow is usually drawn proportional to the amount of the cash flow instance.

Cash flow stream The representation of the (estimated) financial perspective of an alternative

Change-oriented Requirements Engineering (CoRE) A method that involves requirements change and separate requirements into different layers according to several change rates

Cloud computing The delivery of computing as a service rather than a product, whereby shared resources, software, and information are provided to computers and other devices as a metered service over a network (typically the Internet)

Co-Convert A metaphor that refers to the meaningful translation of architectural abstractions of the desired solution

Co-Create A metaphor that refers to the meaningful reflection of the system intervention by the architect

Co-Evolve A metaphor that refers to the meaningful reflection of operation, existence, and growth of the software system

Commit A metaphor that refers to the meaningful reflection of realization of the software architecture in terms of structure and behavior

Common Object Request Broker Architecture (CORBA) A specification and architecture that enables multiple network programming tasks to work together over networks

Communicate A metaphor that refers to the meaningful reflection of software architecture as an architecture description

Component-Based Development (CBD) A methodology that facilitates the reuse of the software components into a new software application

Composite structure diagram A type of structure diagram that represents the internal structure of a class and the possible collaborations

Comprehend A metaphor that refers to the meaningful reflection of the problem situation that is faced by the stakeholders

Conceptual (system) architecture Logical components of a to-be-designed system that relate to user and design requirements

Conceptual model Models of a logical component of a to-be-designed system, usually represented as collaborating objects

Conceptualize A metaphor that refers to the meaningful reflection of the common shared agenda between various stakeholders

Constructive Cost Model (COCOMO) This cost estimation model estimates software development effort as a function of program size.

Converge A metaphor that refers to the meaningful reflection of specific interests and values of stakeholders

COTS software Commercial Off-The-Shelf software whose functionality is acquired from an independent third party

Crosscutting concerns See Quality attribute

Crowd-enabled software engineering Software engineering based on resources provided by crowdsourcing

Crowdsourcing The practice of obtaining needed services, ideas, or content by soliciting contributions from a large group of people, especially from an online community, rather than from traditional employees or suppliers (Merriam-Webster Dictionary)

Depreciation A word that has two different meanings in business decisions. First, it refers to how an asset loses value over time due to effects such as wear and tear and obsolescence. This can more precisely be called actual depreciation. Second, it refers to how the organization accounts for that loss in value. This can more precisely be called depreciation accounting.

Domain entities A type of autonomous object that does not rely on other objects

Domain-Specific Language (DSL) A language that is used to a particular domain, rather than a general-purpose language

Externality A consequence of an economic activity that is experienced by unrelated third parties

Feature models A model that captures and represents the commonality and variability in the software product line

Functional requirements A type of requirements that defines the functionality and tbehavior of a software system

Games with a purpose Human-based computation technique in which a computational process performs its function by outsourcing certain steps to humans in an entertaining way

Goal-oriented software architecting An approach where functional requirements and nonfunctional requirements are refined and treated as goals to be achieved in a software system

Human-provided services Services that allow humans to seamlessly integrate their capabilities into web-scale workflows.

I* framework An agent-oriented modeling language for the representation of social and intentional relationships between the actors in the early life cycle of system engineering

Interest Someone who borrows money from another is usually obligated to return the original amount borrowed plus some additional money. The additional money is the interest.

Interest rate A measure of the rental fee for money in terms of a percentage over some period of time

Knowledge Acquisition in Automated Specification (KAOS) A goal-oriented requirements engineering methodology that enables requirements engineers to build requirements models and to derive requirements documents

Module Dependency Graph (MDG) A graph that represents the dependence relationships between the system modules

Net present value (NPV) An appraisal method used to calculate the total (in and out) cash flows that are linked to the project

Nonfunctional requirements A type of requirements that provides both quality guarantee (such as performance, security, usability, scalability, robustness, and reliability) and constraints (limits on cost, size, regulations) of a software system

Null architecture The architecture that represents basic functional requirements of the system but pays no attention to the nonfunctional requirements

Onion model A model that illustrates the relationship among stakeholders and identifies their roles from the system itself to the wider environment

Pedigreed Attribute Elicitation Method (PALM) A method that is designed to elicit important requirements for architectural business goals

Perspective A method used to ensure that a system provides a particular set of quality attributes

Quality attribute A nonfunctional characteristic of a component or a system

Quality attribute requirements A type of requirements that handles system quality attributes such as reliability, usability, and efficiency

Questions, Options, and Criteria (QOC) The model supporting a representation for rationale behind software engineering decisions

Relative Cost of Reuse (RCR) The ratio of effort needed to reuse the software without modifying the original costs that are normally associated with the development of software for a single use

Return on investment (ROI) An efficiency measure used to describe the periodical rates of benefit (return) from an investment

Risk assessment The methods and activities involved in identifying , analyzing, and prioritizing risk

Self-aware adaptive systems Computer systems that monitor events and states in their environment and then adapt to those events either automatically or through a human user

Service-oriented architecture (SOA) An architectural paradigm in which systems consist of service providers and service users

Social network A social structure made up of a set of actors (such as individuals or organizations) and a complex set of the dyadic ties between these actors

Software architecture The structure of components in a program or system, their interrelationships, and the principles and guides that control the design and evolution in time

Software Architecture Analysis Method (SAAM) The method of software architecture evaluation that carries out context-based analysis through the use of task scenarios

Software product line (SPL) A set of software-intensive systems that share a common, managed set of features satisfying the specific needs of a particular market segment or mission and that are developed from a common set of core assets in a prescribed way.

Stakeholders value Stakeholders can be tangible benefits, profits, savings, social value, feeling, experience, resiliency, innovativeness, and so on, and their importance to the stakeholder dictates their satisfaction. It is the worth of a software system to a stakeholder's problem from the stakeholder's point of view at the time of usage.

Tacit knowledge Knowledge that is informal and based on the experience of individuals

UML class diagram A type of structural diagram that represents the structure of a system at the level of classes and interfaces

Use case A technique that defines interactions from a user's perspective for system requirements study

Value An attitude or belief held by users that describes how they feel about an object, system, organization, or another person

Value articulation/Value matrix representation Representation of the four different perspectives of the value natrix and their relationships in an X-matrix representation.

Value creation A method that involves building and growing business by creating value for the customer and delivering the systems effectively for the software companies

Value-based decision making A methodology that elicits a system's value propositions, reconciles them into a set of satisfactory objectives for the system, and then further obtains achievable architectural solutions with the multi-objective decision support and negotiation techniques

Value-based understanding A method that transitions a software architect to focus on the stakeholders' value that is created by using the software system. Accordingly, the value expected by stakeholders in their value creation context serves as the starting point for software architecture.

Value matrix A view of software architecture based on four different perspectives: Value Proposition, Qualities Specification, Architecture Description, and Architecture Instantiation

Viewpoints A method for guiding the process of developing the views that describe a system's architecture

Virtual team A distributed group of people dynamically selected on-demand, based on their skills and/or abilities to solve specified tasks

Waterfall model A software development process in which progress flow is sequential from the top to the bottom

Author Index

Subject Index

Note: Page numbers followed by "*f*", and "*t*" refers to figures and tables respectively.

Printed and bound by CPI Group (UK) Ltd, Croydon, CR0 4YY

03/10/2024

01040322-0003